"Xfm has always delivered some brilliant music and this book is no exception. It's an honour to be included in it"
Simon Neil, Biffy Clyro

"Xfm has always been about bringing great music to the airwaves that wouldn't get a look-in otherwise, this book brings together the best of the best"
Kele Okereke, Bloc Party

"Contains some of the greatest music ever made"
Tim Burgess, The Charlatans

"What do you mean we've only got two songs in it? Only messing, great book by a great station"
Liam Fray, The Courteeners

"The only reason we are in any book is because of John Kennedy at Xfm, and if we're in a book it must be good"
Dan Le Sac

"A real insight into how some of those truly great songs were written and it's a real honour too that so many of our songs have been chosen by Xfm listeners and have made it into this book"
Andy Williams, Doves

"To be a part of this here book is a lovely thing. We're honoured to be a part of such a great collection of songs and to be in and amongst the pages of a thoroughly top read. God bless Xfm"
Tom Smith, Editors

"A great book about great music from a great radio station"
Guy Garvey, Elbow

"An amazing read and a privileged insight into the stories – and the world – behind the great music Xfm listeners know and love... a must read for any music fan"
Tom Clarke, The Enemy

"Xfm have supported us from the start and it's a real honour to be in this book among so many great artists"
Grant Nicholas, Feeder

THE XFM TOP 1000 SONGS OF ALL TIME

"My collection of music books is now complete. This one will sit at the top of the pile. Some of my songs are in it (four of 'em... that's two more than Shed 7... in your face Rick Witter!) Even better, it's put together by the radio station I love and work for. It's the new Bible"
Clint Boon, Inspiral Carpets

"It's an honour to be in this wonderful book surrounded by such wonderful musicians"
Jamie Reynolds, Klaxons

"It's a privilege to be included in this book. It seems like a long time ago now and for these tunes to be acknowledged in this way is ace. Splendid in fact. So thank you all who voted. Cheers Xfm and all their listeners"
Luke Pritchard, The Kooks

"Thanks Xfm for including 'Walkaway' in your top 1,000 songs of all time. Looking forward to having a little browse and seeing all the great artists and songs within. 'There She Goes' is also included so that's two great songs for starters. Only 998 to go..."
John Power, The La's / Cast

"It's an honour to be in this book, surrounded by some absolute legends and heroes of mine"
Mike Lewis, Lostprophets

"We're touched to have songs in this book. Thank you Xfm"
Felix White, The Maccabees

"Xfm's John Kennedy was the first DJ to play our music, long before we signed to Warp. I'll never get used to the fact that our music has touched so many people, but I'm aware of the big part Xfm has played in its dissemination, which makes them alright by me! Who doesn't love a big list to argue about?"
Paul Smith, Maxïmo Park

"I grew up on Xfm and love everything they do, especially this book"
Ben Lovett, Mumford & Sons

"Xfm is the bo****ks"
Dominic Howard, Muse

"It's a really weird time for music and I think radio is as important as it's ever been. Xfm have supported us since day one and it's a privilege to be part of this"
Blaine Harrison, Mystery Jets

"A great book full of stories behind some amazing music"
Steve Cradock, Ocean Colour Scene

"Xfm has been broadcasting some of the best Anglo-Saxon audio-porn ever created since its inception. I am very proud to have some of my sauciest performances included in this weighty tome"
Brian Molko, Placebo

"Amazing songs. Very flattered to have eight of ours in there! Xfm were the first station to play us and always the coolest"
Johnny Borrell, Razorlight

"Xfm have been at the forefront of launching new music from their inception. The chance to get an insight into what they would choose for their top 1,000 (and how they would choose them) is irresistible"
Scroobius Pip

"Xfm are a leading light in the UK for setting up bands. The fierce loyalty they show towards artists is based around passion for music and paving their own road. The songs of this book are an 'eclection' of the Xfm pulse"
The Temper Trap

"We're totally honoured to have one of our tunes listed in here"
Katie White & Jules De Martino, The Ting Tings

"Great songs are written every second somewhere. This thousand are the ones that didn't slip through the cracks unnoticed. We are both honoured and lucky to feel our music has moved people enough to warrant this kind of recognition and sit amongst both our contemporaries, and our inspirations"
Harry McVeigh, White Lies

"Xfm have always been the ones leading new music and new bands into battle, and long may they continue. A wonderful station, a triumphant book, and an honour to be mentioned... Did we have to pay someone off"
Matthew Murphy, The Wombats

"Xfm used to be my main source of new music while growing up. We feel grateful to have had their backing in our starting out, in particular John Kennedy's support, and feel honoured to be part of this book"
Oliver Sim, The xx

Published in 2010 by Elliott and Thompson Limited
27 John Street, London WC1N 2BX
www.eandtbooks.com

ISBN: 978-1-9040-2796-6

9 8 7 6 5 4 3 2 1

A CIP catalogue record for this book is available from the British Library.
Printed in Italy by Printer Trento

THE XFM TOP 1000 SONGS OF ALL TIME.

General Editor: **Mike Walsh**

Acknowledgements

Mikey Abegunde
Bec Adams
Jim Adkins
Steve Atherton
John Baker
Vicky Ball
Daryl Bamonte
Ed Barfoot
Natalie Barnett
Michael Bennett
Nuno Bettencourt
Reena Bhima
Dave Bianchi
Peter Black
Jim Bob
Simon Bobbett
Clint Boon
Mark Bowen
David Boyd
Anton Brooks
Steve Brown
Max Buckland
Ed Buller
Stuart Cable
Ian Camfield
Cerne Canning
Phil Canning
Andy Cassell
Mark Chadwick
Phil Chadwick
Jim Chancellor
Tom Clarke
Jo Coleman
Austin Collins
Martin Coogan
Faye Copeland
John Coyne
Steve Cradock
Sally Cradock
Karen Dagg
Jonathan Daniel
James Davids
Matt Deverson

Karen Dooley
Lara Drew
Ben Durling
Racheal Edwards
Caroline Elleray
Dave Eringa
Matt Everitt
David Field
Stuart Fletcher
Brandon Flowers
Esme Foster
Simon Fowler
Liam Fray
Dave Fridmann
Malcolm Garrett
Guy Garvey
Jessica Gerry
Alex Gilbert
Alex H.N. Gilbert
Damon Gough
Liz Gould
Rachel Graham
Martin Hall
Martin Harris
Imogen Heap
Dennis Herring
Ben Hopkins
Crispin Hunt
Miles Hunt
Paul Jackson
Alan James
Gary Jarman
Ryan Jarman
Clay Jones
Kelly Jones
Richard Jones
Stephen Jones
Mike Joyce
Alex Kapranos
Yasmin Kerr
Gary Lancaster
John Leckie
Emma Lomas

Pete Lusty
Rob Lynch
Danny MacNamara
Ryan Maher
Kevin McCabe
Jon McClure
Dave McCracken
Alan McGee
Ant McGinley
Zoe McGrory
Alex McHardy
Aisling McKeefry
Chloe Melick
Moby
Kelly Money
Julie Morgan
Gordon Muir
Conrad Murray
Pete Nash
Keith Ormondroyd
Matthew Page
Dimple Patel
Richard Park
Mike Pickering
Sergio Pizzorno
Dave Philpot
Caroline Poulton
Jo Power
Matthew Priest
Jonathan Quarmby
Nick Raphael
Robert Reynolds
Garth Richardson
Dave Rofe
Andy Ross
James Sandom
Hik Sasaki
Peter Shershin
John Silva
Lionel Skerratt
Gaby Skolnek
Slash
Mike Smith

Paul Smith
Luke Steele
Gary Stringer
Claire Sturgess
Rob Swerdlow
Ashley Tabor
Tank
Chris Thomas
Robin Turner
Jude Vause-Walsh
Monique Wallace
Jasper Waller-Bridge
Andrew Walsh
James Walsh
Liam Walsh
Debs Wild
Andy Williams
Nicky Wire
Rick Witter
Mark Wood
Mog Yoshihara

With an extra-
special thank you
to Graham Albans,
for his relentless
endeavour

E&T TEAM
Mark Searle
Olivia Bays
Alex Chappell
James Collins
Rica Dearman
Clive Hebard
Sally Laver
Ellen Marshall
Ben Murphy
Kevin Stewart

Foreword

I've never met a person who didn't have a personal relationship with music. Some of us have deeper ones than others. But we're all in the cathedral. It could have been a band or a voice that first opened the doors. Or maybe it was a rhythm or a melody that called you to the pews. But when we heard that sound, whatever it was, we were transformed. We waved flags.

My older brother Shane had impeccable taste in music. Bands like The Smiths, Depeche Mode, New Order, The Cars, and Talking Heads were always rattling through his bedroom door. When compact discs took over the world he began to replace his collection of cassettes with them. The tapes were then handed down to me. They were my inheritance. I became one of the devout very quickly. They grabbed ahold of me and moulded me into the person that I would become.

Some of the bands that my brother passed on to me are in this book. And there are others whose stories I don't know within its pages. It takes 1,000 of the best tunes from some great bands and fills you in on their experiences at the pulpit. It's not about nostalgia. These memories and conjurings are proof that we existed. Now, sit down, have another Roy Rogers and do what you bought this book to do. Worship.

**Brandon Flowers,
The Killers**

Introduction

Warning: reading this book will compel you to beg, borrow or stream some of the songs written about within. Well, that's the intention anyway. At the very least, we hope you'll find it an enjoyable journey of discovery and rediscovery.

Inside this book you'll find songs that have soundtracked your entire life and songs that you will fall in love with for the very first time. There are first-hand accounts and fascinating facts about the how, where, when and why of some of the greatest music ever made. There will be things that you did know and things that you didn't – stories that have never been told and tales that have been updated. For example, did you know that Blur's string-laden classic 'The Universal' was originally written as a ska-reggae track? Or that the gear shift at 2 minutes and 50 seconds into Doves' 'Pounding' is one of the greatest single moments in modern music? OK, the last bit is merely my opinion, but you get the point. The Blur bit is true.

So why a big list and why now? Well, at Xfm we love a list as much as the next guy and we have produced many over our 18-year history. Xfm listeners have helped us compile the Best British Songs of All Time, the Best Indie Dancefloor

Fillers, the Best Songs of the Decade and more. It was with all this information, topped up by the strident views of Xfm staff, that we decided that 2010 was the year that we would compile *the* list. So here, in your expectant hands, it is. A list that spans from The Rolling Stones in 1965 to The xx in 2009, taking in every great riff, anthemic chorus, clever lyric and adrenalised drumbeat inbetween.

Of course, there will be cries of "Where the hell is…?" and "Are you serious about…?" but isn't that the beauty of it? There aren't many things in life that cause such pulse-quickening debates about subjective taste. In our case, the office arguments were overridden by the ultimate decider: votes from Xfm listeners. Personally I am still a bit miffed about the exclusion of Fountains Of Wayne.

Historically, the songs in this book start with the beginning of "alternative" culture in the mid-1960s. Xfm draws upon a rich heritage of great song-based music that comes from a place of authenticity and with something to say. Music that may often start left of centre but eventually makes a huge difference to the lives of many. From The Who to The Strokes, The Jam to the Arctic Monkeys, this is music that has truly meant something to its creators and its millions of fans. So why more Biffy Clyro than Small Faces? Why Bon Iver over Captain Beefheart? Simply because these are the artists and songs that resonate the most with Xfm DJs and listeners. We know that Dylan and Waits have had a monumental influence on music and culture, but this list is brazenly more about popularity than importance. Nobody can deny the influence of the great groundbreakers but people have voted for what they want to hear more than revere.

Xfm prides itself on passionately championing music that comes from an 'alternative' or 'indie' background that, in some way, influences the broader culture. The first radio station in the world to play The Killers and Kasabian, among many others, is also the radio station that celebrates the success of such era-defining artists. We love it when our friends become successful. Many artists that have enjoyed stadium success over the past ten years received their very first radio support from best-in-class talent spotters like John Kennedy and Eddy Temple-Morris. These longstanding Xfm DJs live and breathe new music and they are dedicated to bringing the best that they find to the airwaves. Xfm is run by a small but dedicated team of music lovers who are driven by a shared enthusiasm for the music that we are lucky enough to broadcast and write about every day. We hope that comes across when you listen to the radio station, browse the website or, indeed, when you read this book.

Many thanks to all our contributors and all the artists, producers, managers and label people who spoke to us specifically for the book. Indeed, our thanks to all of the artists that have ever taken time out for Xfm – to be interviewed, record a session or perform a gig – you really are the reason we all do what we do and we thank you from the bottom of our hearts.

Finally, as Xfm listeners helped us put this outstanding list of music together, this book is dedicated to you; without you, we wouldn't exist. Thanks for listening and taking part. And to anyone who has just picked this book up: many thanks and enjoy the journey.

**Mike Walsh,
Xfm Head of Music**

Authors

TOM BRYANT is a music journalist who has written for *Kerrang!*, *Q* and *MOJO* magazines and *The Guardian*, during the course of which he had an absinthe-fuelled sleepover at Marilyn Manson's house, got attacked by the Red Hot Chili Peppers' bass player and was accused of starting a riot with The Prodigy.

JULIUS HONNOR grew up listening to the rural rhythms of cows and sheep and The Wonder Stuff. Since then he has travelled the world and written about Moroccan Gnaoua music, Italian opera and Bolivian pan pipes. These days you'll find him mainly in London, taking photographs and writing for various books, newspapers, websites and magazines.

OWEN HOPKIN is Xfm's senior interactive editor and joined the station in 2007 having worked as a journalist for *The Fly*, *Melody Maker*, *NME* and *Kerrang!* He also played drums in The Crocketts and The Crimea and is flabbergasted that neither '1939 Returning' nor 'Lottery Winners On Acid' made the final list.

JOHN KENNEDY has been at Xfm since it began. Described by *The Observer* as the "doyen of underground alternative music", as DJ, presenter and producer of Xfm's new music show X-Posure for over ten years, he has given everyone from MIA to Mumford & Sons, Kate Nash to Razorlight their first ever radio play.

MARTIN O'GORMAN is managing editor of Xfm.co.uk, the official Xfm website. He has written for such internationally renowned music monthlies as *Q*, *MOJO*, *The Word* and *Record Collector*, and was a leading contributor to the book *The Beatles: Ten Years That Shook The World* (Dorling Kindersley, 2004).

BUFFIE DU PON has worked in the music industry for over ten years in both the recording and publishing sides of the business. Previously she was head of marketing and branding at Universal Music, working across a range of different music genres. In 2009 she moved to Global Radio to run their record and merchandise businesses.

JIM SALVESON started his career in radio after leaving university in 2000. Six years later he found his spiritual home when Xfm Manchester launched. He has since worked both on and off air on a number of programmes and has produced live sessions for the likes of The Courteeners, Frank Turner and Mumford & Sons. He also owns a Chaka Demus & Pliers album.

MARSHA SHANDUR is one of Xfm's longest-serving presenters and is renowned for her infectious music enthusiasm both on and off the air. She has also worked in various other areas of the music industry, including artist management, A&R, live music promotion and music supervision for a number of TV shows, including E4's *The Inbetweeners*.

MIKE WALSH has 20 years' experience in music and media – from US and UK college radio to head of music at Xfm, where he has been since 2005. In previous roles Mike worked with the likes of Coldplay and Blur in the promotions department of Parlophone Records and programmed various successful radio formats. Mike writes a column for Musicweek. com, regularly contributes to various international music conferences and lives in Cheshire with his wife and a few fish.

STEVE YATES has been writing about music since the mid-1990s, when an all-consuming passion for the records he'd been selling over the counter of a Manchester record shop led him to the pages of acclaimed dance magazine *Jockey Slut*. Since then, he's been a regular online and in print, writing for *The Word*, *Observer Music Monthly* and *Mixmag*, among many others.

ADDITIONAL CONTRIBUTORS
Olivia Bays, Matthew Matranga, Matt Pointon and Mark Searle.

Contents

Contents

AC/DC

AC/DC
Highway To Hell

1979 • 3:32 • Young – Young – Scott

Depending on your sources, 'Highway To Hell' was inspired by either the trials and tribulations of touring life or a treacherous road to a pub from singer Bon Scott's home in Fremantle, Australia. The theme, however, of a devil-may-care attitude to fast-living and its consequences – to which Scott was an enthusiastic subscriber – took on added resonance on February 19th 1980. After a drinking binge, Scott passed out in a car parked outside 67 Overhill Road in East Dulwich, south London, and died after choking on his own vomit. Not only did the song's crunching riff and thundering backbeat become one of rock's finest moments, it sadly also became a glorious epitaph to one of rock's greatest frontmen.

AC/DC
You Shook Me All Night Long

1980 • 3:30 • Johnson – Young – Young

'You Shook Me All Night Long' is a bar-room anthem that typified AC/DC's numbskull genius. A bluesy riff and a fist-pumping chorus soundtracked the re-telling of a 'successful night' with double-entendres and smutty humour to burn. It wasn't big, it wasn't clever, but it rocked. Hard.

AC/DC
Hell's Bells

1980 • 5:46 • Johnson – Young – Young

The ominous portent of chiming bells slowly gives way to one of AC/DC's most foreboding tracks. As the opening song of album *Back In Black*, released barely five months after talismanic singer Bon Scott's death, this was a goose bump-raising tribute to their former frontman. The album's black cover might have symbolised the band's mourning, but AC/DC celebrated Scott's life by unleashing arguably the greatest rock album of all time. In an arsenal of classics, 'Hells Bells' towers as one of the best.

AC/DC
Shoot To Thrill

1980 • 5:26 • Johnson – Young – Young

'Shoot To Thrill' was the staccato-riffed second track on *Back In Black*. Its huge sound was a product of famed producer Robert John 'Mutt' Lange, who helmed previous album *Highway To Hell*. *Back In Black*, however, with its crystal-clear guitars, thunderous low-end and impressive sonic breadth, was his masterpiece. The album, propelled by single and live favourite 'Shoot To Thrill', went on to become one of the biggest albums in history, second only to Michael Jackson's *Thriller*.

It wasn't big, it wasn't clever, but 'You Shook Me All Night Long' rocked

AC/DC
Back In Black

! 1980 • 4:13 • Johnson – Young – Young

Not even the death of lead singer Bon Scott could tear AC/DC away from their formidable blueprint. "If it ain't broke don't fix it" goes the saying, and that's exactly what brothers Angus and Malcolm Young had in mind when they hired Scott sound-a-like Brian Johnson from pub rockers Geordie.

The title track from his first album with the band became its calling card, framed by the unmistakable riff inspired by one of guitarist Angus Young's warm-up exercises. Johnson, AC/DC's new lyricist, was tasked with writing a tribute to his predecessor. "I just wrote what came into my head, which at the time seemed like mumbo jumbo," said the singer, but what emerged struck the mightiest of chords. Both defiant and celebratory, it was a fist-pumping rallying cry that became as much of a mantra for the band as an elegy to a fallen comrade.

AC/DC
For Those About To Rock

! 1981 • 6:47 • Young – Young – Johnson

Usually the band's roof-raising live finale, 'For Those About To Rock' is the title track to AC/DC's eleventh album – the second with singer Brian Johnson. The song's title was cribbed from a Latin phrase from ancient Rome, *"Ave Caesar! Morituri te salutamus"* ("Hail Caesar! We who are about to die salute you"), and turned into the rock fraternity's rallying cry by guitarist Angus Young. The punctuating canon fire in the middle and end of the song has since become a favourite visual staple of the live set. On cue, the band wheel out their replica Napoleonic canons to fire in time with the song. In a scene that sums up AC/DC beautifully, it's also notable for the sight of Johnson, a man of pensionable age, excitedly straddling the ancient weaponry. OH

Aerosmith

Aerosmith
Dude Looks Like A Lady

! 1987 • 4:24 • Tyler – Perry – Child

How many bands have had two separate careers, in two separate generations? Yes, there have been break-ups and reformations for many but in the main those bands tend to keep their previous fanbase, a crowd of faded denim patiently sitting through a song from the new album before being rewarded with a classic from the past. Aerosmith didn't just reform... they were reborn.

'Dude Looks Like A Lady' was the first product of that re-birth. Formed in 1971, the band experienced massive success, but internal conflict and drug-use caused Joe Perry and Brad Whitford to depart. It wasn't until they sobered up and reformed that the band tasted success once more with the release of *Permanent Vacation* in 1987. This time it stuck.

Written with serial songwriter Desmond Child (KISS, Bon Jovi, Alice Cooper), there are various stories about the inspiration behind 'Dude Looks Like A Lady' – the most salient of which comes from Stephen Tyler in the Aerosmith autobiography *Walk This Way*: "One day we met Mötley Crüe, and they're all going, 'Dude!' Dude this and Dude that... 'Dude (Looks Like a Lady)' came out of that session." The album sold more than five million copies, marking Aerosmith's return as "America's Greatest Rock And Roll Band".

Aerosmith & Run DMC
Walk This Way

! 1986 • 3:40 • Tyler – Perry

First released in 1977 and taken from the *Toys In The Attic* album, this single had already been a success for Aerosmith. But their collaboration with Run DMC would expose the band to a new generation and make musical history at the same time. The new version helped to bring rap into the mainstream while giving Aerosmith a younger audience, something which fellow Bostonite and guitarist Nuno Bettencourt told Xfm should not be taken lightly: "To cross the ages and add a whole other next generation of fans, equally as large as the first [is] truly inspiring. It must be the dirty water from Boston."

Aerosmith
Love In An Elevator

! 1989 • 5:39 • Tyler – Perry

Inspired by the success of Aerosmith's preceding album, *Pump* had a positive, fun energy that was reflected in 'Love In An Elevator', the first single release. Supposedly inspired by an experience Stephen Tyler had in a hotel, the song fantasises about sexual experiences in – ahem – "button-down environments". Despite its knowing innuendo and suggestive lyrics, this is no throw-away pop song: there's a great vocal performance from Tyler, tighter than tight harmonies and inspired rock riffs including – unusually for a single release – a two-minute guitar solo from Joe Perry and Brad Whitford. JS

Air
Sexy Boy

⏐ 1997 · 4:59 · Godin – Dunckel

Nicolas Godin and Jean-Benoît Dunckel formed the duo Air after performing in the same college band, Orange, which was also home to other leading lights in the French nu-electronica scene, namely Étienne de Crécy and Alex Gopher. Naming themselves after the phrase "*Amour, Imagination, Rève*" ("Love, Imagination, Dream"), the pair began releasing a series of chilled-out, slightly retro-styled instrumental pieces that referenced 1960s French mood music and the '70s synthesiser experiments of fellow countrymen Space and Jean-Michel Jarre. Their 1998 album *Moon Safari* was a huge worldwide hit and was preceded by the single 'Sexy Boy'. Laden with vintage synths and filtered vocals, the track sounds both dreamlike and stridently sinister. The French lyrics ponder the subject of the "ideal man", asking, "Where are the heroes with bodies like athletes? / Where are your rough-shaven, well-dressed idols?" An accompanying video by the director Mike Mills featured a charming animation of a giant stuffed monkey towering over New York and the song later featured in the film *10 Things I Hate About You*.

Air All I Need

⏐ 1998 · 4:28 · Godin – Dunckel – Hirsch

The biggest single to be taken from the 1998 album *Moon Safari*, 'All I Need' features a guest appearance from Beth Hirsch, a singer from Tampa, Florida, who met the band when she was living in Montmartre in Paris. "They'd heard my demo and invited me to sing on the album," she recalls. "I think they felt they needed a vocalist to come on and add some more colour." Hirsch wrote the melody and lyrics for the track, and supplied the impossibly delicate vocal, while the bassline was taken from an old Air song, '*Les Professionels*'. Now considered a modern lounge classic, the tune is frequently used in TV programmes whenever an air of cool sophistication is required. MO'G

Aqualung
Strange And Beautiful

⏐ 2002 · 3:51 · Aqualung

Matt Hales (also known as Aqualung) could be described as a born musician. Having played piano from the age of four, he has featured in a number of bands over the years (most with terrible names) but it was with Aqualung that he finally found success after 'Strange And Beautiful' was picked as the soundtrack to a Volkswagen advert. Working alongside then girlfriend Kim Oliver, he produced a sorrow-filled love song that manages to walk a fine line between pop and rock. The slow piano waltz is accompanied by yearning lyrics delivered in an irregular rhythm, occasionally pausing as though the singer is thinking about where to go and what to say next. Its style is reminiscent of Radiohead (think 'Karma Police') but with a focus on personal trauma rather than that of the world. Or to put it another way: if Radiohead were butter, Aqualung would be "I Can't Believe It's Not Butter" – a similar taste but with less guilt. JS

Arcade Fire Rebellion (Lies) 2005 · 5:05 · Arcade Fire

A constant changing of personnel is rarely a good thing in music but Canadian musician collective Arcade Fire appear to thrive on it. Fronted by husband-and-wife team Win Butler and Régine Chassagne, the rest of the group are transient – bringing with them different sounds and ideas as they come and go. 'Rebellion (Lies)' was the fourth single to be released from Arcade Fire's debut album *Funeral*, having secured their record deal on the strength of a handful of live shows. This song really set out the Arcade Fire stall: soaring strings, rhythmic piano, rich-layered choruses and Butler's honest, sometimes raw and always passionate vocals.

Arcade Fire
Wake Up

! 2005 • 5:33 • Arcade Fire

Arcade Fire songs often feel like a massive outpouring of emotion. The album *Funeral* was inspired by a series of family tragedies experienced by the band's members and the raw feelings transfer into the opening choral scream of the album's final single, 'Wake Up'. "Something filled up my heart with nothing / Someone told Xfm not to cry" begins Win Butler and from there the track builds and swells into an indie rock symphony, before suddenly

technical error and uploaded the wrong track instead – making 'Black Mirror' available. 'Intervention' starts in typical overpoweringly massive style, with an imposing church organ accompanying Butler's vocals, which have drawn comparisons with Bruce Springsteen. It was the sheer enormity of the song that prompted the band to allow fans to hear it, for the first time, via voicemail on a Freephone number. Singer Win Butler told *Pitchfork*, "I thought it would be an interesting context, to have this huge overpowering thing coming out of a tiny telephone speaker."

  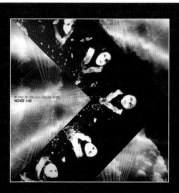

From left: 'Intervention', Keep The Car Running', 'No Cars Go'

mutating into a jaunty pop number complete with accordion accompaniment. It shouldn't work, but it does.

Arcade Fire
Intervention

! 2007 • 4:17 • Arcade Fire

'Intervention' was released ahead of second album *Neon Bible*. Put out as a charity download, the band made a

Arcade Fire
Keep The Car Running

! 2007 • 3:28 • Arcade Fire

Arcade Fire bought a church, converted it into a studio and shut themselves away in order to create their second album *Neon Bible*. 'Keep The Car Running' is probably the track most reflective of that unique environment, with a choir-like crescendo driven along by a pulsing urgent bassline. Although one might assume the nature of the environment in which it was created had influenced the album more widely, Win Butler has described it as a technical, rather than emotional, choice of location: "Most buildings aren't really built with acoustics in mind, and small churches definitely are."

Arcade Fire
No Cars Go

! 2007 · 4:13 · **Arcade Fire**

First released as part of Arcade Fire's self-titled EP, 'No Cars Go' was re-worked and re-issued as part of *Neon Bible*. Along with 'Black Mirror', it was the starting point of the second album. If Arcade Fire can ever be said to get anywhere near a pop song then this is it: soaring strings, crashing guitars, an almost singalong chorus, and what frontman Win Butler has noted as an upbeat, cheerful ending. A shining light in what is, for the most part, a dark and more foreboding album. JS

Arctic Monkeys
I Bet You Look Good
On The Dancefloor

! 2005 · 2:54 · **Turner**

Arctic Monkeys burst onto the UK music scene in 2005, bringing with them not only a new and distinctive sound but

also a change in the way that music was to be consumed. Seemingly appearing from nowhere, the band had built a local fanbase, which then in turn moved online and grew to propel 'I Bet You Look Good On The Dancefloor' to the UK number one spot (and subsequently made *Whatever People Say I Am That's What I'm Not* the fastest-selling debut album in UK chart history). This song was for most their first taste of Alex Turner's "honest" lyrical style, portraying the lives of young men in a north England town in first person prose. Combined with their post-punk sound (which caused comparisons with bands such as The Jam), it helped the band stand out in a landscape dominated by manufactured pop and set them on their way to being one of the most influential British groups of the decade.

Arctic Monkeys
When the Sun Goes Down

! 2006 · 3:20

The band's second single and their follow-up to 'I Bet You Look Good On The Dancefloor', the song was originally titled 'Scummy'. It charts the seedier side of hometown life, inspired by the prostitutes working near the band's studio in the Neepsend district of Sheffield. Starting slowly, the track cranks into the guitar-laden, beat-driven sound that became synonymous with Arctic Monkeys' first two albums.

Arctic Monkeys
Mardy Bum

! 2006 • 2:55 • Turner

Whereas much of *Whatever People Say I Am…* seems to cast an eye over Sheffield nightlife, 'Mardy Bum' deals with the album's other key theme: affairs of the heart. It describes the emotions of a man whose girl has "got the face on" and is written with a bittersweet affection that shows off Alex Turner's dry humour and an understanding of relationships beyond his 19 years. Although never released as a single, 'Mardy Bum' is very much a favourite among Arctic Monkeys fans.

Arctic Monkeys
A Certain Romance

! 2006 • 5:31 • Turner

'A Certain Romance' was one of the first Arctic Monkeys tracks to receive a public hearing. Although not released as a single, it was one of a handful of early demos put out as a free download and is widely considered to be one of the standout tracks on their debut album, despite some critics claiming that the track had lost some of its edge when compared to its raw internet release. The song is perhaps the best example of the way in which the band fused rock, punk and ska alongside Alex Turner's witty lyrics to create their unique sound.

Arctic Monkeys
Fake Tales Of San Francisco

! 2006 • 2:57 • Turner

'Fake Tales of San Francisco' is arguably the band's signature tune, effectively highlighting their charm. In it frontman Alex Turner pokes fun at an invented Yorkshire band, skewering their attempts to pose as a hipper, American version of themselves. Lines such as "I'd love to tell you all my problems / You're not from New York City, you're from Rotherham" highlight everything that the band saw themselves as not being; an effective declaration of intent for forthcoming releases.

Arctic Monkeys
The View From The Afternoon

! 2006 • 3:38 • Turner

As well as being influenced by bands such as The Strokes and The Jam, Arctic Monkeys spent much of their formative years listening to rap music. This is, on occasion, evident in singer Alex Turner's fast-paced, word-heavy delivery: 'View From The Afternoon' – in which Turner observes the local nightlife, such as the "lairy girls hung out the window of the limousine" – is an excellent example.

'Fake Tales Of San Francisco' was a declaration of intent

– Arctic Monkeys

Arctic Monkeys
Leave Before The Lights Come On

❘ 2006 • 3:15

The release of 'Leave Before The Lights Come On' filled the gap between the last single release from Arctic Monkeys' debut album and the first from *Favourite Worst Nightmare*. It was their first without bassist Andy Nicholson. Although a non-album release, it is similar in style to many of the songs on *Whatever People Say I Am...* In some ways it marked a turning point in Alex Turner's writing style; in 2006 he told *NME*: "I remember it's the last song that I wrote about that sort of time, going out and that. My life's not really like that any more."

Arctic Monkeys
Brianstorm

❘ 2007 • 2:50 • Turner

The pressure was on for album number two after the success of *What Ever People Say I Am...* But any doubts were soon

eased by the release of 'Brianstorm', just
eight months after the final single from
their debut album. The track hinted at a
new direction: driven by Matt Helders'
frenetic drumming, it's a much heavier
sound than previous offerings. The
mysterious 'Brian' of the lyrics remains
just that: the band denied his existence
in some interviews and in others claimed
he was a man who turned up in their
dressing room after a gig in Osaka, Japan.

Arctic Monkeys
Fluorescent Adolescent

! 2007 · 2:57 · Turner – Bennett

The second single
from the band's hotly
anticipated second
album *Favourite
Worst Nightmare*
and an answer to
the question of whether Arctic Monkeys
– and Alex Turner in particular – could
maintain their wryly observational
writing style in the face of such massive
success. Here the worldview shifts
from Turner's personal experience to a
broader observation of Britain's working
classes, in this case telling the tale of a
woman losing her sparkle as she ages.
This was the first track on which Turner
relinquished the position of sole lyricist,
creating the song alongside then girlfriend
and Totaliser vocalist Joanna Bennett
while playing word games on holiday.

Arctic Monkeys
Teddy Picker

! 2007 · 2:43 · Turner

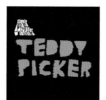

'Teddy Picker' was
the final song to be
released from the
band's second album,
apparently intended as
an aggressive appraisal
of "celebrity culture" and its random, fickle
nature. The band's swagger and confidence
is clear to hear in a song similar in many
ways to 'Fake Tales Of San Fransico', wound
up by fast, skilful drumming and a driving
juicy bassline that wouldn't sound out of
place on a Queens Of The Stone Age single.

Arctic Monkeys
505

! 2007 · 4:13 · Turner

A slower-paced, yearning love song, '505'
brings second album *Favourite Worst
Nightmare* to a close, while perhaps
kick-starting another musical journey.
The track features The Rascals' Miles Kane
on guitar and it would be with Kane that
Turner would later collaborate on musical
side project The Last Shadow Puppets.

Arctic Monkeys
Crying Lightning

! 2009 · 3:43 · Turner

Third album *Humbug*
was released in July
2009. The band decided
to decamp to the
Arizona desert to work
with Queens Of The
Stone Age's Josh Homme as producer for
the record. Meanwhile Alex Turner had
been spending time with side project

The Last Shadow Puppets. The resulting album sounded like the band was further away from Sheffield than ever. Their more mature and darker style was evident in 'Crying Lightning', the first single release. Driven by Nick O'Malley's heavy bass, it has a more vintage sound than previous releases, with Turner's lyrics at times hinting at a Lennonesque surrealism.

Arctic Monkeys
Cornerstone

! **2009 • 3:17 • Turner**

Arctic Monkeys' deepening maturity was increasingly apparent in follow-up single 'Cornerstone'. Alex Turner sounded more like Morrissey than ever and his Yorkshire accent wasn't as evident as on previous recordings – something that drummer Matt Helders put down to his time with The Last Shadow Puppets. He told Xfm: "I think [Alex] had more practise with crooning." This was Turner's "pop song" – written in a major key and lyrically more optimistic with a simple narrative, albeit one laced with metaphorical complexity for those wanting to look beneath the surface. JS

'Cornerstone' is Alex Turner's pop song

Ash
Kung Fu

! 1995 • 2:17 • Wheeler

For a small band, Ash certainly made a big impact with their first single for Infectious Records, 'Kung Fu'. Inspired by Tim Wheeler's love of marshal arts movies, particularly those starring Jackie Chan, it would eventually end up on the soundtrack to Chan's *Rumble In The Bronx* film. It also attracted the wrath of footballer Eric Cantona, who was angry that the single's cover featured a photo of him kicking a Crystal Palace fan. "I spit on your record," was the terse fax the record company claimed to have received from the incensed Manchester United star. That such a short burst of exuberant teen punk should have such an effect clearly delighted all involved.

Ash
Angel Interceptor

! 1995 • 4:04 • Wheeler – McMurray

The quiet before the storm. This was Ash's third single and, while they were very much a buzz band, with two top 20 singles and the support of the *NME* behind them, they had yet to hit the big time. This single came out shortly after a riotous Reading Festival performance in which security stopped the show twice, and preceded both their first world tour and the release of *1977*. Typically youthful for Ash's output at the time, things wouldn't be quite the same again afterwards: a number one album, fame and its subsequent pressures were all soon to follow.

Ash
Girl From Mars

! 1995 • 3:30 • Wheeler

There are fewer simple pleasures than punk-fuelled love songs, delivered with youthful exuberance, which invite everyone listening to jump around with their arms in the air. That is precisely what Ash achieved with their breakthrough fifth single. Frontman Tim Wheeler and bassist Mark Hamilton were both just 18 when the song crashed into the top 40. Ash had delivered a 1990s update to The Undertones' 'Teenage Kicks' – a band who similarly originate from Northern Ireland, similarly full of glee at the thrills and spills of fancying girls. Except, Ash being *Star Wars* fanatics, their girl was not from the neighbourhood, but space instead.

Ash
Goldfinger

! 1996 • 4:32 • Wheeler

Of all Ash's early songs, it was perhaps 'Goldfinger' that most veered from their upbeat template. Reckoned by the band's singer Tim Wheeler to be the best song Ash had then written, it was also the darkest of their initial output, paving the way for the future and yielding their first top 10 single.

Ash
Oh Yeah

! 1996 • 4:45 • Wheeler

As their second album, *1977*, hit the number one spot in the album charts, so 'Oh Yeah' crashed into the top 10 in the singles chart. A perfect summery paean to young love, complete with sweeping strings, guitars and delicious optimism, it's still a live favourite to this day.

lost the plot somewhat, disappearing and refusing to speak to the media. He surfaced in New York where, mostly, he hadn't been behaving himself. He returned to a band who were, financially, on their uppers and they retreated to Wheeler's parents' house to rebuild, in the process writing their strongest collection of songs to date. Written about Wheeler's then girlfriend, 'Shining Light' was the first to be completed: mature, expansive,

> A perfect summery paean to young love, complete with sweeping strings, guitars and delicious optimism
>
> – Ash, 'Oh Yeah'

Ash
A Life Less Ordinary

! 1997 • 4:16 • Wheeler

Riding the wave of successful second album *1977*, Ash were asked to write the title song to the Ewan McGregor film *A Life Less Ordinary*. More importantly, it marked two turning points for Ash – first, it featured new guitarist Charlotte Hatherley; second, its intricate songwriting hinted at new depths.

Ash
Shining Light

! 2001 • 5:09 • Ash – Wheeler

After the success of third album *Nu-Clear Sounds*, Ash's singer Tim Wheeler

but as melodic as ever. It would earn Ash an Ivor Novello Award, whopping single sales and an unlikely fan in Annie Lennox, who covered it in 2009.

Ash
Burn Baby Burn

! 2001 • 3:29 • Ash – Wheeler

Originally intended for *Nu-Clear Sounds*, this was re-written during the same sessions that brought about 'Shining Light'. Despite originally being about suicide, it somehow remains a breezy blast of bubblegum rock. Oozing sunny melodies, it recalls the best of their early celebratory punk while cementing their development into more mature songwriting territory.
TB

Richard Ashcroft
A Song For The Lovers

2000 · 5:26 · Ashcroft

Born in a small town called Billinge, near Wigan, in north-west England in 1971, Richard Paul Ashcroft would go on to become one of the most enigmatic and revered British songwriters of his generation. He formed The Verve (originally called just Verve) in 1989 and they released two epic albums – *A Storm In Heaven* (1993) and *A Northern Soul* (1995) – before splitting up only a few months after the second album's release. They reformed less than a year later and started recording demos with producer John Leckie (Radiohead, The Stone Roses) for an album that would become the world-dominating, multimillion-selling masterpiece *Urban Hymns*. Among the 30 or 40 songs that were demoed in those sessions was this incredibly personal and emotionally candid track, presumably about his newly established relationship with fellow musician Kate Radley of British band Spiritualized. 'A Song For The Lovers' was kept off the final set for *Urban Hymns* but a newly recorded, lush, string-laden version became Ashcroft's debut solo single in April 2000. It was an immediate hit at number three in the UK and spent a healthy six weeks in the UK top 40, perfectly setting up his well-received debut album *Alone With Everybody*. The narrative style, real-time video of Ashcroft in a hotel room was directed by Jonathan Glazer and was actually shot on a specially constructed set on a sound stage at Pinewood Studios. MW

'Wires' is tuneful, anthemic and – most importantly – moving.

Athlete Wires

2005 · 4:05
Pott – Roberts – Wanstall – Willetts

Near-tragedy can have its upsides. In spite of catchy choruses, a quirky, user-friendly sound and even a Mercury Music Prize nomination, south-east London band Athlete failed to make much impact with their debut album, *Vehicles And Animals*. That changed in January 2005 when they released the rousing ballad 'Wires'. Beginning with haunting piano chords overlaid with Joel Pott's breathy vocals, it looms and soars into a fist-in-the-air climax. However, it was the subject matter that really seemed to strike a chord with fans. Singing about the experience of when his new-born daughter had a seizure, Pott's lyrics manage to convey all the terror and urgency of his situation, before reassuring us that everything turned out OK. Released at a time when the UK was in withdrawal from the lack of a new Coldplay or Snow Patrol record, 'Wires' fit the bill perfectly: tuneful, anthemic and – most importantly – moving. MS

The Avalanches
Since I Left You

! 2000 • 4:41 • Chater – Diblasi – Drennen – McQuilten – Salo – Seltmann – Webb

Melbourne-based dance act The Avalanches may well have started life as a punk band but all signs of their instrument-playing past were pushed into the background for 2001 album *Since I Left You*. Its title track is a warm, summer-tinged collection of samples and spoken word, with beats borrowed from Klaus Wunderlich's 'Let's Do The Latin Hustle' and the lead vocal line from the Main Attractions' 'Everyday' (two of more than 3,500 samples Robbie Chater estimates they used on the album). Amazingly this mishmash of sounds comes to a completely cohesive head and the band claim that this track is the one time they managed to write a successful pop song.
JS

The Automatic
Monster

! 2006 • 3:42 • The Automatic

It was with a wry smile that The Automatic watched 'Monster' announce their arrival into the mainstream. The band spent much of the summer of 2006 having the lyrics to their breakthrough hit shouted back at them by fields full of refreshed festival-goers. Most of them perhaps didn't realise – or didn't care – that the song itself was intended to be a critique of laddish drinking culture. "It's a song about lairiness and drunken fools," said the band's guitar player James Frost. "Often you'll be playing that song and there will be a load of drunken fools shouting it back at you. There's a degree of irony." Edgy, angular and featuring a jerky disco-beat and screeched backing vocals courtesy of then keyboardist Alex Pennie, it was an unlikely hit, becoming a staple on radio stations across the summer of 2006 and peaking at number four in the UK singles chart.
TB

Babybird
You're Gorgeous

! 1996 • 3:48 • Jones

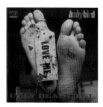

'You're Gorgeous' didn't have much going for it initially. Written for one of his first four albums under the alias "Babybird", Stephen Jones didn't consider the song strong enough to make it onto any of them. It was only after someone else found it on an old C90 compilation and convinced him to re-record it that the track made it onto fifth album *Ugly Beautiful*. Sweet and optimistic-sounding, it's often misguidedly assumed to be a love song: in fact Jones describes it as "a pro-female song against male photographers who want to use women to sell things using sex". That misunderstanding may have helped it to become an international hit – and one that continues to be used in media around the world. Layered with glockenspiel and shimmering guitars, its commercial nature sits in stark contrast to the rest of Babybird's often dark material. The band have gone on to make several albums, most recently featuring Johnny Depp playing guitar on and directing the video for single "Unlovable".
MS

Babyshambles Killamangiro

! 2004 • 3:24 • Doherty

This characteristically open and emotional address from Pete Doherty gave the ex-Libertine a UK top 10 debut single for his new band Babyshambles. The song is said to be Libertine partner Carl Barât's favourite by Doherty; certainly its frenetic energy and big hook stand comparison to some of The Libertines' strongest moments. It is not known whether the lines "On the off chance that you're listening to the radio / I thought you might like to know you broke my heart" refer to Barât or not.
MW

Badly Drawn Boy

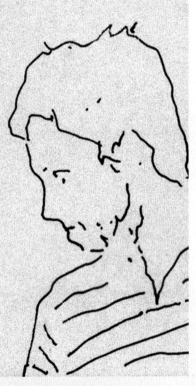

Badly Drawn Boy *Once Around The Block* 2000 • 3:44 • Gough

For the most part, Damon Gough's songs would start life as chords strummed into a tape recorder in his shared four-bedroom house in Manchester. But for 'Once Around The Block' he tried something new, starting with a bass line and working from there. The result would help his debut album *The Hour Of Bewilderbeast* win the Mercury Music Prize and Badly Drawn Boy (a moniker never intended to be used beyond his first EP) to become a household name. A fragile and uneven song, its complicated, improvised melodies give the record a charming naivety. "If I had to pick one achievement," says Gough, "this would be it."

Badly Drawn Boy
Disillusion

! 2000 • 5:10 • Gough

An education in songwriting both lyrically and musically, 'Disillusion' started off life as something very different, with early guitar-heavy demos being compared to the Isley Brothers by Damon Gough. Fellow Manchester band Doves were brought in to play on the track, influencing the song's final disco feel and unique Wurlitzer organ solo at the end.

Gough added simple piano melodies and relaxed breathy vocals that don't hint at the nerves he was feeling about recording in an alien LA environment. "You can hear it on the track," he said, referring to a Jack Daniel's and coke he was drinking while recording his vocal take: "the ice rattling in the glass."

Badly Drawn Boy
Something To Talk About

! 2003 • 3:41 • Gough

! Left: 'Disillusion', 'Silent Sigh', Something To Talk About'

Badly Drawn Boy
Silent Sigh

! 2001 • 4:01 • Gough

Despite being written long before Damon Gough's commission to produce material for the Hugh Grant film *About A Boy*, 'Silent Sigh' became the movie soundtrack's lead single. Using the bassline from Stevie Wonder's 'Supersticious' as a starting point for its composition,

Film soundtracks rarely become standalone albums in their own right, but here the delicate balance between artist, album and film is handled brilliantly, with Gough relating themes and issues in the song to those within the film, while at the same time retaining complete ownership of the track. Possibly the only pop song ever to include the words "ipso facto" – something which Gough jokingly describes as "a lyrical achievement".
JS

BeastieBoys

Beastie Boys
(You Gotta Fight) For Your Right (To Party!)

| 1986 · 4:10
Horovitz – Yauch – Diamond – Rubin

Long before the Beastie Boys were politically correct, painfully cool taste-makers, they were reviled and revered in equal measure following the success of debut album *Licensed To Ill*. As the biggest selling hip-hop album of the 1980s, as well as the first to go to number one in the US, these three white middle class New Yorkers divided opinion like few others.

In the UK, they caused a tabloid-fuelled moral panic, spurred on by live shows that included dancing girls in cages and an inflatable penis. Such was the uproar, Parliament debated the band's entry into the country – revealing a stuffy society struggling to come to terms with hip-hop culture. The kids, however, went potty for the band. Anton Brooks, who went on to become the Beastie Boys' longstanding press officer, saw their two-night stand at London's Brixton Academy with Run DMC. "Even the guard dogs had guard dogs," he told Xfm. "They were worth the hype though, they were absolutely brilliant."

'(You Gotta Fight) For Your Right (To Party!)' was one of the album's singles and clearly illustrated producer Rick Rubin's love of both hip-hop and metal.

The distinctly rocky backing track was a perfect foundation for the band's hilarious, parent-baiting anthem, crowned by an electrifying guitar solo courtesy of Slayer's Kerry King (whom Rubin was also producing). The Beastie Boys may not look back as fondly on this part of their history as others, but '(You Gotta Fight) For Your Right (To Party!)' is a bona fide anthem that continues to connect with millions.

Beastie Boys
Sabotage

| 1994 · 2:58 · Beastie Boys

Such was the success of the Spike Jonze-directed video for 'Sabotage', it's become difficult to decide whether the cop-show spoof is a promotional tool for the song or vice versa. Lauded as one of the greatest music videos of all time, it sees the band running through the streets of LA recreating set-pieces and visual clichés from the much-maligned TV genre.

Incredibly, it was beaten to Video Of The Year in the 1994 MTV Video Awards by ageing rockers Aerosmith. The gaffe was rectified in 2009 when the clip was awarded the newly coined category 'Best Video (That Should Have Won A Moonman)'.

Beastie Boys
Sure Shot

1994 • 3:20
Beastie Boys – DJ Hurricane – Caldato

If their underrated, sample-heavy second album *Paul's Boutique* signalled a reinvention, and third record *Check Your Head* saw the re-introduction of some of the band's early punk influences, fourth album *Ill Communication* was the skilful distillation of the Beastie Boys' entire musical world. 'Sure Shot' was the opening track of this masterpiece, a record that would ensure the band hit the world stage once more. This time, it was for all the right reasons.

Beastie Boys
Intergalactic

1998 • 3:30
Horovitz – Yauch – Diamond – Caldato

By the time the band's fifth album was released, the Beastie Boys seemed less a hip-hop group and more a cultural phenomenon. Their record label Grand Royal would go on to release seminal albums by At The Drive In and Luscious Jackson. *The Grand Royal* magazine's unabashed irreverence would be similarly influential and Mike D's clothing line, X-Large, had become the must-have label in all the right neighbourhoods.

Needless to say, much anticipation greeted their next musical move and 'Intergalactic' left no one disappointed. Its old skool flavour and Vocoded chorus satisfied the faithful and, with a body-popping robot for a video, fans' renewed interest couldn't help but continue furiously.

Beastie Boys
Body Movin'

1998 • 3:13 • Beastie Boys

The band's unrelenting creative hunger fuelled the making of fifth album *Hello Nasty*. With former DMC World DJ Champion Mixmaster Mike in the fold, the band presented a sparser, more retro sound that signalled another musical reinvention. The single 'Body Movin'' was a great example of this restlessness, confirming the Beastie Boys' standing as true hip-hop innovators. OH

!!! Communication was the skilful distillation of the Beastie Boys' entire musical world. 'Sure Shot' was the opening masterpiece

The Beatles

The Beatles Eleanor Rigby

1966 · 2:09 · Lennon – McCartney

One of the bleakest number one singles ever, this dramatic depiction of loneliness is one of Paul McCartney's most acclaimed songs as a Beatle. Initially composed on the piano, the lyric evolved gradually – Father McKenzie was originally Father McCartney, but McCartney's idea to have Eleanor Rigby and the priest meet in the third verse was vetoed by John Lennon. The track boasts only McCartney's vocal and a strident string section scored by producer George Martin, who was inspired by the Bernard Hermann soundtrack to the contemporary sci-fi movie *Fahrenheit 451*.

The Beatles
Tomorrow Never Knows

! 1966 • 2:58 • Lennon – McCartney

Inspired by John Lennon's experiments with the hallucinogenic drug LSD, this is perhaps The Beatles' most complex recording of all. Taking acid guru Timothy Leary's work *The Psychedelic Experience* as a starting point (itself based on *The Tibetan Book Of The Dead*), Lennon used phrases that were intended to guide the curious adventurer through an LSD experience. The music reflected the psychedelic chaos – against a monumentally heavy drum track, various homemade tape loops of sped-up guitar and voices fly in and out, while Lennon intones the lyrics as if he were preaching from the top of a mountain. 'Tomorrow Never Knows' still sounds like nothing else on earth.

The Beatles
Strawberry Fields Forever

! 1967 • 4:07 • Lennon – McCartney

Filming the movie *How I Won The War* in 1966, John Lennon's thoughts turned to his childhood. Between takes, he worked on a song about Strawberry Field, a children's home in Liverpool, which held an annual fête that the young Lennon would frequent. With The Beatles' touring days now officially over, the band reconvened to work on a new album and 'Strawberry Fields Forever' quickly became their most ambitious track yet. Initially recorded in a slow, dreamy style with a memorable intro played on the ancient proto-synthesizer the Mellotron, a dissatisfied Lennon

insisted that the group try again, this time with a heavy drum track and horn section. Still not happy, he persuaded producer George Martin to graft the two versions together. Although Martin had to slow the second version down slightly, by sheer luck the two takes matched seamlessly.

The Beatles
Lucy In The Sky With Diamonds

! 1967 • 3:28 • Lennon – McCartney

Written at the height of John Lennon's infatuation with LSD, this song from *Sgt Pepper* owes a debt to the surrealist fantasy of Lewis Carroll's *Alice In Wonderland*. Featuring some of Lennon's richest lyrical imagery, those in the know claimed the track was pure drug whimsy – after all, didn't the title's initials spell LSD? The true story was simpler. "My son Julian came in one day with a picture he painted of a school friend of his named Lucy," Lennon explained. "He sketched some stars in the sky and called it 'Lucy In The Sky With Diamonds'."

`A Day In The Life` put The Beatles at the forefront of the psychedelic underground

The Beatles
A Day In The Life

! 1967 • 5:04 • Lennon – McCartney

The finale to *Sgt Pepper's Lonely Hearts Club Band*, the genesis of this landmark song was surprisingly random. John Lennon had the *Daily Mail* propped up in front of him at the piano one morning, where he spotted an item concerning the number of potholes in the roads of Blackburn, Lancashire. Beside that was a piece on a coroner's report into the death in a car crash of the heir to the Guinness fortune, Tara Browne. Throwing in a third verse referring to the film *How I Won The War*, which Lennon acted in the previous year, he took the unfinished idea to Paul McCartney. His partner had a song fragment of his own, a brisk slice of life that complemented Lennon's piece perfectly. To bridge the gap between the two sections, Lennon wanted something along the lines of "a musical orgasm". Producer George Martin came up with the idea of employing a 40-piece orchestra, with each member taking their instrument from its lowest note to its highest over the course of 24 bars. The resulting crescendo was phenomenal and the track climaxed with three pianos hitting the heavenly E major chord. The stunning result put The Beatles at the forefront of the psychedelic underground, while propelling them light years ahead of their contemporaries.

The Beatles
All You Need Is Love

! 1967 • 3:50 • Lennon – McCartney

Tasked with composing a song to perform as part of the world's first "global TV show", John Lennon came up with this enduring tribute to the flower-power summer of 1967. Simple and effective, with a communal chorus that featured various celebrities and friends, the band demonstrate how far they've travelled in such a short time by mockingly singing their 1963 hit 'She Loves You' during the fade-out.

The Beatles
I Am The Walrus

! 1967 • 4:36 • Lennon – McCartney

'I Am The Walrus' is a cacophony of startling lyrical ideas, intriguing instrumentation and dazzling studio effects. Written line by line as the fancy took him, John Lennon's stream-of-consciousness gibberish namechecks Lewis Carroll and his 1872 poem "The Walrus And The Carpenter", but the sound is pure 1967. Starting with a muscular rhythm track, Lennon and producer George Martin added growling strings, a vaguely sinister choir (intoning "Oompah, oompah, stick it up your jumper") and a BBC radio broadcast of Shakespeare's *King Lear*. The song was the highlight of the otherwise underwhelming *Magical Mystery Tour* TV movie.

The Beatles
Hey Jude

! 1968 • 7:11 • Lennon – McCartney

The first single on The Beatles' own Apple label was prompted by the turbulent home life of John Lennon, who had recently ended his marriage to live with avant garde artist Yoko Ono. Having visited his partner's estranged wife Cynthia and son Julian, Paul McCartney toyed with an idea for a song called 'Hey Jules'. Changing this to the more "country and western" 'Jude', the track was recorded midway through the *White Album* sessions and quickly became one of the group's biggest hits, thanks mainly to the epic seven minute-plus running time and singalong fadeout.

The Beatles
Revolution

! 1968 · 3:25 · Lennon – McCartney

Written while The Beatles were in India studying meditation with the Maharishi, 'Revolution' ponders the turbulent events of 1968, which saw anti-war demonstrations and student riots across the world. Lennon initially used the lyric "When you talk about destruction / Don't you know that you can count me out... in" as though he wasn't sure of his position on violence. When the band rejected the song as the next Beatles single, Lennon re-recorded the track as an upbeat, grungy rocker, but this time he dropped the "in", committing himself to peaceful protest.

The Beatles
Helter Skelter

! 1968 · 4:30 · Lennon – McCartney

When contemporaries The Who claimed they'd made the loudest rock song ever, Paul McCartney decided to go one better. Initially recorded as a mammoth 27-minute blues jam, 'Helter Skelter' descended into a more streamlined yet chaotic rock thrash that anticipated the rise of heavy metal. With a nonsense lyric using a fairground slide as a metaphor, the whole thing confused psychotic LA hippy Charles Manson who thought the song was an incitement to murder.

The Beatles
Get Back

! 1969 · 3:11 · Lennon – McCartney

Thanks to a bootleg of Paul McCartney satirically riffing on the topically controversial subject of Asian immigration into the UK, 'Get Back' is sometimes unfairly accused of being racist – but don't forget, the Fab Four had spent three months in India the year before and were hardly bigots. McCartney ditched the original lyric, fearing controversy, and wound up with a mid-tempo rocker that concerned a group of misfits and transsexuals. 'Get Back' fitted their latest album idea perfectly, as the band were trying to return to their rock'n'roll roots and was memorably performed during the famous rooftop show on the Apple building in Savile Row in January 1969.

The Beatles
Come Together

! 1969 · 4:20 · Lennon – McCartney

Ostensibly written as a political campaign song for LSD guru Timothy Leary, 'Come Together' is classic freeforming John Lennon and arguably the last great song he wrote as a Beatle. Given a powerful and undeniably funky backing track by Paul and Ringo, Lennon's sketch of a weird hippy character was to get him into trouble, as he adapted the line "Here come old flat top" from 1950s rocker Chuck Berry's 'You Can't Catch Me' – later having to settle with Berry's publishers. Lennon's refrain of "Shoot me" is all but obscured, but the line is still chilling when you consider what was to happen to the Beatle 11 years later in New York.

better. "The relief of not having to go and see all those dopey accountants was wonderful," he recalled in 1980. One of Harrison's most inspirational songs, the feeling of hope shines out of every note.

The Beatles
Let It Be

| 1970 · 3:52 · Lennon – McCartney

Written by Paul McCartney, this quasi-religious song was inspired by a dream in which the troubled bassist's dead

> 'Let It Be' was inspired by a dream in which Paul McCartney's dead mother appeared to him

The Beatles
Here Comes The Sun

| 1969 · 3:06 · Harrison

The early months of 1969 had been rotten for George Harrison. Forced into rehearsing endlessly for the *Let It Be* album and with neither Lennon nor McCartney taking his compositions seriously, being a Beatle wasn't much fun. Having their own company Apple had also become tiresome, so one day Harrison skipped one of the interminable business meetings to hang out with his friend Eric Clapton. As he walked around the guitar hero's garden, the weather took a turn for the

mother appeared to him and told him to forget the business hassles and arguments that were now plaguing The Beatles. Featuring an impressive piano performance from McCartney, the gospel overtones of the track are accentuated by a soulful organ solo from guest musician Billy Preston. The song was released as a single in March 1970 and became the title track of the album and film project that had dragged on throughout the final year of the band's life.
MO'G

Beck

Beck
Loser

| 1994 • 3:54 • Beck – Stephenson

Beck's entry into the pop world sounded like nothing else before it. While Beastie Boys had successfully fused rap, rock and avant-garde funk, no one had thought to place a simple slacker indie song and bottleneck blues over crisp hip-hop beats, courtesy of Carl Stephenson (previously a beatmaker on such friendly fodder as Royal Flush's *"Uh Oh" – Suckers Come To War; Why? To Die*). 'Loser' had myriad inspirations, including the run of dead-end jobs the young Californian had been stuck in for years. But it was hearing his own attempts to imitate Public Enemy's Chuck D that made Beck think "Man, I'm the worst rapper in the world, I'm just a loser". A worldwide hit was born.

Beck
Where It's At

| 1996 • 3:42 • Beck – King – Simpson

The first single from Beck's immense *Odelay* was a flagpole for the album. 'Where It's At' was a hymn to hip-hop, drawing its "two turntables and a microphone" answer/hookline from 1980s hip-hop duo Mantronix, while also sampling a sex education record and cult outfit The Frogs. But amidst the clamour of shouts,

handclaps and Vocoder, the lovely laidback keyboard riff made this one of Beck's most delicious records. Not that American rap fans were won over. As Beck later told the *Irish Times*: "I've met a few rappers; they always think I'm from England."

Beck
Devils Haircut

| 1996 • 3:13 • Beck – King – Simpson

Odelay, Beck's second major-label album and his fifth in all, made explicit the huge debt he owed to patchwork-quilt muses the Beastie Boys. Enlisting the production help of the Dust Brothers (the sampladelic whizzkids behind the Beasties' epochal *Paul's Boutique*), he put the one-hit wonder jibes behind him, returning with an album that both captured and forged the zeitgeist. Eclectic to the point of giddiness, they sampled anything that took their fancy, including, on 'Devils Haircut', two songs by Van Morrison's old R&B band, Them (one replayed in the studio for added oomph).

If the music was a glorious mélange of rap and rock, the lyrics were something else entirely. An exercise in surreal couplets ("Love machines on the sympathy crutches / Discount orgies on the dropout buses"), it provided a stark reminder of Beck's own lineage. Beck Hansen, to give him his never-used full name,

The Beloved
the sun rising

WARNERPLATINUM

was the son of one of Warhol's Factory crowd and grandson of Al Hansen, a leading light of the Fluxus art movement. If Beck's own creations were a little easier on the senses than his ancestors', 'Devils Haircut' retained enough of their playful, anything-goes experimentation to gain the devotion of radio and critics alike. *Odelay*, the album it led off, was a steady success, fuelled in part by an Alternative Album Grammy and regular appearances in best-ever album lists.

Beck
Sexx Laws

¦ 1999 • 3:39 • Beck

The shiny, funky *Midnite Vultures* was possibly the first Beck album to disappoint. But even then it had its moments, principally the hilarious 'Debra' and 'Sexx Laws' – a brassy anthem that looked and sounded like a cross between Mark Ronson and Austin Powers. The lyrics skewed funk's customary machismo with Beck casting himself as a new man, unafraid to cry. He later said the brass on 'Sexx Laws' was inspired by the music at LA Rams football games; the video (which also stars a relatively unknown Jack Black) features a male therapy group-hug, disrupted when a team of helmeted footballers come crashing through the walls.
SY

The Beloved The Sun Rising

¦ 1989 • 5:03 • Marsh – Waddington

The Beloved were just one of the many indie bands who felt the benefit of the "second summer of love" in 1989. Having released a number of unremarkable guitar records on various small labels in the mid-1980s, singer Jon Marsh and keyboard player Steve Waddington pared the band down to a duo and pursued the sort of music that was filtering back into the UK from the clubs out in Ibiza. Based around a classic Chicago house bassline and drum pattern, the song's most distinctive sound is a sample of soprano Emily van Evera singing the beautiful medieval plainsong 'O Euchari'. The publishers of this classic were upset about the uncredited use of the sample, however, and the matter was settled out of court. Arriving at around the same time as 808 State's similarly blissed-out 'Pacific State', this is one of the key British house records of the era.
MO'G

Biffy Clyro

Biffy Clyro
Justboy

! 2001 • 4:22 • Neil –
Johnston – Johnston

These three school friends from
Kilmarnock, Scotland, were signed to
Beggars Banquet after a gig on the
unsigned stage at festival T in the Park.
The wrong-footing verse and sky-scraping
chorus on 'Justboy' laid the foundations
for what was to come and future Xfm
DJ Jim Gellatly – the first to play the
band on radio – quickly seized upon it.

Biffy Clyro
Joy.Discovery.Invention

! 2001 • 3:40 • Neil –
Johnston – Johnston

The opening track to Biffy's debut album,
Blackened Sky, was a fragile, gorgeous
ballad that exploded into a wondrous,
post-hardcore rage. The band toured
relentlessly on the back of it, cosseted
by an independent label happy to see
their popularity grow organically. Another
indication of the band's future success,
'Joy.Discovery.Invention' was clutched
desperately to the hearts of the faithful
and ensured that the rallying cry of "Mon
The Biff!" got louder with each gig.

Biffy Clyro
Questions And Answers

! 2003 • 4:05 • Neil

By the time the band recorded second
album *The Vertigo Of Bliss*, Biffy's endless
time on the road had begun to pay
dividends. Such was their musical synergy,
the album was reportedly recorded in a
day, with 'Questions And Answers' the
dazzling second single to be taken from it.

Biffy Clyro
Semi-Mental

! 2007 • 4:07 • Neil

Since 2002, Biffy Clyro had released
one album a year, but the move from
Beggars Banquet to Warner Brothers
subsidiary 14th Floor Records held up
the recording of fourth album *Puzzle*
for two years. "It was quite a frustrating
time," bassist James Johnston told Xfm,
"but we kept writing, so we had a lot of
songs to choose from." 'Semi-Mental', a
song debuted on previous tours, was the
first taste of the new album. While its
grungy stomp didn't quite give the band's
expansive new sound away, its release as
a download on 25 December – just days
after the album had been completed –
proved a massive hit with their fans.

Billy Clyro toured relentlessly on the back of 'Joy.Discovery.Invention'

Biffy Clyro
Saturday Superhouse

2007 · 3:00 · Neil

The first single proper from *Puzzle* was a visceral indication that the band's tendency to cram countless ideas into one song had been tempered considerably. "When we started playing it, we couldn't stop laughing because it was so simple and fun," frontman Simon Neil said. "When we heard it on the radio, it stuck out a mile as being the most aggressive song on there, but to us it's like a little slice of Girls Aloud."

Biffy Clyro
Living Is A Problem Because Everything Dies

2007 · 5:18 · Neil

Expansive and powerful, confident and humble, clever and dumb, Biffy Clyro's new album was a revelation, and nothing summed it up better than 'Living Is A Problem...' As the album's musically complex opener, it spelt out the record's central theme – the death of Simon Neil's mother – with jaw-dropping skill. "The album's about losing someone that you love very much and trying to cope with it," Neil told Xfm. "With personal issues and the label situation, we were asking ourselves a lot of questions at the time. *Puzzle* seemed to fit the mood of the record perfectly."

Biffy Clyro
Folding Stars

2007 · 4:15 · Neil

An unflinchingly honest song on an unflinchingly honest record, 'Folding Stars' was Simon Neil's most personal moment and also the most difficult to write and record. "This song had to be a pretty song," he once said. "It's a song for someone I love very much and I know they would have liked it. People can say whatever they want about this song. They can get fucked."

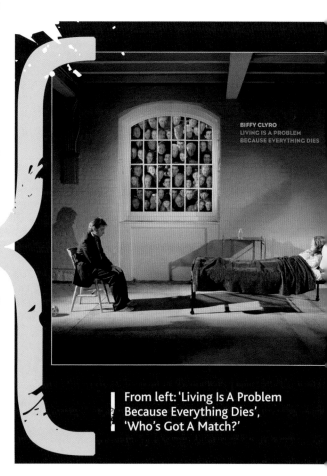

BIFFY CLYRO
LIVING IS A PROBLEM
BECAUSE EVERYTHING DIES

From left: 'Living Is A Problem Because Everything Dies', 'Who's Got A Match?'

Biffy Clyro
Who's Got A Match?

! 2007 · 2:23 · Neil

'Who's Got A Match?', and its dry-as-a-bone guitar riff, seemed to pre-empt the band's touring love-in with Queens Of The Stone Age and their main man Josh Homme's work on Biffy's next album, *Only Revolutions*. The towering desert rock band, however, were the furthest thing on frontman Simon Neil's mind when he wrote the song, telling Xfm: "It always reminds me of the *Airwolf* soundtrack… It's a lot of fun to play, but it's actually about being really mad at things."

Biffy Clyro
Mountains

! 2008 · 3:20 · Neil

Initially seen as a stop-gap between the commercial watershed of *Puzzle* and *Only Revolutions*, 'Mountains' was a very clear sign that Biffy Clyro had become fond of the big hitters' rarefied air. It may have

BIFFY CLYRO / WHO'S GOT A MATCH?

"The golden rule is me and my wife's secret"

— Simon Neil

had a tricky 15/16 time signature in the verse, but the chorus was as universal as anything that Biffy had recorded. The single charted at number five in the UK, their highest position to date.

Biffy Clyro
That Golden Rule

❗ 2009 · 5:40 · Neil

"We've either got parts a toddler can sing or parts that a string section can't play over. It's been the story of our lives", Simon Neil told Xfm. Nowhere was this conflict of styles more obvious than on 'That Golden Rule', where deft musical skill met a gorgeously lamenting chorus. The lyrics may have been a stream-of-consciousness effort by Neil, but that didn't mean they were meaningless. "There definitely is a golden rule," he said cryptically, "but it's me and my wife's secret."

Biffy Clyro
The Captain

❗ 2009 · 3:23 · Neil

'The Captain' saw the band team up with famed string and horn arranger, David Campbell. His dazzling CV may have included work with Marvin

Gaye, Beyoncé and Metallica, but Biffy were also impressed by the fact he was Beck's dad, as singer Simon Neil explained to Xfm: "We sat down with him in his house and we saw pictures of Beck as a kid... That was so weird."

Biffy Clyro
Many Of Horror

❗ 2009 · 4:18 · Neil

There were no left turns on this, a huge arena-filling torch song. It may have been one of Biffy's most emotive songs, but it was typically undermined by the band's mischievous title. "Sometimes we sit around and try coming up with band names for other bands," said drummer Ben Johnston. "Many Of Horror were an imaginary band that played really dark, country songs. The title just stuck."
JS

Big Audio Dynamite
E=MC²

| 1986 · 4:30 · Jones – Letts

After being strapped into The Clash's ejector seat, guitarist Mick Jones had a happier landing than his former bandmates, who followed his departure with the heinous *Cut The Crap*. While Strummer and co went backwards, Jones looked to the future with Big Audio Dynamite – formed with videomaker, DJ and all-purpose punk face Don Letts. 'E=MC²' saw them embracing drum machines, samples and electronics to create one of the era's catchiest singles. Despite Jones rapping the lead vocals like a man thrown into a three-legged race, the song holds the listener's attention, thanks in part to the incredible lyrics, a cryptic reworking of director Nic Roeg's filmography (a continuation of The Clash's own fascination with cinema as inspiration for song). The whole thing rattles along so charmingly, it's one for the whistling bank after only a few listens. It proved to be BAD's biggest hit, leading to a *Top Of The Pops* debut for the old punk boycotter.
SY

The Big Pink
Dominos

❕ 2009 · 3:46 · Cordell – Furze

This London duo were named as one of the BBC's "most likely breakout acts of 2009" and certainly managed to live up to the label with their heroic rock/techno sound. 'Dominos' was the first single to be released from their self-produced debut album *A Brief History Of Love* and it went on to win Best Track of the Year at the 2009 *NME* awards. Although you might have expected a certain pizza chain to pick this up for synchronisation in their media campaign, it was actually Xbox 360 and Jaguar cars who used the song on their TV commercials. Jaguar's strapline of "...an interior that exceeds even the promise of the exterior" actually seems like a fitting description of this promising act.
BdP

Bjork
Human Behaviour

❕ 1993 · 4:12 · Bjork – Hooper

By 1993 the indie world had grown accustomed to seeing its former heroes getting in touch with their much-parodied "dance side" (it became a running joke in the *NME*). But Bjork's was something else again. Retaining the wildly eccentric tone of previous outfit The Sugarcubes (which she dismissed as a joke band), the Icelandic star immersed herself in British house culture, striking up a friendship with Nellee Hooper, previously the very influential producer for Soul II Soul. The album these two fashioned together was as good a pop-house record as you could wish to hear.

The jump-off track and single for the incredible *Debut*, 'Human Behaviour' immediately announced itself as something radically different from Bjork's indie past. Against Hooper's slow, pounding drums and skittering percussion, Bjork incants the lyrics like a small, excited child gazing on the grown-up world with awe and wonder. Perhaps it retained some of that meaning because she wrote the melody as a child, originally presenting it years later under the title 'Murder For Two' to her former band The Sugarcubes, who didn't have a clue how to play on it. Their final album's loss was *Debut*'s gain.

Bjork incants the lyrics to 'Human Behaviour' like a small child – she wrote the melody as a child

Bjork
Venus As A Boy

! 1993 • 4:05 • Bjork

A chilled-out break from the dancefloor rush of *Debut*, 'Venus As A Boy' was a gently sexual tribute to an unnamed friend. With its odd clunky rhythm, it relies for momentum on the brilliantly orchestrated strings and vibraphone and a stunning performance from Bjork. Although she never gets specific about whether this friend was a lover, the way she fondles that egg in the video would be enough to set most male pulses racing. Bjork later admitted she was unhappy with the video director's "cooking" method for the egg, which is eventually fried. "Poached? OK. Boiled? OK. Raw? OK. But not fried," she told *Record Collector*.

Bjork
Play Dead

! 1993 • 3:57 • Arnold – Bjork – Wobble

Although added to later editions of *Debut*, 'Play Dead' originally appeared for the soundtrack of the *Young Americans* film. Written by ex-Public Image Limited member Jah Wobble and future James Bond composer David Arnold, 'Play Dead' took shape when Bjork asked the film director Danny Cannon to fill a page with excerpts of the main character's dialogue, from which she took the title and one more line. The result was markedly different from both her solo and band work, being an epic string-laden piece of aural cinematography that proved a good deal more durable than the film it was written for.

Bjork
Big Time Sensuality

! 1993 • 3:56 • Bjork – Hooper

'Big Time Sensuality' was so brilliantly, breathtakingly immediate, it's amazing it took Bjork's label three singles to get around to releasing it. There's the beginning of the trance sound, before it calcified into pure cheese, a lovely bouncy bassline and an astonishingly gymnastic vocal from Bjork. Despite the title, she insisted the song was a tribute to her purely platonic relationship with producer Nellee Hooper and their shared obsession with, and pleasure in, the job. The video, filmed by photographer Stephane Sednaoui, was also a treat, shooting Bjork for hours on end on the back of a truck in the streets of Manhattan. Even the fact that the video used the Fluke Remix rather than the single version couldn't stop this becoming her break-through single in America.

Bjork
Hyperballad

! 1996 • 4:00 • Bjork – Hooper – De Vries

Despite having no obvious hook or soaring melody to recommend it, 'Hyperballad' topped the vote when Bjork asked fans to select tracks for her 2002 *Greatest Hits* compilation. It's an intense passion play, set to low-key, bubbly, bleepy electronica that builds slowly into a state of delirium. The song concerns a woman who wakes up early every morning, walks to the cliff edge and chucks any old rubbish – "car parts, bottles, cutlery" – off the mountain top, just to purge herself of relationship frustrations so she can go back to her lover happy. Utterly barking, but with an undeniable kernel of truth. SY

Black Grape
Reverend Black Grape

! 1995 • 5:13 • Leveridge – Ryder

When Happy Mondays split following a holiday/recording session/crack binge to forget in Barbados, the smart money was most definitely not riding on the world hearing from Shaun William Ryder again. Though he was an undeniably brilliant lyricist (the greatest poet since WB Yeats,

according to former factory label boss Tony Wilson), not even his mum could love the Bard of Salford's singing, while his well-documented issues with a variety of banned narcotics left him with a reputation best described as "difficult".

Sure enough, when Black Grape formed in 1993 it was without a record deal. Comprising Ryder, the Mondays' non-playing, all-dancing phenomenon Bez, Kermit from Manchester's Ruthless Rap Assassins, drummer Jed Lynch and guitarist Wags from Paris Angels, they might have been mistaken for a Madchester *Wild Bunch*. But incredibly, when that conga drum-roll begins, punctuated by an exultant "yeah" (the accompanying album was called *It's Great When You're Straight...Yeah*), and slides into the harmonica, it's like Happy Mondays had never gone terribly, horribly wrong.

'Reverend Black Grape' is a monster – a danced-up counterpoint to Britpop's retro indie-isms. Black Grape were looser but slicker than Happy Mondays ever were. They also knew how to court controversy: in a song that generally took an axe to organised religion, the lyrics repeat old claims about the Catholic Church's cosy relationship with the Nazis. "Oh Pope he got the Nazis to clean up their messes / He exchanged the gold and paintings, he gave them new addresses". And who was that on the cover of the album? Why, it's notorious international terrorist Carlos the Jackal. Amazingly, the band withstood the ensuing controversy and 'Reverend Black Grape' outsold Happy Mondays at their peak, lodging comfortably inside the top 10 while the album went straight to number one. They were awarded Best Single at the *NME* Brats. True to form, Ryder got smashed and left it in the cab on the way home.

Black Grape
In The Name Of The Father

| 1995 • 4:21 • Saber – Ryder

'In The Name Of The Father' may have begun with a sitar, but that was about as spiritual as the second big hit off *It's Great When You're Straight…Yeah* got. This was another kick-ass stomp through the surreal reaches of Shaun Ryder's brain, speculating on the size of Neil Armstrong's testes and whether he played golf on the moon. It wasn't anything Ryder said on this record that troubled midwest America though – it was the presence of Kermit. Gary Kurfirst, their US label head, said their radio promoters couldn't get the track played unless they took the rap off. Not all America was so conservative, though: Lars Ulrich of Metallica named the album his favourite of the year.
SY

Black Rebel
Motorcycle Club
Spread Your Love

| 2001 • 3:45 • B.R.M.C.

A brutal, fuzzy, stomping rock song, 'Spread Your Love' is one of the highlights from Black Rebel Motorcycle Club's debut album *B.R.M.C.* Named after Marlon Brando's biker crew in classic film *The Wild One*, the trio was based around San Franciscan guitarists Peter Hayes and Robert Levon Been (who went under the name Robert Turner when this record was made). Together with British drummer Nick Jago, the band wore their garage rock influences on their sleeve, paying homage to the likes of The Velvet Underground, The Stooges, The Jesus And Mary Chain and other purveyors of distorted guitar rock. Although partial to the odd introspective and psychedelic moment – their fourth album *Howl* toys with country music in places – 'Spread Your Love' sounds like the bastard child of Black Sabbath and Kasabian, with Hayes and Turner sharing both vocal duties and guitar solos.
MO'G

Black Sabbath Paranoid

| 1970 • 2:45
| Butler – Iommi – Ward – Osbourne

Proof that heavy metal is always best at its simplest, 'Paranoid' was written and recorded in the time it takes to watch an episode of reality TV show *The Osbournes*, part of which all of the band except

> 'Spread Your Love' sounds like the bastard child of Black Sabbath and Kasabian

guitarist Tony Iommi spent out getting lunch. When they returned; Iommi had that famous riff, which opens the song then disappears after 12 seconds, never to return – replaced instead by a chugging, relentless intensity, underlined by the pile-driver blows coming in at the end of the bar. But if the riff and its surrounds were unforgettable, the lyrics were something else again. Tapping into that sense of personal darkness that gripped all the Sabs' best work, 'Paranoid' flew out of the blocks with one of the best (and in light of what we'd subsequently knew about Ozzy Osbourne's woman, most ironic) opening lines ever, in "finished with my woman 'cos she couldn't help me with my mind".

The song was put together so quickly that Ozzy was singing the lyrics while reading them for the first time from the sheet of paper on which they were hastily scrawled by bassist Geezer Butler. The lack of practice may explain why it threw up one of the most misquoted lyrics in rock: "enjoy your life before it's too late" was misheard as "end your life", which sounds funny now but was a lot less so at a time when hard rock bands were being sued for inciting suicide. Not that it had any impact on the song's appeal, proving their biggest hit in the UK and reaching number four. Ozzy used it as an encore long into

Ozzy sung the lyrics while reading them for the first time

his solo career and its enduring popularity was such that it was voted the fourth best hard rock song ever by VH-1 in 2009. Not bad for a tune knocked up during lunch. SY

Blind Melon No Rain

1992 • 3:36 • Graham – Hoon – Smith – Stevens – Thron

When all-and-sundry were donning checked shirts and aping the sound of Seattle, Blind Melon tipped their hat to the more rootsy rock of America's Deep South. Singer Shannon Hoon's friendship with Axl Rose and his backing vocals on Guns N' Roses' *Use Your Illusion* albums certainly piqued interest, but the band's self-titled debut album looked dead in the water until 'No Rain' turned its fortunes around spectacularly. Samuel Bayer, the man behind Nirvana's iconic 'Smells Like Teen Spirit' video, was drafted in to direct the promo. Taking inspiration from the album's cover, a picture of drummer Glen Graham's sister in a bee outfit, Bayer spun a touching story of a similarly dressed tap-dancing girl. It became a huge MTV hit.

However, Hoon's spiralling drug problems would ultimately cut short what seemed to be the beginnings of a dazzling career. On tour promoting second album *Soup* in 1995, he was found dead on the band's tour bus from an apparent drug overdose. OH

Blink-182

Blink-182
What's My Age Again?

❗ 1999 • 2:28 • DeLonge – Hoppus

In a year that saw the release of film *American Pie*, Blink-182 provided the soundtrack (and the figureheads) for a generation of 20-somethings with a fascination for boobs and beer. Three previous albums had failed to ignite the charts and it was *Enema Of The State* that gave the band their first break. Originally titled 'Peter Pan Complex', this was the first single to be released and not only tapped into that culture but coined the band's "anything goes" style, something that Mark Hoppus, speaking to *NY Rock*, argued wasn't entirely justified. "[The record company] really tried to market us as a bunch of guys that will do almost anything for kicks. That's not what we're all about."

Blink-182
All The Small Things

❗ 1999 • 2:48 • DeLonge – Hoppus

Written by Tom DeLonge after a complaint from his then girlfriend that he never wrote songs about her, 'All The Small Things' was Blink-182's breakthrough track (later promoting the re-issue of 'What's My Age Again?'). Much of the song's success was down to exposure on MTV, with a video parodying pop videos from the likes of Backstreet Boys and *NSYNC.

Blink-182
I Miss You

❗ 2003 • 3:47 • Hoppus – Barker – DeLonge

For all their success – and they've had quite a bit, having sold more records than The Clash, The Ramones and the Sex Pistols combined – one thing has eluded Blink-182: the respect of their punk peers. Their 2003 self-titled album was the sound of a band trying to be taken seriously; leaving the locker room humour behind and writing songs of, by and for adults. 'I Miss You' was the standout track from the album and proof that the fratboys of punk were becoming the elder statesmen. The song has a much softer sound than might be expected from the band; its rolling drumbeat is accompanied by downbeat vocals delivering deeper (though not too deep) and more personal lyrics than previous releases. JS

Bloc Party

Bloc Party
Banquet

! 2004 • 3:21 • Bloc Party

Originally forming at Reading Festival in 1999, Bloc Party met a wave of indie love in 2005 when their album *Silent Alarm* was released. The up-tempo, dance-friendly rhythms, strident guitars and Kele Okereke's conversational singing style became a blueprint for a new London sound in the first decade of the century. They took what Franz Ferdinand had made fashionable and ran with it, fast, all the way to *NME* Album of the Year.

The sound of 'Banquet' is clean, the subject less so – "I'm on fire when you come" sings Okereke as drums and guitar riffs build to an impassioned crescendo. A remix of 'Banquet', by The Streets, was included on the later Bloc Party single 'Two More Years'.

Bloc Party
Helicopter

! 2005 • 3:40 • Bloc Party

One of the bounciest songs from *Silent Alarm*, 'Helicopter' made an obvious single. Kele Okereke confidently belts out a cryptic stream of lines about someone not liking chocolate and making the same mistakes as his dad over some wonderfully insistent drumming. Theories

that the song is a criticism of George W Bush have been denied by frontman Okereke in interviews, possibly to avoid alienating American fans. The repeated tagline "Are you hoping for a miracle?" helped it to be chosen for the soundtrack for the football video game *FIFA 06*.

Bloc Party
So Here We Are

! 2005 • 3:53 • Bloc Party

Reaching number five in the UK charts in February 2005, 'So Here We Are' showcased Bloc Party's gentler side. Opening with a beautiful plucked guitar sequence, Kele Okereke's voice is quieter, more muted, as he sings sadly about a relationship gone wrong before, two-thirds of the way through, the tempo and his voice rises, ending the song on an upbeat note.

Bloc Party
Two More Years

! 2005 • 4:28 • Bloc Party

Recorded in summer 2005 and released to coincide with the band's October tour, 'Two More Years' has a poppier feel than the classic *Silent Alarm* tracks, with an extra layer of synths and Kele Okereke sounding a little less strident and raw. But it still has a catchy, energised post-punk feel that's hard not to tap along to. The song deals with a broken relationship, though in hindsight some argue that it was prescient for the band's future.

Bloc Party The Prayer

! 2007 • 3:45 • Bloc Party

BLOC PARTY.
A WEEKEND IN THE CITY

Inevitably, after becoming darlings of indie rock, weighty expectation was heaped on Bloc Party for their second album, *A Weekend In The City*. They coped with some aplomb on this track; adapting their style away from punk towards something a little camper, further away from their post-punk label. 'The Prayer' is an ambitious concoction with a backdrop of monkish chanting, layered with some 1980s-style disco synths and the ever-present heavily percussive beat as singer Kele Okereke prays for dancing feet and the power to dazzle. The song was Bloc Party's highest charting, reaching number four in the UK.

Bloc Party | Still Remember
2007 · 4:36 · Bloc Party

Kele Okereke is a hard man to label. Born in Liverpool to Nigerian parents, he grew up in Essex and has said that he is not proud to be English. He speaks with a stammer. In an indie world of over-confident, white, straight men, he stands out a mile. For Bloc Party's first album, Okereke dodged questions over his sexuality but 'I Still Remember', with its wistful talk of fingers touching and trousers being left by the canal brought them back to the surface and he admitted in interviews to at least a partially autobiographical element to this ballad of unfulfilled love.

Bloc Party Flux
! 2007 • 3:36 • Bloc Party

Though Bloc Party were always fast and rhythmic enough to be dancefloor-friendly, 'Flux' still sounds like a dramatic departure. Having released albums of remixes, their music was suddenly a fully paid-up member of club culture, fusing dance beats and electronic manipulation. 'Flux', produced by Jacknife Lee, an electronica specialist, is startlingly bereft of trademark drums and guitars. "We are in a state of flux" intones Kele Okereke, and clearly they were, big time. Fans weren't entirely bamboozled, however; this is dance music with polished, intelligent panache and it reached the UK top 10. The band also recorded German and French versions of the song.

Bloc Party Mercury
! 2008 • 3:53 • Bloc Party

The video for 'Mercury' features ape scientists creating a strange creature with the head of an ass who then gets elected to the White House, but the meaning of the lyrics is much more opaque. The song has a frenzied energy that occasionally teeters on the edge of instability, while confirming Bloc Party's move away from student bars towards the dancefloor.

Bloc Party
One More Chance
! 2009 • 4:40 • Bloc Party

"The music of Bloc Party came from a very anxious place, an almost neurotic, melancholic place," frontman Kele Okereke told *The Guardian* in June 2010. It wasn't clear whether the One More Chance being begged for here was for a relationship or the band itself, but the level of worry is obvious – both in its insistent house beats and Okereke's strained tones. Kele (having dropped his surname) has since gone solo, and it seems likely that One More Chance may end up being the band's swansong. JK

Blondie
Hanging On The Telephone
! 1978 • 2:23 • Lee

Formed around guitarist Chris Stein and former *Playboy* bunny-turned-singer Debbie Harry, Blondie were one of the bands that frequented New York clubs such as CBGB in the mid-1970s. Their contemporaries were groups like The Ramones and Television, who laid the foundations for punk rock. Originally called Angel And The Snake, Stein and Harry renamed their outfit after the singer's distinctive bleached hairstyle. Achieving a modicum of success in Europe and Australia with first two albums *Blondie* and *Plastic Letters*, the band met up with producer Mike Chapman to work on their third LP. Chapman, who was best known for his work with glam rockers Sweet and Suzi Quatro in the early '70s, found the initial meeting with Stein and Harry difficult. "I found the rest of the band to be pretty accessible," he recalls. "They even knew some of my musical history. To Debbie and Chris, that was somewhat irrelevant."

Chapman gained their trust by turning the embryonic version of 'Heart Of Glass' into pure hit single material, emphasising its dancefloor feel and giving it a gleaming production. The resulting album, *Parallel Lines*, became a new-wave classic and a number one album in the UK. The energetic opening track, 'Hanging On The Telephone', wasn't actually a 'Blondie original but a cover of a song written by Jack Lee for LA band The Nerves in 1976. "After we had the track down, I said, 'You know, we should put a telephone ring on the front of this'," Chapman told *Sound On Sound* in 2008. "The Blondies all thought that was too gimmicky, but I told [the engineer] to call anyone he knew in London in order to record a British phone ring. Once we stuck that on the front of the song they all went, 'Oh, yeah, that does sound pretty cool'."

Blondie Atomic
! 1979 • 3:50 • Harry – Destri

The follow-up to the monster worldwide hit album *Parallel Lines* saw Blondie journeying further into the world of new-wave disco. *Eat To The Beat* appeared a year later in 1979 and the band notched up another UK number one single with 'Atomic'. While the single's title – and post-apocalyptic video – seemed to tap into the fear of nuclear destruction that blighted the early 1980s, Debbie Harry claims that the lyrics were nonsense. "A lot of the time I would write while the band were just playing the song and trying to figure it out," she recalled. "I would just be scatting along with them and I would just start going, 'Ooooh, your hair is beautiful'."

Blondie Rapture
! 1980 • 6:31 • Harry – Stein

While tracks like 'Heart Of Glass' had seen Blondie cast off traditional punk snobbery and embrace disco music, the band's fifth album, *Autoamerican*, saw them take the next step along the road of DJ culture. By 1980, New York was a cultural melting pot of punk – which had turned into more commercially viable new wave – and disco, which was already being derided by a bored public and had started to mutate into something much more interesting – hip-hop and rap. Clubs like The Roxy were bringing punks together with DJs, breakdancing crews and graffiti artists, and the results of this cross-pollination were spilling out into the mainstream via tracks like 'Rapture'. Debbie Harry and Chris

Stein's tribute to the New York club scene, the track has a classic disco bassline, while namechecking super-DJ Grandmaster Flash ("Flash is fast, Flash is cool") and graffiti artist extraordinaire Fab 5 Freddy. Most notably, the song winds up with Harry attempting to rap – although it's not very good and mostly gibbbers on about "The man from Mars" eating "cars and bars", it brought the art to its biggest audience yet. MO'G

The Bluetones Slight Return
1996 • 3:23
Chesters – Devlin – Morriss – Morriss

Arriving a little too late to seem as fashionable as some of their Britpop compatriots, Hounslow's Bluetones are still going strong, though they have never quite matched the impact of this, their singalong debut. It took two attempts to put 'Slight Return' on the musical map – released originally as a double A-side in 1995 together with 'The Fountainhead', it was re-issued the following year, when it reached number two in the UK charts. A traditional male four-piece, guitar and bass jangle sunnily as singer Mark Morriss, one of two brothers in the band, announces that "all this will fade away" and that he's "coming home". The simplicity of the lyrics belie comparisons with the more complex Stone Roses, but it's a song that perfectly captures the sound of 1990s Britain. Though the song was kept off the top of the charts by Babylon Zoo's electronically futuristic 'Spaceman', British music had rediscovered the primacy of the guitar. JH

Blur She's So High
1990 • 3:50 • Albarn – Blur

Blur's debut single was one of the very first songs ever written in the inebriated haze of early meetings between Damon Albarn, Graham Coxon, Dave Rowntree and Alex James. Playing it live, under the band's original name of Seymour, 'She's So High' was one of the songs that helped bring the industry attention that would eventually secure deals with Food Records and MCA publishing. There was another song from those early sessions that almost became Blur's debut single – 'I Know' was a cynical and self-conscious attempt to ape the "baggy" sound of the day that was emanating with great success from Manchester bands like the Happy Mondays and The Stone Roses. For this very reason, 'I Know' was favoured by many of the bosses at Blur's record label and publisher. Thankfully, the band won this early battle and wistful anthem 'She's So High' set the tone for what would become one of the greatest British song catalogues of all time.

there's no other way

Blur There's No Other Way 1991 • 3:14 • Albarn – Blur

Given the battle over whether to release 'I Know' (see left), it was ironic that Blur's first proper chart success was as close as they got to being part of the Madchester "baggy" sound, with their top 10 UK hit 'There's No Other Way'. It's got one of Graham Coxon's most infectious guitar licks underpinned by a rhythm section urging the listener to shuffle their way to the indie disco dancefloor. Damon Albarn described 'There's No Other Way' at the time to Food label boss, Andy Ross, as "a B-side for sure". Luckily, the label got their way this time.

blur
Chemical World

'For Tomorrow' and
'Chemical World' were Blur's
"get out of jail songs"

– Andy Ross

Blur
Popscene

1992 · 3:15
Albarn – Coxon – James – Rowntree

With confidence high on the back of the success of 'There's No Other Way', the band and their team were bullish about releasing the aggressive but hook-laden 'Popscene'. Taking the band back to their punkier art-school roots, the plan was that 'Popscene' was to be the next hit single – a one-off release that would bring them much national attention between the *Leisure* and *Modern Life Is Rubbish* albums. It wasn't and it didn't. Much to their frustration, it only spent one week in the UK top 40 after limping in at a disappointing number 32. It is, however, still regarded as one of Blur's finest moments and hints at the heavier sound that would bring them great international success several years later.

Blur
For Tomorrow

1993 · 4:20
Albarn – Coxon – James – Rowntree

In the words of the band's publisher and confidant Mike Smith, "this was the moment when you knew that Blur were a very special band indeed". 'For Tomorrow' and 'Chemical World' were a pair of songs Damon Albarn created in angry response to his record label telling him that the *Modern Life Is Rubbish* album wasn't good enough. 'For Tomorrow' was written by a hungover Albarn at home in Colchester on Christmas morning

1992. It is undoubtedly the sound of him finding that voice of distinctly English melancholy and lyrical observation that would serve him brilliantly through the next three Blur albums.

Blur
Chemical World

1993 · 6:34
Albarn – Coxon – James – Rowntree

Disappointing sales, a UK press obsessed with American music, an unenthusiastic record label and a soul-destroying US tour had all left Blur a bruised and wounded band. 'Chemical World' was released as a single a month before the band played a legendary and pivotal performance headlining the Melody Maker tent on the Saturday night of the 1993 Reading Festival. A full tent going mental, singing along to every word, lifted spirits and re-galvanised the band. It also turned the heads of the media and the band's label. Food label's Andy Ross later described 'For Tomorrow' and 'Chemical World' to Xfm as Blur's "get out of jail songs".

Blur Girls & Boys

1994 · 4:51
Albarn – Coxon – James – Rowntree

From the opening notes of Alex James's disco bass you knew that this was the start of something different and big for Blur. The song was effectively the opening credits of the Britpop adventure

that would gleefully consume British culture for the rest of the decade. 'Girls & Boys' became the band's first top five UK hit and the omnipresent soundtrack to summer 1994. It marked the start of Blur's ability to mine a seam of intelligent but beery anthems – a laddish pop music that was as much for the heart and the head as it was for the terraces.

Blur
To The End

❙ 1994 · 4:05
❙ Albarn – Coxon – James – Rowntree

The second single from *Parklife* is an early example of the softer, less detached, and more emotionally open side of Damon Albarn. The song's ballroom waltz was the perfect counterpoint to the frenetic energy of 'Girls & Boys' and the album's cartoon-esque title track. In June 1994, 'To The End' was drawing more and more attention to an album that was already being described by the British press, keen to play catch-up on Blur, as a modern classic.

Blur
Parklife

❙ 1994 · 3:05
❙ Albarn – Coxon – James – Rowntree

Originally recorded with Damon Albarn singing all the parts, the song was finally released with the inspired choice of actor Phil Daniels as the voice of the all-knowing cockney geezer. An apt title

track as it nails the image of the album, sitting well with the cover art of dog races and bookmakers to invoke uniquely British personalities and pastimes. Albarn actually co-owned a racing greyhound with Food label boss Andy Ross – they called it Honest Guv – though it is not pictured on the album sleeve.

Blur
End Of A Century

❙ 1994 · 2:46
❙ Albarn – Coxon – James – Rowntree

The last single to be released from *Parklife* is the beautiful and reflective 'End Of A Century'. A seemingly warm and comforting depiction of domestic harmony with an opening line ("She says there's ants in the carpet, dirty little monsters") given to Damon Albarn by his then girlfriend Justine Frischmann (of British band Elastica) after his flat had indeed become infested with ants.

Blur
This Is A Low

❙ 1994 · 5:17
❙ Albarn – Coxon – James – Rowntree

Described by producer Stephen Street, and many Blur fans, as one of the band's finest and most defining moments, 'This Is A Low' was the final track to be recorded for *Parklife*. The music had been around for most of the *Parklife* sessions but Damon Albarn was either reluctant or lost when it came to the lyrics. It was thought by Street that "Damon put off writing that lyric as he knew how good the music

BLUR
END OF A CENTURY

UN-1

BLUE
BATTERIES NOT INCLUDED

6-80

The opening line of 'End Of A Century' came after Damon Albarn's flat had become infested with ants

was". Inspiration came in the form of a handkerchief of shipping districts that gave birth to lines like "On the Mallin Head, Blackpool looks blue and red / and the Queen, she's gone round the bend / Jumped off Lands' End" Bassist Alex James bought the handkerchief for Albarn as the band would sometimes listen to the British Shipping Forecasts while homesick during lengthy American tours.

Blur
Country House
▌ 1995 • 3:57
▌ Albarn – Coxon – James – Rowntree

The first single from *The Great Escape* was originally scheduled to be 'Charmless Man' but the overwhelming response that 'Country House' received on its live debut, at east London's Mile End stadium in June 1995, convinced everyone in the Blur camp that it would be the band's next single only two months later on

August 26th 1995. The release date is significant as EMI brought it forward in order to go head to head with Oasis' 'Roll With It', thus famously turbo-charging the national interest in the brave new Britpop phenomenon. Everyone was a winner from a PR perspective, with both bands featured in TV news and gracing the covers of national newspapers. 'Country House' romped to victory as the UK's number one single. The song is famously about Food Records' ex-label boss Dave Balfe who always had a fractious relationship with the band and who did indeed retire to a very big house in the country.

Blur The Universal
▌ 1995 • 4:00
▌ Albarn – Coxon – James – Rowntree

This epic, string-laden masterpiece started life as a ska-reggae song that was originally demoed for *Modern Life Is Rubbish* album but evolved into

Blur's Country House

It Really Could Happen...

B L U R
PRESENT
"THE UNIVERSAL"

something far more sinister and seductive during *The Great Escape* sessions. It is said to be about a futuristic drug that sedates society. Author John Harris puts it brilliantly: "'The Universal' identified a condition of tranquilised (and very British) denial as the illness of the modern age."

Blur
Stereotypes

| 1996 • 3:11
| Albarn – Coxon – James – Rowntree

After the enormous success of *Parklife* the pressure was on to deliver another album of similar themes very quickly and producer Stephen Street admits that *The Great Escape* was made in a rush. Under the weight of this expectation and against the clock, Damon Albarn was still able to invent more vividly observed and quintessentially British characters, like the suburban swingers that inhabit top 10 single 'Stereotypes'.

Blur Charmless Man

| 1996 • 3:34
| Albarn – Coxon – James – Rowntree

Another great character piece from singer Damon Albarn, but this time more telling of his discomfort with the intense level of fame he was experiencing and the unsavoury characters that it attracted. Winning four Brit awards in one night (a new record in 1995) will certainly increase your "hanger-on" count. With its neat play on The Smiths' 'This Charming Man', 'Charmless Man' is a shining example of Britpop gold and the last single that Blur would ever release in that style.

Blur Beetlebum

| 1997 • 5:05
| Albarn – Coxon – James – Rowntree

The first single from a new age of Blur and one of Damon Albarn's greatest ever vocal performances, 'Beetlebum' was recorded

beetlebum

with their longstanding producer and
friend, Stephen Street, in Albarn's beloved
Iceland. Away from the stresses of London,
Street has described these sessions as
very relaxed with little external pressure.

Blur Song 2

| 1997 • 2:01
| Albarn – Coxon – James – Rowntree

Originally written
and recorded as a
throwaway, the career-
changing two minutes
of 'Song 2' made their
debut at an arena
gig at Dublin's Point Depot in June 1996;
many thousands of teenage girls looked
shocked and confused. Its parent album,
the eponymously named *Blur*, is significant
in its year zero attitude – the "Life"
trilogy was over and Blur were leading
fans out of Britpop and into something
very exciting indeed. "Wooohoo!"

Blur Tender

| 1999 • 7:41
| Albarn – Coxon – James – Rowntree

Although relations
between frontman
Damon Albarn and
guitarist Graham
Coxon were at an
all-time low, they
came together brilliantly for this moment
of transcendent spiritual redemption
to create one of the most moving and
uplifting songs in the Blur catalogue.
From Coxon's perfectly fragile counter-

vocal of "Oh my baby, oh why" to the surge
of the London Community Gospel Choir,
'Tender' is now *the* live moment in most
Blur sets and the song that reduced Albarn
to tears at their Glastonbury 2009 reunion
show. Shamefully it was beaten to number
one by Britney Spears' 'Baby One More
Time' on single release in March 1999.

Blur Coffee & TV

| 1999 • 5:19
| Albarn – Coxon – James w– Rowntree

The only Blur single
with Graham Coxon on
lead vocal and a song
that he was reluctant
to have released as a
single. The track became
the biggest radio hit from the *13* album
and, along with the brilliantly directed milk
carton video, it brought that relatively uncommercial album to a whole new audience.

Blur
No Distance Left To Run

| 1999 • 3:26
| Albarn – Coxon – James – Rowntree

The heartbreaker to end all heartbreakers,
this incredibly raw and emotionally open
song contains Damon Albarn's most
direct lyrics by far about his long-term
relationship and subsequent break-up
with fellow musician Justine Frischmann.
13's producer William Orbit (Madonna)
describes the singer as "being on an
emotional rollercoaster" and remembers
Albarn being in floods of tears when
he sang the opening line "it's over".

Blur Out Of Time

2003 / 3:53 · Albarn – James – Rowntree

'Out Of Time' was recorded in Marrakech at the most strained time in the band's history. Guitarist Graham Coxon had just walked out and, after the enormous international success of his new project Gorillaz, Damon Albarn wondered if he even needed to keep Blur going at all.

Depeche Mode and Elbow producer Ben Hillier was determined to drive the sessions forward and the band recorded 'Out Of Time' in their self-built studio with additional local musicians, Groupe Regional du Marrakech. It's another beautifully reflective song and a benchmark for latter-period Blur.
MW

Bon Iver Skinny Love

2008 · 3:59 · Vernon

What do you do when you split up with your girlfriend, your band breaks up and you've just overcome a serious illness? If you're Justin Vernon, you move to an isolated hunting cabin in the woods of Wisconsin and start writing new music to work through your personal issues. This is how Bon Iver were formed and the album that followed, *For Emma, Forever Ago* is a lament to lost love, following in the tracks of Bob Dylan's *Blood On The Tracks* and Ryan Adams' *Heartbreaker*. 'Skinny Love' is a standout track from the record, focusing on Vernon's failure to make new relationships work, due to the emotions he still harbours towards his previous love. The song contains the acoustic indie/folk sound that is present throughout the album and the lyrics, while vague and somewhat ambiguous, are refreshingly honest. "Now all your love is wasted? / Then who the hell was I?" Rarely has pain sounded more beautiful. MMY

David Bowie Space Oddity

1969 · 5:15 · Bowie

It had taken David Bowie three years of effort and reinvention – he started his musical life inspired by Little Richard, before moving into somewhat dippy psychedelic folk – before this song heralded his arrival into the charts. Finally bringing Bowie to mainstream attention, it was also the song that announced Major Tom and the space themes that would come to dominate the singer's work for the next five years. Released to coincide with the first moon landing in 1969, it told the tale of the fateful spaceman leaving the world and its earthbound obsessions behind – interpreted as a metaphor for drug-taking and a neat prediction of Bowie's forthcoming stellar career.

David Bowie The Man Who Sold The World

1971 · 3:55 · Bowie

The title track of David Bowie's third album marked the point where the singer began to really hit his stride. That it was also the beginning of his collaboration with the musicians who would make up The Spiders, his backing band, is perhaps no coincidence either. Recorded in Bowie's then reportedly 'Dracula-esque' home, the song explores split personalities, horror and fantasy. Given what he would achieve next, perhaps the story might

have ended there but for two notable cover versions. The first was Lulu's cabaret-style version in 1974; the second was Nirvana's on their *MTV Unplugged* performance – an adaption so good some thought it was their song all along.

David Bowie
Changes

▌ 1971 • 3:33 • Bowie

The song that has become David Bowie's calling card and which has come to encapsulate his chameleon-like career. This was Bowie post-flower power, pre-glam rock alien and in the process of attempting to convince the world of his bisexuality – it couldn't have been a more appropriate song for him to be singing. Its release,

first on the *Hunky Dory* album, came just seven months after previous record *The Man Who Sold The World*, and six before the next: *The Rise And Fall Of Ziggy Stardust And The Spiders From Mars*. Three classic albums in just over a year. Extraordinary.

David Bowie
Life On Mars?

▌ 1971 • 3:54 • Bowie

Who knows what on earth David Bowie is singing about here. Sailors fighting in the dance hall; Mickey Mouse's grown-up cow; a god-awful small affair – all make their appearances to render this one of Bowie's most enigmatic set of lyrics. No matter, though, because he chose to bless such nonsense verse with one of his greatest tunes – a rousing, sweeping, glorious melody that simply invites anyone listening to sing along. And if the song's keyboards sound over the top, it's probably because they are – Rick Wakeman, pre-Yes, was on ivory-tinkling duties and over-embellished his part spectacularly, as Bowie has since noted.

David Bowie Starman

! 1972 • 4:16 • Bowie

Perhaps the most important song David Bowie has ever written (or, some have suggested, borrowed from Judy Garland's 'Over The Rainbow'), it was with 'Starman' that he unleashed his Ziggy Stardust persona and changed rock music forever. With this face-painted, flame-haired, androgynous alien onstage and – via *Top Of The Pops* – in the country's faces, glam rock exploded and did away with all the pomp of prog before. Yet, somehow, Bowie had done this by using prog's space-age themes and concepts but blending them with the more minimalist efforts of bands like The Velvet Underground. Soon he would become an untouchable rock idol, the likes of which had never been seen before.

David Bowie Ziggy Stardust

! 1972 • 3:13 • Bowie

If 'Starman' introduced David Bowie's Ziggy Stardust persona, it was with this song that the man who would be dubbed "the high priest of camp-rock" unleashed him. Bowie had, by 1972, become adept at playing the game, manipulating press and hence public opinion. He had told them he was "bi" and, here, in adopting the character of a lady-boy space alien, he was now signalling that he was not even from the same planet as most of those listening to him. It was revolutionary for pop but explosive for Bowie himself, whose new visual image changed his career forever.

David Bowie Suffragette City

! 1972 • 3:25 • Bowie

1972 found David Bowie in generous mood. Not content with entering perhaps his strongest-ever run of inspiration, he was also handing out songs willy-nilly to other bands. Having allowed Peter Noone to have a hit with his 'Oh! You Pretty Things' in 1971, he then offered this thrilling, riff-driven, piano-thumping rocker to Mott The Hoople in order to prevent them from breaking up. They chose 'All The Young Dudes' instead, so Bowie gave them that and took this for himself, inserting it onto *The Rise And Fall Of Ziggy Stardust And The Spiders From Mars* in place of 'Velvet Goldmine'.

Bowie chose to bless such nonsense verse with one of his greatest tunes in 'Life On Mars?'

David Bowie
The Jean Genie

❘ 1972 • 4:02 • Bowie

David Bowie's biggest hit yet was one that started life simply as a riff – archetypically glam rock – for which he had no words. In fact, he thought it rather lightweight when he was piecing the song together in New York, having been inspired by the sounds of The Stooges and, once again, The Velvet Underground. Lyrically, he was writing about his friend Iggy Pop, of The Stooges – or, if not Iggy specifically, a character based upon him. Its similarity to The Sweet's 'Block Buster' – a song which followed it and beat it to the top spot of the charts – was noted at the time.

David Bowie
Rebel Rebel

❘ 1974 • 4:20 • Bowie

Though David Bowie had already said farewell to Ziggy Stardust, killing him off a year earlier, 'Rebel Rebel' still owed a debt to the glam rock embodied by his alien persona. But it was also a song ushering in a new Bowie era – one less inspired by the alien-androgyny of before and more influenced by the likes of The Rolling Stones. It was perhaps this new direction that meant Bowie dispatched with the services of his guitarist Mick Ronson, instead playing the guitar himself here and believing the riff he had written to be one of the best he had ever created.

David Bowie
Diamond Dogs

❘ 1974 • 6:34 • Bowie

With Ziggy Stardust banished (along with the musicians who made up The Spiders), David Bowie set about inhabiting another character – Halloween Jack – and another sound, waving goodbye to glam and ushering in his more raucous, Rolling Stones- and Stooges-inspired direction. As with 'Rebel Rebel', the musical reinvention was in part a result of Bowie's decision to play guitar himself, his less fluid style lending his songs a rougher edge than that embodied by Mick Ronson. The image change was a result of Bowie's time spent in New York alongside the likes of Iggy Pop. Suddenly glam seemed old-hat, while nascent proto-punk was very much the future.

David Bowie
Golden Years

❘ 1975 • 4:00 • Bowie

1975 was yet another year of change for David Bowie. Glam had gone, the raucous New York sound had never been an entirely comfortable fit, and so, on the *Young Americans* album, came an about-face towards Philadelphia soul and disco – a move that few of his fans then much appreciated. This, though belonging to that disco period, appeared on 1976's electro-influenced *Station To Station* and represents the bridge from soul to the colder edge of his Berlin stage. It would also bring about his return to Europe from the depths of a serious and turbulent cocaine addiction while living in Los Angeles.

David Bowie
Sound & Vision

! 1977 • 3:03 • Bowie

Written after David Bowie's nightmarish Los Angeles residency (interviews at the time painted the singer as paranoid, dark, hopelessly hooked on cocaine and thus subsequently introspective and bleak), 'Sound & Vision' ushered in yet another new Bowie direction – this time derived from the motorik new Krautrock sounds of Germany. Lyrically withdrawn – a hangover of his recovery from addiction – he was nonetheless musically inventive, if less expansive than before. Here, cold keyboards stand shoulder to shoulder with processed drums and icy guitars, soundtracking Bowie's words that detailed his solitude and lethargy post-cocaine.

David Bowie
"Heroes"

! 1977 • 3:37 • Bowie – Eno

Recorded in Berlin after David Bowie's relocation to the then West Germany, both this single and the eponymous album from which it was taken are coloured by the Cold War and its subsequent feelings of paranoia, division and isolation. The studio in which Bowie recorded was just yards from the Berlin Wall itself and the track was inspired by the monument and, more specifically, two lovers (his producer Tony Visconti and a woman with whom he was having an affair) meeting in its shadow. Co-written by Brian Eno, '"Heroes"' was perhaps the most successful of the pair's adventures into the early world of synthesizers.

David Bowie
Ashes To Ashes

! 1980 • 4:24 • Bowie

In which David Bowie said goodbye to the 1970s, dredging up the Major Tom character that had launched him to superstardom and then deriding him as a junkie. 'Ashes To Ashes' has been seen as Bowie's less than self-congratulatory appraisal of his own career to that date – he sings of never doing "good things" but never doing "bad things" – but he was also in need of a hit, having failed to trouble the charts unduly with the singles culled from his experimental Berlin albums. This went straight to number one, thus allowing Bowie to take the next two years off as he rebuilt for the '80s. TB

"'Heroes'" was inspired by the Berlin Wall monument and, more specifically, two lovers meeting in its shadow

Billy Bragg

Billy Bragg
A New England

! 1983 · 2:14 · Bragg

If Joe Strummer had never met Mick Jones and Paul Simonon he might well have wound up like Billy Bragg. A one-man band and punk romantic, Bragg took The Clash's iron conviction and early indifference to musical polish and married it with the stripped-back righteous folk of old heroes like Woody Guthrie. 'A New England' wasn't released as a single, emerging instead in 1983 on his debut seven-track mini-album, *Life's A Riot With Spy Vs Spy*. Despite his reputation as a finger-wagging politico, 'A New England' is a beautiful song of love and loneliness built on the chorus: "I don't want to change the world / I'm not looking for a new England / I'm just looking for another girl".

Whether it was Bragg's affecting honesty, a general reaction against the über-gloss of the "new pop" sound of 1983, or its bearing of the anarcho-punk motto "pay no more than £2.99", *Life's A Riot...* was a huge success, and 'A New England' was its flagship track. Bragg became the pin-up (not literally, as he'd be the first to admit) for a new kind of punk-folk fusion, one that soon produced huge stars like The Pogues.

Coincidentally both later worked with Kirsty MacColl – daughter of Ewan, one of Britain's most famous folk songwriters – and it was she who eventually took 'A New England' into the charts, covering it in 1984, with a new verse written by Bragg fleshing it out to radio length.

Bragg may have played the role of the sincerest kid on the block, but he was nobody's fool. A former soldier who bought his way out of the army after a few months, Bragg proved adept at getting noticed. He blagged his way into the offices of his future record label by posing as a TV repair man and into the affections – and playlists – of Radio 1's John Peel by delivering a biryani when the influential complained of hunger on air. Along with the curry, Bragg included a free copy of *Life's A Riot*....

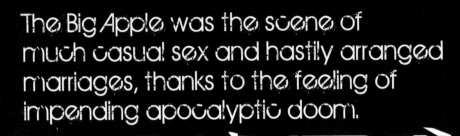

The Big Apple was the scene of much casual sex and hastily arranged marriages, thanks to the feeling of impending apocalyptic doom.

Bran Van 3000
Drinking In LA

1999 • 3:56
Di Salvio – Larson – Vartzbedian

The story goes that Montreal filmmaker James Di Salvio never really intended to form a band when he got 20 or so of his friends together – he was experimenting, having fun and trying to make some money. This spirit of eclectic creativity shines through on Bran Van 3000's debut album *Glee*, a sparklingly carefree and urbane mix of spoken word, samples, rap, trip-hop and – with 'Drinking In LA' – a rock tune that owed something to the best of the Red Hot Chili Peppers and gave the band a worldwide college hit.

The song begins with a mock radio programme giving away tickets to their concert if someone can name "Todd's favourite cheese". They never take themselves too seriously, but on 'Drinking In LA' there is pathos too. Di Salvio has said that the song is autobiographical, about the time he was becoming bored with film and deciding to go into music. In the UK it reached number 36 in the charts in 1998 but was re-released the following year on the back of a Rolling Rock beer advert that propelled it to number three. JH

The Bravery
An Honest Mistake

2005 • 3:41 • Endicott

New York's The Bravery were viewed with some suspicion when they emerged, seemingly fully-formed, back in 2005. However, frontman Sam Endicott had previously been the bassist in NYC power pop outfit The Pasties and moved to vocals when he formed his own group in 2003. The Bravery's first single was 'An Honest Mistake' that rode the wave of glamorous indie rock'n'roll that was being led by The Killers. A driving pop song with pulsing synthesizers and squalling guitar, the lyric appears to be about a simple romantic embarrassment, but was actually inspired by the brief vogue for "terror booty" in post-9/11 New York. In the aftermath of the terrorist attacks, the Big Apple was the scene of much casual sex and hastily arranged marriages, thanks to the feeling of impending apocalyptic doom. 'An Honest Mistake' relates the shamefaced aftermath of one such incident. MO'G

The Breeders
Cannonball

! 1993 · 3:33 · Deal

Following the worldwide success of
American alternative rock giants the
Pixies, bassist Kim Deal found time for
a side project – The Breeders. Initially
featuring Tanya Donnelly of 4AD
labelmates Throwing Muses, the band
released an acclaimed LP, *Pod*, in 1990.
By the time of *Last Splash*, the second
Breeders album from three years later,
the Pixies had split; Donnelly had moved
on to form her own group, Belly; and
Deal had enlisted her identical twin sister
Kelley on guitar. 'Cannonball' was the
lead single and remains The Breeders'
biggest hit. Unusually for the angelically-
voiced Deal sisters, the song opens with

a distorted holler through a megaphone
and swaps between sweet close harmonies
on the verses and a fearsome shriek
on the choruses. However, it's the
phenomenal bassline from Josephine
Wiggs that catches the ear, while the
stop-start rhythm makes the song a
tricky proposition for the dancefloor.
MO'G

Ian Brown
Dolphins Were Monkeys

! 2000 · 5:08 · McCracken – Wills – Brown

Ian Brown met producer/writer and future
collaborator Dave McCracken in May 1999
at Sarm Studios in Notting Hill. Brown
explained to McCracken that he wanted
his new album to be out by the end of
the millennium, which meant that he

! From Left: The Breeders, 'Cannonball'

only had five-and-a-half weeks to make it. The duo based themselves at Sarm and wrote and recorded many of the songs on the *Golden Greats* album there spending a day per song, including 'Dolphins Were Monkeys', which became Ian's second UK top five hit in February 2000.

Ian Brown
Golden Gaze

| 2000 · 3:55 · McCracken – Wills –
Bennett – Wolstencroft – Brown

With 'Golden Gaze', Dave McCracken told me that Ian Brown wanted to write a song that describes seeing someone who inspires you for the very first time. That moment of connection that you know will last for a lifetime. The song was written and recorded in a day. McCracken describes Brown as one of the most spontaneous artists he's worked with and said: "It goes to show just how much can be done with spontaneity, a strong idea and a strong vibe – regardless of how much time you have."

Ian Brown F.E.A.R.

| 2001 · 4:30
Brown – McCracken – Colquhoun

Revered by many as Ian Brown's finest solo work to date, 'F.E.A.R.' is a modern masterpiece of atmosphere and swagger. Sitting in a New York hotel room, inspired by his favourite rappers such as Jay Z and Biggie Smalls, Brown decided to write an entire song using acronyms of only one word. Ian wrote hundreds of acronyms around the word "fear"

and brought them to collaborator Dave McCracken, who already had the perfect set of chords. The strings for 'F.E.A.R.' were recorded by a 32-piece orchestra at Angel Studios in north London – McCracken describes it as an emotional moment: "Ian and I tried to play a game of chess whilst the orchestra recorded but after about three moves we were both almost crying". 'F.E.A.R.' was the first song written and recorded for the *Music Of The Spheres* album and set a pretty high benchmark for the rest of the sessions. MW

Jeff Buckley
Grace

| 1994 · 5:22 · Buckley – Lucas

Lyrically, the title track from Jeff Buckley's only completed album deals with love, mortality and the passionate, resigned acceptance of death. Sonically, a daunting tension is built and relieved – a meandering guitar intro gives way to a rollicking folk-rock riff that rears like a wild animal. Despite him only once meeting his father – 1960s jazz/folk artist Tim Buckley who died from a heroin overdose aged 28 – there are striking similarities between the two. As well as their brooding looks and untimely deaths, both had voices with incredible range: over five octaves and, crucially, the whole spectrum of emotion.

Leonard Cohen's 'Hallelujah' he takes the lyrics of spirituality and sex and expresses faith and betrayal in tones of transcendent joy and heartbroken loss. Pious humility and angelic sweetness turn into spite and gritted-teeth bitterness. The song itself has its own story. Cohen's 1984 original sounds somehow stifled, and it was largely ignored until 1991 when The Velvet Underground's John Cale sang it with a raw emotion that released the power and poetry of the words. Buckley's version built on this and cemented the song's popularity. Incredibly, Buckley's only UK hit came when 'Hallelujah' occupied numbers one and two in the 2009 Christmas chart. Following an internet campaign to keep Alexandra Burke's overblown, histrionic version (complete with unnecessary key change) from the top spot, Buckley lost out to the X Factor winner. Quite the pay-day for Cohen.

Jeff Buckley
Everybody Here Wants You
❕ 1998 • 4:46 • Buckley

Tragically, Buckley drowned in a Memphis river in May 1997, aged 30. He had taken a swim, fully clothed, while waiting for his band to fly in to record the follow-up to *Grace*. What emerged instead was *Sketches For My Sweetheart The Drunk*, a diverse collection of demos. 'Everybody Here Wants You' is a love song of possessive pride, written for girlfriend Joan Wasser (aka New York-based musician Joan As Policewoman) that recalls the sexy soul sound of Prince. MP

Here Buckley shifts from delicate falsetto through silky croon to anguished howls in the song's crescendo. His vocal style proved enormously influential, notably affecting Radiohead's Thom Yorke (who recorded the vocal to 'Fake Plastic Trees' immediately after watching a Buckley show) and Matt Bellamy of Muse.

Jeff Buckley Hallelujah
❕ 1994 • 6:53 • Cohen

Like Jeff Buckley's intimate shows in New York cafés, *Grace* had compelling diversity. Within a moment he could switch from rock god to fragile diva. In his cover of

BUZZCOCKS

ORGASM ADDICT

COLLAGE - LINDER

Buzzcocks

THE XFM TOP 1000 **80** SONGS OF ALL TIME

Buzzcocks
Orgasm Addict

! 1978 • 2:02 • Shelley – Devoto

The Buzzcocks brought punk rock to Manchester. Not just literally with their music (inspired by the likes of The Velvet Underground and The Stooges) but also because, in an effort to find themselves a support slot, they brought the Sex Pistols up from London to play their first Manchester gig. A gig that the Buzzcocks subsequently failed to appear at. Having borrowed £300 from his father, guitarist Pete Shelly recorded and released 'Orgasm Addict', the band's debut single. Quick and exciting with fizzing guitar and fast-paced drums, the energy of the punk movement was present not only in its sounds but also in its process – recorded in just a couple of takes. Banned by the BBC due to its tongue-in-cheek but provocative subject matter, 'Orgasm Addict' helped kick-start not only the punk rock movement but also independent music in north England.

Buzzcocks
Ever Fallen In Love with Someone You Shouldn't've

! 1978 • 2:42 • Shelley

Following the departure of Howard Devoto, Pete Shelley took over on lead vocals for second studio album *Love Bites*, the first single from which became arguably the best-known punk song of all time. Despite taking inspiration from the Sex Pistols, the band did not follow their angry political stylings: instead Shelley wrote a three-minute pop song inspired by the star-crossed lovers in the musical *Guys And Dolls* and a little bit of personal experience. "I did have a certain person in mind but I'll save that for my kiss and tell." he told *The Guardian*.

No stranger to controversy, Shelley originally opened the song with the line "You piss on my natural emotions...", later substituting the word "spurn". The final result was an angst-ridden and confused love song. Although the cover version by the Fine Young Cannibals is possibly better known in the US, the edgier, more energetic original remains the definitive release – demonstrating not only Shelley's ability as a lyricist but also as a songwriter able to match the speed and energy of punk rock with the hooks and sentiments of pop music. After recording four studio albums the band split in 1981 to pursue various solo projects, only to reform eight years later. Since then, the Buzzcocks have undergone various reformations, splits and line-up changes but are still touring with Shelley at the helm.
JS

'Orgasm Addict' was banned by the BBC due to its provocative subject matter

Caesars
Jerk It Out

! 2002 • 3:16 • Joakim Åhlund

The signature tune from Swedish rock band Caesars – in that it has appeared in separate forms on three of the band's six albums – first made its appearance on *Love For The Streets*, which was released under the name 'Caesar's Palace'. Fun and infectious, the track gained notoriety from its appearance in a number of computer game soundtracks and advertisements – most notably for the iPod, which neatly coincided with the release of *Paper Tigers*. Åhlund's discovery of a vintage Farfisa organ has a heavy influence on the band's sound throughout and it is this that kicks off 'Jerk It Out' with a hook reminiscent of Inspiral Carpets (and when performed live played by Börn Yttling of Peter, Bjorn And John). The track builds with choppy guitar, maraca rhythms and quirky, somewhat suggestive lyrics that the band maintain are about letting off steam and going crazy rather than a certain other activity. A guaranteed indie floor-filler. JS

The Cardigans
My Favourite Game

! 1998 • 3:40 • Svensson – Persson

Fronted by striking Scandinavian singer Nina Persson, Sweden's The Cardigans first came to the public's attention in late 1996, when their song 'Lovefool' was included on the soundtrack to the Baz Luhrmann movie *William Shakespeare's Romeo + Juliet*. Their most memorable song, however, was 'My Favourite Game', the lead single from their fourth album, *Gran Turismo*. A driving and distorted rock song, it wasn't always meant to be so heavy, explained producer Tore Johannson: "The first plan was to do it slow with a kind of Neil Young, 'Harvest' shuffle feel to it. We tried that out with the drummer and recorded a drum track. It worked, but it was a bit dull, so we decided to try a more 'rocky' feel." Persson's angelic vocals relate the details of a turbulent love affair over a distinctive two-note guitar riff, played by Peter Svensson. However, strained relationships within the band meant that his minimalist rocking out wasn't universally appreciated. "When Peter first played it, I thought 'that sounds like crap' and I walked out," admitted bassist Magnus Sveningsson. "So there was a lot of tension at that time, and I was grumpy as hell."

The song became an instant success for the band, making the top 20 both in the UK and on the US Modern Rock chart. This was despite the controversial video, directed by Jonas Åkerlund, fresh from producing the notorious 'Smack My Bitch Up' clip for The Prodigy. The

film features Persson recklessly driving an open-top car through the desert, before standing up at the wheel and heading right into the path of an oncoming van... which ironically is carrying the other band members. Needless to say, many broadcasters either banned or edited the video to remove the carnage.
MO'G

Carter USM
Sheriff Fatman

! 1989 • 4:45 • Morrison – Carter

Carter The Unstoppable Sex Machine's songs wrapped social commentary in humour and layered wordplay-heavy lyrics over compelling pogo punk-pop. Initially released ahead of their 1989 debut *101 Damnations*, having signed with Rough Trade and reached number eight in the UK charts with album *30 Something*, 'Sheriff Fatman' was re-issued and became their first hit single. Originally a song about sailing ship adventures inspired by an AA Milne poem, it ended up sounding rather different: a stomping, bile-filled rant against the slumlords of London. The drum machine beat, rousing horns, juddering sequenced bass, punky guitars and JimBob's trademark witty lyrics ("If you flash him a smile / he'll take your teeth as deposit") made it an indie disco smash. The band went on to have four top 10 albums and consistent hit singles. Founding members JimBob and Fruitbat each still play music; JimBob has published two books and Fruitbat presents on community radio.
MS

Johnny Cash
Hurt

! 2002 • 3:38 • Reznor

Johnny Cash may have made his name as a country music star and, arguably, one of the most influential musicians of the last century. But, for many, it will be his haunting version of 'Hurt' that could be classed as his epitaph, if not his legacy. Cash's life and times have been well documented, not least in 2005's biopic *Walk The Line* starring Joaquin Phoenix, which – much to the displeasure of the Cash estate – portrayed him as a man heavily dependent on drink and drugs. There is little doubt that Cash led a turbulent life; a dark side that comes to the surface in this song for an almost cathartic performance.

His early life was dominated by gospel music and it was only when told by a record executive at Sun Records this was unmarketable and he should "Go home and sin then come back with a song I can sell" that Cash did just that and turned his hand to country music. However, 'Hurt' certainly doesn't fall into the traditional country music category. It was recorded by Cash as part of *American IV: The Man Comes*

Around, which formed part of a series of albums recorded under the guidance of producer Rick Rubin (Red Hot Chili Peppers, U2, Metallica) who reinvented his sound in order to appeal to a non-country, younger market. Originally written and recorded by Nine Inch Nails, 'Hurt' was arguably the most successful reworking on a record that featured cover versions of bands such as Depeche Mode and The Beatles. The song is played on a single acoustic guitar (a Martin Dreadnought guitar, as used by Cash throughout his career) with accompaniment via a solo piano note used almost as percussion. The main difference between the Cash version and that of the original is the more melodic tone of the latter (something to do with minor chords and discords, no doubt), but Cash's ownership of the song makes it worthy of a place in this list. Every line is delivered with passion, remorse and wisdom, and with hindsight you can almost hear Cash making his peace with the world (he died a year later). Tackling broken relationships, the end of a life and most significantly drug abuse, the lyrics might as well have been written by the man himself.

The biggest testament to the song's success comes from its author, Trent Reznor, who acknowledged that – despite his fears when approached by Rubin that the song might be seen as a gimmick – Cash's cover has now become the definitive version, likening the scenario to seeing an ex-girlfriend with a new lover. JS

All Change was the last session ever recorded at the legendary Manor Studio in Oxfordshire

Cast
Walk Away

1996 • 3:49 • Power

On hearing that Noel Gallagher was a fan of The La's, lead Cast member and ex-La John Power got himself into the dressing room at an early Oasis show in Liverpool. After passing Gallagher a demo tape of his new band, Oasis invited Cast to support them on a subsequent tour. Cast were soon signed to Polydor Records and became one of the sales success stories of the Britpop era. 'Walk Away' was the fourth and final single from the Liverpool band's million-selling debut album *All Change*. 'Walk Away' could well have been one of the many songs that Power wrote while he was waiting for The La's to come off their seemingly neverending hiatus. *All Change* was recorded with legendary producer John Leckie (The Stone Roses, Radiohead) and was the last ever session in the Manor Studio – a palatial residential studio in the Oxfordshire countryside owned by Richard Branson and used, among many others, by Mike Oldfield to record *Tubular Bells*. 'Walk Away' was released as a single

in March 1996 and went to number nine in the UK charts. By the June of that year it had become a sort of sombre national anthem as it soundtracked endless TV footage of England going out of the Euro 96 semi-final with Gareth Southgate's missed penalty against Germany.
MW

Catatonia
Mulder And Scully

! 1998 • 4:53 • Matthews – Roberts

Catatonia established themselves on the vanguard of the new Welsh invasion after signing to Warner subsidary Blanco Y Negro in the mid-1990s. Formed from the ashes of influential Welsh language bands, and originally featuring Guto Pryce and Dafydd Ieuan from Super Furry Animals, the band came to prominence with a number of independently released EPs before releasing their major label debut, *Way Beyond Blue*, in 1996.

'Mulder And Scully' was the band's second single from second album *International Velvet* and their biggest hit. Reaching number three in the UK chart, its poppy, guitar-driven hooks would begin the band's ascent to mainstream glory, which would culminate in a huge open air show at Margam Park, south Wales, in 1999.

Catatonia Road Rage

! 1998 • 5:09 • Matthews – Roberts

Before the Manic Street Preachers broke down the door, it had been notoriously difficult for Welsh bands to make much headway east of Offa's Dyke. "We dealt with a lot of musical prejudice," Manics' bassist Nicky Wire told Xfm. "There wasn't a great musical lineage to compare yourself to and you'd be castigated for being the 'new Alarm'." The wave of Welsh bands that followed may have hit a commercial pinnacle with Stereophonics' graduation to stadium-slaying status, but the mood of the time was undoubtedly summed up on Catatonia's 'International Velvet' and its chorus of "Every day when I wake up, I thank the Lord i'm Welsh". The album of the same name seemed an inseparable product of the band's background. Cerys Matthews' Welsh accent and sexy rasp stamped its individuality all over Catatonia's breakthrough record and nowhere was her enunciation more prominent than on the album's third single, 'Road Rage'. Tumbling "r"s and stretched vowels drew a brave new line in the sand as Britpop's distinctly English flavour gave way to a more inclusive and 'British' post-Britpop landscape.
OH

If all you've got to do today is find peace of mind ,"Come round, you can take a piece of mine
— Catatonia, 'Road Rage'

The Charlatans

The Charlatans
The Only One I Know

1990 • 3:59 • Blunt – Collins – Burgess – Baker – Brookes

The haircuts, outfits and vaguely similar geography were enough for most people to class The Charlatans as part of the baggy scene when they emerged in the early 1990s. But what would mark them out as something different was their trademark organ sound, their roots in psychedelic rock, funk and soul and their ability to continue in the face of diversity. The band bonded over clubbing all night (at Manchester's Hacienda) then chilling out at home to Pink Floyd. They also shared a mutual favourite record in De La Soul's *Three Feet High And Rising*. From these influences came 'The Only One I Know'. An infectious dance tune, full of the kind of percussive organ that could be found in keyboardist Rob Collins' beloved northern soul, they knew it was huge from early on. "We used to always play it second," singer Tim Burgess told Xfm, "and people would just go mental so we kinda knew that it had something a bit special." It scored them a UK top 10 hit, helped the album get to number one and remains a dancefloor staple.

The Charlatans Weirdo

1992 • 3:40 Burgess – Blunt – Collins – Brookes

Don't always go with your first instinct is an important lesson for a band to learn. Always trust your producer is another. The Charlatans were almost certain they would scrap 'Weirdo', the first song written for their second album. "It wasn't in our minds very good," says Tim Burgess, "but then [producer] Flood did a master mix of the track, we listened and we were all speechless." It gave them a place in the UK top 20 and was their biggest hit in America, achieving the number one spot on the prestigious Billboard Modern Rock Tracks chart.

Everyone has been burned before / Everybody knows the pain

– The Charlatans, 'The Only One I Know'

The Charlatans
Can't Get Out of Bed

1994 • 3:11 • Burgess – Blunt –
Collins – Brookes – Collins

As far as distractions go, being under pressure when recording a new album after a disappointing second album is one thing. Facing a possible eight-year jail sentence is another. Rob Collins had been out drinking with a mate who – unbeknownst to Collins – then decided to commit armed robbery. While awaiting trial, Collins recorded his keyboard parts for The Charlatans' third record, *Up To Our Hips*. Loosely based around a Small Faces riff, this "anti-apathy" song helped the album reach the UK top 10. It came out just as Collins' sentence had finished; within two days of his release he was playing the song live on UK TV show Top Of The Pops.

The Charlatans
One To Another

1997 • 4:32 • Burgess – Blunt –
Collins – Brookes – Collins

Things seemed to be looking up for The Charlatans. Their self-titled fourth album topped the UK charts and proclaimed them back on form. But then tragedy struck. Just a few weeks ahead of the release of 'One To Another', keyboardist Rob Collins was killed in a car crash. "We thought about pulling it, we thought about splitting up," Tim Burgess explained to Xfm. "We thought about everything because that's what death can do. But we wanted to showcase his skill." This song certainly does that. A thundering beast of a track

based around a signature Collins keyboard melody, it reached number three in the UK.

The Charlatans
North Country Boy

1997 • 4:04 • Burgess – Blunt –
Collins – Brookes – Collins

With no keyboard player for their support slots at Oasis' legendary Knebworth shows, the band called on Primal Scream's Martin Duffy to step in. Tim Burgess told Xfm: "Martin Duffy was the unsung hero... He was our shock-absorber. It allowed us four or five months to find someone else." Duffy also contributed to the album, finishing off the keyboard parts that Rob Collins had started. The result, *Telling Stories*, would give The Charlatans their third UK number one album. Ahead of its release, they had another top five single with 'North Country Boy', an optimistic, lolloping track infused with organ and perky guitar riffs. Inspired in part by Bob Dylan's 'Girl From The North Country', Burgess says he "just swapped the gender and wrote a song about a boy from the North Country, which was about me".

The Charlatans
How High

1997 • 3:06 • Burgess – Blunt –
Collins – Brookes – Collins

Long before *The Grey Album* existed, The Charlatans were thinking of combining The Beatles with rap. At least, that was the inspiration behind the band's fourth UK top 10 hit, as Tim Burgess explained to Xfm: "The title was inspired by Method

Man and Redman's song 'How High'. Musically, we wanted it to sound like something from *Sgt. Pepper* but it evolved into something different." A consistent live favourite, the short, vengeful track has Burgess spitting his vocals over winding guitar riffs and crashing drums.

The Charlatans
Tellin' Stories

| 1997 • 5:13 • Burgess – Blunt – Collins – Brookes – Collins

This expansive, airy epic was largely created in Windermere, a small town situated by England's largest lake. Even the words were conceived in the midst of raw nature, although influenced by something far more street: "The lyrics were inspired by De La Soul's first album," Tim Burgess told Xfm. "I was sitting at the top of a tree, thinking about something and dishing out proverbs." The song was completed with what Burgess calls "the incredible Led Zeppelin riff, which Rob [Collins] pulled out of his magical hat".

The Charlatans
Love Is The Key

| 2001 • 4:28 • Burgess – Brookes – Blunt – Collins – Rogers

For a lesser band, it might have been the end. But after everything else The Charlatans had survived, having their singer move halfway across the world wasn't a problem. In fact, it led to their sixth UK top 10 album, *Wonderland*. Recorded in Burgess' new hometown of LA, it was, he says, "a really great experience for the band. We let Los Angeles take us over in every aspect." It was recorded on Wonderland Avenue — formerly home to The Doors, who were to be a big influence on the album. Curtis Mayfield was another key influence: you can hear it all over 'Love Is The Key', from the funky beats and wah wah guitar to Tim Burgess' falsetto vocals.

The Charlatans
You're So Pretty – We're So Pretty

| 2001 • 4:46 • Burgess – Brookes – Blunt – Collins – Rogers

Based around a piano instrumental written by Tony Rogers – the band's new keyboardist – this is an optimistic song, full of funky guitar riffs and ass-slapping beats. Originally on the album *Wonderland*, it was remixed by producer Youth (The Verve, Embrace) for a single release to head up 2006's singles collection *Forever*. MS

"We let Los Angeles take us over in every respect"

– Tim Burgess of The Charlatans recalls recording *Wonderland*

The Chemical Brothers
The Setting Sun

1996 · 4:00
Gallagher – Rowlands – Simons

After making friends as history students at Manchester University, Tom Rowlands and Ed Simons charted a course that immediately marked them out from the pack. In the early 1990s, dance music was steadily fragmenting into smaller and smaller scenes. But Rowlands and Simons were fans of hip-hop, techno and underground rock, and didn't see why they couldn't play the lot. Early DJ sets as the Dust Brothers (taken from the producers of Beastie Boys brilliant *Paul's Boutique* album) were wildly eclectic, and when they made the transition to making their own vinyl, it took the championing of far-sighted DJs like Andy Weatherall to get them noticed. By the time they moved to London and changed their name, they were already on the road to becoming stars.

The Chemical Brothers used to use 'Tomorrow Never Knows' – perhaps the finest track on perhaps the finest Beatles album – as a show-stopping end-of-night anthem when DJing their Naked Under Leather nights in Manchester. So when they got together with Noel Gallagher, no stranger to the Fab Four's back catalogue himself, Lennon's psychedelic masterpiece must have seemed a good ice-breaker. It's no cover but rather a homage, in which air sirens, battering-ram drums and a congested collage of effects and samples replace the original's backwards sitars and guitars. Despite being what allmusic. com described as "easily one of the most

extreme records to reach the British charts", this put the Chemicals and big beat at number one for the first time.

The Chemical Brothers
Block Rockin' Beats

1997 · 3:24
Rowlands – Simons – Weaver

'Block Rockin' Beats' was road-tested at The Chemical Brothers' Heavenly Social residency, a Saturday nightclub in Clerkenwell that pioneered the big beat sound, bringing hip-hop beats and rock riffs into electronic music. This was the Chemical sound *par excellence*; a mash-up of samples and influences from post-punkers 23 Skidoo, old-school rapper

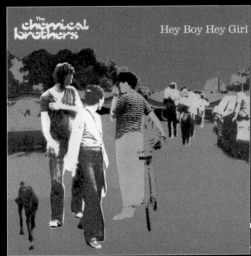

Schoolly D (who supplied the hook and got a writing credit for his pains) and the original funky drummer, Bernard Purdie – proof they didn't need holidaying rock superstars to grab the number one spot.

The Chemical Brothers
Hey Boy Hey Girl

1999 • 4:24 • Rowlands

Two years on from their block rockin' *Dig Your Own Hole* album, things were more complicated for The Chemical Brothers. Their big beat sound had been copied to the point of cliché and the cooler kids had long since moved on. 'Hey Boy Hey Girl' is the same, but different. The old rap vocal is there (this time sampled

from Rock Master Scott & The Dynamic Three), supplying both the name and the more widely used "superstar DJ", which they avoided using as the title for fear of appearing arrogant. But the sound is leaner, less kitchen-sink, more in tune with peers from Van Helden to Daft Punk. From now on, big beat was left to the imitators.

The Chemical Brothers
Let Forever Be

1999 • 3:56 •
Gallagher – Rowlands – Simons

Or 'The Setting Sun Pt II'. The Chemical Brothers' previous collaboration with Noel Gallagher was a commercial and creative triumph, a track that did much to break down the boundaries between rock and dance. 'Let Forever Be' had the air of a sequel rather than a brave new world – the title is clearly a nudge and a wink at 'Tomorrow Never Knows' and the drums are again eerily similar. In tune with the general streamlining of The Chemical Brothers' sound, it was less ferocious than its predecessor, but Gallagher's voice is drastically improved and the introductory coda is a little psychedelic gem.

The Chemical Brothers
Galvanize

2005 • 4:48
Fareed – Rowlands – Simons

Tom Rowlands and Ed Simons' biggest hit of the new century saw them hook up with rapper Q-Tip, a hero since the days of A Tribe Called Quest, and a Moroccan string sample for a beautifully satisfying piece of music. This laid any lingering ghosts of their 1990s' past to rest, as they stretched out their sound into something that was tuneful, danceable and immediate, regardless of genre. As Simons said of their *Push The Button* album, "A lot of electronic music is just about the effect it has and it's all effects and flash, but this has some substance beyond that." 'Galvanize' gained added traction through its use in a long-running Budweiser commercial, but it was perhaps video director Adam Smith who has made most strides since, going on to direct the first episode of *Doctor Who* with Doctor Matt Smith. SY

The Clash

The Clash
White Riot

1977 • 1:56 • Strummer – Jones

"We got searched by police looking for bricks and by a Rasta looking for a pound note", Joe Strummer said of their experience at the Notting Hill Carnival riots in 1976. Recorded the following February and issued just one month later, 'White Riot', their debut single, was two minutes of musical nitro-glycerine, an explosion of punk energy so raw and unbridled that somehow it never dates. Fools thought it was racist, but lines like "Black man gotta lotta problems/ but they don't mind throwing a brick" were sang in tribute, encouraging the white working class to express themselves in the same way.

The Clash
Complete Control

1977 • 3:14 • Strummer – Jones

'Complete Control' was label gripe as insurrection, a three-minute rant against the record company (who insisted they release 'Remote Control' as a single) and manager Bernie Rhodes (for demanding "complete control") that was turned into a call to the barricades. "I don't trust you / So why should you trust me?" shouted

Strummer, his voice scraping across the surface of the background noise, overseen by legendary reggae producer Lee Perry, who seemed baffled by the whole experience. "They were too loud," he later told *NME*. Strummer has a whale of a time, though, comically shouting "you're my guitar hero" at Jones during his sarcastically un-punk axe solo.

The Clash
Janie Jones

! 1977 · 2:06 · Strummer – Jones

Named after a famous singer-turned-madame, 'Janie Jones' mocks the wannabe rebel male locked in a boring job, longing for rock'n'roll and the chance to get stoned. It's particularly poignant since Jones was imprisoned for seven years on the back of a sex-for-airplay payola scandal involving Radio 1 DJs. That aside, it's the white-collar Everyman being sung about here, on one of the group's sharpest, most direct songs, kicking off their debut album and remaining a live favourite to the end. It is the first track mentioned by John Cusack in his side-one-track-one top-five list in the film *High Fidelity*.

The Clash
'White Man' In Hammersmith Palais

! 1978 · 4:00 · Strummer – Jones

There were signs on their debut album, but this is The Clash's harbinger of the greatness to come. 'White Man In Hammersmith Palais' is fabulously ambitious, both musically and lyrically,

with Joe Strummer laying bare his white middle-class guilt, going to an all-night gig expecting hardcore roots only to find "UK pop reggae" and Motown entertainment values. In typical Clash fashion, it's broadened out into a state-of-the-nation rant that takes in everything from The Jam ("they got Burton suits / Huh! You think it's funny? / Turning rebellion into money") to the rise of the National Front. A bold, immense song.

The Clash
Tommy Gun

! 1978 · 3:17 · Strummer – Jones

The Clash's second album was a notoriously unhappy affair. CBS forced American hard-rock producer Sandy Pearlman on them, an association that reputedly began with Strummer onstage dedicating 'I'm So Bored With The USA' to Pearlman's most famous charges, Blue Oyster Cult. Sure enough, this is the closest the west London punks come to American FM rock, with the guitar sound pushed to the full and the militaristic drumming sounding the charge. The lyric reflects on the glamorisation of terror groups and although it sounds like scathing sarcasm ("I'm cutting out your picture from page one"), Strummer himself often wore T-shirts of the Italian Red Brigade, infusing 'Tommy Gun' with ambiguity, to say the least.

The Clash
I Fought The Law

! 1979 · 2:38 · Sonny Curtis

This fantastic cover of an old classic provided The Clash with one of their most memorable singles to date, as well as showcasing the more mature, rounded sound that really came into its own on the *London Calling* album. Originally recorded by Buddy Holly's old backing band, then more successfully in 1965 by Bobby Fuller, it's a milestone in rock fatalism. It was the main track of the *Cost Of Living* EP, released on election day in 1979, and Strummer originally planned to picture that vote's winner, Margaret Thatcher, on the record cover with a swastika superimposed on her.

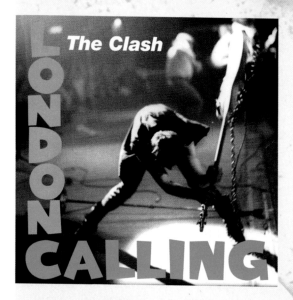

The Clash
Train In Vain

| 1979 • 3:10 • Jones – Strummer

Wholly unexpected in more ways than one, 'Train In Vain' began life as a hidden track on third album *London Calling* after plans to release it as a flexi disc free with the *NME* came to naught too late for them to change the album's artwork. Then its bouncy pop-soul feeling gave the group a surprise top 30 hit in the States, at which point people discovered it was called 'Train In Vain' – despite those words never appearing in the song – rather than the assumed 'Stand By Me'. According to Clash biographer, Pat Gilbert, Mick Jones wrote the angry love song for his former girlfriend, Viv Albertine of The Slits.

The Clash
London Calling

| 1979 • 3:19 • Strummer – Jones

The Clash remained an almost exclusively British proposition for their first two albums, but 'London Calling' was when they went international. Although it deals head on with the threat of nuclear war ("A nuclear error, but I have no fear / 'Cos London is drowning and I live by the river"), it's less an angry diatribe than the baffled observations of a man gobsmacked by everything from phoney Beatlemania to police brutality. The rhythm guitar punches the air, the bassline rumbles and it all carries the pulse and weight of a steam hammer. It closes abruptly, Strummer bouncing around with "I never felt so much-a like-like-like-like", a reference to Guy Mitchell's rock'n'roll-era classic 'Singing The Blues'. But this isn't blues – it's rock at its pummelling, apocalyptic best.

The Clash
Guns Of Brixton

! 1979 · 3:10 · Simonon

Paul Simonon's first composition and vocal for the band was, unsurprisingly, a bass-led reggae track, drawing heavily on the rebel sound he loved. Never fully confident with his instrument, Simonon was so determined to get his debut right that he marked the notes on the fret of his bass, according to engineer Bill Price. The other band members were so taken aback by the novelty of his writing that its working title, immortalised on the *London Calling Legacy Edition*, was 'Paul's Tune'. And yet, the track, with its references to *The Harder They Come*, proved an instant classic, being sampled years later for the Beats International hit, 'Dub Be Good To Me'. The sampled part? The bassline, of course.

The Clash
Bankrobber

! 1980 · 4:33 · Strummer – Jones

'Bankrobber' wasn't the first time The Clash used a reggae producer (see 'Complete Control'), but it was the first time the results sounded somewhere approximate to Jamaican music. This was Joe Strummer in full romantic rebel mode, dreaming of modern-day Robin Hoods over Mikey Dread's authentically bass-heavy backing, which the record company complained "sounded like ['Ashes To Ashes' by] David Bowie backwards" according to Paul Simonon. Although the label initially refused to release it, the track ultimately fared well in the charts, peaking one place below their biggest hit to date and sparking a memorable *Top Of The Pops* in which the absent band (still holding to the punk boycott) were replaced by Legs & Co dance troupe in full stripy-shirted bandit regalia.

The Clash
Rock The Casbah

! 1982 · 3:43 · The Clash

Written principally by drummer Topper Headon, 'Rock The Casbah' became The Clash's biggest hit, especially in the States where it's credited with making them a truly major act. Despite their punkier-than-thou origins, it's essentially a disco-funk track to which Joe Strummer added lyrics about Arabic censorship of Western music. The group later insisted it was intended as a riposte to manager Bernie Rhodes, who complained about their music sounding like a "raga", but it's since acquired favourite status with American jocks at times of tension with the Middle East. Many long-term Clash observers credited the stateside success of the song – and subsequent top 10 status of the *Combat Rock* album – with effectively splitting the band, who felt uncomfortable with their newfound wealth.

The Clash
Should I Stay Or Should I Go

! 1982 • 3:06 • The Clash

The third single off the *Combat Rock*
album is both a plodding Stonesy boogie
and a remarkable demonstration of
the way The Clash worked. Amidst its
ordinariness, there's the fuzzy, gnarly
sound of the bass, Strummer's Spanish
backing vocals and the absurd middle
eight, where it seems to disappear into a
different track altogether. Famously it was
re-released in the 1990s after being used
in a Levi's ad, giving the band a number
one hit for the first time. Distraught at
their apparent sell-out, ex-fan Billy Childish
released a parody as The Stash, called
'Should I Suck Or Should I Blow'. By this
point The Clash were probably past caring.
SY

A&R bidding war. 'We Used To Vacation'
was first released as a track on the *Up In
Rags* EP and showcases the band's talents
as expert storytellers with the tale of an
alcoholic father failing to keep his promise
of sobriety and attempting to make
amends by donations to "tax-deductible
charity organisations" (a line borrowed
from Bob Dylan's 'Ballard Of A Thin
Man'). Nathan Willett's bourbon-soaked,
clattering piano resides over this blues/
rock track of self-loathing and regret.

Cold War Kids
Hang Me Up To Dry

! 2006 • 3:40 • Cold War Kids

After signing to Downtown records, this
was the first single to be released from the
band's debut album *Robbers & Cowards*.
A pop song that breaks all the rules, it

> Self-planned tours and a series of self-released EPs attracted so much praise online that the result was an *A&R* bidding war.
>
> – Cold War Kids, 'We Used to Vacation'

Cold War Kids
We Used To Vacation

! 2006 • 4:01 • Cold War Kids

As with so many bands these days, the
internet played a key role in the success
of Cold War Kids. Self-planned tours and
a series of self-released EPs attracted so
much praise online that the result was an

really shouldn't work with its changes
of rhythm, chaotic piano and Willett's
rasping, pleading vocals helping to paint
a picture of a man on the edge, but its
catchy chorus creates something personal
yet familiar. Modest sales made this gem
even more special, making fans feel part of
a select few to have discovered its charms.
JS

Coldplay

Coldplay
Shiver

2000 • 5:00 • Berryman – Buckland – Champion – Martin

The lead single from Coldplay's debut album *Parachutes* and their first UK top 40 (number 35 in March 2000). Like most of the album, it was recorded with producer Ken Nelson (Gomez, Badly Drawn Boy) during sessions at Rockfield in Wales and Parr Street in Liverpool. The warm rich sound of the album is largely due to Nelson's use of analogue recording equipment and two-inch tape. After a long absence from Coldplay's live sets, 'Shiver' reappeared during their Latin American stadium tour of 2010.

Coldplay
Don't Panic

2000 • 2:17 • Berryman – Buckland – Champion – Martin

'Don't Panic' (originally called 'Panic') was one of the few songs that the band were playing live at their very early gigs and that made it through to the final cut of *Parachutes*. It was a standout song for A&R executive Debs Wild, who helped the band get signed after being one of the first people to see them play live.

COLDPLAY
YELLOW

Parlophone

In September 1998, Coldplay played a tiny bar in Manchester as part of music industry conference In The City; Wild told Xfm in May 2010 that "they looked terrible, proper students, but there was something very special about them – especially the singer, who talked too much but had an incredible singing voice."

Coldplay Yellow

2000 • 4:29 • Berryman – Buckland – Champion – Martin

This was the song that made all the difference. Written during the recording sessions for *Parachutes* in Rockfield Studios and partly inspired by the clear night skies in rural Wales, 'Yellow' was the single that catapulted a relatively unknown British band into national and international recognition within a matter of months. Not only was the song a huge radio hit in the UK, but the video firmly established the charisma of lead singer Chris Martin. Filmed on a deserted and rain-soaked Dorset beach, it shows Martin singing to camera while dawn breaks behind him. A new music star was born.

Coldplay
Trouble

| 2000 • 4:32 • Berryman – Buckland – Champion – Martin

Frontman Chris Martin has suggested that 'Trouble' was written as an apology for his own bad behaviour towards another member of the band. Speculation has suggested that this might be drummer Will Champion, who was almost ejected from the band shortly after they signed their record deal – a situation that Martin has since bitterly regretted. Debut album *Parachutes* is dedicated to Champion's mother who died of cancer in 2000.

Coldplay
In My Place

| 2002 • 3:49 • Berryman – Buckland – Champion – Martin

The first single from Coldplay's second album, *A Rush Of Blood To The Head*. After the huge international success of *Parachutes*, the pressure was on to deliver an equally resonant follow-up. From the first notes of Johnny Buckland's guitar,

fans and record label had nothing to worry about: 'In My Place' made such an anticipated return sound effortless and accomplished. The track was one of the first songs to be written for *A Rush Of Blood To The Head* and was being played live regularly towards the end of the *Parachutes* tour.

Coldplay
The Scientist

| 2002 • 5:09 • Berryman – Buckland – Champion – Martin

A song written about a close friend's relationship, 'The Scientist' is one of Coldplay's most openly romantic and tender songs and features on second album *A Rush Of Blood To The Head*, which saw an even more unapologetic emotional directness in the band's writing. On the *Coldplay Live 2003* DVD, Chris Martin says: "We are fighting for sincere music to be the main thing again. That's what U2 are about and that's what The Beatles were about. We have stopped being shy about how much we love what we do."

Coldplay
Clocks

| 2002 • 5:07 • Berryman – Buckland – Champion – Martin

One of the great live moments of any Coldplay set, the infectious piano and surging rhythm section on 'Clocks' make it perfect for stadiums. Coldplay's 2003 tour saw them perform at some of the biggest and most iconic venues in the world. They played Colorado's Red Rocks amphitheatre exactly 20 years to the day that U2 shot their famous concert there. Two decades apart, it rained on both occasions. Because of its unusual structure, the band were initially against having 'Clocks' released as a single as they doubted it would get much radio play – but the label argued for it and it became the biggest radio hit on the album.

Coldplay
God Put A Smile Upon Your Face

| 2002 • 4:57 • Berryman – Buckland – Champion – Martin

In keeping with the themes of urgency and energy that run through *A Rush Of Blood To The Head*, 'God Put A Smile Upon Your Face' is a far fuller and more driven song than most of *Parachutes*. It was never actually released as a single in the UK but was sent to radio and was accompanied by a video. One of Coldplay's most memorable, the video featured a businessman (played by actor Paddy Considine) becoming invisible as he goes about his day. It was directed by Jamie Thraves who also made the renowned video for Radiohead's 'Just' in 1995.

Coldplay
Speed Of Sound

| 2005 • 4:48 • Berryman – Buckland – Champion – Martin

Coldplay's third album proved to have a more difficult conception than the previous two, with many aborted songs and sessions over an 18-month period

from mid-2003. However, the band's perfectionist determination paid off as *X&Y* went on to become the biggest-selling album in the world in 2005. Lead single 'Speed Of Sound' is a slick piano-driven ode to wonderment, partly inspired by the birth of singer Chris Martin's first child. Outrageously, it was kept off the number one slot in the UK singles chart by novelty act The Crazy Frog.

Coldplay Fix You

Coldplay
Violet Hill

| 2008 • 3:43 • Berryman – Buckland – Champion – Martin

In 2008, Chris Martin told Xfm that, when looking for a producer for the band's fourth album, they called Brian Eno and asked him who he thought the new Brian Eno was. Eno said he wasn't aware of one but would himself like to have a go at being the new Brian Eno. He was duly hired to produce *Viva La Vida Or Death And All His Friends*. Most of the album was recorded in the one studio room at Coldplay's north London base, The Bakery. The chilly Dickensian narrative that is 'Violet Hill' was the first single to be taken from the album and was a top 10 hit on release in the UK in May 2008.

Coldplay Viva La Vida

| 2008 • 4:01 • Berryman – Buckland – Champion – Martin

Coldplay Fix You

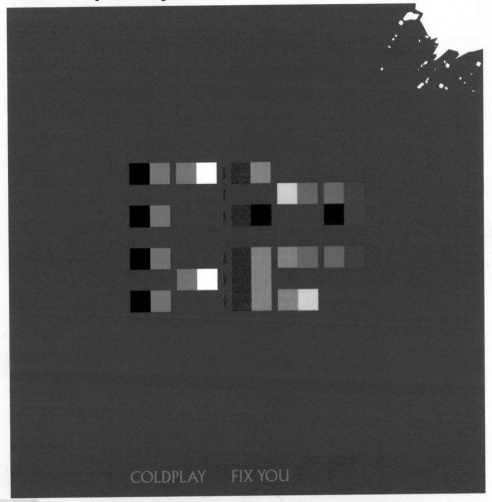

COLDPLAY   FIX YOU

2005 • 4:55 • Berryman – Buckland – Champion – Martin

As a song, 'Fix You' is a masterclass in "the build". It starts with the minimal sound of a church organ and Chris Martin's voice, followed by piano and acoustic guitar, gradually building to a crescendo of electric guitar and heavy drums. The track was said to be written for Martin's wife, actress Gwyneth Paltrow, after the death of her father in 2002. The accompanying video included live footage of the band's performances at Bolton's Reebok Stadium in July 2005.

Chris Martin has alluded to 'Viva La Vida' as the best song Coldplay have ever written and it is certainly one of their most successful. It gave the band their first ever UK number one single and spearheaded an album that became 2008's global bestseller. Chris Martin described the twin title of the album, *Viva La Vida Or Death And All His Friends*, as a choice for listeners as to which title they prefer – "like one of those model aeroplanes that you can't decide which colour to paint," he told Xfm.

Coldplay
Life In Technicolour !!

2009 • 4:06 • Berryman – Buckland – Champion – Martin – Hopkins

This song was originally discussed as the first single from *Viva La Vida Or Death And All His Friends* but felt too obvious. Instead they made a shorter instrumental version of the song the opening track on the album. The full vocal version later appeared as the lead track on the *Prospekt's March* EP, released in November 2008. MW

The Coral

The Coral
Dreaming Of You

! 2002 · 2:21 · Skelly

Formed in their early teens in 1996, by the time The Coral emerged in the early years of the 21st century, there was a justifiably intense buzz around this young and exceptionally talented Liverpool band. Their startlingly mature mix of 1960s psychedelia and folk and the arresting voice of James Skelly ensured that they were the band to watch in 2002. 'Dreaming Of You' was the second single to be taken from their self-titled debut album and was a number 13 hit in the UK in October of that year. *The Coral* was nominated for the 2002 Mercury Music Prize and the band gained famous fans in the likes of Paul Weller and Noel Gallagher.

> Up in my lonely room / When I'm dreaming of you /oh what can I do?

– The Coral, 'Dreaming Of You'

The Coral Pass It On

! 2003 · 2:20 · Skelly

'Pass It On' was the second single from the band's second album, *Magic And Medicine*. An amazingly simple and reflective song, written by a 17-year-old James Skelly in just 15 minutes, without a guitar, while waiting for a train. As with their first album, *Magic And Medicine* was produced by ex-Lightning Seed and Liverpool music legend, Ian Broudie. It entered the UK album chart at number one in July 2003, while 'Pass It On' gave The Coral their first top five single.

The Coral
In The Morning

! 2005 · 2:34 · Skelly

Continuing Liverpool's rich tradition of surrealist experimentation, The Coral's third album *The Invisible Invasion* was more about finding their voice through a group of 12 songs than a string of radio-friendly singles. However, the record did contain The Coral's biggest single to date – the insanely infectious 'In The Morning'. By far the band's greatest radio hit, it was a top 10 single that stayed in the UK top 40 for an impressive six weeks. The band told Xfm in May 2010 that the main hook of the song was written and recorded on a £5 keyboard. MW

It took six months and a Fatboy Slim remix before the public saw the light

– Cornershop, 'Brimful of Asha'

Cornershop
Brimful Of Asha

**1997 • 4:07 • Singh
(Fatboy Slim remix 1998 – 4:03)**

Previously better known for their line in agit-prop than anything resembling a melody, Anglo-Indian Leicester band Cornershop shocked everyone – most of all, you suspect, themselves – with this glorious number one single. It took six months and a Fatboy Slim remix before the public saw the light, though; the initial album version peaked at number 60, hitherto the group's highest chart placing.

'Brimful Of Asha' was simply wonderful in either form, a heartfelt love song to the music of Bollywood in general and the playback singer (whose singing dubbed the main actresses) Asha Bhosle in particular. Her output of some 12,000-plus songs makes her the most recorded vocalist in history. The Indian references may have escaped many, but the undeniable hook ("everybody needs a bosom for a pillow") and a melody so thunderously good it was allegedly plundered as recently as 2007 by The View's 'Same Jeans', certainly didn't. Although it begins as an exclusively Indian affair, it ends up as a celebration of great singles outfits, from T.Rex to Trojan Records. Norman Cook was so smitten he offered to remix it for free, speeding it up, adding a tonne of background noise, but keeping that winning combination of riff, hook and melody in the foreground. SY

The Courteeners
What Took You So Long?

2008 • 4:01 • Fray

Liam Fray spent his time at university playing Manchester's bars and clubs as a singer-songwriter before meeting up with schoolfriend Michael Campbell and deciding to form a band. Thus were the seeds of The Courteeners first sown. A series of sold-out gigs in the band's home city ensued, attracting an army of loyal fans. The result was a record deal and an approach from Stephen Street (Blur, Smiths) to produce their debut album *St. Jude*. 'What Took You So Long?' was the first single to be released from the record, and the Johnny Marr-type guitar and tender vocals from Fray drew comparisons with The Smiths and Oasis. Fray told Xfm in 2009 that his response to such comparisons was as follows: "At sixteen, if you told me I'd be mentioned in the same breath, I would have taken that" – suggesting that the outspoken frontman certainly has more planned for his band.

The Courteeners
Not Nineteen Forever

! 2008 • 3:37 • Fray

If 'What Took You So Long' announced the arrival of the Courteeners, their second single cemented their position on the indie music scene, hitting the UK charts at number 19. Where its predecessor had been gloomy, this upbeat and optimistic track was fuelled by bright guitars and Liam Fray's insightful vocals – reminiscent of The Libertines at their peak – encouraging listeners to seize the day. The band confirmed their status with a sucessful and polished second album *Falcon* and a sold-out show to 10,000 people in Manchester in December 2009. JS

The Cribs
Men's Needs

! 2007 • 3:18 • Jarman – Jarman – Jarman

In 2006, after five years and two albums in the cult punk wilderness, the three Jarman brothers got together in a converted blast furnace and wrote a pop song. Previous releases had been lo-fi and abrasive, but 'Men's Needs' was unashamedly "hooky" with singalong lyrics and toe-tapping rhythm, no doubt influenced by Franz Ferdinand's Alex Kapranos on production duties. Gary Jarman told Xfm that the song set the tone for the rest of the album: "That was like the catalyst song on the record. When you have a few ideas floating around and then one song comes along and that's the direction of the record." The track elevated the band from cult status into the UK mainstream.

The Cribs
Cheat On Me

! 2009 • 3:15 • Jarman – Marr

Much had changed in The Cribs' camp between the release of their third album and the writing of 'Cheat On Me': the band had recruited legendary Smiths guitarist Johnny Marr while Gary Jarman was living in the US during the making of their fourth album, *Ignore The Ignorant*. Demoed as a slow, spacey

I'm not bothered what you say or how you dress / I'm a mess so you've always seemed inviting — The Cribs, 'Men's Needs'

track, which Marr would call "the shoe-gazing song", the final version came about almost by accident. Fuelled by pre-gig excitement, the band played 'Cheat On Me' in sound check much faster than intended, thus reinventing the song. The single showcases the different guitar styles of Ryan Jarman and Marr, with each taking it in turns to contribute their distinctive sound to the record.

The Cribs
We Share The Same Skies

! 2009 • 3:24 • Jarman – Marr

Rather than hindering the creative process, The Cribs seemed to thrive on their intercontinental split with fourth album *Ignore The Ignorant* well received by critics. Not only were the band forced into a different way of writing and recording; being in different locations also inspired themes and subjects. This was certainly the case with the second single from the album, *We Share The Same Skies*. "I remember one day I was back in London," Gary Jarman explained to Xfm. "I just seemed so far from home. I was thinking how depressing it was but it's the same as it is in Portland — I just view it differently." Built around Marr's slick textured riffs married to typically up-tempo guitar scratches, this is the perfect example of the Marr / Cribs union.

JS

From Left:
Ryan Jarman,
Johnny Marr,
Ross Jarman,
Gary Jarman

CSS
Let's Make Love And Listen To Death From Above

! 2006 · 3:31 · Cintra – Lovefoxxx

CSS's full name, Cansei De Ser Sexy, translates into English as "tired of being sexy"; but it's more than just a quirky moniker, it also hints at the band's musical influences. The phrase was allegedly taken from a quote by Beyoncé and it's not just their name that is borrowed from stateside culture. The band turned their back on the limited Brazilian musical scene, preferring to gather ideas from MTV and MySpace to create a sound unfamiliar to their native country. 'Let's Make Love And Listen To Death From Above' (a reference to Canadian band, Death From Above 1979) was CSS's first international release after gaining some popularity via the internet. The song is typical of the CSS sound – reliant on catchy compositions rather than musicianship. Cheeky 1980s synths, bouncy bass and rhythmic suggestive lyrics, delivered by the fantastically named Lovefoxxx, create an edgy party tune that lies somewhere between punk and pop.
JS

The Cult
She Sells Sanctuary

! 1985 · 4:15 · Astbury – Duffy

One of the great British rock acts of the 1980s and one of the few to crack America. 'She Sells Sanctuary' remains The Cult's signature song and was one of the most enduring guitar records of its day. From Billy Duffy's phased opening guitar chords to the clean snap of the snare and Ian Astbury's howl of "Oh the heads that turn", the first 30 seconds of the track is up there with the best. Originally Astbury joined a band called The Southern Death Cult in his hometown of Bradford in 1981. This became Death Cult when he met Mancunian guitarist Billy Duffy, who had previously played with Theatre of Hate and a band called The Nosebleeds with a pre-Smiths Morrissey.

They finally became The Cult in 1984 and released their debut album *Dreamtime*. Second album *Love* (featuring 'She Sells Sanctuary') was produced by Steve Brown, who had just had massive success with ABC and Wham!, which explains why *Love* sounds so brilliantly clean and precise. Most of the album was recorded in rural Surrey, with all the comings and goings of a rock'n'roll band retreat. 'She Sells Sanctuary', however, was recorded in the more serious working environment of west London's Olympic Studios. This is where band and producer knuckled down to get the perfect arrangement and recording of a song that they knew had the potential to be a massive hit. And it was. A number 15 hit in the UK, it stuck around for nine weeks and firmly placed the band on the map. A remix version was released in 1993 and reached the same UK chart position as the original release. MW

The Cure
Boys Don't Cry

| 1979 · 2:38
| Tolhurst – Dempsey – Smith

Before Robert Smith became the tousled-haired godfather of goth of the 1980s, The Cure started life as a young punk trio, hoping to ride the new wave in the suburban English town of Crawley. After an ill-fated spell with German disco label Hansa, the band wound up on new imprint Fiction, founded by A&R man Chris Parry, who had signed The Jam and Siouxsie And The Banshees. However, the expected hits didn't materialise as press reaction to The Cure's witty, yet vaguely pretentious music was almost universally negative. Their debut album featured no track titles, only mysterious icons; their first single, 'Killing An Arab', was a heavyweight dissection of the existential novel *The Outsider* by Albert Camus and was viewed with suspicion in those racially tense days. So when Smith delivered a bona fide classic in 'Boys Don't Cry', the charts remained untroubled. A perfect pop single, which updated the 'Tears Of A Clown' motif for the macho 1970s, it would become one of The Cure's most famous songs many years after the fact.

The Cure
A Forest

| 1980 · 5:55 · Smith – Gallup –
| Tolhurst – Hartley

Having unsuccessfully pitched themselves
as a quirky post-punk act, Robert Smith's
lyrical concerns took a darker turn.
Following a line-up change, The Cure's
second album took its inspiration from the
European soundscapes of David Bowie's
Low and the cold, industrial music of
Joy Division. *Seventeen Seconds* was a
stripped-back, skeletal work, which worried
label boss Chris Parry. "At the time, he
was very disappointed," Smith told Xfm in
2004. "Until he realised that the new stuff
was actually working as well, if not better,
on a commercial level." The standout
track was 'A Forest', an epic six-minute
melodrama powered by unrelenting drums
and a hypnotic bassline. The extended
outro made this a live favourite and
primed The Cure to become the foremost
proponents of gloom-rock in the 1980s.

The Cure
The Love Cats

| 1983 · 3:40 · Smith

Following an ill-tempered European tour,
Robert Smith seriously thought about
winding up The Cure in 1982, but Fiction
label boss Chris Parry convinced him to
continue. Trying to destroy the image
he cultivated over three relentlessly
downbeat albums, Smith delivered a series
of eccentric but fun pop singles and, to his
surprise, found The Cure back in the UK top
20. 'The Love Cats' was the third of these
tracks, and owes much to Disney's *The
Aristocats*. According to Smith, "The idea's
from a book in which a guy puts all these
cats in bags and throws them in a lake…
At first that was the opening line, but I
felt I couldn't sing that in a pop song."

The Cure
In Between Days

| 1985 · 2:58 · Smith

Now enjoying commercial success, Robert
Smith consolidated the ever-shifting
line-up changes of The Cure by inviting
long-time bassist Simon Gallup back into
the fold and writing an excellent album,
The Head On The Door. Lead single 'In
Between Days' is another chart-friendly
Cure track, with a nagging synth riff and
a driving acoustic feel that resembles
New Order's more human moments. The
song still contains a bittersweet edge
that hints at aging and loneliness, but
you wouldn't know it from the exuberant
video, which features an airborne
camera swooping around the band.

The Cure
Close To Me

! 1985 • 3:41 • Smith

Written by Robert Smith about, according to Cure biography *Ten Imaginary Years*, "the end of a day where you feel nothing has been achieved", the song's claustrophobic atmosphere was taken to literal extremes in the famous video by director Tim Pope. The five-strong band were crammed into a tiny wardrobe perched precariously on the edge of a cliff, which inevitably topples over into the sea. "That was an image I had in my mind of the sense that you weren't aware of what was outside and anything could happen," Smith explained in 1991. The song (and video) was remixed in 1990 for the band's experimental *Mixed Up* album.

The Cure
Just Like Heaven

! 1987 • 3:33 • Smith – Gallup – Thompson – Williams – Tolhurst

The height of The Cure's late-1980s' career as oddball pop titans saw them unleash a sprawling double-LP called *Kiss Me Kiss Me Kiss Me*. Often tagged as the 'goth White Album', one of the undoubted highlights is the pure pop of 'Just Like Heaven' – a semi-acoustic ode to a romantic clifftop encounter. Described by singer Robert Smith as trying to encapsulate the feeling that "One night like that is worth 1,000 hours of drudgery", the dreamlike video features his wife Mary as an angelic presence. The romance was missing from Dinosaur Jr's 1989 cover, which flattens the song under grungy thrash.

The Cure
Pictures Of You

! 1989 • 7:29 • Smith – Gallup – Williams – Thompson – O'Donnell – Tolhurst

After the international success of the *Kiss Me Kiss Me Kiss Me* album, Cure spotters were expecting the follow-up to be another series of excellent, if quirky, pop songs. However, when *Disintegration* appeared in 1989, Robert Smith's now-trademark eccentricity had receded in favour of the deeper, more introspective work that The Cure had been known for at the start of the 1980s. With Smith approaching 30, *Disintegration* was a study of growing up, dying relationships and plenty of heartfelt emotion. One of its most moving moments was 'Pictures Of You', a delicate mid-tempo reflection on the passing of time, which was inspired by a fire that took place at the residential studio where The Cure were recording. Once the band had been evacuated, Smith checked through his surviving possessions. "I lost the pictures I always carried around in my wallet," he recalled. "I realised that I'm clutching old pictures of things, even taken before my birth, to give me a sense that things went on then." Harking back to the majestic soundscapes of the band's own *Seventeen Seconds* and *Faith* albums, while owing some of its glittering atmosphere to Joy Division's classic 'Atmosphere', the track was the emotional high point of what is now recognised as The Cure's finest work.

The Cure
Lullaby

1989 • 4:13 • Smith – Gallup – Williams – Thompson – O'Donnell – Tolhurst

'Lullaby' is a typically idiosyncratic and subtly disturbing single based, as so many Cure songs are, on one of songwriter Robert Smith's dreams. Concerning the antics of the spooky "Spider Man", this figure is not the Marvel Comics superhero but – as depicted in the brilliant video – a black-eyed, straggly-haired banshee, portrayed by Smith himself. He appears in the terrified singer's darkened bedroom with a view to consuming him completely. Featuring the frontman at his most grotesque, this concoction of nightmarish lyrics and a slyly appealing tune became the band's biggest UK hit, making number five in April 1989.

The Cure
Love Song

1989 • 3:30 • Smith – Gallup – Williams – Thompson – O'Donnell – Tolhurst

The Cure's biggest hit in the US, 'Love Song' was kept off the top spot stateside by Janet Jackson. Originally written as a wedding present for singer Robert Smith's wife Mary, the song is probably the most accessible on the otherwise emotionally wrenching *Disintegration* album. "[Mary] went away to the other room to listen to it, then smothered me with kisses," he recalled. "It's about love, but also about the inability to never really know someone."

The Cure
Friday I'm In Love

1992 • 3:39 • Smith – Gallup – Thompson – Williams – Bamonte

Probably the most atypical Cure track of all, this is another slick pop song from Robert Smith. 'Friday I'm In Love' takes an almost nursery rhyme-style countdown of the days of the week and turns it into a meditation on the drudgery of life. "It's a dumb pop song," said Smith in 1992, "but it's quite excellent, actually, because it's so absurd." Featuring gleaming production, the song was taken from The Cure's first UK number one album, *Wish*, and is probably the best known of their singles, having taken up permanent residence on the radio airwaves.
MO'G

"It's a dumb pop song, but it's quite excellent, actually, because it's so absurd"
— Robert Smith of The Cure on 'Friday I'm In Love'

Daft Punk

Daft Punk
Da Funk

1995 • 5:35
Bangalter – de Homem-Christo

Some revolutions happen overnight, some take a little while to brew. The French duo of Thomas Bangalter and Guy-Manuel de Homem-Christo rewrote the rules of dance music in the mid-1990s, but 'Da Funk' took a whopping 18 months from initial release on Scottish techno label Soma in the summer of 1995 to become their first hit in February 1997.

Having previously been in short-lived rock band Darling (it was a dismissive *Melody Maker* review that gave them their new name), Daft Punk always had more than a few house beats to their bow. This chugger of a tune rolled in on a huge synth line and spongy bass, delivered in a filter-disco form much imitated – first in the Paris sound they made fashionable, then worldwide. Though The Chemical Brothers were quick to pick up on it, caning 'Da Funk' at their renowned Heavenly Social bashes, de Homem-Christo insisted in a 1996 interview with *Jockey Slut* that the sound owed more to the new jack swing of R Kelly than any big beat scene. That same interview later became legendary when Daft Punk decided they

didn't like the look of themselves on the magazine's cover and ducked behind masks for all future gigs and photo shoots.

Daft Punk
Around The World

1997 • 3:55
Bangalter – de Homem-Christo

Perhaps the least noisy of Daft Punk's earliest hits, 'Around The World' relied on that crystalline bass they did so well, a fluttering synth line and a Vocodered vocal line. Repeated again. And again. And again. Well over 100 times altogether, if you're listening to the full-length album version. Still, it means we can now hear that phrase without automatically thinking of Lisa Stansfield. Or indeed, will.i.am, whose advanced-stage plan to hijack the record and video for his track 'I Got It From My Momma' were scotched when the Punks put taste before moolah and told him no.

Daft Punk
One More Time

2000 • 3:55 • Bangalter –
de Homem-Christo – Moore

Daft Punk's second album, *Discovery*, was all about mixing and matching of influences – and nowhere more so than on 'One More Time'. The intro sounds like a brass fanfare that could've been ripped from an old Stax tune (some thought they knew the exact source, though the French duo always denied using samples), while the vocal took the great deep house singer Romanthony and Auto-Tuned him to buggery. A crime? "Criticising the Vocoder is like asking bands in the 1960s, 'Why do you use the electric guitar?'" Thomas Bangalter told *DJ Times* in 2001. An international dance anthem that can just about be forgiven for bequeathing us T-Pain.

Daft Punk
Harder Better Faster Stronger

| 2001 • 3:43 • Bangalter –
de Homem-Christo – Birdsong

Once they seemed the bitterest of enemies; then for a while you could hardly move in a hip-hop club without bumping into something making flagrant use of European dance sounds. What changed? Kanye West heard Daft Punk's 'Harder Better Faster Stronger' and ripped the idea for his own 'Stronger'. Daft Punk deemed it a meeting of creative minds (will.i.am take note) and the Franco-American alliance later delivered a stellar version of West's 'Stronger' at the 2008 Grammy awards.

If Kraftwerk defined the remorseless image of robots in the 1970s, Daft Punk did it for the noughties. Their sound is a flurry of ideas, a robot voice delivering the words in a variety of pitches, sounding like a sat-nav system steadily sinking into meltdown: what starts as a sparse, decorative vocal soon comes to dominate, while the bass sinks into the background. Although the group recruited famed anime director Leji Matsumoto for the video, the official version was later upstaged by the amateur 'Daft Hands' take, in which a pair of hands (the lyrics written out on the fingers, palms and fists) dance in time with the music. The single reached number 25 in the UK in November 2001; West's version spawned a worldwide number one; the Daft Hands video became one of YouTube's all-time greatest hits. SY

Kanye West heard Daft Punk's 'Harder Better Faster Stronger' and ripped the idea for his own 'Stronger'. Daft Punk deemed it a meeting of creative minds

– Daft Punk, 'Harder Better Faster Stronger'

The Damned
New Rose

1976 • 2:44 • James

Single 'New Rose' was taken from the band's debut album, *Damned, Damned, Damned*, and has since been frozen in time as the first punk single to be released in the UK. It was also the first single issued on Stiff Records, recorded on a simple eight-track deck and produced by the man known as Nick "Cruel To Be Kind" Lowe. A glance through The Damned's discography is highly recommended, not only to understand the challenges that this colourful band have managed to overcome through the years, but also for their album and single sleeve – the essential trip down memory lane for punk and gothic fans everywhere.

The Damned Eloise

1986 • 5:08 • Ryan

Prolific punk band The Damned released their cover of Paul Ryan's track 'Eloise' in 1986, after it was originally recorded by his twin brother Barry in 1968. The group formed in the 1970s and had supported various bands, including the Sex Pistols and T.Rex, but it wasn't until later that they rose to fame with album *Phantasmagoria* in 1985 – their first with major label MCA. It achieved great commercial success and raised the bar for the group's breakthrough potential – so much so that when 'Eloise' was released six months later, it shot to number three in the UK singles chart, helped by MCA's cunning ruse of releasing it on two different 12-inches. BdP

Left to right: Dan Le Sac and Scroobius Pip. Far right: Dan Le Sac Vs Scroobius Pip, 'Angles'

Dan Le Sac Vs Scroobius Pip
Thou Shalt Always Kill

❗ 2007 • 5:19 • Scroobius Pip – Dan Le Sac

Not many songs combine smile-inducing wit, social commentary and common sense-sermonising with a singalong non-chorus and electronic wig-out, but then this is not many songs. Using the Ten Commandments as a blueprint, Scroobius Pip skewers pretension, prejudice and snobbery in calling on listeners to think for themselves while Dan Le Sac cooks up a storm of hypnotic electro. Defying categorisation, the duo created a song that caught people's imagination – and got them chanting "just a band". 'Thou Shalt Always Kill' actually qualifies more than just artistically for inclusion within this book: it was on Xfm's X-Posure in January 2007, mere days after being recorded, that the single got its first ever airplay. Excitement around it has led some media to claim otherwise but only one copy was sent out before the furore, to just one radio station. Not 'just a station' then. JK

The Dandy Warhols
Not If You Were The Last Junkie On Earth

! 1997 • 3:11 • Taylor-Taylor

Despite saddling themselves with a name based on one of the worst puns in rock history, Portland, Oregon's Dandy Warhols have carved out a unique career of slacker rock with the occasional perceptive pop song. Formed in the early 1990s, the band released their debut *Dandys Rule OK?* on an indie label in 1995, before being picked up by major Capitol. Their second album's title, *…The Dandy Warhols Come Down*, was a sly comment on the fact that they'd reportedly blown their advance money within 48 hours. Whatever the truth, the album features some gems, including 'Not If You Were The Last Junkie On Earth' – a sardonic attack on super-scenesters who get into taking heroin as a fashion statement. Singer Courtney Taylor-Taylor's statement that "I never thought you'd be a junkie because heroin is so passé" is both funny and tragic at the same time, while the band work up an authentic garage rock vibe, thanks to some metronomic drumming and a 1960s-style reedy organ.

The Dandy Warhols
Bohemian Like You

! 2000 • 3:32 • Taylor-Taylor

Taken from the Dandys' third album, *Thirteen Tales Of Urban Bohemia*, this song is a witty and acerbic sketch about fashionable types trying to impress each other. Delivered in singer Courtney Taylor-Taylor's trademark drawl, the protagonist tries to affect an air of cool detachment but instead comes across as a little insidious: "I really love your hairdo, yeah / I'm glad you like mine too…" The jangling guitar and Rolling Stones-circa-'Brown Sugar' vibe was instantly appealing – so much so, in fact, that telecoms company Vodafone used it in a TV ad in Europe and Australia. Luckily, the Dandys' credibility remained intact and the move brought them to a wider audience. The song hit number five in the UK singles chart, even though the accompanying video features various fashionistas mentally undressing each other.
MO'G

Death Cab For Cutie
I Will Follow You Into The Dark

! 2006 • 3:09 • Gibbard

Acoustically strummed on a guitar and almost naked in its spare production, Death Cab for Cutie's best song is a ballad about dying and being together. This is no saccharine image of sitting hand-in-hand on pink fluffy clouds, however. Ben Gibbard's afterlife has an unmistakeable bleakness, with "no blinding light, or tunnels to gates of white". There is no easy religious faith in the existence of

heaven or hell, and Catholic school is vicious too: a place of bruised knuckle lessons that "fear is the heart of love". But despite all the darkness, there's a romance here too: whatever there is, or isn't, beyond the grave, love will survive and we'll go together. Performed solo and impromptu at a recording session, the song appears on the band's album *Plans* in mono. It has since been used in several television dramas, including *Scrubs* and *Grey's Anatomy*.
JH

Death In Vegas
Aisha

1999 · 5:53 · Fearless – Holmes – Hellier

Formed by Richard Fearless and Tim Holmes, the music of Death In Vegas owes much to the trip-hop and big beat styles of such contemporaries as The Chemical Brothers, while adding their own unsettling obsessions with psychedelia and the darker side of pop culture. For example, the duo initially called themselves Dead Elvis, until Presley's estate complained; instead they gave the name to their debut album – which mixed various styles with weird samples, such as the stage announcements from the Woodstock festival. Recorded for their second album, *The Contino Sessions*, 'Aisha' is probably their darkest track to date, thanks to a thunderous drum track and the presence of one Iggy Pop. The garage rock legend and "Godfather of

Punk" doesn't sing but offers a spoken-word narration in his distinctive baritone, in which he plays a convicted murderer chatting up the titular heroine. It doesn't go well, as Iggy is convinced a serial killer is on his trail and winds up crying out in what has to be one of the most hair-raising moments in recorded history: "Aisha, I'm confused! Aisha… I'm vibrating!"

Death In Vegas
with Liam Gallagher
Scorpio Rising

2001 · 5:38 · Fearless – Holmes – Button – Rossi – Wiz – Pratt

Continuing the theme of inviting unusual guests onto their records, Tim Holmes and Richard Fearless collected a formidable array of talent for their third album, *Scorpio Rising*. Paul Weller, former Stone Rose Mani and singer Hope Sandoval all contributed, but their biggest coup was for the title track, which saw vocals from none other than Oasis frontman Liam Gallagher. Applying his trademark sneer, the song takes the melody from Status Quo's 1968 psychedelic classic 'Pictures Of Matchstick Men', while the title pays homage to Kenneth Anger's 1964 underground film about satanic bikers. "A lot of the words to the song are actually about aspects of India, where we went quite a bit for the making of the album," Fearless revealed to *The Guardian*.
MO'G

DepecheMode

Depeche Mode
Everything Counts

! 1983 • 4:01 • Gore

If Depeche Mode had split after the departure of chief songwriter Vince Clarke in November 1981, they would be remembered now as a tinkly-pop synth band with a couple of hits. However, the New Romantics from the town of Basildon in Essex carried on with keyboard player Martin Gore taking over the task of writing the music, which would take them into more ambitious and darker areas for 1983's *Construction Time Again*. "I think it was our first combined effort where the Depeche Mode sound was starting to emerge," singer Dave Gahan recalled. The music was heavily influenced by German industrialists Einstürzende Neubauten, and the band began to experiment with sampling "real" sounds from their immediate environment. The record is full of clanks, smashes and hammering, all fed into the Synclavier sampler and used to build rhythm tracks. The approach is at the forefront of the lead single, 'Everything Counts', which opens with a thudding bass drum and groaning, metallic percussion, while the cynical lyrics describe deceitful business practices and anticipates the rise of yuppie culture: "The grabbing hands, grab all they can."

Depeche Mode
Personal Jesus

! 1989 • 3:47 • Gore

At some point in the mid-1980s, Depeche Mode blossomed from a cheerfully naff synth pop band into one of the biggest alternative acts in the world. By 1989, they were a stadium group in the US, while songwriter Martin Gore still managed to get some of the most introspective, private and downright troubling lyrics under the noses of America's teens. No more so than on their single 'Personal Jesus', which was based on the book *Elvis And Me* by Priscilla Presley. "It's a song about being a Jesus for somebody else, someone to give you hope and care," explained Gore at the time. "It's about how Elvis was her man and her mentor and how often that happens in love relationships; how everybody's heart is like a god in some way, and that's not a very balanced view of someone, is it?" Unusually for the Mode, the main riff is played on a guitar rather than a synthesizer, which must have appealed to the deeply religious country legend Johnny Cash, who covered the song in 2002. The track remains one of the biggest-selling records in the history of the band's American label, Warner Brothers.

It's a song about being a Jesus for somebody else, someone to give you hope and care — Martin Gore on 'Personal Jesus'

Depeche Mode
Enjoy The Silence

1990 • 4:18 • Gore

One of Depeche Mode's biggest worldwide hits, songwriter Martin Gore originally wrote the song as a slow, mournful ballad played on a creaking old harmonium. When the rest of the band were convinced that the track had potential as a single, Gore resisted attempts to speed up the song, feeling that it didn't suit the tone of the lyrics – a serious meditation on communication (or lack of) in relationships. He eventually capitulated and added a distinctive guitar riff that recalled their contemporaries New Order.

The song became Depeche Mode's first UK top 10 single since 1984, and their only Billboard top 10 hit in the US.

Depeche Mode
I Feel You

1993 • 4:34 • Gore

Following the huge success of 1990's *Violator* album, Depeche Mode settled comfortably into the life of stadium rock superstars. For the follow-up, 1993's *Songs Of Faith And Devotion*, the band moved even further away from their electronic roots. While starting life as an all-synthesizer band, guitars and live drums had been creeping their way back into their music. 'I Feel You', the first track and lead single from the new album, was their heaviest-sounding track yet. It was a perfect sound to take out on the road, but the subsequent *Devotional* tour saw singer Dave Gahan take the "rock god" lifestyle too seriously, and the band almost split following his near-death experiences with heroin addiction. MO'G

Dodgy
Staying Out For The Summer

⁞ 1994 • 3:12 • Clark – Priest – Miller

Considered part of the Britpop scene, Dodgy never took themselves as seriously as others often did. Their debut album, *Homegrown*, was produced by The Lightning Seeds' Ian Broudie, who would go on to make albums with The Coral and The Zutons. Like those bands, Dodgy's sound had a lot of heart but was infused with a sense of fun. Originally released *after* the summer in November 1994 (a misguided decision by the label), this single didn't come into its own until the following year. After three top 40 hits, it received a more timely re-issue at the beginning of summer 1995. Written "literally in five minutes" at frontman Nigel Clark's girlfriend's house, it's a joyful indie stomper with a bounding guitar riff and the odd touch of melancholy. Throughout, Dodgy's trademark harmonies underpin lyrics about longing to shake off the day job, with a little heartbreak thrown in.

Dodgy
Good Enough

⁞ 1996 • 3:59 • Clark – Priest – Miller

Jaunty, warm keyboards, lush harmonies and positive sentiments make this one of the ultimate feel-good tracks. As sunny and fun as the lyrics seem, the line "Keep your eyes on the prize" is actually lifted from a folk song about the American Civil Rights Movement, at the time quoted frequently by drummer Matthew Priest's dad. It instantly became a huge radio hit. In 1996, Britpop was raging, but commercial stations were still afraid of the hand-break turn that playlisting an Oasis track would mean. 'Good Enough' was the perfect solution. The sound was sufficiently user-friendly not to scare such stations off, while Dodgy's status as a guitar band meant they ticked the Britpop boxes. It gave the band their biggest hit and continues to be a staple of radio station playlists more than a decade on. After briefly splitting, the band reformed in 2007; they continue to write and perform. MS

A joyful indie stomper with a bounding guitar riff and the odd touch of melancholy

– 'Staying Out For The Summer'

The Doors

The Doors
Break On Through (To The Other Side)

1967 • 2:26 • Densmore – Krieger – Manzarek – Morrison

Formed in 1965 in Los Angeles, The Doors would go on to become one of America's finest exports. Fronted by the charismatic and wild Jim Morrison, keyboardist Ray Manzarek, drummer John Densmore and guitarist Robby Krieger completed the lineup to create the controversial rock act.

'Break On Through...' was the first Doors' single to be produced, perhaps aptly released on New Year's Day in 1967 as a seven-inch. As with so many great bands, this first release from debut album *The Doors* failed to set the world alight, though it certainly functioned as an introduction to frontman Jim Morrison's epic new sound. The track limped into the Billboard charts at number 101, but has stood the test of time and to this day remains one of the band's signature songs. A perennial staple on film soundtracks, it has featured in *Forrest Gump*, *21*, *Jarhead* and *The Simpsons*, among many others.

The album version of 'Light My Fire' was originally almost seven minutes long

The Doors
Light My Fire

1967 • 2:52 • Densmore – Krieger – Manzarek – Morrison

From the album *The Doors*, 'Light My Fire' was released as a single in April 1967. It spent an impressive three weeks at number one in the US Billboard charts. It was the track that brought the band worldwide acclaim and remains perhaps their best-known song. The album version of 'Light My Fire' was originally almost seven minutes long, but record company Elektra felt this was too long to get any radio play, so the transfixing guitar and organ solos were edited down to shorten the track as we know it today. Elektra did, however, leave the longer version on the album, encouraging serious fans to purchase both the album and the single.

The Doors
L.A. Woman

1971 • 7:59 • Densmore – Krieger – Manzarek – Morrison

The title track of the last Doors album featuring the original line-up, recorded six months before the death of Jim Morrison. The LP was recorded at the band's "workshop" in Los Angeles, which was actually a cramped office space. Morrison taped his vocals in the bathroom to get a fuller, more rounded sound. A frenetic tribute to the seedier side of California, Morrison repeats the name Mr Mojo Risin' at the climax – actually an anagram of his own name.

The Doors
Riders On The Storm

1971 • 4:35 • Densmore – Krieger – Manzarek – Morrison

Doors producer Paul Rothchild parted company with the band on hearing this track, claiming it was "cocktail music". The rest of the world disagreed, and the climax to the *L.A. Woman* album remains The Doors' eeriest moment, thanks to Morrison's sinister vocal and Ray Manzarek's dreamlike keyboards. Some claim that the song relates to the case of Billy Cook, a hitchhiker who killed an entire family in 1960. It was the last Doors song to feature Morrison – the singer died in mysterious circumstances in Paris in July 1971 and the band limped on for two more albums without him. In 1978, the surviving members put new music to a series of poems that Morrison had recorded earlier in the decade and released the finished product as *An American Prayer*.
BdP / MOG

A frenetic tribute to the seedier side of California, Morrison repeats the name Mr Mojo Risin' at the climax – actually an anagram of his own name.

– The Doors 'L.A. Woman'

Doves

Doves Here It Comes

1999 • 4:51
Goodwin – Williams – Williams

Manchester band Doves are Jimi Goodwin (bass/vocal) and the Williams twins Andy (drums) and Jez (guitar). Under their previous moniker, Sub Sub, they achieved great success in the dance world and had a number three UK hit in 1993 with 'Ain't No Love, Ain't No Use'. In 1996, partly inspired by the indie bands they saw play Manchester's Hacienda club, they rented New Order's old rehearsal space and started writing songs. One of the first to appear was 'Here It Comes' – a dark piano-led swagger that wore the band's love of Northern Soul proudly on its sleeve.

Doves Catch The Sun

2000 • 4:50
Goodwin – Williams – Williams

An unusually straightforward song for Doves, and one that the band omitted from their live set for many years for that very reason. Its parent album, their debut *Lost Souls*, received a Mercury Music Prize nomination in 2000 but lost out to Badly Drawn Boy's *The Hour Of Bewilderbeast*. Ironically, Doves were helping out as Badly Drawn Boy's backing band only two years before.

Doves There Goes The Fear

2002 • 6:54
Goodwin – Williams – Williams

Writing their second album, *The Last Broadcast*, Doves retired to a series of remote rural cottages in Wales and across north England. This established a method of writing in isolation that would continue for the next few albums. Doves rarely stick to one studio for the recording of each album and 'There Goes The Fear' was recorded in a Stockport studio that they had only used once before – when they made their number three Sub Sub hit 'Ain't No Love, Ain't No Love Use'. Almost exactly ten years later they recorded 'There Goes The Fear' in the same place. It became Doves' biggest hit to date at... number three.

Doves Pounding

2002 • 4:45
Goodwin – Williams – Williams

Approximately two minutes and 50 seconds into 'Pounding', just after Jimi Goodwin sings "Seize the time / cause it's now or never baby", the drums get harder, the guitar kicks into a higher, sky-reaching riff, and the whole song ascends to a new level of euphoria.

This, for many people, is one of the greatest moments ever produced from the rich musical city of Manchester.

Doves
Caught By The River

2002 · 5:55
Goodwin – Williams – Williams

Andy Williams describes the writing sessions for *The Last Broadcast* as a joyous and unlaboured period in the band's history. With confidence boosted by the success of *Lost Souls*, all three band members were having a creatively prolific time with songs like 'Caught By The River' written rapidly and with ease. Williams wrote the lyrics about a very close friend who was having a particularly bad time, but he was still keen for the song to be an uplifting experience. Although the band never thought of the song as a potential single, it ended up being one of Doves' most successful releases on American radio.

Doves
Black And White Town

2005 · 4:15
Goodwin – Williams – Williams

The first single from Doves' third album *Some Cities* and their second UK top 10 hit. An intense and powerful video capturing the lives of local youths on Glasgow's Summerston estate was shot for the song by acclaimed Scottish film director Lynne Ramsay (*Morvern Callar* and *Ratcatcher*). Ramsay was not happy with the final edits made by the record label

and some reports suggest that she even took her name off the piece, leaving it to the official pseudonym "Alan Smithee", which directors use when they no longer want to be associated with a work.

Doves Kingdom of Rust

2009 · 5:12
Goodwin – Williams – Williams

After a five-month break from each other, Jimi Goodwin and the Williams brothers retired to their newly-built studio barn conversion between Liverpool and Manchester to write and record *Kingdom Of Rust*. The first single and title track of the album was one of the first songs to appear in these sessions and was described by Tom Rowlands of The Chemical Brothers, who was collaborating with the band at the time, as "having a northern spaghetti western feel to it".
MW

> The drums get harder, the guitar kicks into a higher, sky-reaching riff, and the whole song ascends to a new level of euphoria
>
> – Doves, 'Pounding'

'Killing Moon' was both a breakthrough and, at least until their successful reunion, a finale

Echo & The Bunnymen
The Cutter

1983 · 3:53 · De Freitas – McCulloch – Sergeant – Pattinson

Alongside 'Nothing Lasts Forever', 'The Cutter' is the Bunnymen's highest UK chart placing at number eight, perhaps surprisingly for a record that was deemed an all-round disappointment at the time. But 'The Cutter' has aged well, boldly probing psychedelic territory with its Indian strings (courtesy of Sri Lankan violinist Shankar) and a keyboard fanfare that sounds uncannily like bagpipes. But 'Mull Of Kintyre' this ain't, despite the cover picturing the band somewhere in deep-freeze territory. With its cryptic lyrics and magnificent production, courtesy of Will Sergeant's flatmate and future Lightning Seed Ian Broudie, it hasn't dated a day.

Echo & The Bunnymen
Killing Moon

1984 · 5:45 · De Freitas – McCulloch – Sergeant – Pattinson

Some seven years after punk, many of its precepts still held sway. Keep the chords minimal, the time short, and whatever you do, stay away from the orchestras. The Bunnymen junked the lot on their fourth album, *Ocean Rain*, of which 'Killing Moon' was the undoubted centrepiece. The Liverpudlians had been pegged as post-punk's underachievers, the band who should've been U2. Certainly they had the epic widescreen sound down more convincingly, and Ian McCulloch was a natural-born superstar, not least in his own mind.

'Killing Moon' was both a breakthrough and, at least until their successful reunion, a finale. The *Ocean Rain* album was accompanied by a PR campaign branding it the best ever made, and with its experimental structure and a 35-piece orchestra, this was about as big as they could go (over nine minutes on the 12-inch), with Ian McCulloch's vocal almost parodically dramatic. It peaked at number nine in the UK charts, which must have been a disappointment, for this is the sound of a band pulling out all the stops. But the song acquired an afterlife via film soundtracks such as *Donnie Darko* and *Grosse Pointe Blank*, where it's been used to symbolise teen angst and doomed romance.

Echo & The Bunnymen
Nothing Lasts Forever

1997 · 3:54
Sergeant – McCulloch – Pattinson

There was something inevitable about 'Nothing Lasts Forever', the signature tune of the Echo & The Bunnymen reunion. The definitive Liverpool band of the early 1980s, their split a decade later had been unhappier than most, made ridiculous by the band's attempt to carry on without frontman Ian McCulloch, and tragic when drummer Pete De Freitas died in a motorbike accident. McCulloch's solo career, meanwhile, seemed like one long build-up to the reunion, working first with former Smiths legend Johnny Marr, then Bunnymen guitarist Will Sergeant as Electrafixion. When original bassist Les Pattinson joined up, reviving the Echo & The Bunnymen name was the obvious option.

What couldn't be predicted, though, was just how successfully they'd revive the sound and image. The sleeve of the album, *Evergreen*, was shot in the woods, deliberately echoing their *Crocodiles* debut, while even the title 'Nothing Lasts Forever' was a playful nod to their awkward break-up. And the song could've fallen straight off the *Ocean Rain* sessions, repriving that yearning, epic, windswept sound they'd done so well. Marr claimed the tune, which was originally to be called 'Never, Never, Never', stemmed from their sessions, but agreed to go without a credit.

Echo & The Bunnymen
Bring On The Dancing Horses

1985 · 3:59 · De Freitas – McCulloch –
Sergeant – Pattinson

With the band suffering writer's block following the epic *Ocean Rain*, 'Bring On The Dancing Horses' was the only new song to emerge in the three years between their fourth and fifth albums. Recorded for the *Pretty In Pink* soundtrack, it proved a valuable introduction to American teens. It would have fit sweetly into the former, having the same epic sheen but with a new reverb-heavy production reminiscent of the Cocteau Twins. They weren't the only new Scottish band the Bunnies were listening to: the brilliant B-side, 'Over Your Shoulder', was an unabashed lift of The Jesus And Mary Chain's feedback-soaked rock.
SY

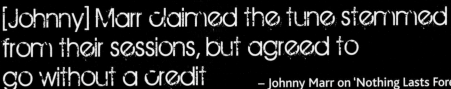

[Johnny] Marr claimed the tune stemmed from their sessions, but agreed to go without a credit

– Johnny Marr on 'Nothing Lasts Forever'

Editors

Editors
Bullets

2005 · 3:10
Smith – Urbanowicz – Leetch – Lay

Birmingham's Editors were initially compared with post-punk legends Joy Division, thanks to singer Tom Smith's deep baritone and Chris Urbanowicz's icy guitar, which recalled the legendary Mancunians' work at the end of the 1970s. However, Editors distinguished themselves as purveyors of epic, dark rock and were an impressive live band to boot. Originally called Pilot, the band were known as Snowfield when they produced a demo of 'Bullets', but changed their name to Editors when they signed to Kitchenware. An excellent debut single, 'Bullets' opens with an assured guitar fanfare and showcases Smith's distinctive voice.

Editors
Munich

2005 · 3:46
Smith – Urbanowicz – Leetch – Lay

Second single 'Munich' consolidated the band's successful formula – driving drums from Ed Lay, a sturdy bassline from Russell Leetch, ringing guitar from Chris Urbanowicz and a passionate vocal from Tom Smith, who dissects an unhealthy relationship: "People are fragile things / You should know by now". First released in April 2005, the song was re-issued in 2006 and made the UK top 10.

Editors
Blood

2005 · 3:29
Smith – Urbanowicz – Leetch – Lay

Originally called Pilot, the band were known as Snowfield when they produced a demo of 'Bullets'

– Editors, 'Bullets'

Editors' third single from July 2005, issued just prior to the release of their acclaimed debut album, *The Back Room*. The song contains a biting lyric from singer Tom Smith, offering the rather cold sentiment: "Blood runs through our veins / That's where our similarity ends". "It's an out-and-out pop song for us, but kind of dark, lyrically very dark," Smith explained to Xfm at the time. "But it's got a bit of a dancefloor element and there's a lot of melody in it."

Editors
All Sparks

2005 • 3:34
Smith – Urbanowicz – Leetch – Lay

Released as the fourth single from *The Back Room* in March 2006, this is probably the most Joy Division-esque of all Editors' songs, as the strident rhythm and pumping bass recalls the Manchester band's 1980 track 'A Means To An End'. However, Tom Smith's lyric seems slightly sad on closer inspection, as it concerns a friend or lover who seems to be growing distant or who is set for a spectacular fall.

Editors
Smokers Outside The Hospital Doors

2007 • 4:58
Smith – Urbanowicz – Leetch – Lay

Editors' second album, *An End Has A Start*, saw the group expand their sound and the first single, 'Smokers Outside The Hospital Doors', was unusual in that it uses major chords – a departure from the downbeat sound of the first album. The track also features a choir of various band members and studio staff that brings the song to an uplifting climax. The lyrics explore universal fears of death and mortality, as singer Tom Smith explained to Xfm: "It's an image of visiting hospital as a child and something that's stuck with me. When you're a lot younger, disease, illness and ultimately death seem a long way away. Only when you're forced to visit that environment do you think, things do come to an end. As you get older, you come to realise that even more. Yes, it's scary, but there are equally scary things going on in the world."

Editors
An End Has A Start

| 2007 • 3:46
| Smith – Urbanowicz – Leetch – Lay

The title track of Editors' second album, this song is described by bassist Russell Leetch as "a pop nugget – we wanted it to be a rush". Singer Tom Smith admits that the song was an attempt "to be New Order, because they wrote great songs", but explained that the lyrics mined the same vein of dark material as the rest of the album, with its refrain of "You came on your own / That's how you leave". "It's about being aware of things ending," he told Xfm. "It's not looking at the bright side of death, because that's a really nasty way of looking at it. But appreciating what you have while you have it, in light of thinking about the scary stuff."

Editors
The Racing Rats

| 2007 • 4:18
| Smith – Urbanowicz – Leetch – Lay

Featuring a plaintive piano intro, 'The Racing Rats' is one of the more optimistic songs on the album, *An End Has A Start*.

According to frontman Tom Smith, the song "touches on being in planes and visiting London, Tokyo and touring... Being in these vastly overpopulated cities with millions of people. You step away from it and they look like ants or rats. But as scary as it is, it's exciting at the same time."

Editors
Papillon

| 2009 • 5:26
| Smith – Urbanowicz – Leetch – Lay

"Papillon" is French for "butterfly" and the first single from Editors' third album *In This Light And On This Evening* recalls the famous novel and film of the same name. Written by Henri Charrière in 1969, the story recounts the author's time spent in prison for a murder he didn't commit and was made into a film with Dustin Hoffman. "I've never read the book," singer Tom Smith told Xfm, "but I remember watching the film with my dad quite a lot as a kid. The song touches on escape and it came rushing back when I was writing." The song highlighted the band's interest in synthesizers, with a heavily-sequenced riff propelling the track and a scorching Minimoog refrain on the chorus. "They're great-sounding things," said Smith of the technology. "In a way, we were trying to humanise these machines, to make them feel not so robotic."
MO'G

Eels

Eels
Novocaine For The Soul

! 1996 • 3:08 • Everett – Goldenberg

Following two albums and a modestly successful career as a solo artist, Mark "E" Everett enlisted the help of bassist Tommy Walter and drummer Jonathan "Butch" Norton to piece together his next creative vision, Eels.

As one of the first acts to be signed to the newly formed Dreamworks record label, Everett was indulged his eclectic sonic palette and introspective lyrics by producer John Simpson, one-half of formidable creative partnership The Dust Brothers (the Beastie Boys' *Paul's Boutique*, Beck's *Odelay*). Unsurprisingly, the album was a cutting-edge mix of grungy rock with a hip-hop sheen, and spawned first single 'Novocaine For The Soul'. Embraced wholeheartedly by the UK on its release, the band went on to win a Brit award in 1998 for Best International Breakthrough Act. Much consternation by the stiff hierarchy of the awards body ensued after discovering that Walter had begun using the gong as a stand for his triangle.

Eels
Mr E's Beautiful Blues

! 1999 • 3:58 • Everett – Simpson

Following the bleak tour-de-force of second album *Electro-Shock Blues*, a record inspired by the death of E's sister and his mother's cancer diagnosis, Eels lightened the mood a little with third record *Daisies Of The Galaxy*. With Dust Brother John Simpson still on board, the album took a more folky, countrified direction and was put on the map by its biggest single, 'Mr E's Beautiful Blues'. Musically, it was a ray of sunshine compared to *Electro-Shock Blues'* dismal downpour, but lyrically it was anything but. Initially, E had earmarked the song for

> Much consternation ensued after discovering Walter had begun using the gong as a stand for his triangle
>
> — Eels misuse of their 1998 Brit award

following album, *Souljacker*. The record company, fearing another album bereft of commercial singles, tried persuading him to include it on *Daisies...* Unhappy that the record's coherent themes and feel were being upset by this new addition, he finally agreed to tag it on to the end of the album as a "bonus song". It appeared a full 20 seconds after the main body of the album had finished. OH

in among the distortion and clatter was a song that exuded more intelligence and wit than the entire class of 1993 put together. That it was a sub two-and-a-half-minute chastising of a drunken lover unable to perform, and that singer/guitarist Justine Frischmann was seeing Blur's Damon Albarn at the time, did the song's infamy no harm whatsoever. The band's collection of unlikely characters – a scruffy rock chick, a pouting indie starlet, an androgyne, a bloke – and this hastily recorded demo that cost record label Deceptive £500 truly embodied everything great about Britpop.

Elastica
Stutter

| 1993 · 2:24 · **Frischmann/Elastica**

Elastica became one of Britpop's defining bands with a self-titled debut album full of razor-sharp, spike-pop nuggets and four brilliant singles that were born for the seven-inch. 'Stutter' was the first, and

Elastica
Line Up

| 1994 · 3:15 · **Frischmann**

Elastica's first top 20 UK hit saw them catapulted into the blinding glare of Britpop's spotlight. Requests for magazine front covers and TV appearances began flooding in as they were caught up in

Post-punk legends Wire, Elastica's heroes, took the band to court

the era's heady days. "That would have been the start of all the tabloid stuff with Justine and Damon," Deceptive co-owner and promotional guru Alan James told Xfm. "They were like a Posh and Becks for the music industry." Not everyone was so enamoured of the band, however. Post-punk legends Wire, Elastica's heroes, took the band to court citing similarities between 'Line Up' and their own song, 'I Am The Fly'.

Elastica
Connection

! 1994 • 2:20 • Frischmann/Elastica

Another top 20 hit for the band in the UK, 'Connection' also made some headway in the States too. Unsurprisingly, Britpop's cultural references weren't entirely grasped by America, but the might of Elastica's US label Geffen, as well as the song's universal quiet/loud dynamic and nagging keyboard refrain, ensured that Justine Frischmann and her

bandmates were one of the few English acts of the time to make a significant commercial impact across the pond.

Elastica
Waking Up

! 1995 • 3:15 • Frischmann – Stranglers

Despite protestations by the band, who wanted 'Car Song' as their fourth single, 'Waking Up' became Elastica's biggest hit. It reached number 13 in the UK charts and would precede the self-titled album shooting straight to number one.

With the benefit of hindsight, 'Waking Up''s opening line – "I work very hard but I'm lazy, I can't take the pressure and it's starting to show" – seemed oddly prophetic. The band began to unravel with the trappings of success and, after multiple lineup changes, eventually delivered a so-so second album five years after their incandescent debut. OH

Elbow

Elbow Newborn

2001 • 7:36
Garvey – Potter – Potter – Turner – Jupp

Incredibly, for a song of such understated power and maturity, 'Newborn' was one of the first songs ever written and recorded by the newly-named Elbow (they were called Soft for a while). A demo version of 'Newborn' was recorded by Clint Boon (Inspiral Carpet and Xfm presenter) in his attic studio in his house in Rochdale in early 1997. Boon told Xfm: "This tiny attic would get so hot that we had to have all the windows open whilst recording which meant that all of my street would have heard Guy [Garvey,

> "All of my street would have heard Guy belt out the really loud bit"

— Clint Boon on Elbow's recording sessions

singer] belt out the really loud bit at the end of 'Newborn' – nobody complained."

Elbow
Fugitive Motel

2003 • 5:52
Garvey – Potter – Potter – Turner – Jupp

Undoubtedly one of Guy Garvey's most plaintive songs, with characteristically wistful Elbow atmospherics. A transmission of loneliness from "somewhere in the dust bowl", this is a tale of being far from home in a place of interchangeable, and insalubrious, anonymity. Elbow have always been a hard-touring band and have trekked through most of America regularly since their first album in 2001.

Elbow
Forget Myself

2005 • 5:22 • Elbow – Garvey

This was the first single to be taken from Elbow's third album, *Leaders Of The Free World*, which was recorded and self-produced at Salford's Blueprint Studios. Blueprint became a base for the band and the place they would record and produce their next album, the Mercury Music Prize-winning *The Seldom Seen Kid*. Originally from Bury,

Elbow have since adopted Manchester as their hometown and a consistently rich source of inspiration. 'Forget Myself' is a wonderfully vivid description of a night out in the city, with crowds of people "scented and descending from the satellite towns" and doormen with "heads like Mars" – while the perennially lovelorn singer Guy Garvey looks for "a plot where I can bury my broken heart".

Elbow
Leaders of the Free World

2005 · 6:11
Garvey – Potter – Potter – Turner – Jupp

The title track of Elbow's third album, and its second single, is one of their darkest, most aggressive and most powerful songs. "It was written as a reaction to the illegal allied invasion of Iraq," Guy Garvey told Xfm, and it is one of surprisingly few anti-war songs released at that time. Even with its anthemic chorus and muscular guitars, it's a somewhat off-kilter song with an eerie and apposite feeling of discontent throughout. The guitar solo is Garvey's only solo in the entire Elbow catalogue. Its anti-war message is summed up in the key lyric "I think we dropped the baton like the 60s didn't happen".

Elbow
Grounds For Divorce

2008 · 4:00
Garvey – Potter – Potter – Turner – Jupp

The band built this incredibly powerful and infectious song around a gritty, bluesy groove that guitarist Mark Potter had had for some time. 'Grounds For Divorce' is about the period shortly after the death of Elbow's good friend and fellow Mancunian musician Bryan Glancy (the titular *Seldom Seen Kid*), which was – as frontman Guy Garvey explained to Xfm in 2008 – "a horrible time when everyone was drinking themselves half to death". The "hole in my neighbourhood down which of late I cannot help but fall" is famous locally as one of Elbow's favourite Manchester pubs: the Temple of Convenience on Great Bridgewater Street – a converted public toilet.

Elbow
One Day Like This

2008 · 6:34
Garvey – Potter – Potter – Turner – Jupp

The Seldom Seen Kid, as with all of Elbow's work, glues together brilliantly as an album. You can tell that Elbow really believe in the album as a concept (which is a very different thing to believing in concept albums). This passion for "the album as art" would partly explain their well-earned Mercury Music Prize win in 2008. Although they are not a band who think in terms of singles, with 'One Day Like This' they created one of the greatest British singles of the decade.

Elbow
The Bones Of You

| 2008 • 5:12
Garvey – Potter – Potter – Turner – Jupp

One of the sharpest ever descriptions of how a song can literally stop you in your tracks and, with breathtaking emotional clarity, take you back to a time and a place. In Guy Garvey's case, he was taken back to a previous relationship that had not worked out. However, unbeknown to him at the time, he was about to be reunited with this lost love, who then became the subject of the next track on *The Seldom Seen Kid*, the deliriously romantic 'Mirrorball'.

Elbow
Mirrorball

| 2008 • 5:50
Garvey – Potter – Potter – Turner – Jupp

The elation of a new love, or a re-kindled one in this case, is perfectly portrayed here as a taller, brighter and better person walks home after a night with their loved one. Experiencing the world through different eyes and ears ("We made the moon our mirrorball / the streets an empty stage / the city sirens – violins / everything has changed"), the narrator is ultimately saved by the redemptive power of love. MW

Electric Six
Danger! High Voltage

| 2003 • 3:35
Frezza – Nawara – Selph – Tyler

It's easy to dismiss Electric Six as a novelty band. Flashing codpieces and pole-dancing Abraham Lincolns don't paint the Detroit six-piece as anguished poet types, but it would be remiss to write off the band's fusion of disco, pop and glam rock as 'novelty'. 'Danger! High Voltage', their debut single in the UK, is an insanely catchy fusion of disco guitars with Dick Valentine's classic rock-style vocals and is rumoured to feature Jack White on backing vocals – credited to the mysterious John S O'Leary – a rumour that has both been dismissed and confirmed by the band on numerous occasions. Infectious and fun, this is by far the band's biggest commercial success, reaching number two in the UK singles chart. Despite the release of six studio albums to date, they have yet to replicate it. JS

ELECTRIC SIX

Danger! High Voltage

! Electric Six, 'Danger! High Voltage'

Electronic
Getting Away With It

! 1989 • 5:16 • Sumner – Marr – Tennant

Expectations were high when it was announced that New Order frontman Bernard Sumner and ex-Smith Johnny Marr were to form their own group. It came as a surprise to many, however, when the two guitarists called their project Electronic and concentrated mainly on keyboards. There was no need to panic, though – their first single from November 1989 was a stellar affair, featuring a guest spot from Neil Tennant of the Pet Shop Boys. 'Getting Away With It' takes a humorously self-deprecating Sumner lyric and a chorus featuring Tennant's unmistakable vocals. Throw in some lightly funky Marr guitar licks and you have an instant indie-disco classic.

Electronic
Get The Message

! 1991 • 5:20 • Sumner – Marr

"Songs like 'Get The Message' [have] ended up being more than the sum of their parts," recalled Bernard Sumner in 1991.

"It doesn't just sound like New Order and The Smiths fused. It was important that we were more than just a formula combing the two groups." He was right: 'Get The Message' may be full of gleaming guitar, but this is no battle of the axemen. Instead, you get a glorious summery pop tune, complete with synth brass stabs. The dour Manchester vibe seeps through, however, when Sumner mutters: "You're too expensive, girl, to keep".
MO'G

Embrace
All You Good Good People

! 1997 • 6:06 • McNamara – McNamara

The word "anthem" can get bandied about a little too easily sometimes but for this song, there's no better description. Crashing straight in, it has drum rolls,

"It doesn't just sound like New Order and The Smiths fused. It was important that we were more than just a formula"

– Bernard Sumner on 'Get The Message'

trumpet blasts, gang vocals and strings. As a debut single it was quite a statement, coming out on legendary label Fierce Panda. Certainly, it was enough to get Embrace signed to Virgin subsidiary Hut, with whom they would release three albums. The first line, "I feel like I'm at something", was written at a Placebo gig (they were labelmates). The initial plan was to begin with a rap inspired by a Dirk Bogarde film, but that was then replaced by Danny McNamara's rewritten verse. It was a smart move – the song hit the top 10 in the UK and paved the way for a UK number one album with *The Good Will Out*.

Embrace
Ashes

! 2004 • 4:22 • McNamara – McNamara

After failing to replicate the success of their debut album, Embrace were dropped by Hut in 2002. Later signing to Independiente, the band made a triumphant comeback with hit single 'Gravity'. However, as that song was written by (friends of the band) Coldplay, cynics debated whether Embrace could keep this success up. They needn't have worried: from its first second, 'Ashes' was destined to be the kind of hit that would be used on TV sports montages for years to come. Urgent guitars, pacey drums and Danny McNamara's soaring vocals – even the lyrics had relevance, being as they were about rising from the, well, ashes. Ironically, it was almost shelved – it was in fact Chris Martin who encouraged them to go back to it. He would sing it to

McNamara's answerphone and was very vocal about making sure it got onto the record. Luckily it did: it helped make album *Out Of Nothing* go double-platinum in the UK and is their bestselling record to date. MS

"You need a song like that to open doors"

– Derry Brownson on 'Unbelievable'

EMF
Unbelievable

! 1991 • 3:30
Atkin – Brownson – Bench – Foley

The very first single to be released by EMF (an acronym that the band claimed stood for 'Epsom Mad Funkers'; the label 'Every Mother's Favourite'; and the tabloid press something completely different). Despite the band's Gloustershire base, their fusion of dance and rock often saw them associated with the Madchester scene and bands such as

The Stone Roses and Happy Mondays.

Featuring an instantly recognisable guitar riff, this track was the band's most successful and poppiest release, which keyboard player Derry Brownson told *Designer* magazine was a necessary evil rather than their finest music moment: "You need a song like that to open doors." However, despite that opinion, the single was a 1990s party classic, using US shock comedian Andrew Dice Clay's samples of "oh" and the key line "You're unbelievable" to irresistably catchy effect. With chart success on both sides of the Atlantic, 'Unbelievable' may well also be responsible for the most swearing ever heard in one song on the airwaves. The almost indecipherable vocal during the chorus asks "What the fuck / What the fuck" and was never edited for radio.

Despite never splitting officially, the band have "gone on hiatus" on numerous occasion, most recently in 2009, but with their rock/dance style, sideways caps and baggy shorts, they remain a symbol of the '90s.
JS

Empire Of The Sun
Walking On A Dream
2008 • 3:16 • Sloan – Littlemore – Steele

Empire Of The Sun is a collaboration between Australians Luke Steele (of band Sleepy Jackson) and Nick Littlemore (of Pnau). 'Walking On A Dream' was co-written with Donnie Sloan (bassist in another Australian band, Sneaky Soundsystem). No one can describe the creation of the song better than Steele himself – this is what he told Xfm in 2010: "Donnie sent over this track, which we loaded up at about 9.45 and immediately I had a melody like my voice box had whizz-fizz rivers. It demanded height, so I reached for my tightest Bee Gees pants and hit the vocal highlands. Nick had some lyrics he'd been writing down, inspired by being apart from his girlfriend who was trekking through the Brazilian jungle and had fallen ill. It was like the words were a prayer, 'cause they talked of the future, they talked of when two people become one. It was like one lightning bolt of a prayer we are not going to forget anytime soon. By 10.30, the track was finished. We all knew straightaway there was something very magical about this track. It was so simple; it had nothing really going on. No real build-ups – it kinda rolled along like some sleepy sexy walrus."
MW

It kinda rolled along like some sleepy sexy walrus

– Luke Steele on 'Walking On A Dream'

TheEnemy

The Enemy
Away From Here

! 2007 • 3:03 • Clarke

In April 2006 Tom Clarke, Andy Hopkins and Liam Watts were three 18-year-old Coventry lads on their way to an early band rehearsal in Hopkins' battered Ford Fiesta. They were frustrated with their day jobs, worried about how to pay for the £8-an-hour practice room and bemoaning the lack of big chorus songs on the radio. Fifteen minutes later, and without the use of instruments, they had written their first hit single – 'Away From Here' – which was a UK top 10 release the following April. A year or so on and singer/guitarist Clarke has bought his first flat near a nightclub in Coventry city centre and is now often woken up at closing time with chants of "A away a way oh oh oh away from here". He doesn't seem to mind: "You can't complain about having your sleep disturbed by your own song," he told Xfm in May 2010.

The Enemy Had Enough

! 2007 • 2:29 • Clarke

A song written in three minutes (approximately the time it takes to play it) in the aforementioned Coventry practice room. Singer Tom Clarke believes that he was so pissed off with his girlfriend at the

> "You can't complain about having your sleep disturbed by your own song"
>
> – Tom Clarke on 'Away From Here'

time that he just opened his mouth and the whole song just came pouring out.

The Enemy
We'll Live And Die
In These Towns

! 2007 • 3:55 • Clarke

The title track of The Enemy's debut album, which won the Xfm New Music Award for Best UK Debut Album Of The Year 2007. Although the song was understandably perceived as social commentary, the lyrics actually stem from a phone conversation that Tom Clarke was having with his then fiancée while he was starting to record the band's album in London. He says that she pretty much gave him every line in the song while telling him about the miserable time she was having at home in her run-down flat in Coventry. MW

Faith No More

Faith No More
We Care A Lot

1987 • 4:03 • Faith No More

Originally recorded in 1985 for the band's debut album of the same name, 'We Care A Lot' made significant waves after its re-recording and re-release on the band's second album – their major label debut, *Introduce Yourself*. One of the earliest and most successful examples of the cross-pollination of genres way before it became a trait of the alternative rock explosion, the record marked Faith No More out as true innovators and visionaries. Written in the wake of Live Aid, singer Chuck Mosley's lampooning of do-good rock stars hits comical proportions with his disdainful bleat while the band seamlessly knit funk, metal, hip-hop and punk to devastating effect.

Faith No More
Epic

1989 • 4:55 • Faith No More

The band's pioneering genre-mashing reached a completely new level, both artistically and commercially, with the introduction of new singer Mike Patton, formerly of Mr Bungle. 'Epic' may have been the band's commercial apex, but they went on to become a huge influence on other bands, most notably those on nu-metal's vanguard. Some, however, weren't impressed: the year after 'Epic' was released, Anthony Kiedis – who'd been ploughing a similar musical furrow with Red Hot Chili Peppers – told *Kerrang!* magazine: "My drummer says he's gonna kidnap him [Patton], shave his hair off and saw one of his feet, just so he'll be forced to find a style of his own." OH

Faithless
Insomnia

1995 • 8:42
Armstrong – Bentovim – Maxi

In the midst of the retro-inspired guitar movement that was Britpop came a British dance act who would place their music firmly into the live arena and become one of the biggest-selling British electronic acts of all time. Built around a brilliantly complementary trio of dance music veterans – Rollo, Sister Bliss and Maxi Jazz – Faithless went on to sell more than 12 million albums worldwide. But 'Insomnia' was arguably the song that brought Faithless centre stage, with a UK number three hit on its re-release in October 1996. A formidable live act, the sound of those 'Insomnia' keyboard stabs have provided some of the most exhilarating festival moments for hundreds of thousands of people around the world. MW

Fall Out Boy
Sugar, We're Goin Down

2005 · 3:49
Hurley – Stump – Trohman – Wentz

It was with 'Sugar, We're Goin Down' that Fall Out Boy announced their rise to the big time. Inspired by the pop-punk of Blink 182, in singer Patrick Stump Fall Out Boy had a songwriter with a seemingly effortless ability to pen pure pop songs then spin them through a punk filter. Added to the mix was a clutch of bitter break-up lyrics written by the band's pin-up bassist Pete Wentz, a man with an endless array of cute phrases to go with his boyband looks. The track was the band's first top 10 US single.

Fall Out Boy

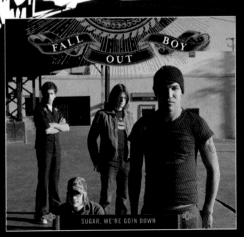
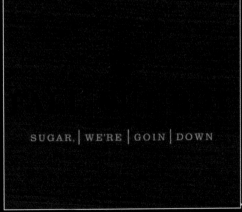

Sugar, We're Goin Down: single and album artwork

Fall Out Boy
Dance, Dance

2006 • 3:01
Hurley – Stump – Trohman – Wentz

The falsetto chorus from Fall Out Boy's second single from their album *Dance, Dance* could be dropped successfully into any number of chart-topping pop songs. Such was the secret behind the group's appeal: their songs were sugary,

Fall Out Boy
This Ain't A Scene, It's An Arms Race

2007 • 3:32 • Fall Out Boy

With the release of their fourth album, *Infinity On High*, Fall Out Boy found themselves credited with leading a new wave of emo. Despite the album sales such scene-setting status earned them, the band professed themselves to be rather

From left: 'Dance, Dance', 'This Ain't A Scene It's An Arms Race'

commercial and immaculately crafted, but they were delivered by an emo band who appeared anything but. Always marked by their lyrical eloquence – despite this song's protestations of being no good with words – Fall Out Boy tended to concentrate their words on one main topic: that of breaking up with girls. It followed 'Sugar, We're Goin Down' into the US top 10.

less than delighted with their newfound position. "Make us the poster boys for your scene, but we're not making an acceptance speech", Patrick Stump sang in 'Thriller'. In this new slice of scene ambivalence, the band attempt to further divorce themselves from the genre but, erm, do so in a song that would come to define it. TB

The Farm

The Farm
Groovy Train

! 1990 · 4:07 · Grimes – Hooton

Along with the likes of Flowered Up and indie-pop chameleons Blur, The Farm were geographical anomalies of the musical genre known as "baggy". Formed in Liverpool in 1983, deriving their name from the disused barn where early rehearsals took place, they had been through several phases without success. That is, until they put traditional North/West rivalries aside and fare-dodged their way on the gravy train to Madchester with, ironically, a song about bandwagon-jumping. The number six hit gave a snapshot of the scene it annexed, mentioning the essential "baggy jeans" and exhorting us to "get on the groovy train". Production from Graham "Suggs" McPherson of Madness and legendary house DJ Terry Farley (fresh from working with the Happy Mondays and Primal Scream) meant a sample-heavy mix of big shuffling beats, trippy looping guitars, tight bass-driven grooves and a singalong chorus – the result was a classic indie floor-filler.

The Farm
All Together Now

! 1990 · 5:41 · Grimes – Hooton

A moving and uplifting retelling of the famous Christmas Day truce of 1914,

A moving and uplifting retelling of the famous Christmas Day truce of 1914

– The Farm, 'All Together Now'

which saw British and German troops call an unofficial ceasefire and play a friendly game of football between the First World War trenches. Lifting its chord progression from classical piece Pachelbel's 'Canon', it had a keyboard sound pitched somewhere between church organ and house piano. It was thought-provoking but still got us onto the dancefloor. The song peaked at number four in December 1990. With terrace-friendly themes of war, football and togetherness, it became associated with the beautiful game. Incredibly, singer and devout Liverpool FC fan Peter Hooton allowed Everton to record a version as their FA Cup song in 1995. DJ Spoony's remix was England's Euro 2004 single, reaching number five (England lost on penalties in the quarter finals). Debut album *Spartacus* charted at number one in March 1991, a feat matched in the baggy scene only by The Charlatans.
MP

Fatboy Slim

Fatboy Slim has been banned from playing Brighton beach since a quarter of a million people turned up in 2002

Fatboy Slim
Rockafeller Skank

1998 · 3:59 (radio edit)
Barry – Fatboy Slim – Terry

A rather unlikely candidate for dance superstardom, Norman Cook grew up in unpromising surrounds in leafy Surrey. An omnipresent innovator in British pop since the 1980s, Cook went from The Housemartins to Beats International before becoming Fatboy Slim. One of the stand out tracks on his 1998 *You've Come A Long Way, Baby* album, 'Rockafeller Skank' is a big beat journey through hi-energy sound and northern soul. The vocal line

"Right about now, the funk soul brother, check it out now, the funk soul brother" comes from New York rapper Lord Finesse. Cook has said that, because of the deals he struck to use the four samples in the song, he himself receives no royalties for the track. Speeding up like a malfunctioning robot, at one point the song threatens to overheat, at which point he pulls it right back and it starts to build again. Famous for his huge raves, Fatboy Slim has been banned from playing Brighton beach since a quarter of a million people turned up in 2002. Asked for the secret of his success, Cook once said: "I like to party, and I have more fun than the audience." His infectious musical enthusiasm shines through on this track more than any other.

Fatboy Slim
Gangster Tripping

1998 · 5:20
Davis – Dust Junkys – Fatboy Slim

No late-1990s party really kicked into action until the feast of sounds and beats that is 'Gangster Tripping' came on. It contains samples from DJ Shadow, himself a famous sampler, as well as a 1973 song by Ann Robinson. Norman Cook, always a producer with fingers in many musical pies, clearly had a lot of fun making this one – as have all the people who've danced to it ever since.

The song had two videos: the first, directed by Roman Coppola, son of Francis Ford, features a toilet exploding in slow motion.

Fatboy Slim
Praise You

1998 • 5:17 • Fatboy Slim – Yarbrough

A number one in the UK, 'Praise You' has more of a traditional song structure than Fatboy Slim's other dance hits, heavily featuring vocals from a 1975 track by previously uncelebrated singer Camille Yarbrough. Al Gore used the song while campaigning for president in 2000. The video, featuring Spike Jonze, was filmed guerrilla-style outside a cinema in California and features an unappreciative employee who comes and turns off the music halfway though. Despite costing only a reported $800, it was a multiple award winner at the 1999 MTV Video Music awards, including best choreography. Fatboy Slim himself features in the video as a bystander.

Fatboy Slim
Right Here, Right Now

1999 • 3:56
Fatboy Slim – Peters – Walsh

Reaching number two in the UK charts in spring 1999, big beat single 'Right Here, Right Now' was very much a song of the moment, surging to success on a wave of end-of-the-millennium excitement. Taking a vocal sample from the 1995 science fiction film *Strange Days*, the track layers beats and effects to dramatic, futuristic effect. The video for the song, a speeded-up animated version of the evolution of life on earth, culminates with homo sapiens discovering fast food and becoming fat and sedentary – an image that also adorned the cover of album *You've Come A Long Way, Baby*, from which the track is taken. The food-toting cardboard cut-out in the video is Norman Cook himself. With 'Right Here, Right Now' Fatboy Slim captured the musical mood of the times, with fizzing, toe-tapping sounds that saw in the new century.
JH

Despite costing only a reported $800, the video was a multiple award winner at the 1999 MTV Video Music awards

– Fatboy Slim, 'Praise You'

Feeder

Feeder
Buck Rogers

! 2001 • 3:12 • Nicholas – Lee – Hirose

Feeder almost gave this song away. Originally written for American band Radio Star, the intention was, according to singer Grant Nicholas, "to make a song in the same style as the Pixies on a very comic book level". Luckily, says Nicholas, "producer Gil Norton smelt a hit" and convinced them to keep it for themselves. The song reached the UK top five, became an indie disco staple and helped their third album, *Echo Park*, go on to reach platinum status. Most distinctive for its repetitive vocals ("It's got a CD player / player / player / player"), the lyrics are about a successful film director who fancied one of the band's girlfriends.

Feeder
Just A Day

! 2001 • 4:05 • Nicholas – Lee – Hirose

'Just A Day' began life on the soundtrack for Playstation 2's *Gran Turismo 3*. When it was later released as a single in its own right, Feeder launched a competition on their website, asking fans to send in unedited videos of themselves singing along to the song, which they then compiled. The resulting clip received heavy MTV rotation and has since become a cult internet classic. Tragically, this was the last Feeder song to be recorded featuring drummer Jon Lee, who committed suicide a month after it was released.

Feeder
Just The Way I'm Feeling

! 2002 • 4:26 • Nicholas

After the suicide of drummer Jon Lee, Feeder seriously considered calling it a day. Bassist Taka Hirose went back to Japan and singer Grant Nicholas began furiously working. "I started writing songs very soon after he died and I was still in shock to be honest... I went straight into the studio and drove the engineer mad by just working every hour. If I hadn't done that I don't know whether the band would have been able to carry on." One of the last tracks to be written for the album, it's an epic, string-laden, melancholy rock song. The emotional tone connected with their audience, becoming their second top 10 hit.
MS

The Flaming Lips

The Flaming Lips
Race For The Prize

! 1999 • 4:18 • The Flaming Lips

At a crossroads following the departure of guitarist Ronald Jones, Wayne Coyne and The Flaming Lips set about reinventing their sound in the most glorious Technicolor fashion. Inspired by their "Parking Lot Experiment" (where 40 car stereos simultaneously played the same song) and the four CD set of *Zaireeka* (again to be played at the same time), album *The Soft Bulletin* took on a neo-psychedelic, gonzo-symphonic hue that seemed utterly groundbreaking. "We made that record fully expecting it to be our last," producer Dave Fridmann told Xfm. "It's a very good attitude to have in the studio." 'Race For The Prize', the album's opening track and

Declared the official rock song of Oklahoma, The Flaming Lips' home state

– The Flaming Lips, 'Do You Realize??'

first single, was the first taste of the band's new vision. It proved an instant critical hit and made the weird, incongruous indie band hiding on Warner Brothers' roster suddenly one of its greatest assets.

The Flaming Lips
Do You Realize??

! 2002 • 3:29 • The Flaming Lips

Recorded quickly in a couple of days and disregarded until those around the band signalled its importance, 'Do You Realize??' quickly became one of The Flaming Lips' most dearly loved songs. Inspired by guitarist Steven Drozd's attempts to quit heroin and the death of frontman Wayne Coyne's dad, the optimistic, life-affirming song was declared the official rock song of Oklahoma, The Flaming Lips' home state.

The Flaming Lips
The Yeah Yeah Yeah Song

! 2006 • 4:06 • The Flaming Lips

Eleventh album *At War With The Mystics* was, according to their producer Dave Fridmann, the point where the band had "finally, collectively got control of the studio and were doing exactly what they wanted". 'The Yeah Yeah Yeah Song' was the album's opening track and, despite many people thinking it was a swipe at former President George W Bush, head Lip Wayne Coyne maintained it had a broader meaning. "It's about anybody who has a lot of power and is too inexperienced for the power given to them," he said in 2006. OH

FleetFoxes

Fleet Foxes
Mykonos

2008 • 4:35 • Pecknold

It's not often that the words "Seattle" and "baroque" are used in the same sentence, but with the arrival of Fleet Foxes, it seemed the US city had finally thrown off the shackles of being forever equated with grunge. Formed by Robin Pecknold and Skyler Skjelset, the band's combination of close harmony vocals and 1960s ambience makes their music sound as if The Beach Boys had slipped back in time to the Middle Ages. Taken from their *Sun Giant* EP, which was recorded after

Unsettlingly haunting and stunningly beautiful... 'White Winter Hymnal' is brief yet captivating

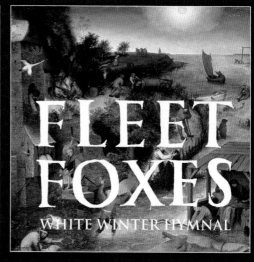

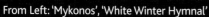
From Left: 'Mykonos', 'White Winter Hymnal'

their self-titled debut album but released beforehand, 'Mykonos' has an overwhelming mystical pagan vibe. However, the more traditional folk-rock coda reveals the band's stylistic debt to artists like Neil Young and Crosby, Stills And Nash.

Fleet Foxes
White Winter Hymnal
2008 • 2:27 • Pecknold

Taken from Fleet Foxes' debut album, 'White Winter Hymnal' starts with a choral round that evokes the snowy landscapes of the title, but – like the Pieter Bruegel painting that adorns the LP cover – the delicate beauty hides a darker undercurrent. The song seems to depict children trudging through the icy wastelands, but something troubling occurs: "Michael, you would fall / And turn the white snow red as strawberries / In the summertime". Unsettlingly haunting and stunningly beautiful at the same time, 'White Winter Hymnal' is brief yet captivating. MO'G

Florence And The Machine

Florence And The Machine
Kiss With A Fist

! 2008 • 2:04 • Alchin – Summers – Welch

Noughties indie-garage-rock queen Florence Welch (and let's not forget her Machine) came to mass public attention in 2008. Her debut album *Lungs* brought a fresh new sound and feel to the female indie-rock scene. The single 'Kiss With A Fist' was released on June 9th 2008 through Moshi Moshi Records and brought Welch a giant wave of press attention, new fans and industry interest. The lyrics provoked some controversy with phrases like "I broke your jaw once before / I split your blood upon the floor", "My black eye casts no shadow", and "A kick in the teeth is good for some" leading many to assume the song was about domestic violence, but Welch denies this: "'Kiss With A Fist' is *not* a song about domestic violence. It is about two people pushing each other to psychological extremes because they are fighting but they still love each other. The song is not about one person being attacked, or any actual physical violence, there are no victims in this song…".

Florence And The Machine
Dog Days Are Over

! 2008 • 4:12 • Ford – Summers

'Dog Days Are Over' was the second single to be released by Florence And The Machine. The original release date was moved back one week to December 1st 2008 on download and seven-inch. (The B-side was the band's version of well-known house track 'You've Got The Love', of which more later.) Then the track was re-released on April 2010, alongside a new video. When Florence Welch was asked why a second video was shot for the re-release, she replied: "The original was so cheap… It was a video camera in a forest, with my dad and Marks & Spencer sandwiches."

Florence And The Machine
Rabbit Heart (Raise It Up)

! 2009 • 3:52 • Epworth – Welch

In an interview with the *Times*, singer Florence Welch explained the origins of the band's name: "The name Florence And The Machine started off as a private joke that got out of hand. I made music

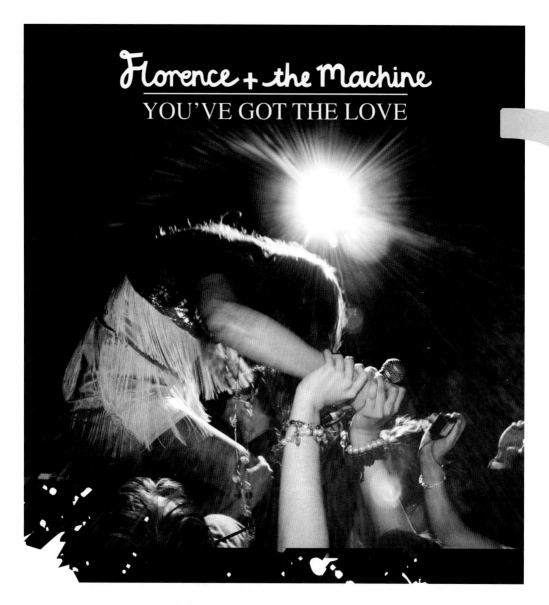

Florence + the Machine
YOU'VE GOT THE LOVE

with my friend, who we called Isabella Machine to which I was Florence Robot. When I was about an hour away from my first gig, I still didn't have a name, so I thought, 'OK, I'll be Florence Robot Is A Machine', before realising that name was so long it'd drive me mad." The single

'Rabbit Heart (Raise It Up)' was released on June 22nd 2009 and reached number 12 in the UK singles chart. Although the track is upbeat, the lyrics and title are about fear, with lines such as: "This is the gift, it comes with a price / Who is the lamb and who is the knife".

Florence And The Machine
Drumming Song

2009 • 3:43 • Ford – Hunt

From launch to date, Florence And The Machine have won more awards and accolades than I've had hot dinners – a tribute to her label, Island Records, for getting it *so* right. So far the mantelpiece in the Welch household has three Brit awards (one in 2009 and two in 2010), a UK Festival award, a Meteor award (the Irish equivalent of a Brit award), an Elle Style award, a *South Bank Show* award... the list goes on. 'Drumming Song' is the fourth single from this multi-talented band and was released on September 13th 2009.

Florence And The Machine
You've Got The Love

2009 • 2:48 • Stephens

After it had already appeared as a B-side, the fans were keen to show Florence And The Machine just how much they loved her cover of 'You've Got The Love', originally released by The Source featuring Candi Staton, with DJ Eren later producing the house mix version for which the song is best known. Released on November 16th 2009 in the UK, it was the fifth single from their debut album. It wasn't until the second week in January 2010, though, that the track reached number five in the UK after featuring in an episode of the cult BBC TV show *Gavin And Stacey*. It became Florence And The Machine's bestselling single to date and was the highest chart entry for the band until a unique

collaboration on an extended version of the song – renamed as 'You've Got The Dirtee Love' – with Dizzee Rascal at the Brit awards in early 2010, was released as a download. It propelled the band up to the number two spot in the UK singles chart. BdP

Flowered Up
Weekender

1992 • 12:56
Dorney – Jackson – Maher – Maher

The Madchester band not from Manchester, this London five-piece fit the bill anyway: their sound was psychedelic/ indie/dance crossover; they wore floppy hats; and they even had their own Bez in the form of "dancer" Barry Mooncult. Success would be short-lived for Flowered Up, but 'Weekender' reverberated way beyond a scene. A sprawling, 13-minute epic, it encompasses guitars, euphoric trumpets, dub, white-boy funk and some of the squelchy acid house that soundtracked the clubs referred to in the lyrics, spat out by frontman Liam Maher. It was a top 20 hit, later achieving cult status. The song directly addressed the kids experiencing the aftermath of the "second summer of love" in late 1980s Britain, working all week in mindless jobs in order to get off their faces at the weekend. Soon after its release, much-publicised drug problems caused the band to split. Keyboard player Tim Dorney went on to find success after forming Republica, while sadly Maher died of a heroin overdose in October 2009, aged 41. MS

FooFighters

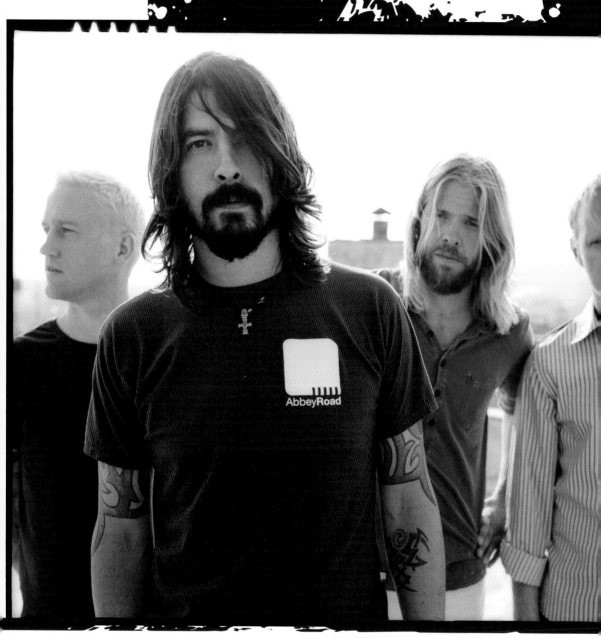

Foo Fighters
This Is A Call

! 1995 · 3:52 · Grohl

"What's the last thing the drummer said before he was kicked out of the band?" quipped Dave Grohl once. Answer: "I wrote a song we should play." In the wake of Kurt Cobain's death, though, the former Nirvana drummer could only find solace in writing and playing his own music. Though not initially intended for release, he realised the instrumental melodic, pop-rock classics he'd composed deserved an audience but, more pressingly, needed lyrics. Hence nonsense verse about fingernails and acne medicine Minocin, rather than words about his grief. "I didn't want to say anything," Grohl admitted. "I was afraid people would read things into what I was trying to say."

Foo Fighters
Monkey Wrench

! 1997 · 3:51 · Grohl

With the viability of the Foo Fighters assured by the overwhelming positive reaction awarded to Dave Grohl's essentially solo first album, he felt on firmer ground with the second. However, these were still troubled times for Grohl – his first marriage broke down, he alienated the band's drummer William Goldsmith and his guitarist, Pat Smear, left the band. Not that 'Monkey Wrench' would give any indication of such turmoil – despite detailing his matrimonial disharmony, this is perfect power-punk: taut, to the point and, in the effect it would have on its audiences, almost the opposite of the angst that had inspired it.

Foo Fighters Everlong
! 1997 · 4:10 · Grohl

Written by Dave Grohl during a break in the band's recording schedule for their second album *The Colour And The Shape* at home in Virginia, 'Everlong' marked an evolution in the former drummer's songwriting ability. Instead of the (admittedly stunningly effective) riff-based music he had so far composed, this seemed a real song – growing, swelling, collapsing then exploding. Rumoured to be about a short-lived relationship with Veruca Salt singer Louise Post, Grohl has remained tight-lipped as to its inspiration – except to clarify that the whispered words during the breakdown are not, as thought, a love letter but, rather less romantically, from a technical manual.

Foo Fighters
Breakout

2000 · 3:21
Grohl – Mendel – Hawkins

From the outside, Foo Fighters had hit the heights by 1999. On the inside, all was still turmoil. Band members had come and gone, Dave Grohl was sick of living in Los Angeles and unsure as to whether the glitzy Hollywood life to which he had been exposed was really him. So Foo Fighters decamped to Virginia, put a mixing desk in the basement of Grohl's house and recorded an album alone. The neighbours weren't amused as the frontman laid down this song's vocals (about, he claims, acne); they threatened to phone the police to "complain that someone was getting murdered".

Foo Fighters
Learn To Fly

1999 · 3:55
Grohl – Mendel – Hawkins

Number one on the Billboard Hot Modern Rock Tracks chart, a top 40 UK hit, a massive fan favourite and, erm, one of Dave Grohl's least favourite Foo Fighters songs. Having endured a difficult couple of years since the inception of Foo Fighters, by 1999 Grohl felt both the band and he personally had hit rock bottom – in fact he joked third album *There Is Nothing Left To Lose* was once going to be called "Fuck It". This was his song about the search for inspiration in such tricky times. It's about the "signs of life that will make you feel alive," he said before, bafflingly, dismissing it as rubbish.

Foo Fighters
Next Year

2000 · 4:37
Grohl – Mendel – Hawkins

The final single from *There Is Nothing Left To Lose* was a breezy, delicate and whimsical ballad, drifting along from start to finish. Maintaining much of the album's downbeat nature, it found singer Dave Grohl in introspective mood, thinking about his time on the road, his own ego, and his desire to get back home. It's another song from the album that, despite finding considerable favour among the band's fans, Grohl has brushed off as not particularly good. "'Next Year''s a piece of shit! That song is so stupid. It's weird," he said, somewhat uncharitably.

Foo Fighters
All My Life

2002 · 4:24
Grohl – Hawkins – Mendel – Shiflett

There are riffs, and there are guitar lines like those on 'All My Life'. The first single from the Foo Fighters' fourth album is perhaps one of the 1990s' greatest rock tracks, from its staccato opening chug and its clattering drums to its majestic unfurling. The band themselves clearly like it so much they more or less stop the song halfway through, deconstruct the riff then rebuild it and unleash it again: this time, twice as good. Listen carefully, and in the line "I love it but I hate the taste" you'll get some idea of Dave Grohl's preferences while in the sack.

FOO FIGHTERS

ECHOES, SILENCE,
PATIENCE & GRACE

88697 11516–2

The neighbours weren't amused;
they threatened to phone the police
to "complain that someone was
getting murdered" – Neighbourly reaction to Foo Fighters' 'Breakout'

Foo Fighters
Times Like These

2003 · 4:26
Grohl – Hawkins – Mendel – Shiflett

Despite the bombast of some tracks on the Foo Fighters' fourth album *One By One*, the record was written in a hurry with Dave Grohl unsure whether he wanted to remain in the band. A sabbatical playing drums for Queens Of The Stone Age helped but Grohl has since refused to play much of the album live. 'Times Like These' was different: a thrilling, emotive and revealing look into Grohl's life, which he has claimed as the best he's written. So, when George W. Bush borrowed it for his 2004 re-election campaign, the singer was not pleased. "It's like being raped in the ass", was his considered response.

Foo Fighters
Best Of You

2005 · 4:16
Grohl – Hawkins – Mendel – Shiflett

Inspired by Dave Grohl's time on the presidential trail with George W Bushs' 2004 rival John Kerry, 'Best Of You' was the first single from the Foo Fighters' fifth album. Taken by many to be a love song, Grohl actually intended it to be more political and inspirational. For a long time Grohl refused to write particularly meaningful lyrics, preferring to keep songs' motivations to himself, but 'Best Of You' changed that. "The most important part of a song now, to me, is the lyric," he said afterwards. "The [songs] that stand out are the ones that say something."

Foo Fighters
The Pretender

2007 · 4:28
Grohl – Hawkins – Mendel – Shiflett

Echoes, Silence, Patience & Grace, the Foo Fighters' sixth album, was marked by its more lyrical focus and songs designed to be listened to, "rather than music made for pummelling the person next to you" as Dave Grohl put it at the time. Except 'The Pretender'. Because this song was designed entirely for jumping around to. As Grohl himself says: "The album needed a four-minute blast of rock. We threw this together in an hour. It's the sort of song this band is all about. It's not 'Bohemian Rhapsody'; it's a basic four-part rock song with a Chuck Berry break-down in the middle. I love it."
TB

Franz Ferdinand

Franz Ferdinand
Take Me Out

2004 • 3:57 • Kapranos – McCarthy

The song that kicked it all off for the Glasgow-based band, 'Take Me Out' hit number three in the UK charts, cracked the US Billboard Hot 100 at number 66 and was voted the number one song of the year by listeners to Australia's influential Triple J radio station. It also spearheaded a debut album that went on to win that year's Mercury Music Prize and sell more than 3.5 million copies worldwide. The lyrics were inspired by a film that singer-guitarist Alex Kapranos saw about snipers; as he explained to Xfm, he liked the idea of the phrase "take me out" also applying to a relationship. 'Take Me Out' is only ever written on Franz Ferdinand set lists as 'The Scottish Song' – an in-joke referencing superstitious theatre luvvies who only ever refer to Shakespeare's *Macbeth* as "The Scottish Play".

Franz Ferdinand

MATINÉE

"You'll find me in the matinée /
the dark of the matinée"

Franz Ferdinand
Matinée

2004 · 4:03
Kapranos – McCarthy – Hardy

With lyrics based around Alex Kapranos' childhood memories of walking to school, the band were keen to shoot their video in a school. Kapranos asked his old school in Glasgow for permission to film there but was rather bluntly refused by the school secretary. It was only then that he realised that the same school had recently been at the centre of the "Brandon Lee" scandal in which a 32-year-old man masqueraded as a 17-year-old schoolboy. Understandably the school would not have welcomed four 30-something blokes dressed as school kids prancing around their corridors!

band's eponymous debut album and their third UK top 20 hit. The song is a description of a night out in which two of frontman Alex Kapranos' male friends become romantically linked and the characteristically staccato guitar and bass makes it a perfect indie dancefloor-filler.

Franz Ferdinand
This Fire

2004 · 4:15 · Kapranos – Huntley –
McCarthy – Thomson – Hardy

'This Fire' was partly responsible for the formation of Franz Ferdinand. Alex Kapranos had had the basic song idea since 2000 and about a year later he decided to use a bass guitar that he had recently been given by Mick Cooke of Belle &

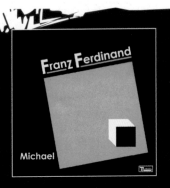  

From left: 'Michael', 'This Fire', 'You Could Have It So Much Better'

Franz Ferdinand
Michael

2004 · 3:21 · Kapranos – Huntley –
McCarthy – Thomson – Hardy

The fourth single to be taken from the

Sebastian to teach the song to his mate. Bob (Robert) Hardy had never played an instrument before but soon picked up the bass part to 'This Fire' and the first two members of the as yet un-named Franz Ferdinand were looking to start their band.

Franz Ferdinand
Do You Want To

2005 • 3:35 • Kapranos – Huntley – McCarthy – Thomson – Hardy

"So here we are at the Transmission Party / I love your friends / They're all so arty". On December 19th 2004, Franz Ferdinand completed the second of two triumphant sold-out gigs at the SECC arena in their hometown of Glasgow. These two shows (with support from Kaiser Chiefs) marked the end of an incredible year during which they had toured the world in support of their massively successful debut album. The end-of-tour party that night was held at Glasgow's Transmission Gallery and the lyrics of 'Do You Want To' are simply, as Alex Kapranos put it to Xfm, "some of the dafter things that some people had said to me that night".

Franz Ferdinand
Walk Away

Franz Ferdinand
No You Girls

2009 • 3:41 • Kapranos – Huntley – McCarthy – Thomson – Hardy

'No You Girls' is the first single taken from the third album *Tonight: Franz Ferdinand*. Yet another of those big-chorus indie disco classics that Franz do so well, 'No You Girls' is inextricably linked to the last track on the album, a song called 'Katherine Kiss Me'. Singer Alex Kapranos told Xfm that "both songs tell the same story but in different ways to different people".
MW

From left: 'Do You Want To', 'No You Girls'

Franz Ferdinand Walk Away

Franz Ferdinand
WALK AWAY

Domino

⏐ **2005 • 3:36 • Kapranos – Huntley – McCarthy – Thomson – Hardy**

One of Franz Ferdinand's simpler and more haunting songs, Alex Kapranos wrote the track by himself on an acoustic guitar in a dressing room in Hamburg after a rather awkward meeting with the female subject of the lyrics. After trying a number of different, more creative arrangements, the band did something that they often found themselves doing when in the studio, and returned to the more straightforward and direct arrangement of the original composition.

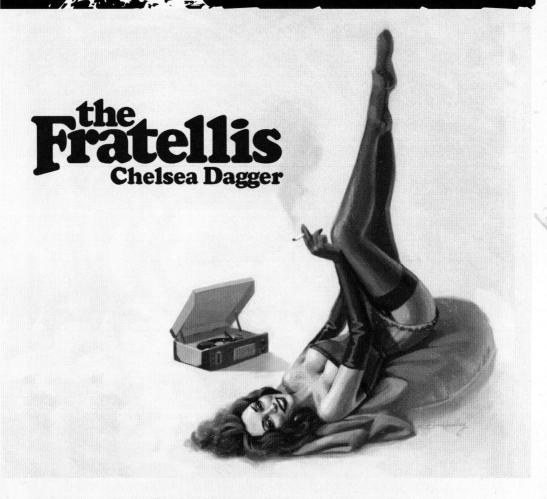

The Fratellis Chelsea Dagger | 2006 · 3:35 · Fratellis

Energetic and crazily catchy even from the first few bars, Scottish band The Fratellis entered the collective national consciousness with this strutting, guitar-heavy, testosterone-fuelled, three-and-a-half-minute burst of hedonism. For some, 'Chelsea Dagger' became so ubiquitous that its upbeat sprightliness began to annoy, but it's hard not to be sucked in. The title is an apparent reference to lead singer Jon Fratelli's wife, who danced burlesque under the stage name Chelsea. Celtic FC and the Scottish national side are among many football teams to have adopted the track as a singalong goal celebration.

The Fratellis
Whistle For The Choir

2006 • 3:36 • Fratellis

Where 'Chelsea Dagger' had do-de-do-ing, 'Whistle For The Choir' had whistling, and a similarly catchy tune. A little gentler in sound, it ploughed the same rich thematic furrow of slightly raunchy romance. The single's cover design is a reference to the song's original title, 'Knickers In A Handbag' and the song deals with finding a girl irresistible at 3am in the morning. The band, all of whom changed their surnames to Fratelli, have responded to accusations of pub-rock shallowness by pointing out that popular music is supposed to be fun. JH

Friendly Fires
Paris

2007 • 3:54 • Friendly Fires

Formed from the ashes of First Day Back (the band's first incarnation as 14-year-old schoolboys), Friendly Fires got started after band members' return from university and began to reinvent themselves, leaving their younger post-punk sounds behind and instead opting for disco grooves and rich synthesizers. Taking their name from a track on a Section 25 album (a band signed to

Manchester's Factory Records), the group attracted a large following from their live shows and previous releases. 'Paris' features backing vocals from members of US indie band Au Revoir Simone; it's a typical Friendly Fires song, with fast samba beats and pulsing synths combined with some damn catchy pop hooks.

Friendly Fires
Jump In The Pool

2008 • 3:37 • Friendly Fires

The first release from the band's self-titled Mercury Music Prize-nominated album. Richer in harmonies than tracks such as 'Paris', here the band stick to their core subject matter of love and relationships, rather than tackling the world's weightier issues. As singer Ed Macfarlane explained, this was a product of their environment rather than a conscious decision: "I think romance and relationships is a theme that runs through the album. Because I've got more

FRIENDLY FIRES
PARIS

FRIENDLY FIRES
"JUMP IN THE POOL"

FRIENDLY FIRES
KISS OF LIFE

From Left: 'Jump In The Pool', 'Kiss of Life'

experience of [romance and relationships], than say, American politics." The result is closer to New York than St Albans; an ultra-cool party tune with more cowbell than you could shake a glow stick at.

Friendly Fires
Kiss Of Life

2009 • 4:10 • Friendly Fires

If the band's previous work was samba-tinged then 'Kiss Of Life' is soaked in it. Latin rhythms run from start to finish, something that Ed Macfarlane told Xfm didn't hint at the band's future plans: "I don't think we're going to do a samba-influenced album because that might be a little bit annoying, but we wanted to do something that was a progression from 'Jump In The Pool'." It's certainly true that those beats, combined with rich, layered harmonies and Friendly Fires' ability to create addictive hooks, create an amazing indie-pop record.
JS

Fun Lovin' Criminals
Scooby Snacks

1996 • 3:04 • Fun Lovin' Criminals

As New York as yellow taxis, Fun Lovin' Criminals formed almost by accident when Brian Leiser and Steve Borgovini (who were already making techno music together) met Huey Morgan at the Limelight in New York City, where Morgan worked behind the bar. They started playing together; filling in for no-show acts at the bar, and it was as a result of those shows that the band signed a record deal. Their debut album *Come Find Yourself* was released in 1996 – a mixture of hip-hop, rock and blues – and 'Scooby Snacks' was the first single to be taken from it. A flop in their home country, they had considerable success in the UK with the track, which takes a wryly humorous look at the dark side of New York (the lyrics talk of robbing banks while high on Valium), punctuated by samples from Quentin Tarantino movies *Reservoir Dogs* and *Pulp Fiction*.

However, Morgan told Toazted.com that the relationship between band and director was not a happy one: "He took advantage of us. Made us give him 40 per cent of the song and made us write on the album that we wrote the song with him and we didn't write it with him... we're looking to kick his ass." Morgan's casual, almost lounge poet rap is the epitome of cool and teamed with the singalong chorus, this is arguably the band's signature tune.

Fun Lovin' Criminals
The Fun Lovin' Criminal

1996 · 3:11 · Fun Lovin' Criminals

Diversity seems key to the Fun Lovin' Criminals' music and this, the third single to be taken from the band's debut album, takes its inspiration from the world of blues with double bass, harmonica and a catchy blues guitar riff mixed in with the hip-hop sound unique to the mid-1990s. The band's continued references to crime and recreational drugs in their lyrics paints a picture of New York similar to that depicted in the movies and perhaps hints at why the band have enjoyed more success away from their own country.
JS

The Futureheads
Hounds Of Love

2005 · 3:05 · Bush

"Uh oh oh – uh oh oh – uh oh oh / UH OH OH – uh oh oh / UH OH OH – uh oh oh / UH OH OH – uh oh oh / UH OH OH" – if you haven't already started to join in then you're not familiar with

The Futureheads' re-imagining of the Kate Bush classic as a post-punk, power-pop singalong in three-part harmony. Rectify this immediately as it's one of the highlights of the indie noughties.

Forming as teenagers in Sunderland in 2000, The Futureheads' first foray abroad as a band was the following year on a tour of squat clubs in Germany and Holland with North East DIY legends Milky Wimpshake. Bassist David "Jaff" Craig's tour compilation included 'Hounds Of Love' and Milky Wimpshake's bass player Christine said it would be a great idea to cover the song. Back home the band decided to have a go; the arrangement came easily and once aired live it became a staple of their shows. Although recorded by The Futureheads for their first ever radio session on X-Posure Xfm in September 2002, the band were reluctant to release it at that point in case it put them in some "wacky cover group" pigeonhole. Later it got a vinyl outing as a one-track seven-inch given away at a Christmas gig in Newcastle in 2004. Newly mixed, it was then included on the debut album and finally released as a proper single in February 2005. It went straight in at number eight in the UK charts and was named Best Single of 2005 by *NME*. The band still happily play it today, knowing it helped create their success, re-working it for ever larger venues and in so doing turning a song about the fear of falling in love into an audience participation anthem.
JK

Garbage

Garbage
Only Happy When It Rains

! 1995 • 3:56 • Garbage

Starting out as a humble jam session between the producer trio of Butch Vig, Duke Erikson and Steve Marker, Garbage went on to sell more than four million copies of their debut self-titled album. The band formed officially in 1993 (after Vig's success producing classic Nirvana album *Nevermind*) and a year later, following initial sessions with Vig on vocals, recruited Shirley Manson as a frontwoman after seeing her singing with Scottish alt-rock band Angelfish on television. It was this move that gave the outfit their defining sound, with Manson's aggressive breathy snarl bringing character to Garbage's guitar-based rock-pop as demonstrated on this, their breakthrough UK single. An ironic look at the band's obsession with depressing subject matter, Manson holds court from the first second with only an instantly recognisable beat preventing a capella performance both alluring and intimidating at the same time.

Garbage Queer

! 1995 • 4:36
! Erikson – Manson – Mariler – Vig

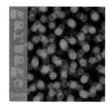

Slightly different in style to the band's previous release, 'Queer' holds back on the heavy guitars in favour of synths and a trip-hop beat, giving the record a laidback feel with Shirley Manson's slurred, sometimes slightly offkey vocals again the star. The song samples Single Gun Theory's 'Man Of Straw' – their second choice after it was decided that using a Frank Sinatra sample would prove too expensive. It went on to become the band's first top 20 hit in the UK, peaking at 13.

Garbage Stupid Girl

! 1995 • 4:18 • Erikson – Manson –
! Marlier – Vig – Strummer – Jones

One of the tracks formed before singer Shirley Manson's introduction to the band, 'Stupid Girl' arose from early jamming sessions between Butch Vig, Steve Marker and Duke Erikson. With a classic bassline from Marker and 1990s Britpop-style guitar courtesy of Erikson,

it was only when Vig introduced a drum sample from The Clash's 'Train In Vain' that the song really took shape. "I knew the song was good," Vig told *Kerrang!* magazine, "when I kept playing the same rough mix over and over again on my car stereo for months." An education in apathy, the track connected with a teenage subculture – an anthem for those who didn't "fit in" but who didn't care anyway.

Garbage Push It

1998 · 4:02

Erikson – Manson – Marlier – Vig

Although second album *Version 2.0* was not met with the same critical acclaim as their first, 'Push It' became Garbage's third consecutive top 10 charting single in the UK. It's a more ambitious track with faster techno-style beats; the response "Don't worry baby" to Shirley Manson's call of the same line is an interpolation from The Beach Boys' record of the same name – an interesting juxtaposition of Brian Wilson's sunny songwriting with this song's more gloomy production.
JS

The Gaslight Anthem The '59 Sound

2008 · 3:10 · The Gaslight Anthem

Rarely do bands emerge fully formed but when The Gaslight Anthem released their 2008 album *The '59 Sound*, theirs was a sound so timeless it was as though it had existed forever. So strong was it that, unconcerned by the fact that virtually nobody in the UK knew who the New Jersey punks were, *Kerrang!* magazine immediately slapped them on their front cover. Curiosity piqued, the record-buying public immediately investigated this song, the title track. They discovered a record inspired, sonically, as much by the 1950s soul music beloved of the band's singer Brian Fallon as by that other New Jersey legend, Bruce Springsteen. This was blue-collar music, written from the heart, delivered from the hip and imbued with real feeling. Lyrically, it was written in tribute to a friend of the band who died while they were away on tour. Live, the memory of that friend lived on as the chorus became a singalong favourite of crowds across Europe and America.
TB

It was only when a drum sample from The Clash's 'Train In Vain' was added that it all came together

— Garbage, 'Stupid Girl'

Glasvegas Geraldine

GLASVEGAS · GERALDINE

2008 · 3:24 · Allen

The 2009 winners of Xfm's New Music award, Scottish four-piece Glasvegas made a splash in 2007 with a number of live shows and some rave reviews courtesy of Creation Records co-founder and the man who signed Oasis. Alan McGee described them on his MySpace page as "The most important band of the last 20 years". 'Geraldine', the first release from their self-titled debut album, is an eerie, guitar-rich track that could easily have come from the production booth of Phil Spector. The song is frontman James Allen's tribute to the efforts of social workers, in particular his sister's colleague Geraldine Lennon, after whom the song is named.

Glasvegas
Daddy's Gone

2008 • 4:27 • Allen

First released on Sane Man Recordings in 2007, 'Daddy's Gone' was re-recorded and re-released as the second single from the band's debut album. The original release, a limited edition seven-inch, prompted interest from a number of record labels as well as from Lisa Marie Presley, who went on to ask the band to record with her. With a sound not dissimilar to Arcade Fire, 'Daddy's Gone' is a rich and emotionally charged song, its guitars and accent-heavy vocals swimming in atmospheric reverb and a pulsing bassline. JS

GLASVEGAS · DADDY'S GONE

Gnarls Barkley
Crazy

2006 • 2:58 • Burton – Callaway

Brian Burton and Thomas Callaway weren't major-label fodder when they wrote 'Crazy'. Burton, better known as

"'Danger' was number one with Gorillaz and I was number one with Pussycat Dolls"

— Cee-Lo of Gnarls Barkley

Danger Mouse, was a little-known hip-hop producer slowly on the way up. Callaway, aka "Cee-Lo", was a rapper and singer on the way down from Atlanta hip-hop act Goodie Mob, despite two fine psychedelic solo albums. They shopped their Gnarls Barkley collaboration around, to the sound of polite refusals and closing doors. Then everything changed. The song 'Crazy' – a rumination on madness with a strong 1960s' soul flavour powered by an extraordinary falsetto vocal – generated some interest and they all came running. "Which was perfect timing," Cee-Lo said in 2006, "because Danger was number one with [Gorillaz'] 'Feel Good' and I was number one with Pussycat Dolls [Cee-Lo wrote their 'Don't Cha' hit]. The negotiating leverage was all in our court."

The rest was all records – selling and breaking. 'Crazy' was the first single to top the British charts on downloads alone, the longest ever to stay at the top of the download charts (11 weeks) and, at nine weeks, the longest regular chart-topper since 1994. It might have been longer, but the duo deleted the single to prevent people getting sick of it. They might be crazy, but they're not stupid. SY

Gomez
Whippin' Piccadilly

Gomez
Whippin' Piccadilly

1998 • 3:12 • Ball – Blackburn – Gray – Ottewell – Peacock

The third and final single to be taken from the band's debut album *Bring It On*, and the first of a total of six UK top 40 singles for Gomez. *Bring It On* is a richly musical and innovative album that exceeded all commercial expectations in the UK and around the world. It also beat off stiff competition from Massive Attack's *Mezzanine* and The Verve's *Urban Hymns* to win the Mercury Music Prize of 1998. The band were signed by Dave Boyd (The Verve, Placebo, Smashing Pumpkins) to his Hut label, based on a five-song demo that was recorded on basic four-track equipment in a garage in the band's hometown of Southport. MW

José González
Heartbeats

2003 · 2:39 · The Knife

Unknown outside his Swedish homeland, until an advert for high-definition TVs, José González's arrival chimed with a rediscovery of the joys of folk. In particular, the Swede with Argentine parents brought a quiet intimacy to people sick of being deafened by the loudness of wars being waged in almost every genre, from rock to urban to dance. 'Heartbeats' was one such example: written by the mercurial Swedish brother-sister duo The Knife, in its original form it was a perfect squall of competing electronic noises. But González found the song that lurked within and his classical acoustic guitar and warm, whispered vocals proved the perfect soundtrack to images of multicoloured balls bouncing down hilly streets. The ad, screened in 2005, earned his *Veneer* album and the single a UK release in 2005 and 2006 respectively, both breaking into the top 10. SY

Gorillaz

Gorillaz Clint Eastwood

2001 · 5:40 · Gorillaz

Charting at number four, this sounded like pop from another dimension; a loping dub groove, whimsical lyrics delivered lethargically, spaghetti western melodica (hence the title) and a haunted house Wurlitzer building spooky tension like a heavily sedated version of The Specials. This zombified stoner's anthem threatens to grind to a halt before being hijacked by Californian rapper Del Tha Funkee Homosapien (Ice Cube's cousin). Damon Albarn of Blur and Jamie Hewlett, the comic book artist who co-created *Tank Girl*, came up with the concept for Gorillaz while watching MTV. Dismayed by the vapid procession of pop stars, they created the ultimate manufactured pop – a virtual band. Together they conceived the dysfunctional histories of 2D, Murdoc Niccals, Noodle and Russel Hobbs. Albarn enrolled hip-hop producer

Dan "The Automator" Nakamura for the beats. Meanwhile, Hewlett designed a grotesquely cool cast of urban outlaws and directed the videos. This risky project could have alienated music fans by seeming pretentious or condescending, but the tunes were so infectious that "sunshine in a bag" was echoing round heads and homes before scepticism could intervene.

Gorillaz
19/2000 (Soulchild Remix)

! 2001 • 3:27 • Gorillaz

A speeded-up reworking of the album track, this release developed Gorillaz as a multimedia phenomenon. In addition to blanket TV and radio play, and in place of band members fulfilling tiresome promotional duties, we got groundbreaking videos and an interactive website that was a rewarding, immersive experience for fans. The video caught the band on a road trip that spiralled into a CGI version of *Wacky Races*. Along with an outrageous number of catchy, childlike hooks, stomping piano and "nah-nah" backing vocals, a place on the soundtrack to the EA Sports video game *FIFA 2002* widened the band's cultural catchment area even further.

Gorillaz Feel Good Inc.

! 2005 • 3:41 • Gorillaz – Jolicoeur

This was a clear signal that *Demon Days* would be a more coherent album than the Gorillaz' debut. The sound had matured – here, melancholic, oppressed verses contrasted with the dreamy, organic innocence and optimism of the acoustic chorus. Chart success and impressive live shows had collaborators queuing up: the colourful rap and maniacal laughter come courtesy of De La Soul. Between albums, Damon Albarn had recorded *Think Tank* with Blur but without Graham Coxon, and it became clear who the boss was in his projects. He selected producer Danger Mouse on the evidence of Danger's *Grey Album* bootleg, his first major commission (he would later form Gnarls Barkley and produce The Black Keys and Beck). The song made history as the first to chart through downloads alone when the band released 300 seven-inch singles four weeks early to fulfil the rule that a physical product must be on sale for a single to qualify. In at 22, it rose to number two when fully released.

Gorillaz DARE

! 2005 • 4:04 • Gorillaz

Living (or thereabouts) cartoon character Shaun Ryder guested on this dirty slab of disco, which gained mass appeal by adding the nation's favourite indie rogue/genius to a perfect pop blend of intoxicated, swooning keyboards, twinkling percussion and sleazy bass. Ryder's expectant refrain originated in the studio as he was recorded requesting his headphones be turned up; "It's coming up... it's coming up... it's there" mutated to "it's DARE". Straight in at number one, this was the first time either Gorillaz or Ryder had topped the charts. Imagine the celebrations (if you DARE). MP

Gossip
Standing In The Way Of Control

! 2005 · 4:16 · Gossip

Having spent almost a decade in the indie rock underground and produced two studio albums, it was Gossip's single 'Standing In The Way Of Control' (and the accompanying album of the same name) that finally brought them to the attention of the world. After escaping the US bible belt in favour of studying in Washington, the trio of frontwoman Beth Ditto, guitarist Brace Paine and drummer Hannah Billie (who joined the band after previous drummer Kathy Mendonca left) went about making music to make people dance.

Hardly shrinking violets, the band were receiving as much attention for Ditto's appearance and sexuality (not to mention her naked cover shoot for *NME* or tales of eating squirrels as a kid) as they were for their songs. But despite all the publicity, the music was the real star. From the opening thrashed guitar and drums of 'Standing In The Way Of Control' and the instantly memorable and toe-tappingly funky bassline, it was easy to tell that here was a band offering something different; dance-based punk-rock with Ditto's sometimes soulful, sometimes banshee-like vocals creating a point of difference from their indie contemporaries.

Ditto has no qualms about the media attention, often using the band's profile as a soapbox from which to air her views. 'Standing In The Way Of Control' was written as a response to the proposed US ban on same-sex marriage, said Ditto: "I wrote the chorus to try and encourage people not to give up... It's a scary time for civil rights, but I really believe the only way to survive is to stick together and keep fighting." A worthy message within a funky, punk-disco track, delivered by a rodent-eating lesbian – you can't get much more unique than that.
JS

Grandaddy
The Crystal Lake

! 2000 · 5:00 · Lytle

There was something about Grandaddy that always conveyed the sense of opposites colliding to good effect. They were the rural, anti-technology songwriters who told of the dangers of computers but did so by merging electronic bloops and squiggles with their lo-fi, rough-hewn, country-tinged indie. They were also decidedly anti-mainstream, refusing to have anything to do with major labels or venues with corporate affiliations. Yet somehow they shone regardless. In 'The Crystal Lake' their slow-burn aesthetic lurked under shimmering, tinkling synthesizers as Jason Lytle sang "I've got to get out of here" with the air of a desperate man caught up in a tangle of modern life that he doesn't comprehend. There was always a sense they were swimming against the stream, their break-up in 2006 being a sad but inevitable day.
TB

Green Day

Green Day
Welcome To Paradise

! 1994 • 3:45 • Armstrong – Green Day

Green Day exploded from nowhere in 1994. Nobody was expecting a song about moving out of your parents' house and into a squat (by three no-mark Californian punks) to tee up what would become one of the decade's biggest-selling albums in *Dookie*. But it did. Post-Nirvana (Kurt Cobain had committed suicide six months earlier) it turned out that people didn't necessarily want their rock music serious, making Green Day – with their juvenile interests, suburban rebellion and knack with a three-and-a-half minute pop-rock song – the perfect choice. Originally recorded for their previous album, *Kerplunk*, in this guise 'Welcome To Paradise' would introduce Green Day to the world.

Green Day
Basket Case

! 1994 • 3:03 • Armstrong – Green Day

If 'Welcome To Paradise' tentatively opened the door for Green Day, 'Basket Case' charged through it, raided the fridge, then peed on the carpet. A supremely snotty – and supremely catchy – burst of radio-friendly punk that offered throw-yourself-around guitars and a breeziness that belied the fact that for once Billie Joe Armstrong wasn't singing about masturbation. Instead, this was Armstrong in serious mode, wondering if the panic attacks he suffered meant he was cracking up. Despite the intent, it was a mosh pit classic, hurtling into the top 10 around the world and helping Green Day shift more than seven million copies of third album *Dookie*.

Green Day
When I Come Around

! 1995 • 2:58 • Armstrong – Green Day

By 1995, Green Day had become superstars, filling the post-grunge void seemingly overnight. It meant that the Berkeley punk scene from where they originated immediately and vehemently turned their backs on them. Green Day's only choice then was to plough on for bigger and better things. 'When I Come Around' hit the top of America's Billboard Modern Rock Tracks chart, becoming a radio classic in an instant. But, more than that, in its slower-paced chug and more introspective lyrics, it proved there was more to Green Day than 200mph songs and the juvenilia that marked some of their previous output.

GREEN DAY american idiot

For once it wasn't Billie Joe Armstrong
singing about masturbation, but it
still became a mosh pit classic

– Green Day, 'Basket Case'

"The older I get, the more I try to make my anger have a direction"

– Billie Joe Armstrong

Green Day
Good Riddance (Time Of Your Life)

! 1997 • 2:33 • Armstrong – Green Day

Tiring of their image as the gurning, grinning goofs of pop-punk, Green Day took an abrupt left turn with their more political sixth album, 2000's *Warning*. Their confidence in doing so stemmed from the acoustic 'Good Riddance (Time Of Your Life)', which had paved that path some years before. Sweeping strings, laidback balladeering and stripped-down simplicity had not been Green Day's hallmarks until that point; however, the change in direction was an important one, allowing the band the room to manoeuvre that their power-chord approach elsewhere forbade them. That 'Good Riddance' still remains their live closing number of choice says something about its enduring appeal.

Green Day
Minority

! 2000 • 2:48 • Armstrong – Green Day

Where the punk of Bad Religion, The Replacements and Operation Ivy had coloured their earlier work, *Warning* saw Green Day turning elsewhere for influence. In came snippets of Bruce Springsteen, The Who, Bob Dylan and Tom Waits, and with them a warmer, acoustic and more organic sound. What they lost in fan numbers – *Warning* was their first album since their 1990 debut not to go platinum – they gained in maturity, and the American-Irish stomp of 'Minority' was a first step towards the more political songwriting that would become the band's hallmark with the advent of 'American Idiot' in 2004.

Green Day
Warning

! 2000 • 3:41 • Armstrong – Green Day

Initially an attempt to pen a set of lyrics made up entirely of warning signs, 'Warning' further cemented the fact that Green Day had moved on from the knockabout punk of old and into territory deemed more serious. The band's singer Billie Joe Armstrong explained: "The older I get, the more I try to make my anger have a direction." It was in tracks like 'Warning' that he achieved this, though with a new wave of pop-punks spearheaded by the likes of Blink-182, the challenge was that their fans were not entirely happy to move with them into such mature waters.

Green Day
American Idiot

! 2004 • 2:56 • Armstrong – Green Day

With much of their fanbase indifferent after *Warning* and others intrigued by a new generation of younger, hungrier and more fun pop-punk bands, Green Day could easily have slipped off quietly into the night before *American Idiot*. Instead, they ripped up the template of the band they were supposed to be and recorded the most ambitious album of their career – a make-or-break move that paid off in spades. An epic, theatrical concept record ensued, of which this was the lead and standout track: a George W Bush-bating punk-rock stormer that reintroduced them to the world in spectacular fashion.

Green Day
Boulevard Of Broken Dreams

¦ 2005 · 4:20 · Armstrong – Green Day

The overriding emotions behind *American Idiot* were anger and despair, but there was also ambition and a desire to achieve something widescreen – in part an attempt to shrug off the bounds in which *Dookie* had wrapped the band since 1994. A grand concept album, inspired by The Who, Meatloaf and Queen, wasn't a bad way to do so. 'Boulevard Of Broken Dreams', written about the loneliness the album's everyman protagonist Jesus Of Suburbia in the big city, was *American Idiot*'s emotional and musical turning point. The song's title was stolen from the famous James Dean picture of him walking alone through a rainy Manhattan.

Green Day
Holiday

¦ 2005 · 4:03 · Armstrong – Green Day

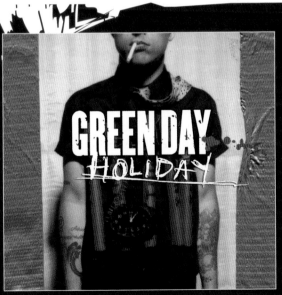

¦ From left: 'Holiday', 'Wake Me Up When September Ends'

Conceptually, 'Holiday' celebrated the moment *American Idiot*'s hero, Jesus Of Suburbia, ditched the small-town life of which he was sick to move to the city. Bored of his hometown and its narrow politics, he hits the bright lights and revels in his rebellion and rage. For the band's singer Billie Joe Armstrong, though, it was in part a metaphor for America's involvements in Afghanistan and Iraq, conservative politics and vote-buying in Congress. A return to the simple power-punk of old, coupled with delicious tunefulness, propelled the song to number one in the US and into the top 10 virtually everywhere else.

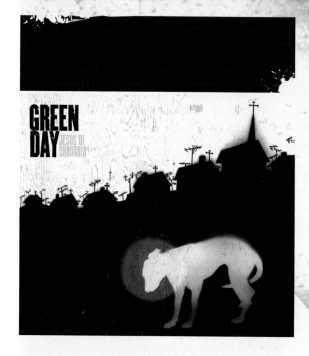

Green Day
Wake Me Up When September Ends

! 2005 • 4:45 • Armstrong – Green Day

A departure from much of the rest of *American Idiot*, 'Wake Me Up When September Ends' takes a step back from the political sloganeering and righteous anger to allow Billie Joe Armstrong time to address the death of his truck driver and musician father. "He died when I was 10-years-old," Armstrong told *Kerrang!* "It seems funny it's taken me this long to write about him." Recalling 'Good Riddance (Time Of Your Life)' all those years earlier, it proved Armstrong could handle emotional sincerity equally as adeptly as he could point the finger of blame at the country's leaders.

Green Day
Jesus Of Suburbia

! 2005 • 9:08 • Armstrong – Green Day

For those already turned off by the new Green Day sounds *Warning* introduced, 'Jesus Of Suburbia' would be an absolute horrorshow. The band who had made their name with three-minute blasts of power-chords and melodies were now playing ambitious nine-minute rock marathons inspired by The Who, and introducing the character who would drive much of the subsequent rock opera that followed in *American Idiot*. Made up of five movements, none of its parts were initially intended to be joined. But, as the band's bassist, Mike Dirnt, explained: "It just grew from us getting comfortable in the studio and connecting pieces together."

Green Day
21 Guns

! 2009 • 5:21 • Armstrong – Green Day

The success of *American Idiot* was both a blessing and a curse for Green Day – suddenly they faced the strain of topping what had been their biggest critical achievement. "Pressure was always something that was lurking in the back of my mind a little," admitted Billie Joe Armstrong. "But you have to hit it head-on. You have to drive yourself a little crazy." They addressed the stress by penning another rock opera, of sorts, following a couple struggling to live everyday American life. '21 Guns' would be the album's second single and earned the band a Grammy nomination to boot. TB

Guns N' Roses

! Slash

Guns N' Roses
Welcome To The Jungle

! 1987 • 4:31 • Guns N' Roses

'Welcome To The Jungle' was Guns N' Roses' hymn to the mean streets of Los Angeles and remains one of rock's all-time greats. "It was the first song I ever played Axl [Rose, singer]," guitarist Slash told Xfm recently. "It was a song that wrote itself. We had three hours to rehearse and it was done in that time." As the band's first single, it clearly set them apart from the hair-metal hordes doing the rounds at the time. Guns may also have been using enough hairspray to halt a charging rhino, but their adoption of punk's attitude and the Stones' outlaw posturing made them electrifyingly exciting and genuinely terrifying. A classic rock'n'roll band in other words, and 'Welcome To The Jungle' was their confirmation.

Guns N' Roses
Sweet Child O' Mine

| 1987 • 5:55 • Guns N' Roses

The band's smash hit and the song that would set *Appetite For Destruction* on a course to become the biggest-selling debut album in history. Written in the period between signing their record deal with Geffen and recording the album, it was pieced together in a shared rented house which the band had enthusiastically "customised". Or, "we'd trashed it", as Slash said to Xfm. "There was no electricity, no power, no hot water and the furniture was upside down. I was just sitting around the house playing my guitar and I came up with this melody which Izzy [Stradlin, rhythm guitarist] put some chords behind." Axl Rose was listening intently upstairs and scribbled a set of lyrics dedicated to then girlfriend Erin Everly (daughter of Everly Brother, Don). Coupled with Slash and Stradlin's tune in a rehearsal room – "again, it sorta wrote itself", said Slash – 'Sweet Child O' Mine' became the band's passport to stadium glory.

Guns N' Roses
Paradise City

| 1987 • 6:46 • Guns N' Roses

The song's iconic video showed a band entirely comfortable with large stadiums and huge crowds, even if they weren't their own. Filmed at the 1988 Monsters of Rock Festival while supporting Aerosmith in the States, the grainy tour footage of the band playing to thousands did the perception of Guns N' Roses no harm whatsoever. Written much earlier in their career, Slash remembers 'Paradise City' to have come together on the journey home from a show at San Francisco club The Stone. For a band famed for their volatility, the guitarist recalls the song's genesis as a harmonious and collaborative affair: "It was one of those moments where the camaraderie of the band was so tight. We were just enjoying our time together and I look back at that trip, and that creative spark that happened between us, with fond memories."

Guns N' Roses
Patience

| 1988 • 5:56 • Guns N' Roses

While *Lies*, the band's second official album, would court controversy with the outrageously homophobic and racist 'One In A Million', acoustic ballad 'Patience' did wonders for their commercial clout. An Izzy Stradlin number that captured Guns N' Roses "as naked and as raw as possible", according to Slash, it signalled the end of the gritty rock band seen on *Appetite*… and began a period of reinvention that would culminate in the release of third album, the twin set of *Use Your Illusion I* and *Use Your Illusion II*.

Guns N' Roses
Live And Let Die

| 1991 • 3:03 • McCartney – McCartney

The Wings song and James Bond theme, not known for its subtlety, gets an OTT makeover here as Guns N' Roses' sonic ambition hits unprecedented levels. A favourite of both Slash and Axl Rose, and featured on the first *Use Your Illusion* album, 'Live And Let Die' was destined for the stadiums and open spaces that would play host to the band's enormous tour in support of the twin records.

Guns N' Roses
November Rain

! 1991 • 8:57 • Rose

They may have been out-of-step with the time – the explosion of Nirvana and *Nevermind* had begun to usher in a far more modest and musically temperate age – but 'November Rain' was Guns N' Roses' defiant King Canute-like stance against a rising tide. "Axl had that song for a long time," Slash told Xfm. "Tom Zutaut [the band's A&R man] even had to talk him out of putting it on *Appetite...*" 'November Rain' was the realisation of *Use Your Illusion*'s ambition in one glorious/ridiculous nine-minute epic. Even the

similarly OTT video – still one of the most expensive of all time – was one part of a trilogy. "That's right'" said Slash, "'Don't Cry', 'Estranged' and 'November Rain' were all supposed to tell one story, just don't ask me what it was!" Excess all areas reigned; 'November Rain' was Guns N' Roses' one last stab at musical immortality before their inter-band relationships began to disintegrate. They'd never reach the same heady heights again.

Guns N' Roses
Knocking On
Heaven's Door

! 1991 • 5:36 • Dylan

The most dangerous band in the world take on Bob Dylan's classic and give it a stadium-ready arrangement. Like 'Live And Let Die', this was also a firm band favourite. It was, however, debuted years before its release on *Use Your Illusion II* at the band's legendary three-night stand at London's Marquee in 1987. OH

"It was one of those moments where the camaraderie was so tight. We were just enjoying our time together"
— Slash on writing 'Paradise City'

HappyMondays

Happy Mondays
24 Hour Party People

1987 · 4:40 · Happy Mondays

Happy Mondays led the Manchester label Factory back into the charts and established 'baggy' as the main musical preoccupation for Britain at the dawn of the 1990s. The title track of their first album saw the band's embryonic indie-dance formula take root, and was given a no-nonsense production by former Velvet Underground man John Cale. A skewed take on funk, complete with seedy lyrics howled by singer Shaun Ryder, it later achieved fame as the theme song to the Factory Records biopic of the same name in 2001.

Happy Mondays
Wrote For Luck

1988 · 6:06 · Happy Mondays

Collaborating with former Joy Division producer Martin Hannett, Happy Mondays' second album, *Bummed*, brought the band's attempts at mashing indie with dance to life. 'Wrote For Luck' had a hypnotic, shuffling rhythm, while Shaun Ryder supplied an ambiguous lyric that took inspiration from the 1974 movie *Stardust*, which featured David Essex as a

successful rock star who hits rock bottom. At one point, Essex's character emerges from sleeping clothed in a full bath. "You're all wet," says his manager. "Yeah," replies Essex. "But I'm getting drier." "That movie started me off thinking about getting into the music business," Ryder reveals. "I was about 13 and thought, that game's for me. I wanted sex, drugs and rock and roll."

Happy Mondays
Hallelujah

1989 · 2:39 · Happy Mondays

'Hallelujah' was the lead track of an EP from November 1989 and featured vocals from Kirsty MacColl. The late singer-songwriter's husband was producer Steve Lillywhite, who was mixing the track, and it was suggested that she contribute. "She wasn't keen," remembers Shaun Ryder. "She said 'I'll jinx it'... She wasn't having any hits at the time. But it was our first shot on *Top Of The Pops*." MacColl joined the band for their landmark slot on the UK music TV show, which also saw an appearance by their fellow Mancunians The Stone Roses on the same edition. Madchester had arrived.

HAPPY MONDAYS

"She wasn't keen," remembers Shaun Ryder. "She said 'I'll jinx it'... She wasn't having any hits at the time"

– Shaun Ryder on Kirsty MacColl

...ondays

...py Mondays – Demetriou – Kongos

"'Step On' was a fluke," says Shaun Ryder of Happy Mondays' biggest hit, which is a cover of John Kongos's 1971 single 'He's Gonna Step On You Again'. In the middle of recording their third album *Pills'n' Thrills And Bellyaches*, the band's American label Elektra suggested they take part in a 40th anniversary tribute to the company. "They sent over a tape with lots of songs from the back catalogue of Elektra," says Ryder. "We thought, this is the last thing we need. We stuck the tape on and 'Step On' was either first or second on the tape. We said, right that'll do! We'll just get some drum on it and send it off to Oakey." Producer Paul Oakenfold added his magic, Ryder overdubbed random cries such as "Call the cops!" and a baggy classic was born.

Happy Mondays
Kinky Afro

! 1990 · 3:59 · **Happy Mondays**

 Taking the refrain from disco classic 'Lady Marmalade' and adding some soulful vocals from the Mondays' new backing singer Rowetta, 'Kinky Afro' emerged at the height of baggy madness in the autumn of 1990. Factory label boss Tony Wilson later claimed that the opening couplet was worthy of the best poetry England had to offer: "Son, I'm 30 / I only went with your mother 'cause she's dirty." "I was about 27 or 28 when I wrote that one," reveals Shaun Ryder. "It's not really autobiographical. It was just a story, really."

Happy Mondays
Loose Fit

! 1990 · 4:57 · **Happy Mondays**

 Another track culled from the excellent *Pills'n' Thrills And Bellyaches* album, 'Loose Fit' is an ode to a gentleman who favours the baggier trouser and is typical of Shaun Ryder's eccentric lyrical style. "Like all my songs, it's just a story," he says. "Some of them have little meanings – they have subliminal messages, shouts to people who know who we're talking about, but nobody else does... a big mish-mash of comic strip sort of songs." MO'G

You know you talk so hip man / You're twistin my melon man

– Happy Mondays, 'Step On'

Hard-Fi

Hard-Fi
Living For The Weekend

! 2005 • 3:42 • Archer

The best thing to have come out of the commuter-belt town of Staines since Ali G, Hard-Fi's soaring anthem revels in the glories of going out. It has been much used by TV and advertising companies since being released in 2005, to help sell everything from Carling beer to the Winter Olympics. Melding indie and dance influences, a rousing rhythm and a stadium-friendly beat accompany Richard Archer's vocals. The prominence of 'Living For The Weekend' helped send the band's debut album, *Stars Of CCTV*, to number one in the UK and gain a Mercury Music Prize nomination.

The song has been covered by the Sugababes, who recorded the track live and included it as the B-side to their single 'Follow Me Home'. Their version is noticeably more soulful, emphasising the sadder side of a track that has more depth than you might at first think. This is a world where work is unrewarding, where the weekend is the only release from the pressures of life and where "my clothes are all counterfeit" and "my name isn't on the list". It's a celebration of six o'clock on a Friday night but also a wry indictment of working-class, suburban living in 21st-century Britain: a Mike Leigh movie in music. JH

Imogen Heap
Hide And Seek

! 2005 • 4:29 • Heap

In July 2004, Imogen Heap was having a
long and frustrating night in her south
London home studio. A few ideas hadn't
worked and her laptop mother-board had
just melted. Although it was 4am, Heap
was determined to stick to her own rule
of always leaving the studio on a positive
so she turned to a new bit of kit she had
borrowed called a harmoniser. With it
she was able to use her own synthesized
vocals as the only instrument on the track.
With the tone set, 'Hide And Seek' then
came to her very quickly. At the very end
of the recording you can hear the first
train of the day pulling its way out of
Waterloo station, not far from her studio.

Heap told Xfm that the song is about
the loss of someone very dear to her and
one that she did not previously believe she
was brave enough to write. Few songs stop
you in your tracks on first hearing and this
is one of them. Chilling yet full of human
warmth, it's a unique-sounding track that
beautifully conveys a universal emotion.
MW

The Jimi Hendrix Experience
Hey Joe

! 1966 • 3:30 • Roberts

Jimi Hendrix seemed to magically appear
on the planet in the mid-1960s, sent
from heaven with a supernatural ability
to make the guitar sound like nothing
else on earth. In fact, the former US army
serviceman had been paying his dues in a
number of bands for several years. When
ex-Animals bassist Chas Chandler moved
into management and was looking for an
artist to record the rock standard 'Hey Joe',
he chanced upon the guitarist. Already a
favourite of US bands such as The Leaves,
The Byrds and Love, Hendrix recorded his
version soon after Chandler brought him
to London in late 1966. A bluesy tale of
a slighted man extracting fatal revenge
on his cheating "woman", the single
shows little of Hendrix's trademark guitar
trickery, but lays the foundation for one
of the most incendiary careers in rock.

The Jimi Hendrix Experience
Purple Haze

! 1967 • 2:50 • Hendrix

As 1967's summer of love began in
earnest, several key records soundtracked
the seismic cultural and musical changes
underway. One of these was 'Purple Haze'
by Jimi Hendrix, which gave full rein to
the guitarist's incredible skill. Although the
phrase 'purple haze' apparently appears
in Dickens' *Great Expectations*, the song
was taken by most people to reference
some kind of drug experience, especially
with the show-stopping line: "S'cuse me,

while I kiss the sky". From the discordant intro to the shrieking fade, 'Purple Haze' allows Hendrix to wring new and amazing sounds from the electric guitar.

The Jimi Hendrix Experience
All Along The Watchtower

! 1968 • 4:00 • Dylan

One of the rare occasions where a cover version eclipses the original, Jimi Hendrix's take on Bob Dylan's classic was an apocalyptic re-telling of an already haunting allegory. Originally on Dylan's 1967 album *John Wesley Harding*, Hendrix added his own unmistakeable guitar pyrotechnics to the tale. Initially recorded in January 1968 in London,

The Jimi Hendrix Experience
Crosstown Traffic

! 1968 • 2:19 • Hendrix

One of Jimi Hendrix's more poppier moments, taken from the last Experience album, *Electric Ladyland* and featuring an energetic performance that puts more emphasis on vocals and piano than Hendrix's legendary axe skills. The opening refrain was recorded with makeshift kazoos made from toilet paper and combs, while Dave Mason of contemporary rock band Traffic joins in on the choruses. Meanwhile, Hendrix's laidback vocal equates trying to get a girl with dodging busy traffic and a number of car-based puns ram the point home.

> One of the rare occasions where a cover version eclipses the original.. Dylan himself was impressed: "It overwhelmed me, really," he later admitted — The Jimi Hendrix Experience, 'All Along The Watchtower'

Hendrix travelled to New York for a series of long and tortuous recording sessions that tried to capture the sound he heard in his head. And it was well worth the effort – as the penultimate track on the epic *Electric Ladyland* double album, it became one of the greatest rock performances of all time and Dylan himself was impressed: "It overwhelmed me, really," he admitted later.

The Jimi Hendrix Experience
Voodoo Chile (Slight Return)

! 1968 • 5:13 • Hendrix

By the time 'Voodoo Chile (Slight Return)' made number one in the UK charts in the autumn of 1970, Jimi Hendrix had already died from an accidental overdose of prescription drugs and alcohol on September 18th. It was a fitting tribute to the man who reinvented the way electric guitar was played. The song was initially recorded for the *Electric Ladyland* album back in 1968 and was the follow-up to a longer piece, titled simply 'Voodoo Chile'. The original was a 15-minute blues jam; the "slight return" was recorded the following day while a TV crew filmed the band. From the moment the track fades in with Hendrix's phenomenal use of the wah-wah pedal, this is one of rock's wildest showmen at the height of his powers. The obscure lyrics ("Well I stand up next to a mountain / And I chop it down with the edge of my hand") only heighten the impression that Hendrix has become some kind of rock'n'roll shaman. MO'G

The Hives
Hate To Say I Told You So

! 2002 · 3:12 · Fitzsimmons

It's mid-2001 and ex-Creation Records boss Alan McGee is bored. He's on a European promo tour for his new label Poptones, he's been sober for several years and he's staying in a Berlin hotel room wondering why German music TV is so crap. Suddenly and without warning, the television bursts into life. A great-looking singer is strutting like Mick Jagger crossed with Iggy Pop while his band explode into the most earth-shatteringly cool garage

rock song. McGee cannot believe what just hit him and immediately starts making phone calls. The singer was called Pelle Almqvist, his band were The Hives and the song was 'Hate To Say I Told You So'.

After a bit of asking around, McGee was astonished to discover that the band were practically unknown outside Germany and their home country of Sweden. The Hives were soon signed to Poptones and started their international career in the UK with a series of gigs and some major TV shows (McGee knew that TV would be important to their success). They arrived at a time when the term "garage rock" was being used to describe a number of hot new bands such as The White Stripes, The Strokes and The Vines, but the UK press was less interested in The Hives. This would change as the band's live reputation spread. Poptones released the brilliantly titled *Your New Favourite Band*, which was a compilation of The Hives' previous two albums (*Barely Legal* and *Veni Vidi Vicious*). The record kept on selling with the increased exposure the band got via TV, radio and touring, and eventually exceeded platinum sales in the UK. The band's live reputation soon spread around the world and The Hives became a hot ticket in every major territory. It's worth noting that McGee has never met The Hives' "mythical" manager and songwriter, Randy Fitzsimmons, and firmly believes that he does not exist.

The Hives
Main Offender

! 2002 · 2:33 · Fitzsimmons

Just like 'Hate To Say I Told You So', 'Main Offender' is an irresistible indie disco floor-filler and a standout live song, with those heavy, raw yet tightly controlled riffs that are capable of taking the roof off any venue. Like all great rock'n'roll it is instinctive and even slightly sinister, yet ruthlessly focused on getting the listener to move. As frontman Pelle Almqvist would say in one of his famous onstage quips: "Bad music is the devil and I will be your exorcising priest, helpin' you out!" MW

Hole Doll Parts

| 1994 · 3:33 · Hole

The rollercoaster life of Hole frontwoman Courtney Love reached a series of extremes in 1994. The suicide of her husband, Nirvana's Kurt Cobain, in the April of that year was followed by the fatal heroin overdose of her friend, and Hole bassist, Kristen M Pfaff only two months later. Both events took place against the backdrop of the snowballing success of Hole's second album, the prophetically titled *Live Through This*. 'Doll Parts' was the first and most successful single from the album. It's a deeply emotive song of painful introspection that Love wrote in 1991 after first meeting Cobain and believing that her feelings were unrequited. With its key lyric – "I love him so much it just turns to hate / I fake it so real I am beyond fake / Someday you will ache like I ache" – the song naturally took on a new poignancy after Cobain's death, shortly before the single's release. There were many rumours at the time about

how much of the album was actually written by Cobain – claims that Love reacted to with disdain. She made sure that all future Hole releases were very explicit about who wrote which songs.

Hole Celebrity Skin

| 1998 · 2:43 · Corgan – Love – Erlandson

After the global success of *Live Through This*, a more refined and revitalised Hole was ready for action in 1998. Even with the usual fractious in-fighting, the band were back with a more ambitious sound and some of their strongest songs to date. During an interview with Jules Holland on his BBC TV show *Later...*, singer Courtney Love joked that the album was titled *Celebrity Skin* because she had "touched a lot of it". The song was co-written with Hole guitarist Eric Erlandson and Love's on/off love interest, Billy Corgan of Smashing Pumpkins. 'Celebrity Skin' became a US radio hit and launched the band's most successful album. Considering the mixed reception Love had recently received as the "rock star widow" and unsuitable parent, 'Celebrity Skin' opens with her most defining line: "Oh, make me over / I'm all I wanna be / A walking study / In demonology".

Hole Malibu

| 1998 · 3:50 · Corgan – Love – Erlandson

Another co-written track with Billy Corgan and Hole guitarist Eric Erlandson, on this song Courtney Love's lyrics are explicitly about late husband Kurt Cobain's treatment for heroin addiction

be copied to the present day. The song's lyrics, though, were curiously historical and political, written by Harris about the forced removal of Native American land by the American army. Not exactly the subject matter of your everyday heavy metal band.

'Run To The Hills' formed the centrepiece of perhaps the most important heavy metal album ever to have been written and went on to become the band's first top 10 hit. British hard rock had been in a lull before the song arrived – Deep Purple had gone, Judas Priest were arguably about to pass their peak, and bands like Def Leppard were too commercial for many. In Iron Maiden, though, there was something British, something genuine, and something that pulled no punches. Metal would never be the same again. TB

The Jam

The Jam
David Watts

! 1978 • 2:56 • Davies

At the age of 14 a young Paul Weller, inspired by legendary British bands like The Beatles, formed a band that would go on to become one of the most successful groups to come out of the late 1970s punk era. The early incarnations of The Jam featured Weller on bass; it would not be until some years later, after time spent on the working man's club circuit, that Weller would be joined by Rick Buckler (drums) and Bruce Foxton (bass), enabling him to take up his position front of stage and, in 1977, sign to Polydor Records.

Having spearheaded a revival of the mid-1960s mod style, the band's cover of The Kinks' song 'David Watts' was the first single to be released from third album *All Mod Cons* and a nod to one of Weller's key influences, Ray Davies. Weller had spent much of the writing time for the album listening to old Kinks records and the LP has the sound of "British invasion" pop running throughout, not least on this bouncy cover version in which Foxton takes over on lead vocals. Only released as a single after the record company turned down the band's preferred choice of 'Billy Hunt', the track remains faithful to the original but is laced with The Jam's trademark fizz and attitude.

The Jam
Down In The Tube Station At Midnight

! 1978 • 4:45 • Weller

The final track on *All Mod Cons* is arguably one of Paul Weller's most accomplished songs and the perfect example of his ability to produce entertaining social commentary. The song tells the story of a vicious mugging in a London tube station by two thugs who "Smelt of pubs and Wormwood Scrubs / And too many right wing meetings". The song starts with the sounds of a London Underground station before the hi-hat takes over the rhythmic noise of the train and an R&B bass riff drives forward. Weller juxtaposes a jaunty, upbeat tempo and early images of domestic life with the song's dark subject matter. The single's B-side was a cover of The Who's track 'So Sad About Us' and the back of the LP featured a photo of The Who drummer Keith Moon, who died one month before the single's release. 'Down In The Tube Station...' performed well and reached number 15 in the UK charts.

The Jam
Eton Rifles

! 1979 • 3:59 • Weller

Despite being very much associated with the punk movement, The Jam had a more sophisticated sound that gave them a longevity way past that period. Rich in melody and demonstrating frontman Paul Weller's desire for the band to evolve, 'Eton Rifles' was the only release from album *Setting Sons*. Inspired by the "right to work" marches of the time, this was Weller's most assured work to date, combining working class slang terms and a complex narrative in an exploration of class war. The track peaked at number three in the UK and was the first of a run of four hit singles: each would define the band and all became classics in their own right.

The Jam
Going Underground
! 1980 · 3:34 · Weller

By the time The Jam released 'Going Underground', they were alreadfy fully-fledged superstars. Still, the song cemented their status, going straight into the top of the UK charts – although success in the US still eluded them. Originally intended as a B-side, a mix-up in the pressing plant saw it released as a double A-side with 'Dreams Of Children'; ultimately it was the more melodic 'Going Underground' that had the

largest impact. Striking the right balance between aggressive punk posturing, Beatle-esque guitar and catchy singalong pop to create perfect harmony, the single would become the The Jam's defining release.

The Jam
Start
! 1980 · 2:16 · Weller

The Jam followed up the success of 'Going Underground' with their second chart-topper, 'Start'. Released as a teaser to the ambitious *Sound Affects* album and once more taking inspiration from The Beatles (this time 'Taxman'), the track was a punk-tinged gesture to 1960s rock, which hints at the work Paul Weller would later produce with The Style Council.

The Jam
That's Entertainment
! 1981 · 3:34 · Weller

Sound Affects would be The Jam's high-watermark on the US charts, yet it still did not bother the top 50. 'That's Entertainment' was one of the standout tracks on the album and entered the

Sound Affects would be The Jam's high-watermark on the US charts, yet it still did not bother the top 50

singles chart without even being released. Despite being one of the Jam's best known songs, its sound is markedly different to previous releases; Paul Weller's ambitions to move the band forward led him to abandon the driving rhythms and choppy electric guitars in favour of psychedelic backwards acoustics twinned with his trademark cynical world view.

The Jam
A Town Called Malice

! 1982 · 2:55 · Weller

The Gift was to be The Jam's final studio album. Paul Weller was once more pushing the band into unknown territory with jazz, funk and soul influences throughout. The album was given a mixed reception, with fans keen to hear more of their trademark original sound, but 'A Town Called Malice' was universally accepted as one of their finest tracks and saw them collect their third UK number one single, keeping The Stranglers' 'Golden Brown' off the top spot. The song is a rebel cry from Weller written about tough times for families in his hometown of Woking under the Thatcher government of the time.

The Jam
The Bitterest Pill

! 1982 · 3:35 · Weller

Another departure from the band's roots, 'The Bitterest Pill' is often called a Style Council song pretending to be a Jam record – arising from Paul Weller's desire to write more melodic and soulful material. Despite The Jam being one of

the biggest bands in the country by this point, Weller was frustrated by the group's limitations. With the single still at number two in the charts, he shocked fans (and fellow band members) by announcing The Jam would split at the end of the year.

The Jam
Beat Surrender

! 1982 · 3:25 · Weller

The Jam released their farewell single 'Beat Surrender' on November 26th 1982 and it quickly became their fourth single to go straight to the top of the charts. Once more frontman Paul Weller's soul influences were clear and he would go on to explore this sound further in future projects. Laced with backing vocals and sax reminiscent of Stax records, the track leaves the band's punk and rock influences well behind, a far cry from the rawness of their early releases (such as *In The City*) and testament to how Weller had developed as a songwriter in just five years.

After a series of sold-out shows, and with 'Beat Surrender' still at number one, Weller walked away from the biggest band in the UK at the time to form The Style Council before later moving on to a successful solo career. Bassist Bruce Foxton and drummer Rick Buckler later reformed the band without Weller to play under the name "From The Jam"; there appears to be little chance of a full reunion, with Weller describing the reformation as "a bit cabaret". JS

James

James Born Of Frustration

1992 • 4:21 • James

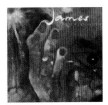

The success of their third album, *Gold Mother*, saw James break through to mainstream success and the band were soon back in the studio to work on its successor. 'Born Of Frustration' became the opening track on fourth album *Seven*. From the euphoric "Woooowooooowoooooowooo" of the opening line and the use of triumphant horns, 'Born Of Frustration' sets the tone for the new direction taken on *Seven*, with the album sounding grander and more ambitious than previous works. The lyrics speak of the frustration of being in a relationship when the parties are not getting along. Released as the second single from the album, 'Born Of Frustration' reached number 13 in the UK charts.

> # The catchy chorus "you think you're so pretty" ensured success
> — James, 'Laid'

James Laid

1993 • 2:36 • Baynton-Power

After huge success with albums *Gold Mother* and *Seven*, James drafted in producer Brian Eno and created a more experimental sound on fifth album *Laid*. The title track is one of the few commercial songs on the album, although the lyrics were rather risqué for mainstream radio: "This bed is on fire with passionate love / The neighbours complain about the noises above / But she only comes when she's on top". The catchy chorus "you think you're so pretty" ensured success in both the UK and the US, where it remains James' most recognised track.

James Sit Down

1991 • 4:07
Booth – Glennie – Gott – Whelan

Originally released as a seven-minute single in 1990, 'Sit Down' failed to make an impact, reaching a disappointing number 77 in the UK charts. It was only after the rise of the Madchester scene, led by fellow Mancunians The Stone Roses and

With the world at their feet, they all fell out and, somewhat anticlimactically, split

– Jane's Addiction's
swift rise and fall

Happy Mondays, that James – seeing that the eyes of the music press were on their home city – decided to record a shorter version and re-released 'Sit Down'. That decision proved to be a masterstroke. It became the biggest hit of James' career, reaching number two in the UK chart in March 1991 and only kept off the top spot by Chesney Hawkes' 'The One And Only'. Anthemic and engaging, 'Sit Down' captured the spirit of Madchester and was a precursor to the all-consuming Britpop scene lurking around the corner.

James Come Home

1989 · 5:04 · Booth – Glennie – Gott

Taken from third album *Gold Mother* and originally flopping as a single in 1989, 'Come Home' was re-released in 1990; it gave James their biggest hit to that date, peaking at number 32 in the UK chart. This punchy and perhaps rather aggressive song had double-edged lyrics about a broken relationship and, more personally, singer Tim Booth's time as a member of restrictive sect Lifewave.
MM

Jane's Addiction Been Caught Stealing

1990 · 3:34 · Jane's Addiction

The story the album charts tell of late 1980s/early '90s rock music is that hair metal was in the ascendancy, stadium bands were kings, and the underground was irrelevant. Jane's Addiction, alongside Nine Inch Nails and – to a lesser extent – the Red Hot Chili Peppers, would herald the change that led to the door being opened for grunge. Though formed in 1985 and having already released a seminal album in 1988's *Nothing's Shocking*, it was with their second record *Ritual De Lo Habitual* that they cracked the mainstream. The song that did it was the chirpy, spiky and occasionally funky 'Been Caught Stealing', a paean to juvenile delinquency and petty theft complete with barking guard dogs. It became an MTV hit, pricked hair metal's pomposity, made Jane's Addiction stars, then teed up a 13-month tour during which, with the world at their feet, they all fell out and, somewhat anticlimactically, split.
TB

The Jesus And Mary Chain
April Skies

| 1987 · 3:11 · Reid – Reid

Glasgow's The Jesus And Mary Chain caused uproar and outrage when they emerged in the mid-1980s. Managed by Creation label boss Alan McGee, their sub-15-minute live shows were confrontational attacks of pure feedback that often erupted in genuine riots while the leather-clad Reid brothers – William and Jim – looked on. Their provocative stance didn't last long, however, and the band soon moved on to writing "proper" songs, resulting in the classic 1985 debut album *Psychocandy*. Still using plenty of fuzzy guitar and reverb, the Mary Chain's music had one eye on influential garage bands like The Velvet Underground and the other on classic 1950s rock'n'roll. 'April Skies', from their second album, *Darklands*, is a chugging ballad with an epic guitar solo. The effect is pleasingly retro, but the widescreen sound of the music masks the downbeat lyrics: "Sun grows cold, sky gets black / And you broke me up, and now you won't come back". MO'G

Jet
Are You Gonna Be My Girl!

| 2003 · 3:33 · Cester – Muncey

When they emerged in 2003 on the back of this song, Jet were not a band with complicated ideals. Formed around two brothers, ebullient drummer Chris Cester and more thoughtful singer Nic, they grew up in Australia blaring AC/DC and The Beatles, drinking and having fun. It was from little more than this background that they formed Jet and set about continuing to enjoy themselves. Alongside other Australian bands like The Vines, they were briefly tagged as part of an Antipodean scene, with riff-rockers like New Zealand's The Datsuns thrown into the mix, and it was with such endorsements ringing in their ears that they flew to Los Angeles to make their debut album.

Get Born, the result, was a slice of classic garage rock in which the band's influences – The Rolling Stones, AC/DC and T.Rex – could plainly be heard. But it was lead single 'Are You Gonna Be My Girl' that earned the band the most attention, in part because of its use on a widely aired iPod advert. Opening with a beat and bassline that recalled Iggy Pop's 'Lust For Life', it was initially criticised as sharing a bit too much of that song's DNA. It was a charge denied by the band, who said that they were more inspired by Motown than Iggy Pop. "We do wear our influences on our sleeves," said Nic. "Most of the time I don't give a shit though. If you think that, then fuck you. Check out our bank balances, we sell too many records to give a shit." It may have been an aggressive rebuttal but, at that point, it was also true. The exuberance and good-time guitars on 'Are You Gonna Be My Girl' made it a radio hit around the world, generating three million sales for *Get Born* in the process. TB

Jimmy Eat World
The Middle

**2001 • 2:46 • Adkins – Burch –
Lind – Linton – James – Lucia**

Inspired by a note left on the band's
message board by a bullied female fan,
Jim Adkins (vocals/guitar) wrote 'The
Middle' as a message to anyone who felt
that they didn't fit in. He wrote the song
in early 2000 and told Xfm that because
it was so simple and easy to write, he was
nervous about taking it to the rest of the
band. He now knows that it is always the
best songs that come that quickly. Adkins
also said that he was looking at a signed
Bruce Springsteen poster at the time and
so believes that he "channelled his inner
Boss". 'The Middle' became Jimmy Eat
World's breakthrough track in the US and
set up their multimillion-selling career.

Jimmy Eat World
Big Casino

**2007 • 3:40
Adkins – Linton – Burch – Lind**

Singer Jim Adkins explained to Xfm that,
while writing 'Big Casino', he pictured
an older guy in a music instrument
shop who was "still keeping the dream

alive" and imparting useless advice to a
younger, much better musician. The title
of the song and opening lines "Before
this world starts up again / It's me and
night / We wait for the sun / The kids and
drunks head back inside" were inspired
by the street cleaners in Las Vegas who
clear the Strip every day just before
dawn; Adkins imagined this older failed
musician to be one of those cleaners.
MW

Joan Jett & The Blackhearts
I Love Rock N' Roll

1982 • 2:55 • Merrill – Hooker

By the age of 15 Joan Jett had formed
The Runaways, an all-girl punk group
that was tearing up the LA rock scene
of the mid-1970s. In 1979, aged 19, Jett
produced the seminal LA punk band The
Germs' first and only album. The Germs
featured guitarist Pat Smear who went on
to play with Nirvana and the Foo Fighters.
When The Runaways split in 1980, Jett
moved to New York to form new band
The Blackhearts. Within a year they were
to have a US number one hit with this
classic single – a cover of 'I Love Rock N'
Roll', which was originally a B-side for
'70s English group The Arrows. A Britney
Spears version hit the UK charts at number
13 in 2002 – Ms Spears' lowest chart
entry to date, which serves her right for
tinkering with such a rock'n'roll treasure.
MW

Joy Division

Joy Division
Transmission

! 1979 • 3:36 • Joy Division

 Joy Division were one of the many bands inspired by the arrival of punk. Formed by guitarist Bernard Sumner and bassist Peter Hook, they were lucky enough to discover a visionary frontman in Ian Curtis and a metronomic drummer, Stephen Morris. The band issued their own EP in early 1978 and then recorded a whole album with major label RCA that ultimately remained unreleased. One of the LP's highlights was a new track, 'Transmission', which saw the group move away from punk-thrash and into unexplored areas. That the song was something special quickly became apparent to Hook when they played it during a soundcheck for one show. "People had been moving around, and they all stopped and listened," he told MOJO. "I was thinking, 'What's the matter with that lot?' That's when I realised it was our first great song." Initially celebrating the power of radio, the lyrics become more frantic and desperate as the music assumes a vital connection between lovers. Played slowly and menacingly on the RCA album, the song was speeded up for

a Factory single release in October 1979, while Curtis's shamanistic dancing added extra urgency to its live performances.

Joy Division
She's Lost Control

! 1979 • 3.57 • Joy Division

"A girl used to come into the centre where Ian worked to try and find work. She had epilepsy and lost more and more time through it. One day she just didn't come in any more. He found out later she'd had a fit and died." Bernard Sumner recalls the genesis of one of Joy Division's most unsettling songs, which was given extra poignancy when singer Ian Curtis subsequently developed epilepsy himself. Included on the band's acclaimed debut album *Unknown Pleasures*, the track was reworked a year later for a 12-inch release aimed at clubs and was effectively covered by disco diva Grace Jones.

Joy Division
Atmosphere

! 1979 • 4:11 • Joy Division

Recorded midway between Joy Division's debut album and its follow-up, *Closer*, 'Atmosphere' is one of the most graceful records to come out of the whole post-punk genre. With its symphonic string synthesisers and celestial percussion, this song demonstrates how far the band had travelled from their punk roots in such a short space of time. The lyrics – delivered in Ian Curtis's deep baritone – seem to concern his favourite themes of alienation and isolation. Originally issued as an ultra-rare single in France, the song became more famous in 1988, when it was reissued with a baffling Anton Corbijn video featuring hooded monks.

forceful Peter Hook bassline and an elegiac synthesizer riff from Bernard Sumner, the recording of the song was unusually problematic, with two entirely different versions completed. Factory boss Tony Wilson lent Curtis a copy of a Frank Sinatra album to listen to the evening before the final session, and the legendary crooner's influence can be heard on the finished take, which made number 13 in the UK charts

From left: 'Love Will Tear Us Apart', 'Atmosphere'

Joy Division
Love Will Tear Us Apart

1980 · 3:27 · Joy Division

Joy Division's most famous song was born from the turbulent life of singer Ian Curtis. Constant touring was exacerbating his epilepsy, while his marriage was running into problems. 'Love Will Tear Us Apart' is a heatbreaking lament for a dying relationship, and the confusion and despair felt by the people involved. Powered by a

in June 1980. By then, Curtis was dead. He had committed suicide on the eve of the band's first US tour on May 18th and the song literally became his epitaph. Factory were accused of bad taste when the single was released, as the sleeve appeared to depict a tombstone. Nevertheless, the song remains the band's most enduring legacy and has been covered by artists as diverse as 1980s' heartthrob Paul Young and acoustic troubadour José González. MO'G

The single won best video at MTV Europe's awards, prompting the first of Kanye West's "it-should've-been-me" tantrums

– Justice vs Simian, 'We Are Your Friends'

Justice
D.A.N.C.E

2007 • 3:54 • Augé – Chaton – de Rosnay

Two long-haired Frenchmen dressed in black leather, Justice look like the last people you'd expect to be writing songs dedicated to the greatness of Michael Jackson. The duo of Gaspard Augé and Xavier de Rosnay even admitted that their French label grimaced when they played them the song, complete with vocals supplied by the Foundation for Young Musicians, a London-based youth choir. Certainly with its staccato strings, nimbly funky bassline and air of impossibly good, discofied cheer, it's a mile away from their first single 'Waters Of Nazareth' or most of their album *t* (alternatively known as *Cross*), which was described by BBC online magazine *Collective* as "intoxicatingly pitched between Daft Punk and actual daft punk".

But the track became an internet phenomenon in the summer of 2007, powered by an endless series of unofficial remixes. One, by Mark Ronson-affiliated rapper Wale, was described by Justice to *Pitchfork*, with no apparent hint of irony, as "the best thing that ever happened to this track… it sounds like Will Smith".

Despite the acclaim, 'D.A.N.C.E' flopped on its UK release, with many critics pointing to the complete stranglehold of indie rock on national radio at the time. The magazines still loved it though, with *Rolling Stone* naming it fourth best tune of 2007 and *Vice* magazine releasing it on their US record label.

Justice Vs Simian
We Are Your Friends

2006 • 2:40 • Justice Vs Simian

'We Are Your Friends' began life as a remix by the French duo of the English electro-rock band's 'Never Be Alone', entered into a 2003 competition. Picked up by DJ Hell for his Gigolo label, it gathered steam until eventually re-issued under its new name in the UK, becoming a huge hit with its unforgettable hook and rattling synths. Simian had by then been reinvented as Simian Mobile Disco and were sounding a lot like Justice, a new breed of indie dance that was heavier on the dance than the indie. The single won best video at MTV Europe's awards, prompting the first of Kanye West's "it-should've-been-me" tantrums.
SY

Kaiser Chiefs

The second time round
was a much better result
for the boys from Leeds

— Rereleasing 'Oh My God' gave the Kaiser Chiefs their first hit

Kaiser Chiefs
Oh My God

**| 2004 • 3:43 • Baines – Hodgson –
Rix – White – Wilson**

Having served time in also-ran Leeds band Runston Parva, Ricky Wilson, Andrew White, Simon Rix, Nick Hodgson and Nick "Peanut" Baines decided to have one last shot at indie fame by renaming themselves Kaiser Chiefs and writing a whole new set of songs. Despite support from Xfm, their debut single 'Oh My God' in May

2004 failed to set the charts alight… until it was re-issued on the B-Unique label and hit the top 10 nine months later.

Kaiser Chiefs
I Predict A Riot

**| 2004 • 3:52 • Baines – Hodgson –
Rix – White – Wilson**

As the strategy of releasing and re-releasing a track had worked well for Kaiser Chiefs with 'Oh My God', they saw no reason not to try it again. Second

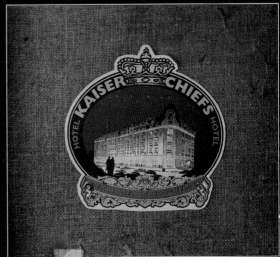

From left: 'I Predict A Riot', 'Every Day I Love You Less And Less'

single from debut album *Employment*, 'I Predict a Riot' was first put out on November 1st 2004 (reaching number 22) before being re-released as a double A-side on August 22nd 2005, when it moved up to number nine in the UK. The story behind the single came about from drummer Nick Hodgson's time as a DJ in Leeds. After driving past a fight one night he created the song's riff and a first few words. The rest was inspired by a band at his club one night, as he explains: "They were going mad and so were the crowd. You could see the bouncers moving in and I said to the club's boss, 'I predict a riot'. The structure was there, then everyone invented their own parts. We thought maybe it was too punky but our manager thought it sounded like 10cc meets The Clash. I was pleased with that."

Kaiser Chiefs
Every Day I Love You Less And Less

| 2005 • 3:37 • Baines – Hodgson – Rix – White – Wilson

The first track on album *Employment*, 'Everyday I Love You Less And Less' was released as single number three on May 16th 2005 and gave Kaiser Chiefs their second top 10 single of the year. The bandmates (most of whom you'd probably be happy to take home to meet your mum) chose their name after Leeds United defender Lucas Radebe was transferred to the South African football team "Kaizer Chiefs".

Kaiser Chiefs
Ruby

| 2007 • 3:23 • Baines – Hodgson – Rix – White – Wilson

After a busy year of touring – which included a career-making Pyramid Stage slot at Glastonbury 2005 – Kaiser Chiefs retreated into the studio to record their second album. *Yours Truly, Angry Mob* kept the patented Chiefs formula of acerbic lyrics and joyous pop tunes, and the lead single 'Ruby' became the band's first number one hit. "To be honest," guitarist Andrew "Whitey" White told Ultimate Guitar, "It's our most radio-friendly song. It's got everything in there." BdP / MOG

KAISER CHIEFS *Ruby*

The Kaiser Chiefs' first number one single in the UK. To date, it has sold more than 375,000 copies

– Kaiser Chiefs, 'Ruby'

Kasabian

Kasabian
Processed Beats

! 2004 • 3:18 • Karloff – Pizzorno

Few bands made an impact on the first decade of this millennium like Kasabian; their imagination, ambition and ability have set them apart from many of their peers. The song that began their rapid trajectory from bedroom to festival headliners was 'Processed Beats'. Guitarist and writer Sergio Pizzorno told Xfm that he wanted to create "psychedelic hip-hop with traditional '60s British songwriting". Written and demo-recorded at home on "the most basic computer program", Pizzorno believed that 'Processed Beats' marked the beginning of what Kasabian were going to become. The band were played on radio for the very first time by Eddy Temple-Morris in 2003 when he was given a demo of 'Processed Beats'.

Kasabian
Club Foot

! 2004 • 2:57 • Karloff – Pizzorno

With a record deal in place, Kasabian moved to a remote Leicestershire farmhouse in 2003 to write and record their debut album. The band loved the freedom and isolation of their new rural retreat and the songs came thick and fast. According to Serge Pizzorno, 'Club Foot' (their first UK hit), "just arrived one typically stoned evening at the farm".

Kasabian
Cutt Off

! 2004 • 4:38 • Pizzorno – Karloff

Although most Kasabian songs convey a life-affirming euphoria, their lyrics are often – as the band put it – "on the darker side of happy". The conspiratorial paranoia of 'Cutt Off''s lyrics came from an FBI book that Serge Pizzorno had been reading. The John in the first line of the song is a

"Psychedelic hip-hop with traditional '60s British song writing"

– Serge Pizzorno's idea behind 'Processed Beats'

fictitious spy character and not the John Lennon that many people assumed.

Kasabian
L.S.F.

! 2004 · 3:20 · Pizzorno – Karloff

In early band rehearsals Kasbian's invincibly charismatic singer Tom Meighan would jump off amps and shout things like "C'mon Glastonbury!", and as Serge Pizzorno points out: "you are never going to get there if you can't see it". This drive, focus and confidence would serve them well as they made progressively more ambitious (and successful) albums. Originally written on an acoustic guitar, 'L.S.F.' is one of Kasabian's earlier songs that has since taken on a life of its own when played live – the refrain of "Oh c'mon, we got our backs to the wall" has been sung vehemently by fans everywhere from Glastonbury to Fuji Rocks.

Kasabian
Empire

! 2006 · 3:24 · Pizzorno – Karloff

Kasabian's second album was written and recorded in a speedy three months during the winter of 2005/6. Title track 'Empire' was based on a riff that guitarist Serge Pizzorno had had for a while and was one of the first songs to emerge from these sessions. Singer Tom Meighan had recently been using the word "empire" to describe things that he thought were amazing – from music to films to trainers. The album's original title was *British Legion* but the label insisted that it be changed to avoid any nationalist misinterpretation. Seemingly missing the irony of then calling it *Empire*.

Kasabian
Shoot The Runner

! 2006 · 3:27 · Pizzorno

The writing and recording of new album *Empire* was straight off the back of a lengthy world tour, of which the final leg was a North American stint supporting Oasis in large legendary venues like the Hollywood Bowl and Colorado's Red Rocks Amphitheatre. These gigs left a huge impression on Kasabian and drove them even harder to write bigger and heavier songs to fill large spaces. The road had taught them what was required to make a great live song and the glam-rock stomp of 'Shoot The Runner' is a perfect example.

Kasabian
Vlad The Impaler

! 2009 · 4:42 · Pizzorno

Buoyed by *Empire*'s success, Kasabian were determined to push things further with a bolder and broader third album.

Writer Serge Pizzorno told Xfm that he had been listening to a lot of M.I.A. at the time of writing *West Ryder Pauper Lunatic Asylum*, and the resulting genre-blending anti-rock is best personified on 'Vlad The Impaler' – a twin-vocal monster of a song. Thoroughly unique and modern, Pizzorno describes it as "wanting to take rock'n'roll to the sword".

Kasabian
Fire

! 2009 • 3:47 • Pizzorno

'Fire' was based on an idea that Serge Pizzorno had as a potential B-side from the *Empire* sessions, but was so enraptured with its bizarre structure that he decided to hold it back. It re-emerged while he was writing and recording new album material in his new home studio in Leicestershire. He said that "it was the song that everyone I played it to went 'what the fuck is that?' – it just didn't sound like anything else". It became Kasabian's biggest UK hit to date, reaching number three in June 2009.

Kasabian
Where Did All The Love Go?

! 2009 • 4:24 • Pizzorno

About three-quarters of the *West Ryder Pauper Lunatic Asylum* album was written and recorded in Serge Pizzorno's home studio before the band flew to San Francisco to work with legendary hip-hop producer Dan The Automater. Pizzorno describes the ensuing track 'Where Did All The Love Go?' as "a mad dark disco record".

Kasabian
Underdog

! 2009 • 4:30 • Pizzorno

The opening track on *West Ryder Pauper Lunatic Asylum*, and the album's third single, 'Underdog' was apparently intended as Kasabian's modern take on The Rolling Stones. The swagger of early Stones is apparent throughout the album as is the experimentation of a band like Can, and the glorious psychedelia of Silver Apples and The Pretty Things. MW

Keane

Keane
This Is The Last Time

2003 • 3:31
Chaplin – Hughes – Rice-Oxley – Sanger

Originally 'This Is The Last Time' was released on October 13th 2003 through Fierce Panda Records, but the version that the UK public came to know and love would be released on November 22nd 2004 by Island Records as Keane's official

fourth single and a hit from their debut album *Hopes And Fears*. The track was written in G major and the lyrics suggest a beautiful concoction of confusion, regret and chance. Pianist Tim Rice-Oxley described the song as dealing with the difficulties involved in making decisions about a relationship and the internal conflict and confusion such choices can inspire: "You have a bond with someone but you don't want to stay with them

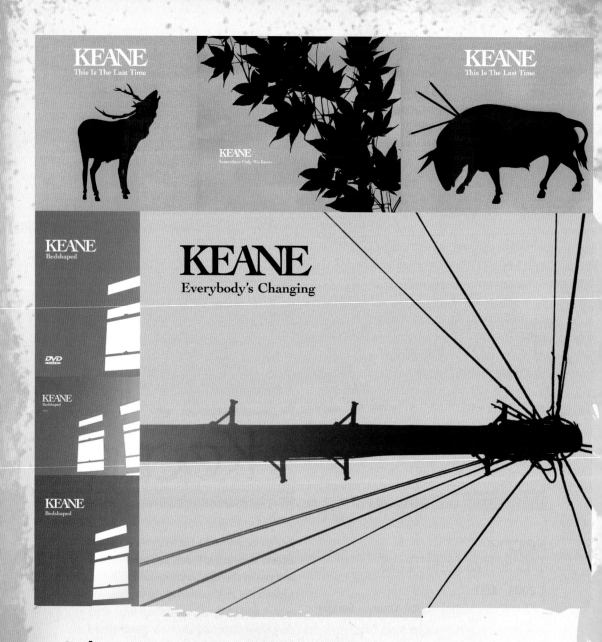

Top: 'This Is The Last Time', 'Somewhere Only We Know', 'This Is The Last Time' (DVD).
Side left: 'Bedshaped' (DVD), 'Bedshaped', 'Bedshaped' (Vinyl). Centre: 'Everybody's Changing'

forever, so you decide to go. But you're not saying 'I hate you and I'm leaving'... you're trying to say 'I think you're great but I've seen that there's something more perfect and magical out there for me and I need to find it. But I will always be your friend if you need me'."

Keane
Everybody's Changing

▌ 2003 • 3:32
▏ Chaplin – Hughes – Rice-Oxley

Another dual release date for another iconic anthem from Keane: 'Everybody's Changing' was first released on May 12th 2003 and then re-released almost exactly a year later in May 2004. The chart positions speak for themselves: it reached numbers 122 and four respectively, so Jon Turner and his team at Island Records knew exactly what they were doing. Years later, at the launch of the Conservative Party's 2010 election campaign, the track was played after leader David Cameron's speech. Drummer Richard Hughes made his feelings clear via Twitter: "Am horrified. To be clear – we were not asked. I will not vote for them." Lesson learned – once your music's out there, it's out there.

Keane
Somewhere Only We Know

▌ 2004 • 3:57
▏ Chaplin – Hughes – Rice-Oxley

'Somewhere Only We Know' was the first single to be released from Keane's debut album *Hopes And Fears* and its simple piano backing, mixed with the haunting voice of Mr Tom Chaplin, introduced listeners to a new sound from an exciting new band. Amazingly for any release, let alone a debut, 'Somewhere Only We Know' went straight into the UK singles charts at number three, and still to this day remains one of Keane's bestselling singles. After its UK success, Island Records went on to release the single internationally, with similar results: the single remained in the top 10 of the Mexican airplay chart for 18 weeks.

Keane
Bedshaped

▌ 2004 • 4:38
▏ Chaplin – Hughes – Rice-Oxley – Sanger

Another single release from *Hopes And Fears*, 'Bedshaped' was released on August 16th 2004 and sold nearly 22,000 copies in the first week of sales. A beautiful string-based anthem, piano accompaniment and Tom Chaplin's effortless vocals round this track off and complement its thought-provoking lyrics. Particularly poignant is the end of the song, which fades with the line: "But what do I know? What do I know? I know". Written mainly by pianist Tim Rice-Oxley in 2001, he explained the motive behind the track as follows: "I think I'm right in saying that in hospital when someone is ill and has to spend a lot of time in bed they can become 'bedshaped'. It sounds a bit depressing, but in the context of the song I wanted to suggest old age and frailty." BdP

The Killers

The Killers
Mr Brightside

2004 • 3:43 • Flowers – Keuning –
Stoermer – Vannucci

In 2002 a 21-year-old college drop-out called Brandon Flowers had just been abandoned by his first band (a synth-pop outfit called Blush Response); he was a Vegas hotel porter and was suffering the acute sting of his first broken heart. "At an all-time low – right in the trenches" is how Flowers described it to Xfm in May 2010. After seeing Oasis play The Joint in Vegas in the April of 2002, Flowers decided that he wanted to be in a rock'n'roll band and so, via a press ad, he met up with Dave Keuning (influences cited as Oasis and The Cure). Weeks later, Flowers was driving to work in his battered 1992 Geo Metro when he put on one of the home-recorded cassettes that Keuning had sent him. Out of the speakers rushed a bright pulse-quickening guitar riff and suddenly, with lyrics that he had been nurturing from his recent heartache, Flowers was singing along at the top of his voice. 'Mr Brightside' – and the next biggest band in the world – was born.

If you love good music it will find you anywhere

– Brandon Flowers

The Killers
Jenny Was A Friend of Mine

2004 • 4:04 • Flowers – Stoermer

'Jenny Was A Friend of Mine' became the opening track on The Killer's debut album *Hot Fuss*, and featured on a demo tape that also included an early version of 'Mr Brightside' and a song called 'On Top'. Most US record labels had passed on the band but a tape had been picked up by a UK music industry scout called Alex Gilbert who then passed it to his friend Ben

'Somebody Told Me' became the song that really broke The Killers in the UK – charting at number three on its re-release in January 2005. It was a huge cross-over success, achieving much pop radio airplay and it remains one of their great live moments. Frontman Brandon Flowers describes it as having a lot of sexual energy and the song that is most influenced by their hometown of Las Vegas. The Killers took their name from the imaginary band in the video for New Order's 2001 single 'Crystal'.

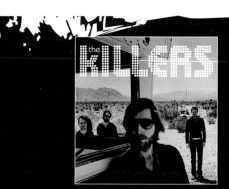  

From left: 'When You Were Young', 'Bones', 'Read My Mind'. Right: 'Smile Like You Mean It'

Durling. In August 2003, The Killers signed to Durling's UK indie label Lizard King. The band agreed a deal with Island Records in the US two months later. Although never a single, 'Jenny Was A Friend of Mine' received heavy airplay on Xfm.

The Killers
Somebody Told Me

2004 • 3:17 • Flowers – Keuning – Stoermer – Vannucci

The Killers
All These Things That I've Done

2004 • 5:02 • Flowers – Keuning – Stoermer – Vannucci

On July 2nd 2005, The Killers performed 'All These Things That I've Done' on stage at Hyde Park as part of Live 8, in front of an estimated global audience of more than three billion. The song's opening lines took on a new poignancy: "When there's

SMILE LIKE YOU MEAN IT

nowhere else to run / Is there room for one more son / If you can hold on". The live crowd's response in Hyde Park was amazing while television viewers around the world gaped at this explosive new band, before humming the line "I got soul but I'm not a soldier" non-stop for the next few days.

The fourth single from *Hot Fuss* and a number 11 hit in the UK in September 2004. 'Smile Like You Mean It' is typical of the album's inspired mix of 1980s synths, muscular indie-rock guitars and Flower's detached, almost weary, voice delivering lines about lost love: "And someone will drive her around / Down the same streets that I did".

The Killers
Smile Like You Mean It
⚡ 2004 · 3:55 · Flowers – Stoermer

The Killers
When You Were Young

2006 · 3:39 · Flowers – Keuning – Stoermer – Vannucci

"I never saw my hometown until I stayed away too long" sings Tom Waits on 'San Diego Serenade' (from 1974's album *The Heart Of Saturday Night*): this is how Brandon Flowers best describes the writing of The Killers' second album. If *Hot Fuss* was British in its influences and outlook, *Sam's Town* was most definitely American. "We had never left our home country and then we had been everywhere – I wanted to write something that represented where I am from," Flowers said in May 2010. This re-appreciation of the US informed a more observational lyrical approach inspired by great American storytellers like Springsteen, Tom Petty and the aforementioned Waits. Full of confidence after the phenomenal success of their debut album, The Killers wrote 'When You Were Young' very quickly and early on in the *Sam's Town* sessions. A strident chest-out smash hit of a song, Flowers describes 'When You Were Young' as one of the band's most collaborate efforts and one of their proudest moments. "After writing that," he says, "everything else on that album was just gravy."

The Killers Bones

2006 · 3:46 · Flowers – Keuning – Stoermer – Vannucci

The second single from *Sam's Town* and the first music video ever directed by acclaimed filmmaker Tim Burton.

The award-winning video shows CGI skeletons re-enacting famous beach scenes from classic films *10* and *From Here To Eternity*. The video also featured actors Michael Steger and Devon Aoki.

The Killers Read My Mind

2006 · 4:03 · Flowers – Keuning – Stoermer – Vannucci

Sometimes referred to by singer Brandon Flowers as the best song he has ever written. Lyrically, 'Read My Mind' embodies much of the American storytelling that runs through *Sam's Town*, with wonderfully vivid nods to Springsteen such as "I never really gave up on / Breaking out of this two-star town / I got a green light, I got a little fight / I'm gonna turn this thing around". The Pet Shop Boys did a remix that appeared as a B-side of the single and featured on the duo's own 2007 album, *Disco Four*.

The Killers Human

2008 · 4:05 · Flowers – Keuning – Stoermer – Vannucci

Frontman Brandon Flowers says that 'Human' was written in direct response to the criticism that the band received over *Sam's Town*. Much of the world's press misinterpreted the album as a cynical attempt to establish themselves in their home country after their success in Europe. The band were hit hard by this critical mauling and, although *Sam's Town* sold well, Flowers was determined to make a more playful and less serious third album. It appealed to him however that the first single would be the most European of their hits – the pop-dance radio smash 'Human'. The track was recorded with producer/collaborator Stuart Price (Madonna, Kylie Minogue) very quickly after the band's first meeting with him in London. The line "Are we human, or are we dancer?" is said to be inspired by a remark from revered maverick writer Hunter S Thompson about America "raising a generation of dancers".

lots of space and be playful". The playful pop approach is summed up in the album's second single, the infectious melting-pot that is 'Spaceman'.

The Killers
A Dustland Fairytale

2008 · 3:46 · Flowers – Keuning – Stoermer – Vannucci

From left: 'Spaceman', 'All These Things that I've Done', 'Human'

The Killers
Spaceman

2008 · 4:45 · Flowers – Keuning – Stoermer – Vannucci

Brandon Flowers talks about The Killers' third album, *Day And Age*, as being more fun and varied; a record that draws upon "60 years of great popular rock and pop music that we love – why would we limit ourselves to just one genre or style?" He also told Xfm that during the sessions for *Day And Age* they were listening to "Roxy Music and Talking Heads, we wanted the album to have

The '61 that singer Brandon Flowers refers to in the opening lines of 'A Dustland Fairytale' is the year that his parents met and started their 49-year relationship – a partnership that only ended when his mother passed away in 2010. Although the song is not specifically about them, Flowers told Xfm that it is about something they, and their relationship, represent: "an ideal that they left behind, an ideal that is dying in the world. Their commitment and their values that don't seem to exist any more as we become more fleeting in what we want from the world."

Kings Of Leon

Kings Of Leon
Molly's Chambers

2003 · 2:15
Followill – Followill – Angelo

"My Dad was a travelling preacher," began drummer Nathan Followill, when asked by Xfm about his three brothers' unlikely musical beginnings. "My mom played piano and sang, my dad played guitar, bass and sang. We spent a lot of time on the road with him, but every church we'd go to, I'd just sit and watch the drummer the whole time." While rock'n'roll was a strict no-go area – "they didn't want us to listen to it in case it was about drugs or sex", said Nathan – an uncle with a secret penchant for Chuck Berry opened the brothers' eyes to the wider musical world. 'Molly's Chambers', however, was the wider world's first taste of Kings Of Leon, the band of three brothers and cousin Matthew. As the lead track from the *Holy Roller Novocaine* EP, its taut Southern groove blew a fresh hole in the music scene... a small, mouthwatering taster of what was to come.

Kings Of Leon
Red Morning Light

2003 · 3:03
Petraglia – Followill – Followill

Naysayers still balked at the "new Strokes" tag, poking fun at the band's drainpipe jeans and their heroically hirsute appearance, but 'Red Morning Light' towered over such petty criticism. Here was one of the most unique voices in music, resplendent in a three-minute romp of gritty guitars, a lackadaisical Southern drawl and a brutally honest production. "When I was 16 I couldn't have told you the difference between a Rolling Stones song and a Led Zeppelin song because that world didn't exist to us," said drummer Nathan Followill told Xfm, but 'Red Morning Light' seemed to distil 40 years of rock'n'roll's essence into one bite-sized chunk. It was, as we suspected, love at first sight and the romance has barely wavered since.

Kings Of Leon
California Waiting

2003 · 3:29
Followill – Followill – Angelo

'California Waiting' was a pivotal moment in the band's live set where, with tiny amplifiers, zero production trickery and the minimum of fuss, Kings Of Leon tore up the world's venues with a frightening chemistry and dazzling conviction. With its soaring chorus, the song was the soundtrack to the penny dropping; in Camden's tiny Electric Ballroom, Kate Moss, Stella McCartney and Sadie Frost swayed elegantly at the side of the stage. "We don't really keep up with [our success] that much," singer Caleb Followill told Xfm in 2003. "The way we can tell is by the shows – it's always been pretty crazy over here but now it's starting to show in random, weird places."

Kings Of Leon
Wasted Time

2003 · 2:45
Followill – Followill – Petraglia

They may have had a sheltered upbringing but by the release of 'Wasted Time', the Followills were rock'n'roll stars indulging fully in the perks of the job. "We had to chase girls around in their underwear in the dark'" said Nathan, explaining the concept behind the single's video. "It doesn't get much more fun than that!"

Kings Of Leon
The Bucket

2005 • 2:55 • Followill – Followill – Followill – Followill

"We're not as bad as people say," Caleb Followill told Xfm as their second album *Aha Skake Heartbreak* hit the shelves. "We're tired of all the stories and the celebrities showing up at gigs, we just wanted to get home and do the album." Recorded once more with producer Ethan Johns in LA, 'The Bucket' was the first taste of the band's hotly anticipated second album. While it didn't have an orthodox stadium-filling chorus, its joyous, country-tinged lollop did the Kings' reputation no harm whatsoever.

Kings Of Leon Four Kicks

2004 • 2:08 • Followill – Followill – Followill – Followill

This ramshackle racket with a harsh, rough exterior hinted at a bravery to broaden the band's sonic palette. A new candid lyrical approach was also clearly evident. According to Caleb Followill: "It's a more honest account about some of the things that have happened, no matter how embarrassing they may have been."

"We had to chase girls around in their underwear in the dark"

– Nathan Followill on the 'Wasted Time' video

Kings Of Leon
King Of The Rodeo

2004 • 2:27 • Followill – Followill – Followill – Followill

Aha Shake Heartbreak may have been thin on conventional singles in the vein of 'Molly's Chambers' or 'California Waiting', but it was full-to-bursting with great songs like 'King Of The Rodeo'. Adding a new depth to the Kings Of Leon oeuvre, the song and album were the sound of a band's musical stock rising before their assault on the mainstream began in earnest.

Kings Of Leon
On Call

2007 • 3:21 • Followill – Followill – Followill – Followill

"It's hard for me to pick a single and to put a face on a record," said Caleb Followill of third album *Because Of The Times* and its lead single 'On Call', "but this was a simple song with a powerful statement." In a reverse Samson-type effect, the new-look, less shaggy Kings had produced the album and single of their careers thus far. Which prompted Xfm to speculate whether an entirely shorn Kings would yield further success. "Matt may shave his back," joked brother Nathan. "World peace will definitely follow when he does that."

Kings Of Leon
Fans

2007 · 3:36 · Followill – Followill – Followill – Followill

Caleb Followill told us this track was "about me quitting being so hard on myself... When you go home you feel like everyone's forgotten about you [and] at the end of the day, we've still got you guys." On an album of intense beauty, unbridled ambition and steadfast confidence, 'Fans' was a touching ode that swelled the hearts of supporters and spurred the Kings' phenomenon on to ever greater heights.

Kings Of Leon
Charmer

2007 · 2:56 · Followill – Followill – Followill – Followill

A wider set of musical influences were clearly evident on 'Charmer' as the band went on a furious sub-three-minute orbit around the Pixies' planet of sound. That the album was beautifully coherent despite such a left-turn was testament to the undeniable quality of the record and the band who had produced it.

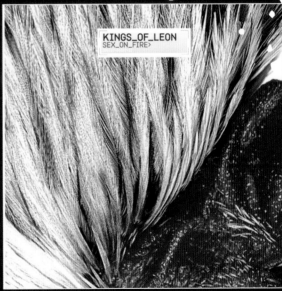

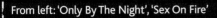
From left: 'Only By The Night', 'Sex On Fire'

Kings Of Leon
Sex On Fire

2008 · 3:23 · Followill – Followill – Followill – Followill

Having brought Glastonbury festival to its knees with a storming headline set in June 2008, the swelled ranks of fans were crying out for an anthem to celebrate Kings Of Leon's arrival at rock's top table. Enter 'Sex On Fire': the distillation of the band's hard work in one roof-raising, fist-pumping moment. "When it was only the music, it sounded like Gang Of Four with punchy bass and drums," bassist Jared Followill told Xfm. With Caleb's vocals, it became the anthemic staple of countless more headline festival slots.

Kings Of Leon
Use Somebody

2008 · 3:47 · Followill – Followill – Followill – Followill

If 'Sex On Fire' smashed down the doors to the mainstream music scene, 'Use Somebody' was the sound of squatters taking up permanent residence. It was the band's first song to make any real headway in the States, taking up residency in the Billboard Hot 100's top five. "When we first recorded this song, I took away a rough mix and listened to it for the first time," guitarist Matt Followill told Xfm. "I immediately called Jared and said this was the best song we'd done in our career."

Kings Of Leon Revelry

2008 · 3:22 · Followill – Followill – Followill – Followill

The band may have matured over four albums but 'Revelry' hinted that the old wanton ways were still alive and well, as bass player Jared Followill coyly explained to Xfm: "It's about being in a relationship with somebody… You could be having a great time, but in the back of your mind you're thinking about how good it was beforehand when you were out partying."

Kings Of Leon Notion

2008 · 3:01 · Followill – Followill – Followill – Followill

Only By The Night was the album that saw bassist Jared Followill jump to the fore. Nowhere were his snaking basslines and increasing confidence as a songwriter more in evidence than on 'Notion'. "I got the most boring instrument, so I try and make my parts memorable," he told Xfm. "My playing sticks out the most on 'Notion', probably because the song started with the bass."

Kings Of Leon Manhattan

2008 · 3:24 · Followill – Followill – Followill – Followill

Notable for its distinctive, drawn-out guitar punctuations, 'Manhattan' betrayed Matthew Followill's debt to U2's The Edge. "If you're in a rock band, I don't think you can help but be influenced by The Edge," he said. "We even have U2 names: Hairy Mullen Jr, The Curve, J Damn Clayton and Wino!" OH

The Kinks

The Kinks
You Really Got Me

1964 • 2:14 • Davies

'You Really Got Me' may have been The Kinks' third single, but it was the one that propelled them into the big league. It went straight in at number one in the UK charts and reached the top 10 in the US. A stomping, rave-up R&B number, it's often cited as the track that "invented heavy metal", thanks to the searing guitar riff – an effect achieved by Dave Davies after he slashed his guitar amp with a razor. A persistent rumour that the solo was played by future Led Zeppelin axeman Jimmy Page (then a mere session musician) has been denied by all concerned.

The Kinks
All Day And All Of The Night

1964 • 2:23 • Davies

Knowing they were on to a good thing with their Transatlantic hit 'You Really Got Me', The Kinks refined the formula for the follow-up with another slice of scorching British R&B – and bagged a UK number two hit for their trouble. Much of the record's impact is down to Dave Davies' rip-roaring guitar and producer Shel Talmy's distorted production – a trick he'd repeat later with The Who.

The Kinks
Waterloo Sunset

1967 • 3:16 • Davies

'Waterloo Sunset' was one of The Kinks' biggest UK successes. It went into the UK charts at number two, missing out on the number one spot thanks to The Tremeloes' 'Silence Is Golden'. Headed up by the supremely talented singer-songwriter Ray Davies and his powerhouse guitarist brother Dave, The Kinks took a youthful interest in classic American R&B and gave it a uniquely British spin. Hailing from Muswell Hill in north London, the band created some of the most quintessentially English songs of the 1960s and set the blueprint for what was to become Britpop. The lyric "Terry meets Julie, Waterloo station / Every Friday night" is often thought to be about the relationship between actors Terence Stamp and Julie Christie, however Davies told *Uncut* magazine in 2009 that "it was a fantasy about my sister going off with

'Waterloo Sunset' epitomises the 1960s for many

The track that invented heavy metal?

– The Kinks, 'You Really Got Me'

her boyfriend to a new world and they were going to emigrate and go to another country." While the rest of the country was going ape for Liverpool and Mersey Beat, 'Waterloo Sunset' is firmly set in London, with Davies offering an outsider's view of the hubbub that surrounds the famous railway station of the title. Marking the end of the band's relationship with producer Shel Talmy, this was the first sign of The Kinks forging a new identity of their own.

The Kinks Lola

! 1970 • 4:03 • Davies

As The Kinks, the Davies brothers released a host of commercially and critically successful singles and albums, building a reputation from Ray Davies' poetic and observational writing style. One of the singles that helped the band maintain their longevity was the track 'Lola', written about a transvestite.

According to The Kinks' official biography, the idea for the track came to Davies after their manager got drunk at a club one night and started dancing with a woman (or so he thought). Towards the end of the night, the transvestite's stubble started to show but their manager had had one too many drinks to notice by that point... Released on June 12th 1970, the lyric

"You drink champagne and it tastes just like coca cola", had to be re-recorded as "cherry cola" since the BBC flatly refused to air the reference to a commercial brand. Along with the equally quirky 'Apeman', 'Lola' marked the end of classic-period Kinks. While Ray Davies continued to experiment with concept albums he wouldn't bag another bona fide hit until 1982's 'Come Dancing'. BdP / MOG

Klaxons Golden Skans

! 2007 • 2:45 • Klaxons

It's a sign of the times that Klaxons were first played on Xfm (on February 6th 2006) from a demo downloaded from their MySpace. The excitement around the band was such that we couldn't wait for any officially sanctioned recordings. The ecstatic ramshackle chaos of their live shows was even reflected in their name, then still in its full version: Klaxons (Not Centaurs). By the time 'Golden Skans' came out, the frenzy around the band had switched to a cautious optimism – the hope being that the band would be able to deliver on the hype that had grown around them in the preceding 12 months and that had helped lead to their apparently sizeable record deal with Polydor. Deliver they did, with a song that confounded expectations and showed that at the heart of the band was a love of pop. Instead of the frenetic uptempo and noisy madness of previous singles, here was a mid-paced number with a funky bassline breakdown and an instantly catchy wordless vocal refrain that, once heard, was never forgotten. Their biggest hit to date, it peaked at number seven in the UK charts a week before the release of their debut album *Myths Of The Near Future*.

Klaxons
It's Not Over Yet

! 2007 • 3:35 • Oakenfold – Davis

Klaxons were always open about their influences. Their debut single included a cover of the proto rave tune 'The Bouncer' by Kicks Like A Mule, and

their early gigs were parties where the soundtrack of early 1990s jungle combined with electro was as vital an ingredient as the band itself. No wonder the term "new rave" stuck. 'It's Not Over Yet' reworked and renamed the 1995 trance pop hit 'Not Over Yet' by Grace, epitomising the band's knack for welding guitars to dance in a way that taps into the naïve euphoria at the heart of all rock'n'roll. JK

The Knack
My Sharona

! 1979 • 3:58 • Fieger – Averre

One of the biggest songs of 1979, The Knack hit gold with their debut single from album *Get The Knack*. Formed by singer Doug Fieger after he made the decision to move to Los Angeles to start a band, they found almost instant stardom. Ironically, the demo of 'My Sharona' had been rejected by many record labels before The Beatles' label, Capitol Records, signed them up. This association – along with a Beatle-

'It's Not Over Yet' reworked and renamed the 1995 trance pop hit 'Not Over Yet' by Grace

like pose on the back cover of the album, which Fieger described as "a tongue-in-cheek joke" – led to unfavourable comparisons with Lennon and co. when, in fact, the band perhaps owed more to the likes of The Who and The Kinks. Beginning with its iconic guitar lick, which guitarist Berton Averre had written some time before, the track takes on a train-like rhythm, its pent-up nervous energy expressing Fieger's lust for the mysterious Sharona. Despite only costing $18,000 to make, the album was a classic and went on to sell six million copies worldwide. JS

The Kooks
Naïve

2006 • 3:23
Garred – Harris – Pritchard – Rafferty

Hailing from Brighton, The Kooks were signed to Virgin within three months of forming. They take their name from a Bowie song and have impeccable indie-pop credentials, though suffer slightly from repeated comparisons to Arctic Monkeys, with whom they have an ongoing rock tiff. The two bands released their debut albums on the same day and lead singer Luke Pritchard has claimed that he "had to kick Alex [Turner, Arctic Monkeys' singer] in the face after he tried to pull the leads out of my guitar pedals while we were on stage". The fourth and most successful single from their debut album, 'Naïve' was written by Pritchard when he was 16. It proved poppy and catchy enough to help win them an MTV Europe award for Best UK Act in 2006. Lily Allen and former Sugarbabe Mutya Buena have both covered the song.

The Kooks
Ooh La

2006 • 3:30
Garred – Harris – Pritchard – Rafferty

Echoes of The Kinks show through on The Kooks' sixth single from debut album *Inside In/Inside Out*. Acoustic guitars and a light touch belie the story of a pretty girl that the world "chewed up" and "spat out". Popular theories that the song is about Audrey Lindvall, an American model killed while out cycling, do not stand up to interrogation, as it was recorded a year before her death. Others, rather more convincingly, point to Luke Pritchard's ex-girlfriend Katie Melua as potential subject matter for the song. The Kooks have always used myriad influences in their music, and have never quite settled on a sound to call their own. In 'Ooh La', their thoughtful, sensitive lyrics find something like a natural home; they could do much worse than use this as a blueprint. JH

Kraftwerk
The Model

| 1978 • 3:43 • Hütter – Bartos – Schult

It's hard to underestimate the influence Kraftwerk had on music in the late 1970s and early '80s, especially in Europe. Hailing from Dusseldorf in West Germany and emerging from the progressive rock scene of the '60s, the quartet of Ralf Hütter, Florian Schneider, Karl Bartos and Wolfgang Flür brought electronic music to a mass audience and inspired a whole generation to tinker with keyboards, drum machines and sequencers. They came to the world's attention with the *Autobahn* album, whose 22-minute title track used synthesizers and homemade electronic percussion to evoke the mood of a motorway journey. Its hypnotic rhythms and deceptively simple German lyrics made it a chart hit in the UK. Subsequent albums – produced in the band's own Kling Klang studios – refined the formula, but Kraftwerk had an eye to the dancefloor and they moved away from their prog roots to experiment with more heavily-sequenced beats. 1977's *Trans-Europe Express* was later appropriated by New York DJ Afrika Bambaataa for the early hip-hop classic 'Planet Rock', while other celebrity admirers included David Bowie, who would play the band's albums before his live shows.

However, Kraftwerk's biggest hit came about by accident. Amid the sci-fi trappings of robots and futuristic cityscapes of 1978's *The Man-Machine* was 'The Model', a brief sketch concerning a character's infatuation with a woman he'd seen in a fashion magazine. In the meantime, Kraftwerk's presence had made itself felt in the UK – initially with bedroom synth-dabblers such as Cabaret Voltaire and The Human League, who took the blueprint laid out by the Germans and put their own British twist on the music. This new electronica suited itself perfectly to the burgeoning New Romantic genre which took hold at the turn of the '80s – the cold, clinical sound of the synthesizer reflected the highly fashion-conscious, yet seemingly emotionless world of the club kids. When, in 1981, EMI needed a B-side for the new Kraftwerk single 'Computer Love', they dipped into the band's last album... and found 'The Model'.

While the original German lyric is dryly sarcastic – Hütter even affects a silly voice at one point – the icy detachment of the English translation fitted the mood of Britain's club culture perfectly, and radio programmers found themselves overlooking 'Computer Love' and playing the flipside instead. 'The Model' quickly became a club classic, sitting perfectly alongside homegrown electronic acts like Depeche Mode and Gary Numan. The song shot to number one in the UK charts in February 1982 and Kraftwerk became the acknowledged godfathers of synth-pop. They weren't one-hit wonders, however, as their early records were later picked up by house and techno DJs in Europe and the US as perfect examples of the music of the future. MO'G

The La's
There She Goes

1988 • 2:39 • Mavers

The story of The La's is one of the most frustrating in rock history. They recorded just one album, which contains one of the most perfect pop tunes of the last 30 years – 'There She Goes'. But there was no follow-up, no superstardom. So what went wrong?

Formed in Liverpool in the early 1980s by original member Mike Badger, the band gave themselves a colloquial name in "La's" – as in the local way of saying "lad". A debut single, 'Way Out' was released in 1987 to a blaze of indifference, but their second single, 'There She Goes' was an instant classic. It first emerged in November 1988 and while it didn't make the "proper" charts, it was a monster indie hit.

Based around a deceptively simple guitar line, the track makes fine use of the soaring harmonies between Lee Mavers and guitarist John Power. At odds with the post-Smiths indie scene, their scruffy appeal made them look as if they'd been beamed in from the set of some 1950s skiffle movie.

Even when rumours started flying that the song was actually about heroin use – thanks mainly to the line "pulsing through my vein" – it didn't dent the appeal of the song. The band denied the drug reference anyway. The group then spent the best part of two years demoing, recording and then re-recording their debut album. They saw off experienced producers like John Leckie and Mike Hedges in pursuit of the perfect sound. One story had Mavers insisting on using authentic 1960s recording equipment, because it would have authentic 1960s dust on the valves inside and therefore give the music an authentic 1960s sound. Or something.

Finally, they arrived at the studio of Steve Lillywhite, who had launched U2's stellar career and it was these sessions that became the band's self-titled, debut album in November 1990. Despite the trauma, a re-issued 'There She Goes' was duly sent to where it belonged: the top 20.

Subsequently, The La's went into hibernation. Or, rather, Lee Mavers did, working with a revolving-door set of musicians. Power, meanwhile, formed Cast and cheerfully rode the wave of Britpop. Despite a brief and underwhelming reunion in 2005, rumours still abound that Mavers has a second album up his sleeve. But, as producer Mike Hedges told *The Guardian*, "[Lee's] standards were so high that you're never going to reach them. At some point you have to say, 'That's it, it's finished'."
BdP / MOG

Ladyhawke
Dusk Till Dawn

2008 • 2:37
Brown – Gabriel – Gray – Robinson

Who is Ladyhawke? Given that name one might be tempted to envisage a

Lady Gaga-type character with hawk claws and big eyes... scary. She is in fact the mysterious and enigmatic Pip Brown from New Zealand who complements her music with stunning, carefully thought-through artwork. 'Dusk Till Dawn' is from Ladyhawke's self-titled debut album. According to co-writer Hannah Robinson,

single on December 8th 2008. It turned out to be Pip Brown's most successful single to date (at the time of writing) in particular, reaching the top 10 spots in her native New Zealand and Australia. On her website, Ladyhawke (her stage name was taken from the 1985 Richard Donner film) gives some insight into

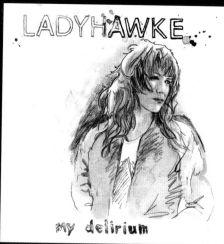

From left: 'Dusk Till Dawn', 'My Delirium'

inspiration for the track came from rather prosaic quarters: "... at the time Pip had just landed off a flight from New Zealand and was feeling very jet-lagged."

Ladyhawke
My Delirium

2008 • 4:19

Brown – Gabriel – Gray – Robinson

'My Delirium' is also from debut album *Ladyhawke* and it was released as a

the songwriting process for the track, similarly inspired by her exhaustive travelling: "I wrote the song a year and a half ago after days of no sleep due to terrible jetlag. I felt like I was going out of my mind. I was missing my friends and family back home, and I was basically living to hear my phone ring in hope that it would be one of them calling. So 'My Delirium' came out of me thinking I was going crazy from lack of sleep!" BdP

The Last Shadow Puppets
The Age Of The Understatement

! 2008 · 3:07 · Kane – Turner

'The Age Of The Understatement' was the first single to be released from the debut album of the same name by The Last Shadow Puppets. Alex Turner of Arctic Monkeys, Miles Kane of The Rascals and Simian Mobile Disco member James Ford put together the side-project band. They told the *Daily Record*: "We got the name The Last Shadow Puppets because a friend of ours was on the phone lying on her bed and she was doing shadow puppets on the wall. We thought it would be a good name and put the 'The' on to make it dramatic." The single raced to number nine in the UK singles chart and the album was released just a week later, going in at number one in the UK album chart. The album was also nominated for the 2008 Mercury Music Prize. BdP

LCD Soundsystem
Daft Punk Is Playing At My House

! 2005 · 3:28 · Murphy

You'd think that being offered the chance to be the first staff writer on *Seinfeld* would be your one shot at the big time. Not for James Murphy. When he turned down that opportunity he had his sights firmly set on one thing: a career in music. Since the age of 12, Murphy had spent his life playing in a number of bands such as The Extremes (thrash metal), Pony (punk) and Speedking (a rock band who refused to pose for photos), and later formed his own record label, DFA, working with acts from Britney Spears to N*E*R*D. No wonder then that the sound of Murphy's own project, LCD Soundsystem, so effortlessly breaks down the boundaries of rock, punk, rave and any other genre you care to throw into the mix.

The perfect example of this expert blending of musical differences is 'Daft Punk Is Playing At My House'. The fifth single to be released from LCD Soundsystem's self-titled debut album, the track is just as sharp as first single (and satirical dissection of what it is to be cool) 'Losing My Edge'. Listeners are transported to a teenage house party, with Murphy's punchy rock-rap vocals narrating from the host's point of view over the funkiest of basslines and handclaps.

Considering the importance of lyrics in LCD Soundsystem songs, Murphy has a casual approach to their conception. Talking to *Prefix* magazine about his work on the soundtrack for Noah Baumbach's 2010 film *Greenberg*, he confessed: "I don't know how to really write a song. Most of the lyrics I write are improvised or written on the day they're sung." Whatever his claims to lyrical amateurism, few dance/indie crossover acts are able to combine genres so effortlessly and effectively as LCD Soundsystem. JS

"The lyrics I write are improvised or written on the day they're sung" – James Murphy

Led Zeppelin

Led Zeppelin
Good Times Bad Times

1969 • 2:48 • Bonham – Jones – Page

As a means of introducing your new band to the world, the opening salvo that 'Good Times Bad Times' offers is not a bad one – especially when its bombast is followed by Robert Plant's air-raid siren voice exploding not far behind. In 1968, guitarist Jimmy Page and bassist John Paul Jones had already established themselves as session players of prominence, while drummer John Bonham was doing the same. This track, written by Jones after they had joined forces, would lay down the seeds of metal to come but, more importantly, would invent a heavy blues style that would counterpoint and accelerate the end of 1960s psychedelia.

Led Zeppelin
Whole Lotta Love

▌ 1969 • 5:34

▌ Page – Plant – Bonham – Jones – Dixon

If Led Zeppelin's debut album split its listeners into camps – those who disliked it (critics, generally) versus those who dived headlong into its hard blues, eastern and folk influences – *Led Zeppelin II* marked their arrival into the big time, even knocking The Beatles off the top of the US album charts thanks to the success of this, its lead single. It remained "just" an album track in the UK, thanks to Led Zeppelin manager Peter Grant's refusal to release British singles. It started with Jimmy Page's riff, unfurling into his dive-bombing guitars, leaving singer Robert Plant scratching around for lyrics. So he nicked some from the Willie Dixon-penned Muddy Waters song 'You Need Love', which cost them a court case come 1985.

Led Zeppelin
Immigrant Song

▌ 1970 • 2:25 • Page – Plant

Though Jimmy Page has protested that Led Zeppelin should not get the blame/credit for being heavy metal's forefathers, in tracks like 'Immigrant Song' the band find themselves without a leg on which to stand. Its hard, pummelling rhythm has become a staple rock tempo and Robert Plant's battle-cry lyrics about Vikings and Valhalla have since inspired countless metal acts to write about the very same topics. Penned after a classic gig in Iceland, Plant also made mention of "the hammer of the gods", an appropriate sobriquet for the very sounds Led Zeppelin were making and the future title of a lascivious biography detailing their more outrageous exploits.

Led Zeppelin Black Dog

▌ 1971 • 4:56 • Page – Plant – Jones

Led Zeppelin III's folk-orientated influences, written after the band had decamped to Bron-Y-Aur cottage in Wales, highlighted their diverse sound but, really, it was hard blues rocking that most of their fans wanted. Hence when their fourth album opened with this weighty riffathon, few were disappointed. Not until they tried to dance to it, anyway. Despite appearing to consist of bludgeoning simplicity, John Paul Jones' song winds through various complicated, shifting rhythms requiring intricate fretwork and some invention from drummer John Bonham. Robert Plant, however, eschewed the track's subtleties, writing instead about trying to get a girl into bed.

Led Zeppelin
Rock And Roll

▌ 1972 • 3:41

▌ Page – Plant – Jones – Bonham

Where 'Black Dog' left off, 'Rock And Roll' took up. Following hard on the heels of *Led Zeppelin IV*, it's a straight-ahead stomper, featuring boogie-woogie piano courtesy of The Rolling Stones' ivory-tinkler Ian Stewart. The song itself is just a simple 12-bar blues track given a hefty wallop of Led Zeppelin boot and came courtesy of the frustrating recording sessions for another album track, 'Four Sticks'. Beaten by that song's complex rhythms, drummer John Bonham hammered out the beat to 'Good Golly Miss Molly' instead. A 15-minute jam later, Led Zeppelin had knocked this together – perhaps one of their most well-known live classics.

Led Zeppelin
Kashmir

! 1975 • 8:29 • Page – Plant – Bonham

Having been tinkering around with a sitar and various Moroccan and Indian influences for a while, Jimmy Page finally layered them all together into one fabulous, exultant riff that simply soared from the grooves of Led Zeppelin's sprawling 1975 double album *Physical Graffiti*. As his guitars, a sweeping orchestra and various Mellotrons and keyboards unfurl, though, it is in drummer John Bonham's brilliantly simple beat – remarkably in a different time signature – that the song is unified. The band believed the song to be their finest, an amalgamation of everything that made Led Zeppelin what they were.
TB

Leftfield
Open Up

! 1993 • 3:48 • Barnes – Daley – Lydon

Old punk stars never really got to grips with the house revolution. Despite being repeatedly told acid house was the punk of its times, few tried and even fewer succeeded. In fact, there was perhaps only one example (unless you count musician-turned-manager-turned-JAMs/ KLF prankster Bill Drummond), when progressive house duo Leftfield finally coaxed John Lydon into the studio for 'Open Up' after two years of trying. Lydon had hit the end of the road with Public Image Limited and was yet to reform the Sex Pistols, when Neil Barnes of Leftfield approached him through John Grey, a friend since Pistols days.

Lydon turned up in the studio ready to go. Barnes later said: "I remember he came with all the lyrics written out – he'd hate me for saying that but he did, he had the whole thing written out from beginning to end, and he just went in and did it, he's a proper 'pro', I think the word is." 'Open Up' was brilliant, with Lydon's voice at its most demonic as he wailed "burn Hollywood, burn" against the piercing flares of Leftfield's electronics. It was an instant underground favourite, but its path to success wasn't clear. For starters Lydon's label had first dibs on any release, meaning the duo's own Hard Hands indie had to wait while they pondered. But they baulked at the asking price, giving Hard Hands a clear run, until the real world intervened in the form of fires raging through southern California the week of

He would always resent the song that made the band's name

– Evan Dando's ambivalence towards 'Mrs Robinson'

release. 'Open Up' was deemed a little too close to the truth, and dropped from the airwaves in a burst of sensitivity that was, probably unavoidable. It didn't stop the record climbing to number 13 in the UK charts, giving Leftfield their first proper hit and Lydon his first top 20 hit since 'Rise'. SY

The Lemonheads
It's A Shame About Ray

❗ 1992 • 3:07 • Dando – Morgan

Five albums, nine years and more than a few band members into their career, melodious indie rock band The Lemonheads – or, Evan Dando really, as he was by then the sole original element – finally struck on something approaching mainstream gold. Written with Tom Morgan, the singer of Australian indie band Smudge, this was Dando at his most winning: jangly, catchy pop-rock with a melancholic undertow. About a club owner who called everyone Ray because he has, as the song goes, "Never been too good with names", it would gently announce Lemonheads to a wider circuit, though it would take their next single, 'Mrs Robinson' to spread that influence.

The Lemonheads
Mrs Robinson

❗ 1992 • 3:44 • Simon

If Lemonheads singer Evan Dando had his way, the world would not necessarily have heard his band's version of this Simon and Garfunkel classic. Without it, though, chances are not much of the world would have heard of The Lemonheads.

In 1992, the band were languishing in the minor leagues of the indie circuit. They were an anomaly – too tuneful for grunge, too rock-inspired for most other genres. Formed in 1983 by Dando – born to a model mother and real estate agent father – they had bounced around from their Boston birthplace without really capturing anyone's attention other than to draw comparisons to Dinosaur Jr Noisy indie, melodic punk and then – after several band members had come and gone and a major label deal had been signed – a country direction had been tried. But Dando has always been a contrary soul and so, after that major label debut, he split the band, reformed it, disappeared to Australia, returned, then wrote arguably his best ever album in *It's A Shame About Ray*. It was a masterclass in pop-grunge, immediately accessible yet marked by a lingering darkness amid the breezy melodies. It was critically well-received, its creators were delighted with it, the band's existing fans loved it – but no one bought it. It skulked in the lower reaches of the album charts until Dando's record company, Atlantic, noticed that the band had recorded a pop-rock cover version of 'Mrs Robinson' and, despite The Lemonheads' resistance, released it as a single. The song, a beefed-up, riffed-up version of the acoustic original, made Dando a household name after it was added to the re-issued *It's A Shame About Ray*. However the pressures of that success sent Dando into a world of drug abuse, and he would always resent the song that made the band's name, reluctantly playing it live only when forced. TB

John Lennon

John Lennon
Plastic Ono Band
Give Peace A Chance

! 1969 · 4:51 · Lennon – McCartney

1969 saw John Lennon and Yoko Ono take to their beds in an attempt to campaign for peace via a series of high-profile events. During their second "bed-in" in Montreal, they decided to write a song for the movement, which they hoped would be adopted by anti-war protesters. The result was 'Give Peace A Chance', featuring another Lennon stream-of-consciousness lyric, combined with a communal chorus of friends, celebrities

and hangers-on. The result was so effective, it's still used as a rallying cry to this day.

John Lennon
Instant Karma!

! 1970 · 3:21 · Lennon

Written and recorded in the same day, and given an authentic 1950s sound by producer Phil Spector, this was John Lennon's third solo single and his last before The Beatles' split was officially announced. "I'm fascinated by commercials," he explained years later in an interview for *Playboy*. "The idea was like instant coffee, presenting something in a new form."

John Lennon
Working Class Hero

! 1970 · 3:51 · Lennon

The angriest song from John Lennon's debut solo album, this bitter diatribe against authority sounds like a twisted Bob Dylan track, thanks to its bare bones acoustic guitar. The f-word is deployed twice, making this track feel as far from the carefree days of The Beatles as is humanly possible.

John Lennon
Imagine

! 1971 · 3:04 · Lennon

John Lennon's most famous solo song – and his most misunderstood. Usually attributed as being part of his peace campaign, 'Imagine' was actually written two years later, when the former

Beatle became heavily involved with Britain's "new left" campaigners, and has more in common with 'Power To The People' than 'Give Peace A Chance'. While detractors scoffed at the line "Imagine no possessions" coming from a multimillionaire, the heart of the song is in the power of positive thinking. "If you can imagine a world at peace," he explained in 1980, "with no denominations of religion, then it can be true." The other inspiration came from Yoko Ono's 1963 conceptual book *Grapefruit*, which carried a series of haiku-like instructions. MO'G

The Levellers
One Way

! 1998 • 3:25 • The Levellers

Owing more to The Clash than The Saw Doctors, The Levellers' brand of insurrectionary folk-rock struck a universal chord in the early 1990s with their song 'One Way'. Written by bassist Jeremy Cunningham about life in Crawley with his dad, the song was set off by singer Mark Chadwick's rousing chorus. "I was living in Havens-Oost in Amsterdam and I'd met a girl in the worst circumstances," Chadwick told Xfm. "We had no money, it was terrible and she just said to me, 'Mark, there's only one way of life, and that's your own'. I thought, 'That's a lyric, I'll have that!'" The song was seized upon by new-age travellers as an anthem, but Chadwick maintains that wasn't the way

it was originally intended. "It was just supposed to be a brilliant statement," he told Xfm. "It can be interpreted any way. It could be a right-wing anthem, a left-wing anthem, an anarchist anthem... it falls into all the boxes."

The Levellers
What A Beautiful Day

! 1997 • 4:03 • The Levellers

In some ways, the song 'What A Beautiful Day' was The Levellers' greatest achievement. The sugar-coated chorus propelled one of the band's most politicised songs into the mainstream and became a huge hit. "Most people just hear the chorus – what a beautiful day," singer Mark Chadwick explained to Xfm. "The verses are actually talking about the history and politics of anarchy and revolution." It was a song written by Chadwick in the band's Metway studio complex in Brighton. Bashed off quickly, "about as long as it took me to play it". The song's potential became immediately apparent. "There was a guy upstairs who came down and said, 'That's a hit.' I told him I'd only taken four minutes to write it. He said, 'It's the first time I've heard it and I'm whistling it now. It's a hit.'" OH

"I'd only taken four minutes to write it"

– Mark Chadwick, 'What A Beautiful Day'

The Libertines

The Libertines
What A Waster

! 2002 • 2:58 • Barât – Doherty

The Libertines were one of the cornerstone bands of the new millennium. Formed in 1999, this English punk revival band comprised Pete Doherty (vocals/rhythm guitar) and Carl Barât (vocals/lead guitar), backed by bassist John Hassall and Gary Powell on drums. The legendary Mick Jones of The Clash produced both of their two albums for Rough Trade.

'What A Waster' was the very first single The Libertines produced; however, it wasn't initially included in debut album *Up The Bracket*. It was released on June 3rd 2002 in CD, seven-inch and download formats, but like other Libertine singles after it, suffered from significant returns due to the excessive swearing that featured in the lyrics – as was made clear from the opening lines: "What a waster, what a fucking waster / You pissed it all up the wall / Round the corner where they chased her". As a result, the song struggled to get any airplay across many UK radio stations, with many steering clear for fear of upsetting listeners. Eventually it was included as track 13 on *Up The Bracket* upon re-issue many months later.

The Libertines
Up The Bracket

! 2002 • 2:38 • Barât – Doherty

The title track of The Libertines' debut album, 'Up The Bracket' was made a single in its own right in September 2001. By now, the British music press was completely enamoured with the band, particularly Pete Doherty's tales of the fictitious "Albion", which found echoes in the patriotic days of Britpop. "A punch up the bracket" is a peculiarly English term, being a favourite of legendary Brit comic Tony Hancock.

The Libertines I Get Along

! 2002 • 2:51 • Barât – Doherty

The 12th track on the *Up The Bracket* album, the video for this track features the band performing in a clinical studio environment. A group of model-like girls storm into the room taking pictures of the band – who seem to be missing Pete Doherty – and crowding around each of the musicians. The to-the-point lyrics require little explanation ("I get along singing my song, people tell me I'm wrong... Fuck 'em!") and appealed squarely to their core audience of angst-ridden teenagers across the UK.

The Libertines
Time For Heroes

! 2003 • 2:40 • Barât – Doherty

Released on January 13th 2003, 'Time For Heroes' was the third single from album *Up The Bracket*. It went to number 20 in the UK and was one of the most requested tracks during The Libertines' live gigs. It's said that the lyrics for this track are based on Pete Doherty's experiences of brutality at the London May Day riots of 2001, hence the amusing line: "There are fewer more distressing sights than that / Of an Englishman in a baseball cap". Sadly, The Libertines' success would be eclipsed by their internal conflict, and the band went on to split up at the end of 2004.

The Libertines
Don't Look Back Into The Sun

2003 • 2:58 • Barât – Doherty

The lyrical 'Don't Look Back Into The Sun' was the fourth single The Libertines released on the Rough Trade label. Produced by Bernard Butler, former guitarist with Suede (as was original single 'What A Waster'), it was available as a single, but surprisingly not included on any albums.

The Libertines
Can't Stand Me Now

2004 • 3:23 • Barât – Doherty

'Can't Stand Me Now' – the first and most successful single from the album simply entitled *The Libertines* – went to number two in the UK singles chart, followed by the album reaching number one.

Despite the band's success, this song carries a bittersweet undercurrent. Doherty's romance with drugs was now at its height and relationships between the band members began to sour. Barât wrote the lyrics, which are shocking in their brutal honesty: "An end fitting for the start / You twisted and tore

> The bond between them couldn't be broken and the duo found themselves playing impromptu shows together

our love apart..." To hear Doherty sing the words is almost heartbreaking.

The Libertines
What Became Of The Likely Lads

2004 • 5:53 • Barât – Doherty

A typically ramshackle stormer, 'What Became Of The Likely Lads' was the final Libertines single to be released, in October 2004. Two months later, the band played a show in Paris before winding up, acrimoniously. Harking back to the classic 1970s British TV comedy *Whatever Happened To The Likely Lads*, the song is unbearably poignant as Barât and Doherty reflect on their career together. But it wasn't the end of the story. The pair went their separate ways – Barât to Dirty Pretty Things and Doherty to Babyshambles – but the bond between the two songwriters couldn't be broken and the duo found themselves playing impromptu shows together. In 2010, they announced a full-blown Libertines reunion at the Reading and Leeds festivals and even promised new material.
BdP / MOG

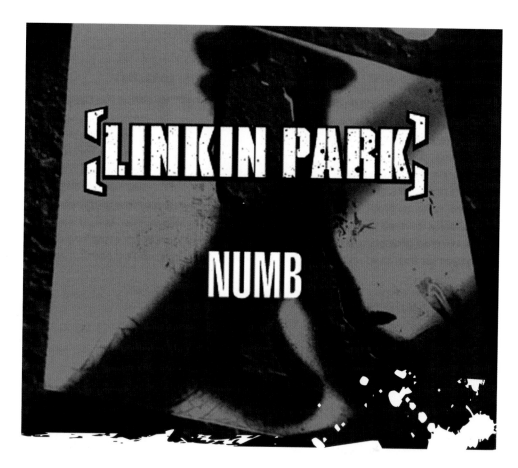

Linkin Park
In The End

! 2001 • 3:37 • Linkin Park

'In The End' was, ironically, the song with which Linkin Park cemented their arrival. From the mulch of turn-of-the-century rap-rock bands emerging from the US, this immediately stood out. There was something real in singer Chester Bennington's impassioned pleas, a vastness in the guitars and more than a little in the very marketable sound Linkin Park created that flung them headlong towards rock stardom. As the single clambered to top 10 chart positions around the world, there were red faces at the band's record company — they had urged a change in sound. "We had such a battle, it was really brutal," said Bennington. "This was sweet vengeance for us."

Linkin Park
Numb

! 2003 • 3:08 • Linkin Park

It was probably with this song that nu-metal reached its watershed moment.

With it, Linkin Park appeared to have concentrated their blueprint to such a point that, not only had they released perhaps their definitive track, but they also realised they could take the template no further. This is classic Linkin Park, from the opening synth ditty, through slick, giant riffs, singer Chester Bennington's self-loathing lyrics and Mike Shinoda's rap. 'Numb' proved nu-metal had come as far as it could and, perhaps appropriately, it closed the band's second album, *Meteroa*, prompting a change in direction for their third record.

Linkin Park
What I've Done

! 2007 • 3:25 • Linkin Park

'What I've Done' marked an adjustment in Linkin Park's sound. Even they had tired of the nu-metal template they had honed to stasis. They were cautious that their third album proper, *Minutes To Midnight*, shouldn't be seen as the completion of a trilogy in which their fans had lost interest.

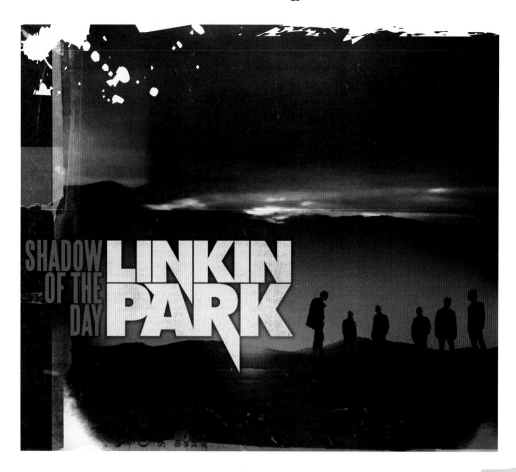

Out went the old way of working and this – epic, straightforward, less jiggered about by DJs and written chiefly by frontman Mike Shinoda and guitarist Brad Delson – was the result. "We wanted a song that encapsulated the feel of the whole record and I think this is that song," said Shinoda of their newfound deeper presence.

Linkin Park
Shadow Of The Day

| 2007 • 4:50 • Linkin Park

Lo-fi computer beats, ambient sounds, vocals not hewn from a full-blown crisis? Surely this can't be Linkin Park. Gone are the raging guitars, gone is the rapping, gone is everything that once defined this band. In fact, in its orchestral sweeps and gentle but catchy melody line, it sounds like Snow Patrol doing U2. This is Linkin Park mark two, the music derived from their decision to distance themselves from their nu-metal past. Released as the third single of their *Minutes To Midnight* album, their fans took a while to readjust and it charted moderately in the US but failed to crack the top 40 in the UK.

Linkin Park
New Divide

| 2009 • 4:30 • Linkin Park

Written specifically for the film *Transformers: Revenge Of The Fallen*, this was Linkin Park's first foray back into the studio after the release of their third album. The results were a curious mix of their desire to move forward into more classic rock territory, and an

Their fans took a while to readjust, and it charted moderately

– Linkin Park, 'Shadow Of The Day'

easing back into old habits. While there were few of the hip-hop influences that defined their early career, this was a song much affected by computers – from Chester Bennington's digitally tweaked voice to an electronic splurge of chaos midway through. All of which, perhaps, is appropriate given the plot of the film: a human caught up in a war of machines. TB

Longpigs

Longpigs She Said

1995 • 3:44

Hunt – Boyle – Stafford – Hawley

As obstacles to releasing a debut album go, your singer being involved in a car crash that puts him in a three-day coma is a big one. As is your record label going under. Such was the position the Longpigs found themselves in. Crispin Hunt having survived intact, they were picked up by U2's label, Mother Records. After re-recording the album, 'She Said' came out as their second single. Woozy guitars and repetitive piano chords are overlaid with unhinged vocals about, according to Hunt, "people who don't live up to their clothes, myself included". Although it made little impact then, a re-issue just after the album had been released gave the band their second UK top 20 hit and ensured their place in the indie halls of fame.

Longpigs On And On

1996 • 4:16

Hunt – Boyle – Stafford – Hawley

A beautiful love song with bittersweet lyrics, jerking guitar licks, swooning keyboard chords and heart-wrenching harmonies, this was the Longpigs' breakthrough hit. It gave them a UK top 20 hit, got them radio play on both sides of the Atlantic and made it onto the *Mission: Impossible* soundtrack. After the subsequent success of their debut album, a combination of strong personalities within the band, drink and drugs meant that, by the time their second album was released two years later, tensions had reached breaking point. Shortly after its release, the label folded and the band split. Guitarist Richard Hawley is now a Mercury Prize-nominated solo artist and singer Crispin Hunt is a writer and producer who has worked with Ellie Goulding and Natalie Imbruglia.
MS

> Woozy guitars and repetitive piano chords are overlaid with unhinged vocals about, according to Hunt, "people who don't live up to their clothes"
>
> – Peter Hunt on 'She Said'

Lostprophets
Last Train Home

! 2004 · 4:35 · Lostprophets

That Lostprophets were branded the UK's response to nu-metal says much about the state of British heavy rock at the turn of the century. The Welsh sextet came from the hardcore punk scene, counted a DJ among their ranks and were avowed Duran Duran fans. Simply, they didn't fit into a pigeonhole – so they were wedged into one instead. 'Last Train Home', the second single from their second album, meant pigeonholing became unnecessary. Slick, crafted and possessed of an effortless chorus, it was a definitive piece of post-millennium rock – radio-friendly,

inclusive and, above all, catchy. The single reached number eight in the UK but, more impressively, it topped the US Billboard Alternative Song chart, breaking the band in America, where they remain one of this country's more successful rock exports. The problem? Many in Britain thought the band *were* American after this track, something at which the Welshmen baulked.
TB

Liam Lynch
United States Of Whatever

! 2003 · 1:31 · Lynch

Probably the daftest song to ever break the UK top 10 (and that's quite an achievement, considering Britain's illustrious history of chart nonsense), 'United States Of Whatever' is a silly vignette that immortalises garbled Valley Girl speak and throws in a heap of distorted punk rock for good measure. Performed by comedian and former Liverpool Institute of the Performing Arts graduate Liam Lynch, the song originally appeared on his bizarre low-budget MTV sock puppet show *Sifl And Olly* in 1999 and was apparently improvised in one take. The song depicts a cocksure hoodlum protagonist encountering various peers or authority figures and silencing their admonishments and inanities with the deathless retort: "Yeah, whatever!" Part of the track's charm is its quaint 1950s *Grease/Happy Days* ambience that sees Lynch "on the corner, wearing my leather" or "throwing dice in the alley". If the Fonz had made a record, it would sound like this.
MO'G

The Maccabees

The Maccabees
About Your Dress

2007 • 2:14 • Jarvis – Thomas – Weeks – White – White

Forming in Brighton while at university, but with strong roots in south London, The Maccabees took their name at random from the Bible without any consideration of the possible religious connotations. Not that those were negative. Being named after Jewish rebels of the second century BC who rose up to defend their faith has a certain rock'n'roll resonance to it and seems particularly fitting for a band who inspire devotion. 'About Your Dress' is a good example of their appeal; the tiny details of a first encounter combined with anthemic guitars to powerful effect.

The Maccabees
Precious Time

2007 • 4:18 • Jarvis – Thomas – Weeks – White – White

It's the combination of the intimacy of Orlando Weeks' voice and the twin guitars of brothers Hugo and Felix White that is key to The Maccabees' magic. Against a powerful rhythm section, their songs twist and turn, breaking down to build back up to a series of rousing climaxes. On 'Precious Time', the guitars chime delicately while Weeks' intones "let's make time work for us"; the drums then rise to a crescendo before coming to an abrupt halt as the group join him to implore "let's take our precious time about it," as the crescendo begins again, finally exploding in soloing guitars. Played live, the crowd goes wild.

The Maccabees
Can You Give It

2009 • 2:54 • Jarvis – Weeks – White – White

Faced with the task of following up their propulsive debut album *Colour It In*, The Maccabees chose to create more light and shade for the follow-up, working with Markus Dravs who produced Arcade Fire's *Neon Bible*. *Wall Of Arms* is seen as darker and less bright-eyed than its predecessor, but the core ingredients of the band's sound remain. 'Can You Give It' is another rousing singalong, with an almost military drum pattern providing the foundation for shimmering guitars and their biggest chorus to date. Once again The Maccabees conjure a sense of friendship for those who want it.
JK

Magazine
Shot By Both Sides

1978 • 4:04 • Devoto – Shelley

"I'm not stupid and I refuse to pretend to be," proclaimed Howard Devoto, punk's most unashamed intellectual, in Magazine's first *NME* interview. Devoto had already quit Buzzcocks ('Shot By Both Sides' has the same riff as their 'Lipstick') to escape three-chord limitations and his new group were among the first definitively *post*-punk outfits. This, though, is one of their simplest, most brilliant, records, made in a brief period between keyboardists and with traditional driving guitar energy. Sparked by a political row with his girlfriend, 'Shot By Both Sides' was all about the individual in the heart of the mob, rejecting both sets of dogma, "on the run to the outside of everything". Devoto's contempt for entertainment's norms was such that their breakthrough *Top Of The Pops* performance turned to disaster, when he stood stock-still throughout the mime show. 'Shot By Both Sides' fell down the chart from number 41. Magazine never got so high again.
SY

Manic Street Preachers

Manic Street Preachers
You Love Us

1990 • 4:16 • Manic Street Preachers

The Manic Street Preachers arrived on the British music scene of the early 1990s in an explosion of stencilled shirts and eyeliner. Their proto-glam punk, allied to a fierce lyrical intelligence, was a breath of fresh air in a world bereft of real rock stars and music to truly believe in. The media may have been a little sceptical, but 'You Love Us' was Manic Street Preachers' glorious two-fingered salute to the non-believers.

"The song stemmed from the title," bassist Nicky Wire told Xfm. "We weren't exactly loved at the time and the song just seemed like a brilliant,

MANIC STREET PREACHERS
MOTORCYCLE EMPTINESS

"We can play anywhere and people know 'Motorcycle Emptiness', and that's really gratifying" – Nicky Wire

romantic, nihilistic statement of self-belief." Fans (or disciples), however, clung to every word of rock's four new ideologues. Here was clearly the beginning of a full-blown phenomenon.

Manic Street Preachers
Motorcycle Emptiness

1992 • 6:05 • **Manic Street Preachers**

Undoubtedly the centrepiece of debut album/manifesto *Generation Terrorists*, 'Motorcycle Emptiness' was where the band made good on their unswerving self-belief. Cut from the cloth of two old songs, 'Go Buzz Baby' and 'Behave Yourself Baby', James Dean Bradfield's neverending guitar solo kicked off a tune that suddenly made the Manics' claim that they would self-destruct after selling 17 million records (the number of copies Guns N' Roses' *Appetite For Destruction* had sold) believable.

"Although we were never going to sell our millions of records and split up, it certainly connected everywhere around the world," said Nicky Wire to Xfm recently. "We can play anywhere and people know 'Motorcycle Emptiness', and that's really gratifying."

Manic Street Preachers
From Despair To Where

1993 • 3:34

Bradfield – Moore – Wire – James

Second album, *Gold Against The Soul*, was the sound of a band in transition. A stepping-stone between the glitter-explosion of *Generation Terrorists* and

the intensely inward-looking *The Holy Bible*, 'From Despair To Where' was perhaps its most obvious manifestation. Classic rock motifs peppered the thrilling music, but guitarist Richey James' key lyric, "I try and walk in a straight line", was a sign that both he and the band were heading to darker places.

Manic Street Preachers
La Tristesse Durera
(Scream To A Sigh)

1993 • 4:13

Bradfield – Moore – Wire – James

Even in the process of musical transition, the band managed to unleash what's still widely regarded as one of their greatest singles. Having lifted the title from Van Gogh's suicide note (translated, "the sadness will never go away"), Nicky Wire handed the lyrics over to Richey James to complete. Coupled with a gently lilting drum track and a scorching guitar solo this, as Wire himself pointed out, felt like a band really coming together.

Manic Street Preachers
A Design For Life

1996 • 4:21 • Bradfield – Moore – Wire

'A Design For Life' was Manic Street Preacher's defining song under the worst possible circumstances. Following the disappearance of guitarist, lyricist, and chief conspirator Richey James, the band responded to a period of huge uncertainty by retreating to producer Mike Hedges' studio in the south of France. What emerged – a Phil Spector-influenced sweep of strings, chiming guitars, enormous choruses – was simply stunning. Touching on themes of class and privilege, and of the lack of social cohesion in a post-Thatcher Britain, 'A Design For Life' became an unofficial anthem for south Wales. Officially, it was the greatest musical comeback in history. "It was the song that made us carry on," Nicky Wire told Xfm. "Had we not have written something that good, I'm not sure we would have bothered any more."

near the Severn Bridge, an infamous suicide spot. Officially "presumed dead" on November 23rd 2008, the band had lost an integral part of its make up. If 'A Design For Life', however, was a sign that the band could carry on without their former provocateur, 'Everything Must Go' was its letter of explanation. "It was a big move," Nicky Wire told Xfm. "I think the worst thing we could have done was try to be the band on *The Holy Bible*. This was our way of explaining that."

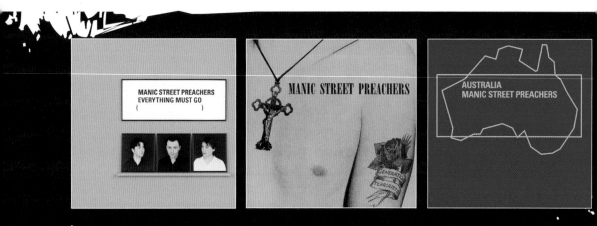

From left: 'Everything Must Go', 'Generation Terrorists', 'Australia', *This Is My Truth Tell Me Yours*

Manic Street Preachers
Everything Must Go

1996 • 3:41 • Bradfield – Moore – Wire

James Dean Bradfield and Richey James checked in to a hotel on Bayswater Road in London ahead of a promotional trip to America in early 1995. At 7am on the day of departure, February 1st, James checked out of the hotel. His car was found two weeks later parked at a service station

Manic Street Preachers
Kevin Carter

1996 • 3:25
Bradfield – Moore – Wire – James

Another brave move for the band as Sean Moore's plaintive trumpet refrain and skipping beat lays the foundation for one of the five sets of Richey James' lyrics that made it on to *Everything Must Go*. Crowning a hat-trick of top 10 singles

THIS IS MY TRUTH TELL ME YOURS
MANIC STREET PREACHERS

(a fourth would arrive with 'Australia'),
'Kevin Carter' was inspired by the Pulitzer-
prize photographer and represented an
assured musical step in an uncertain time.

Manic Street Preachers
Australia

❘ 1996 · 4:03 · Bradfield – Moore – Wire

Despite the band admitting that
'Australia' was destined to soundtrack
TV sports programmes like *Match Of
The Day*, the lyrics provided a more
personal account of Nicky Wire's state
of mind in the post-Richey James
fallout. Following the press furore
that followed James' disappearance,
'Australia' was the bassist's metaphor
for escape to the furthest place he
thought possible. "I only went to
Torquay in the end," Wire told Xfm.
"Not quite as glamorous is it?"

Manic Street Preachers
If You Tolerate This Your Children Will Be Next

! 1998 • 4:51 • Bradfield – Jones – Moore

'If You Tolerate This…' was originally destined for a B-side until a wily Sony executive sniffed a hit. Inspired by the Spanish Revolution and a homage to The Clash's 'Spanish Bombs', it became Manic Street Preachers' first number one and would go down in history as the chart topper with the longest title. Having seen 'A Design For Life' beaten to number two by 3,000 measly copies of Mark Morrison's 'The Return Of The Mac', this victory over pop group Steps was a huge achievement. "We were immensely proud of that song in every way," said Nicky Wire.

Manic Street Preachers
You Stole The Sun From My heart

! 1998 • 4:22 • Bradfield – Jones – Moore

This Is My Truth Tell Me Yours was the Manics' first album without any contribution from guitarist Richey James. Nicky Wire bore full lyric-writing duties as a result, which saw the album explore a more orthodox, poetic style as opposed to the densely-packed lyric sheets of his friend. Influenced by Welsh poet RS Thomas, it allowed Wire, by his own admission, to write this "love song, but a very negative one".

Manic Street Preachers
Tsunami

! 1998 • 3:50 • Bradfield – Jones – Moore

With its epic sweep, 'Tsunami' was the fourth and final single to be taken from *This Is My Truth Tell Me Yours*. It featured the use of a yangqin – an ancient Chinese hammered dulcimer – to create the song's distinctly oriental flavour. Hired in for the sessions at Rockfield Studios with producer Dave Eringa, the instrument prompted much scratching of heads before providing the key to unlocking this glorious song. "It was absolutely impossible to play," Nicky Wire remembered, "but it sounded fantastic."

Manic Street Preachers
Your Love Alone Is Not Enough

! 2007 • 3:55 • Manic Street Preachers

In a career that had contained more unexpected twists and turns than most, 'Your Love Alone Is Not Enough' heralded one of the sweetest. Admitting that they lost their way as a band during the recording of seventh album *Lifeblood*, Nicky Wire and James Dean Bradfield took a break to record solo albums. It clearly rejuvenated the Manics for the making of eighth album, *Send Away The Tigers*. This track with Cardigans singer Nina Persson brought about another resurgence in the band's popularity more than 18 years after their first single (a state of affairs nicely summed up by the title of another song on the album, 'Indian Summer'). "The idea was always that we'd do a duet with Nina that was going to be a massive radio hit and end up saving our career," said Nicky Wire to Xfm. "All of those things came true." OH

Marilyn Manson

Marilyn Manson
The Beautiful People

! 1997 • 3:45 • Manson – Ramirez

Like some crazed creature from the deepest darkest corner of the underworld, Marilyn Manson has always been what so many tousle-haired metalheads could only dream of becoming: a genuinely scary man. Not because he swears or shouts or wears an alarming quantity of make-up, though there's plenty of that too, but because you feel that you probably don't want to see what's inside his head. Marilyn Manson is both the name of the band and the lead singer: a deliberate conjugation of sex symbol and serial killer, which is fairly typical of their courting of controversy and relentless desire to shock. It also underlines their status as the ultimate misfits.

Generally considered as one of the band's strongest and most successful original songs, 'The Beautiful People' was a top 20 hit in the UK and regularly features in lists of the greatest ever heavy metal tracks. Manson himself has said that "I knew we'd arrived at our defining sound when we wrote it". A rocking, there's-a-train-coming drumbeat opens the track, soon to be followed by aggressively percussive riffing. "The beautiful people", Manson breathily rasps, over and over, with scorn and just the slightest hint that he might want to eat them. Throwing vitriol on the self-selecting "beautiful people" may not be that radical, but the zest with which Manson rails against the "fascism of Christianity" and the "fascism of beauty" has a mesmeric zealousness to it. Nietzschean themes of master-slave morality and the Superman run through the band's *Antichrist Superstar* album and here they particularly come to the fore, pushing the notion that the weak are oppressed by, and justify the existence of, the strong. At times as a band Marilyn Manson cross into shock-rock self-parody, but here their genuine belief in their own anarchic punk streak comes through. JH

"I knew we'd arrived at our defining sound when we wrote it"

Mansun
Wide Open Space

! 1996 • 4:34 • Draper

Some bands have fans; some have obsessive fans. Mansun's definitely fall into the latter category. When the band split during the final recording session for their fourth album, their fans successfully petitioned to have EMI release the unfinished album. 'Wide Open Space' came years prior to this, when relations were good between the four lads from Chester. Their sixth single – a haunting, upbeat song driven by a two-note riff that plays throughout – took a long time to finish. "I struggled for six months to find the lyrics for this song," recalls singer and guitarist Paul Draper. "I eventually got them from absorbing someone talking on TV which gave me the title, then I painted the imagery around that." Such imagery, along with their serious, cerebral sound, marked Mansun out as different from bands they'd previously been grouped with as part of a second wave of Britpop. It also led to their first album, *Attack Of The Grey Lantern*, debuting at number one in the UK album charts. A semi-concept album based around a fictional English village, it was as well received critically as it was commercially.

Although 'Wide Open Space' was not their biggest hit in terms of chart position and sales, it gave them some success in America (reaching the top 30 in the Billboard Modern Rock Tracks chart) and has become their best-known track. This was in part helped by alternative versions of the song appearing on Mansun's next four releases. Paul Oakenfold's 'Perfecto' remix made it a classic dance anthem, introducing the band to an entirely new demographic. After releasing two more successful albums, Mansun disbanded in 2003. At the time, no reason was given, but Draper revealed in 2008 that it was due to bassist Steve "Stove" King being sacked "for defrauding [their] accounts which led to the band splitting up".
MS

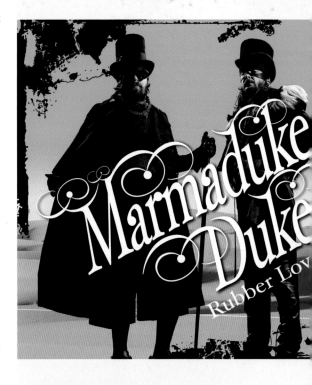

Marmaduke Duke
Rubber Lover

2009 • 1:54 • Reid – Neil

When Biffy Clyro singer Simon Neil and Sucioperro frontman JP Reid take time off from their day projects, they do so in admirably batty fashion. Their side project, Marmaduke Duke, is named after a Portuguese duke of the pair's own invention who travels the world partying and prophesying. Rarely do tracks written by two hairy rockers messing about in their downtime become summer club anthems yet, somehow, 'Rubber Lover' managed it. In Marmaduke Duke, Neil and Reid operate under the names The Atmosphere and The Dragon, and this song was written under

equally outlandish circumstances: ie at night while several sheets to the wind. "The next morning, we didn't really know what we'd made," said The Dragon. In fact, they had fashioned some classic dance-pop: sugary, eminently danceable and the polar opposite of their normal output. That a song ostensibly about a sex-doll received widespread airplay somehow only added to the project's subversive nature. TB

the kind of household where singing and performing were a part of every family get-together. He wrote this anthem while doing construction and landscaping jobs during school holidays, trying out words as he worked the machinery. A quietly building, chugging rhythm on guitar leads into Mason's dreams of a brighter world. "We can do better than this" is the message, sung in a voice and manner that doesn't preach or

> [Mason] articulated the thoughts of his generation, with a song that led him to being described as the new Bob Dylan

Willy Mason
Oxygen

! 2005 • 3:03 • Mason

Hope was a scarce commodity in pre-Obama America. Reeling from 9/11, caught up in a senseless war and with President Bush still in power, it was no wonder that many in the artistic community – from Neil Young to R.E.M. – felt it imperative to create some form of response. But it was a teenager from Massachusetts who really articulated the thoughts of his generation, with a song that led him to being described as the new Bob Dylan. The son of disaffected folk singers who left New York in favour of the rural idyll of Martha's Vineyard, Willy Mason grew up in

lecture, but is more like a friend offering advice. He moves from personal hopes to wider concerns from line to line, each so quotable that they'd all need to be printed here to do them justice.

Mason was 19 when he released the song himself as a solo acoustic recording in 2004 on what became known as the *G-Ma's Basement* EP. He re-recorded it for his debut album *Where The Humans Eat* with his brother Sam on drums, and it entered the UK singles chart on its release in 2005. 'Oxygen' is the kind of song that stops you in your tracks the first time you hear it and continues to do so way beyond the era in which it was created. JK

Massive Attack

Massive Attack
Unfinished Sympathy

1991 • 5:12 • Marshall – Vowles – Del Naja – Sharp – Nelson

Massive Attack were formed from the embers of Bristol collective The Wild Bunch. Although only three in number, Grantley "Grant" Marshall ("Daddy G"), Andrew Vowles ("Mushroom") and Robert Del Naja ("3D") believe in a collaborative approach and often work with other artists on their tracks. They pioneered a new style of dance music, commonly termed "trip-hop," although the band have never liked that term or recognised themselves as founders of the genre.

Debut album *Blue Lines* was released in 1991 to widespread critical acclaim and has gone on to be hugely influential in British dance music. The standout track on the album is 'Unfinished Sympathy', which remains one of the most moving pieces of dance music ever written. It begins with a simple slow beat before bursting into life with percussion and strings. Shara Nelson's vocals define the track, with a wonderfully rich and emotive voice that sounds like it would be more commonly found on a soul track coming out of Detroit, rather than a dance track from Bristol. 'Unfinished Sympathy' was released as a single in

February 1991 under the temporary band name, Massive – following threats of censorship due to the ongoing Gulf War conflict and fears within the band that the name Massive Attack might give the wrong impression that the band supported the war. The song was accompanied by a music video, which became pioneering in its own right. Shot in Los Angeles and featuring Nelson singing the song through the streets, oblivious to the goings on around her, it was one of the first music videos to use one continuous shot and has been mimicked numerous times since, perhaps most notably by The Verve on 'Bittersweet Symphony'.

Massive Attack
Teardrop

1998 • 5:31 Del Naja – Marshall – Vowles – Fraser

The release of Massive Attack's third album *Mezzanine* in 1998 saw a change in musical direction. The album was darker than previous works and for the first time guitars were prominent. 'Teardrop' stood out as a song with a lighter touch, predominantly due to the sugar-sweet vocals of ex-Cocteau Twin Elizabeth Fraser. Robert Del Naja revealed that the lyrics, written by Fraser, were a poignant eulogy to her good friend Jeff Buckley. The track gained wider recognition through the accompanying video, featuring an unborn baby floating gently through the womb and singing along to the lyrics, making it a regular feature in "best video" polls. 'Teardrop' was the second single to be released off the album and reached number 10 in the UK charts in April 1998. MM

Maxïmo Park

Maxïmo Park
Apply Some Pressure

2004 • 3:20
English – Lloyd – Smith – Tiku – Woolle

Released a few months ahead of debut album *A Certain Trigger*, the breathless urgency of 'Apply Some Pressure' crashes straight in – sharp guitars and Paul Smith's almost shouted vocals don't detract from its instant catchiness. Producer

Mark Ronson was such a huge fan of the band that he decided to include the track on his breakthrough album *Version*. However, unlike most of the songs on that album, he felt no other singer could match Smith so invited him to sing on the cover. The song was re-released nine months later. Although its chart position was only improved by three places, it led to increased airplay that ultimately helped the album reach platinum status.

MAXÏMO PARK

BOOKS FROM BOXES

"You would put down your drink and run to the dancefloor before the vocals kicked in"

– Paul Smith explains the term, a "pint dropper" song

Maxïmo Park Graffiti

2004 · 3:05

English – Lloyd – Smith – Tiku – Woolle

Being asked to meet someone in a park who then tells you your song is a "pint dropper" is an odd way to start an illustrious musical career, but so it was for Maxïmo Park. Having heard their self-funded debut release, Steve Beckett from Warp Records did exactly that. "He meant," explains singer Paul Smith, "that if you were in a club and it came on the sound system, you would put down your drink and run to the dancefloor before the vocals kicked in." Given a Paul Epworth-produced makeover for its 2005 re-release, none of that effect was lost, thanks to the song's wall-of-sound guitars and frantic organ chords battling with Smith's strong voice and pronounced Newcastle accent.

Maxïmo Park Our Velocity

2006 · 3:18

English – Lloyd – Smith – Tiku – Woolle

For such a big indie disco hit, the subject matter of this track is bleak. "When I was writing the lyrics to this song, war was pretty inescapable on TV," said Paul Smith. "I tried to think about what it must be like to be away from home and also how the people in charge must feel when they make massive, life-changing decisions." The first single to come from what would be their second double-platinum-selling album, it flits between juddering keyboard sounds and crashing guitars. Their first UK top 10 hit, the

song also made it onto two computer games: an incarnation of *Guitar Hero* and Xbox 360's *Project Gotham Racing 4*.

Maximo Park
Books From Boxes

2007 · 3:28
English – Lloyd – Smith – Tiku – Woolle

A personal favourite of singer Paul Smith's, he describes the song as "our early-R.E.M. moment". Gentler than the frantic pace of many of their other tunes – though not quite slow enough to be classed as a ballad – it's a melancholy ode to the inevitable end of a romance. The second single to come from the Gil Norton-produced album *Our Earthly Pleasures*, it became their fifth UK top 20 hit.
MS

The MC5

The MC5
Kick Out The Jams

**1969 · 2:49 · Davis – Kramer –
Smith – Thompson – Tyner**

Without The MC5, it's likely there'd have been no punk and the musical landscape of the last 30 years would have been very different. Their deeply political take on dumb garage-rock emerged at a time when the counter-culture was on the rise in the US and while their discography wasn't huge and their actual hits were few and far between, their rabble-rousing music left a significant legacy. The band were formed in the Detroit area in the early 1960s by guitarists Wayne Kramer and Fred "Sonic" Smith. They were joined by singer Rob Tyner, who also coined the band's name – The MC5 – which stood for "Motor City Five," in tribute to Detroit's car-manufacturing history.

Known for their uproarious live shows, the band soon forged affiliations with various radical political groups, including the White Panthers. Founded by John Sinclair (later immortalised in a John Lennon song), this collective supported the Black Panthers, the revolutionary African-American organisation dedicated to racial equality. In their first manifesto, Sinclair famously stated: "Our programme of rock and roll, dope and fucking in the streets is a

programme of total freedom for everyone." And The MC5 were to be his standard-bearers. In the politically turbulent year of 1968, the band performed a staggering eight-hour set during the protests at the Democratic Convention in Chicago, which preceded a week of violence and riots. Such publicity brought the group to the attention of Danny Fields of Elektra Records, who signed The MC5 and their "little brother band" The Stooges.

The '5's debut album, *Kick Out The Jams*, was recorded live at the Grande Ballroom over two nights in October 1968 and features the band at their powerful best. The title track is a raging garage rock rant notorious for Tyner's opening declaration to "KICK OUT THE JAMS, MOTHERFUCKERS!" "We first used the phrase when we were the house band at a ballroom in Detroit," Kramer explained to the press at the time. "We played there every week with another band from the area. We got in the habit, being the sort of punks we are, of screaming at them to get off the stage, to kick out the jams, meaning stop jamming." While the record label offered a censored version of the album against The MC5's wishes, the statement has echoed down the age as an expression of anarchic frustration and the group has influenced countless bands, including The KLF who sampled Tyner's words for the opening of their rave anthem 'What Time Is Love?' The song remains a rock'n'roll rallying cry and was fittingly the first record to be played on Xfm following its official full-time station launch in September 1997.
MO'G

McAlmont & Butler
Yes

! 1995 • 4:53 • McAlmont – Butler

One of the most exhilarating but short-lived partnerships of the 1990s produced one of the highlight singles of the decade. After breaking up his indie duo Thieves, singer David McAlmont joined forces with guitarist Bernard Butler, who had recently quit from Suede. They recorded a few EPs' worth of songs, including the majestic 'Yes' (a UK top 10 hit) and 'You Do' (a UK top 20 hit) before acrimoniously splitting and vouching never to work together again. This left the label with a collection of EPs and other material, which made up the platinum-selling album, *The Sound Of McAlmont & Butler*. As it turned out the duo did work together again for another album in 2002 called *Bring It Back*.
MW

The Members
Sound Of The Suburbs

! 1979 • 3:15 • Carroll – Tesco

I grew up in a town called Camberley, in the heart of the London commuter belt – the very same suburbs where The Members formed. There isn't a statue or plaque, but there is a great big Tesco supermarket, which perhaps in some way is a tribute to band frontman Nicky Tesco. Tesco had hastily put together the band within days after a chance meeting at a party led to the offer of an audition. It would not be until two years later that the band settled on their final lineup, headed by Tesco and guitarist Jean-Marie Carroll (Tesco being

the only remaining member from those first auditions). A Sex Pistols-inspired punk record, 'Sound Of The Suburbs' became the band's signature tune – full of energy, lyrics spat out by Tesco with suitably boisterous cockney-lad swagger. It went on to sell 250,000 copies. Carroll once said it was also a song the band were originally reluctant to use: "I have to say, it took me a long time to persuade them to play ['Sound Of The Suburbs']. The first time we played it the crowd went bananas and we kind of knew that it would be a hit."
JS

Mercury Rev
Goddess On A Hiway

| 1998 · 3:45 · Donahue

Mercury Rev shocked everyone, perhaps themselves most of all, by making a hit album in *Deserter's Songs* after ten years of earnest plugging away at the margins. 'Goddess On A Hiway' was its opener – an exuberant, elegiac voyage into anything from a doomed relationship to Mother Earth. Despite the sense of a group finally finding their feet (the occasional presence of two members of rock legends The Band can't have hurt), the album was recorded while singer Jonathan Donahue was strung out on heroin and guitarist Grasshopper decamped to a Jesuit Spanish monastery to sort his head out. It obviously worked.

Mercury Rev
The Dark Is Rising

| 2001 · 3:54
| Donahue – Grasshopper – Mercel

After the commercial breakthrough (in the UK at least; they remained strictly on the sidelines in their American home) of *Deserter's Songs*, Mercury Rev delivered what was for them the biggest surprise of all – more of the same. This most fractious of bands have always had a tendency to wander off – sometimes leaving the stage mid-song, just to get a drink. But after lead singer David Baker departed, the remaining members acquired a kind of stability, settling into a sound somewhere between The Flaming Lips (with whom singer Jonathan Donahue had once played) and the grandiose rock of 1970s Pink Floyd.

'The Dark Is Rising' begins like a Bond theme, with an orchestral crescendo crashing into Donahue's fey falsetto. The strings keep returning at the end of every verse, effectively playing the role of the chorus. Just as the band find their most expansive sound, Donahue seems to be mocking their own pretensions. "I always dreamed of big crowds / Plumes of smoke and high clouds" he sings over the gentle piano, before the orchestra answers him with a bang. Incredibly, such an uncommercial song provided the band with their biggest hit, breaking into the top 20. Though it was business as usual in the States, where the album's sales weren't helped by its release date, September 11th 2001.
SY

Metallica
Enter Sandman

1991 · 5:32
Hammett – Hetfield – Ulrich

'Enter Sandman' and the eponymous Metallica album (known as *The Black Album*) heralded a strange new dawn for Metallica. For the past ten years they were the uncompromising and unsightly metal band who may have had a devoted set of fans, but whose music remained very much of a defined scene. Household names they were not, despite impressive record sales. What they were known as, though, was the "people's band". Over four previous albums they gave up and put out for their fans and, though they were still successful, they symbolised what could be achieved without "selling out". That most of the rest of America had no clue who they were was almost part of the appeal.

But 'Enter Sandman' would change that. From its opening riff to its elemental chug and knife-sharp soloing, it would become exactly the sort of metal track that people that didn't much care for metal liked. And so, just as Guns N' Roses and AC/DC had done before them, Metallica would cross over quite spectacularly into the mainstream, leaving a fair few bitter diehard fans muttering in their wake. Developed from a riff written by the band's quiet lead guitarist Kirk Hammett,

'Enter Sandman' showed a new resolution in Metallica to head for simpler, more commercially fertile waters. Previously their work had grown from thrash into a more complicated musical beast. Here though, the formula was straightforward – write a good riff in the first place, then stick with it. It lured in those non-metal fans who had previously dismissed the band, inviting them to spend time with the rest of an album that was a heavier listen than many would normally contemplate. And what they heard, they liked. Almost immediately, Metallica went from the leaders of the underground to a stadium-sized, world-conquering act.

Metallica
Nothing Else Matters

1992 · 6:29
Hetfield – Hammett – Ulrich

The Black Album had already elevated Metallica from the shadows to wider world attention but, with Nirvana and grunge already exploding, the perch of the biggest metal band in the world was not a stable one. Or at least it wouldn't have been had Metallica not had a range of contours and contrasts. 'Nothing Else Matters' provided exactly the depth that would keep people listening as Kurt Cobain and co. slayed the rest of hair metal. Sweeping orchestras, a pretty guitar line and James Hetfield's hushed vocals were as welcome as they were surprising to those who had Metallica pegged as unruly riff merchants. TB

MGMT
Time To Pretend

2007 • 4:21
VanWyngarden – Goldwasser

After bonding over a love of music at Wesleyan University, Connecticut, Ben Goldwasser and Andrew VanWyngarden slowly began piecing together their own vision under the moniker Management. The indie release of their *Time To Pretend* EP piqued interest in taste-making circles large enough for Columbia Records to sign the pair. Having shortened their name to MGMT, the band were packed off to work with venerable producer Dave Fridmann, famed for honing The Flaming Lips' similarly kaleidoscopic musical palette. A re-recorded 'Time To Pretend' was the first taste of album *Oracular Spectacular*, with its lampooning of rock star excess, chiming synths and other-worldly effects. Suddenly, the idea of a new "summer of love" seemed like a very good thing indeed.

MGMT Electric Feel

MGMT
Kids

2007 • 5:02
VanWyngarden – Goldwasser

A minor furore engulfed the band's most well-known song when, in 2008, it was used without permission by French President Nicolas Sarkozy's political party, the UMP. Band lawyer Isabelle Wekstein described the song's use (at a party conference and in two online videos) as "acts of counterfeiting", which she swiftly dealt with. Despite the controversy, 'Kids' was universally well received and, as well as topping numerous end-of-year polls, it was nominated for a Best Pop Performance Grammy. OH

MGMT Electric Feel 2008 • 3:49 • VanWyngarden – Goldwasser

The critical success of *Oracular Spectacular* and second single 'Electric Feel' stoked up the fervour surrounding MGMT to hysterical levels. One of the few publications in the world to maintain a cool head, however, came from surprisingly close quarters. Bruce VanWyngarden, lead singer Andrew's dad and editor of the *Memphis Flyer*, admitted the conflict of interest might be awkward for music writers on his paper, stuck between a rock and a hard place over how to critique his son's band objectively. "No matter that MGMT has been praised and dissed and profiled by every major music publication and music blog around the globe," he wrote in his blog, "it's still a ticklish deal for our guys."

Moby

Moby
Why Does My Heart Feel So Bad?

! 1999 · 3:44 · Hall

After the critical beating and lack of commercial success received by his 1996 punk-rock album *Animal Rights*, Moby (born Richard Melville Hall) genuinely believed that new record *Play* would have no audience. As he told Xfm in June 2010: "*Play* was supposed to be this weird marginal record that nobody would review, let alone buy." It went on to sell over ten million copies and is the biggest-selling album of its genre. 'Why Does My Heart Feel So Bad?' was originally recorded in 1992 as, in Moby's own words, "a very tacky techno record".

Moby Natural Blues

! 1999 · 8:09 · Hall

'Natural Blues' was one of a number of songs on 1999 album *Play* that were inspired by, and used samples from, a 1993 album called *Sounds Of The South* – a compilation of field recordings of traditional blues and gospel singers from the American South. Moby says that he wanted the music on 'Natural Blues' to pay homage to the original vocal of American folk singer Vera Hall, which appears on the track and which was recorded in 1937.

Moby Porcelain

! 2000 · 4:00 · Hall

'Porcelain' started life as an instrumental that Moby had written for a film in 1998 but, inspired by New Order's *Power, Corruption & Lies* (one of Moby's favourite albums), he decided to put a vocal on it. He told Xfm that he was very unsure of the song and had to be convinced by his manager even to include it on the album. He explained: "At the time I was quite intimidated by the perfection of club records by The Prodigy and The Chemical Brothers, and the radio was full of very loud bombastic music by the likes of the Backstreet Boys and Limp Bizkit. I didn't think that *Play* was particularly well mixed or recorded by me, at home, and I was a little embarrassed by it." Nowadays, he says, he realises that it's the imperfection of songs like 'Porcelain' that gives them an "unfinished, earnest and honest emotional connection". 'Porcelain' became Moby's biggest hit single to date – reaching number three in the UK in June 2000. MW

The Mock Turtles
Can You Dig It?

! 1991 · 3:56 · Coogan

This was the standout single for Manchester band The Mock Turtles, enjoying two spells in the chart – 'Can You Dig It?' was re-released in 2003 after being featured in a Vodafone advertising campaign. Starting life as a B-side, the record came about largely by chance because, as singer Martin Coogan (brother of comedian and actor Steve) explained to Xfm, they needed to come up with the flip-side to 'Lay Me Down': "We had a single release date and because of the length of time it took to print the sleeve, I had to come up with the title before I'd written it." Having settled on 'Can You Dig It?', Coogan wrote the song that night, taking time out from a dinner party to complete the lyrics. After the band signed their first "major" record deal, the track was re-released as a single and was well received, only outsold during its time in the charts by Chesney Hawkes' 'The One And Only'. JS

Modest Mouse
Float On

| 2004 · 3:28 · Brock – Modest Mouse

Formed in 1993 in Issaquah, a suburb of Seattle, Modest Mouse collected indie achievements like an enthusiastic Scout collects badges. They recorded singles for the ultra-cool Sub Pop and K record labels; bluesman Seasick Steve produced early

"The record company were kinda fearful there wouldn't be a record at all"

records; they kick-started a resurgence in Portland's influential music scene; and, more importantly, they pushed American indie back into the mainstream at a time when it seemed dead and buried. 'Float On' was the catalyst for these musical darlings to go spectacularly overground. When Modest Mouse moved to Oxford, Mississippi, to record parent album *Good News For People Who Love Bad News*, however, the signs were anything but encouraging. "The band was in a shambolic state when they showed up," said producer Dennis Herring. "They had a drum set but no drummer, they only had one or two songs that they could play from start to finish and the record company were kinda fearful there wouldn't be a record at all."

Once Herring and Modest Mouse began stitching together pieces of ideas, however, the band's new sound and vision slowly came to life. "They definitely wanted to take Modest Mouse to a new place, and in that way the process felt really good," remembers Herring. 'Float On' arrived after the record company had granted the band a little more time to record two extra tracks. Starting with just the distinctive guitar line and a few of singer Isaac Brock's excellent lyrics, the team put together a song that would become Modest Mouse's first commercially significant single and push the album to platinum status. It was an unlikely victory, catapulting a distinctly odd band into the hearts of mainstream America. And perhaps most bizarrely of all, it led to a commissioned painting of Brock, in lederhosen, being hung in the mayor of Portland's office. OH

Morrissey
Suedehead

! 1988 • 3:55 • Morrissey – Street

When Johnny Marr announced that he'd
left The Smiths, the world wondered if
the band would carry on without him. It
was not to be – the group officially split in
September 1987 and Morrissey embarked
on a glittering solo career. His choice of
collaborators for his first album *Viva Hate*
raised some eyebrows – Vini Reilly, who, as
the Durutti Column, had released a string
of delicate instrumental albums on the
Factory label, and former Smiths producer
Stephen Street. Any worries about their
ability were quashed when 'Suedehead'
appeared in February 1988. With a title
lifted from Richard Allen's 1971 novel of
skinhead life, elliptical lyrics based on a
needy relationship, and a shimmering Reilly
guitar riff, Morrissey's solo years were
off to a flying start. The nation remains
divided as to whether Moz sings "It was
a good lay" on the fade out, however.
The man himself wasn't saying, although
he once claimed that such a line "might
amuse someone living in Hartlepool".

Morrissey
Every Day Is Like Sunday

! 1988 • 3:36 • Morrissey – Street

Morrissey's lyrical
world seems stuck in
the early 1970s, with
camp TV personalities,
power cuts and
unfashionable trousers
prevalent. So his ode to gloomy seaside
summer holidays is hilariously bleak,
comparing it to the Sabbath before the
Sunday trading laws changed. In an echo of
John Betjeman's famous line, "Come, friendly
bombs, and fall on Slough!" Morrissey
daydreams about the whole wretched town
being flattened in a nuclear explosion.

Morrissey
The Last Of The Famous
International Playboys

! 1989 • 3:42 • Morrissey – Street

It was a relief for Moz-watchers to find
their hero's obsession with 1960s icons
continued unabated into his solo years.
This single fantasises about notorious
gangsters the Kray twins – Reggie and
Ronnie – who alternately charmed and
terrorised the East End of London until
their imprisonment in 1969. "The level of
notoriety that surrounded them," Morrissey
said in 1989, "the level of fame they gained
from being unreachably notorious. When
you reach that stage, you are admired."
MO'G

Morrissey
The More You Ignore Me,
The Closer I Get

! 1994 • 3:43 • Morrissey – Boorer

Morrissey's fourth solo album since leaving
The Smiths, *Vauxhall And I* found him in
contemplative mood, wondering whether
to continue with his career and plumbing
a depth of emotion he would never again
reveal with such intimacy. He spent much
of the record sardonically investigating his

life, not necessarily liking what he saw. Here though he appears to be taking a swipe at his former bandmate, Mike Joyce, who would soon take Morrissey to court over The Smiths' songwriting royalties. "I bear more grudges / Than lonely high court judges", run Morrissey's soon-to-be prophetic words.

Morrissey
Irish Blood, English Heart

! 2004 • 2:37 • Morrissey – Whyte

 Absent for seven years – at least in terms of studio output – Morrissey had much to prove on his return in 2004. In that time away he had found himself without a label, involved in an ongoing debate about his views on race, and with the bitter aftertaste of a court case surrounding songwriting royalties of his former band The Smiths. 'Irish Blood, English Heart' was his first foray back into the limelight and the track brought with it a newly polished and more overtly commercial sound than before. It worked, too; Morrissey's exploration of his heritage went to number three in the singles charts, the highest he had ever achieved.

Morrissey
First Of The Gang To Die

! 2004 • 3:38 • Morrissey – Whyte

With interest in Morrissey reasserted by the success of *You Are The Quarry*'s first single 'Irish Blood, English Heart',

'First Of The Gang To Die' – its second single – found a receptive audience keen for more Moz. They also got a better song, too. A dissertation on street crime it may have been, but it also featured some of the sharpest writing Morrissey had unveiled in years – something for which he can thank Alain Whyte, his longstanding co-conspirator. Here was Morrissey in accessible mode, demonstrating that a lightness of touch, musically, need not diminish lyrics detailing dark subject matter. TB

Motörhead
Ace Of Spades

! 1980 • 2:47 • Clarke – Kilmister – Taylor

The metal band even punks liked, Motörhead ditched the excesses of the genre (no dungeons and dragons or hour-long guitar solos here) for heads-down speed rock and uncomplicated biker imagery. This was their anthem, a fabulous celebration of gambling that sounded like a 'Viva Las Vegas' for people who would've been frogmarched from casinos. Though frontman Lemmy Kilmister admitted he was more of a fruit machine man than a card-player, no one ever doubted this former Hendrix roadie and Hawkwind bassist walked it like he talked it. It got them a rare *Top Of The Pops* appearance, but is best remembered for turning up in anarchic 1980s TV sitcom *The Young Ones* when the flatmates race off to appear on *University Challenge*. SY

Mumford & Sons
Little Lion Man

2008 · 4:05 · Mumford & Sons

With influences including Miles Davis, Bob Dylan, Coldplay, Arcade Fire and the songs of long-time friends Noah And The Whale and Laura Marling, it's not hard to see how Mumford & Sons' music manages to feel simultaneously novel and familiar.

The band emerged from a country and folk club in west London, run by banjo player Winston Marshall. School friends Marcus Mumford, keyboardist Ben Lovett, and Noah And The Whale's Matt Owens would cram in alongside bassist Ted Dwane and other musicians, all taking it in turns to get up and play with each other. Eventually, the four of them began playing, writing and then releasing Lovett-produced EPs on Chess Club Records. 'Little Lion Man' first appeared on their second EP, *Love Your Ground*. A storming, banjo stomper with angry lyrics, it caught the attention of critics and fans in the UK and Australia, where it was voted number one in Triple J's Hottest 100 for 2009 – a poll of 1.1 million listeners.

Mumford & Sons
The Cave

2009 · 3:33 · Mumford & Sons

Described by Marcus Mumford as "one of my heroes", Markus Dravs (Arcade Fire, Coldplay) was called in to produce their debut album. *Sigh No More* came out in late 2009: it entered and then re-entered the top 10, and stayed in the UK top 40 for several months. Initially

released as lead track on their final EP for Chess Club, 'The Cave' – a rambunctious hoe-down full of the band's trademark four part harmonies and urgent banjo chords – made it onto the record. Re-issued in 2010, it repeated the success of former singles in both the UK and Australia.

Mumford & Sons
Winter Winds

2009 · 3:40 · Mumford

With its blowsy horns and soaring choruses, 'Winter Winds' is a rousing but more reflective song than previous singles. The song was heavily influenced by the Avett Brothers' album *Four Thieves Gone*. Banjo player Winston Marshall explained that it "was written after listening to that album for like three, four times a day for a week".
MS

Muse

From left: 'Uprising', 'Undisclosed Desires', 'Time Is Running Out'

Muse Muscle Museum

1998 · 4:23 · Bellamy

It was 'Muscle Museum' that started the ball
rolling for Muse, reaching number three in
the indie charts on its release. Re-recorded
for their debut album *Showbiz*, it was an early
example of Muse's trademark of underpinning
frontman Matt Bellamy's flamboyance
with exemplary rhythmic solidity.

Muse Unintended

1999 · 3:57 · Bellamy

Muse's debut album, *Showbiz*, had been
dogged by comparisons to the then
ascendant Radiohead. The criticism centred
chiefly on the similarities between Matt
Bellamy and Thom Yorke's voices, but in
songs like this gentle, floating acoustic
ode to love, the differences between
the bands were clear to anyone except
those drawn to simple assessments.

Muse Plug In Baby

2001 · 3:40 · Bellamy

When Muse first emerged, they were three
shy kids. After first album *Showbiz* sealed
tours with the Red Hot Chili Peppers and
Foo Fighters though, they found their feet.
'Plug In Baby' was second album *Origin
Of Symmetry*'s standout track, a blizzard
of outrageous guitars and screaming
falsetto that paved the way to the future.

Muse Feeling Good

2001 · 3:20 · Bricusse – Newly

It seemed an odd cover version for
Muse to be taking on – a song written
for a musical and then made famous
by Nina Simone – yet their version
so beefed up this old standard that it
became very much their own. The band's
frontman, Matt Bellamy, had long been
a Simone fan and saw this as a tribute.

Muse
Stockholm Syndrome

! 2003 · 4:56 · Muse

During the recording of Muse's third album *Absolution*, they told *Kerrang!* that their work in progress was "fat as fuck. Our producer kept telling us to make our riffs more fucking heavy." They did so by recording drums in a swimming pool and guitar parts in a field, and ransacking a castle for cartwheels and cattle prods to use as instruments. Then they were baffled when they were described as being somewhat eccentric. This, the album's lead single, was an impressively tumbling, rumbling, rhythmic masterpiece of power, precision and attitude. More striking still was the fact the group now sounded like absolutely no other band on earth.

Muse
Time Is Running Out

! 2003 · 3:56 · Muse

From its groove-based, fuzzily electronic opening bassline to its finger-clicking beat, it was obvious that with 'Time Is Running Out' Muse were keen to explore increasingly diverse influences. In this case the band's bassist, Chris Wolstenholme, had apparently been influenced by Michael Jackson, yet it was in the song's explosive and belligerently heavy guitars that live crowds wallowed. Because of that, this was the song that allowed Muse to emerge from the shroud of underground respect they had earned in America and become fully-fledged stars there. Understatement has never been something of which

Muse could be accused and here they were beginning to revel in their exuberance.

Muse Hysteria

Muse Sing For Absolution

! 2004 · 4:55 · Muse

Heartbreaking and beautiful, 'Sing For Absolution' proved that amid the bombast, the Devon three-piece could also be relied upon to produce transcendent works of dark majesty. Founded on Muse's simple blueprint – solid rhythm over which Matt Bellamy's vocal-, piano- and guitar-based imagination can soar – this was the band at their emotive best.

Muse
Supermassive Black Hole

! 2006 · 3:29 · Bellamy

Muse's fourth album, *Black Holes And Revelations* suffered a troubled birth. In order to write it, the band had decamped to Chateau Miraval, a remote French 17th-century castle overrun with bats. They had ended up with songs they claimed sounded like "classical jazz" and which, preposterously, Matt Bellamy deemed as "too mental... even by our standards". So they disappeared to New York, immersed themselves in the club scene for a little while, explored a lot of science-fiction and conspiracy theories, and

Muse Hysteria 2003 • 3:47 • Muse

Coinciding with Muse's growing reputation for debauchery and flamboyance came this,
a singularly debauched and flamboyant slice of spectacularly over-the-top rock indulgence
that just happened to be brilliant. By the time Muse released their third single from
Absolution, they had earned a reputation for being a bit loopy – singer Matt Bellamy
had professed to his fondness for Ouija boards, groupies and cladding himself in fancy-
dress costumes while at home alone – and the growing lunacy and daring of their music
somehow seemed to cement the fact that no one was combining raging guitars with
thrilling ambition in quite the same manner as Muse.

returned with songs like this one, dominated by dance beats, electronica and paranoid lyrics. The direction change worked and 'Supermassive Black Hole' romped straight into the top 10 when released as a single.

Muse Starlight

! 2006 • 4:00 • Bellamy

Black Holes And Revelations found Muse, initially, banging their heads against a creative wall and they credit 'Starlight' as being one of the album's toughest tracks to complete – despite the fact it was written a good couple of years before recording sessions began for their fourth album. Intended to be a love song, its themes were somewhat at odds with the topics of global politics, underground resistance and governmental suspicion found elsewhere on *Black Holes*… Yet the blend of its cold beats and bassline with the warmth of Matt Bellamy's voice and piano somehow sum up much of what Muse wanted to achieve with the album.

Muse
Knights Of Cydonia

! 2006 • 6:07 • Bellamy

The last song on *Black Holes And Revelations* may be a sprawling, ridiculous work of imagination but, frankly, anything the song achieves before its three-quarter point becomes instantly forgettable in the face of the riff Muse subsequently choose to unleash. Perhaps the most exciting guitar line they've ever written ends this six-minute epic in rampant style.

Muse Invincible

! 2007 • 5:00 • Bellamy

Inspired by David Bowie's 'Heroes' in subject matter, though not sound, 'Invincible' was the fourth single released from *Black Holes And Revelations* and, along with 'Take A Bow', was the only track to emerge from Muse's period recording in France. Clearly its military drums, ethereal guitar and subsequent

! From left:
'Sing For Absolution',
'Starlight'

lightness of touch were not among those songs deemed "too mental" by the band. In fact, buoyed by the fact nobody knew what to expect from Muse any more, the band were delighted to find themselves free to do whatever they wanted – hence a guitar solo here sounding much like a helium-infused kazoo player.

Muse
Map Of The Problematique
| 2007 • 4:19 • Bellamy

For the two days before the unhinged and conspiracy-fuelled pandemonium 'Map Of The Problematique' was released as a single, Muse had found themselves playing the biggest shows of their lives at Wembley Stadium. It was an unlikely celebration of their dominance: a song based on the book *The Limits To Growth*, a 1972 study on the earth's inability to sustain the human race.

Muse Uprising
| 2009 • 5:05 • Bellamy

Muse decided to close ranks for their fifth studio album and went to town, producing a sprawling, original and utterly crackers record all on their own. As the album's opener and first single, 'Uprising' was the way in and somehow managed to sound like the theme tune to *Doctor Who*, Blondie's 'Call Me' and Billy Idol's 'White Wedding' without at any point sounding like it was created by anyone but Muse. A baffling state of affairs. It also found the band's frontman Matt Bellamy in characteristically paranoid mood, calling

the world to arms against the powerful who pull the strings behind the scenes.

Muse
Undisclosed Desires
| 2009 • 3:56 • Bellamy

Inspired by the R&B of producers such as Timbaland, Matt Bellamy wanted to explore a more dance-orientated side of Muse – hence shuffling electronic beats, syncopated slap bass and a repeated staccato orchestral figure that marked an abrupt left turn from the guitar histrionics that defined much of Muse's previous work.

Muse
United States Of Eurasia
| 2009 • 5:47 • Bellamy

"There were definitely moments where we thought, 'Are we going to get away with this?'" said Matt Bellamy of the writing and recording of their fifth album *The Resistance*. "On 'Eurasia', we definitely felt that," he added, perhaps unnecessarily for a track that blended Queen, Chopin and Balkan folk music with the band's commitment to rampant overstatement. Bellamy had immersed himself in former US policy adviser Zbigniew Brzezinski's 1998 book *The Grand Chessboard*, in which he attempts to define a means for Eurasian countries to maintain power, and was shocked into writing this response. "It was like reading something written by Dr Strangelove," said Bellamy. "These people really are megalomaniacs!"
TB

My Chemical Romance
I'm Not OK

! 2004 • 3:08 • My Chemical Romance

The second single from My Chemical Romance's breakthrough second album, *Three Cheers For Sweet Revenge*, was initially written as an anthem for outsiders. "It was," as the band's singer Gerard Way claimed, "a declaration for the kids who would become our fans." It became an all-pervasive hit, its subversive high-school video, teen-uproar sentiments and sheer melodicism generating it an audience way beyond those original outsiders, and sending it to number 19 in the UK singles chart. "That song was like an infiltrator," said Way. "It was normal people who got it, people who were tired of pretending to be something they're not."

My Chemical Romance
Welcome To The
Black Parade

! 2006 • 5:11 • My Chemical Romance

After the album *Three Cheers For Sweet Revenge* had propelled My Chemical Romance to fame, many assumed they

would take its formula – dark-hewn, emotional, but melodically driven rock – and repeat it. They were wrong. Instead, the band unveiled a grand rock opera, centred on a character known as "The Patient" and including death, reincarnation and occasional high-kicking camp. This slice of explosive, epic abandon was the album's centrepiece but was, curiously, written years beforehand and was originally called 'The Five Of Us Are Dying'. "It was a plea for help," said Gerard Way, "that sentiment turned into something quite empowering."

My Chemical Romance
Teenagers

| 2007 • 2:42 • My Chemical Romance

Evidence that My Chemical Romance had a sense of humour – and perhaps access to the records of Status Quo – came towards the end of their third album, *The Black Parade*. Opening with the sort of chugging guitar riff of which Francis Rossi would be proud, the band proceed to deliver a tongue-in-cheek but nonetheless scathing assessment of the relationship between America's youth and their elders. Despite the apparently light-hearted flourishes in the song – its guitar sign-off, its Nirvana-referencing video – it was a song in part born from

singer Gerard Way's fear of getting old and losing touch with his past. TB

Mystery Jets

Mystery Jets
Two Doors Down

| 2008 • 3:36 • Trivedi – Fish – Rees – Harrison – Harrison

Having your dad around is something teenagers usually avoid at all costs. Blaine Harrison invited his to join his band. After signing to 679, the band's debut album *Making Dens* scored them critical acclaim and a place in the UK top 40 album chart. For second album *Twenty One*, the band employed electro DJ Erol Alkan as producer then ditched their prog rock sound in favour of 1980s-style indie-pop. 'Two Doors Down', their biggest hit to date, is a sunny, optimistic, shimmering love song about the girl next door. Heavily influenced by Aztec Camera, Roxette and Phil Collins, the band consider it their "homage to one-hit wonders". They told Xfm that Alkan says of the tune, "every time he thinks about the song he hates it, but every time he listens to the song he loves it". Perhaps not entirely dissimilar to how a teenager might feel about having their dad in their band? MS

The band consider it their 'homage to one-hit wonders'

– Mystery Jets on 'Two Doors Down'

Kate Nash
Foundations

2007 • 4:05 • Nash – Epworth

Commenting on the ups and downs of a relationship with the wit and wisdom of one much older than her years, Kate Nash caught the public imagination with this song to such an extent that it reached number two in the UK charts a few weeks before her 20th birthday. The release date of her debut album, *Made Of Bricks*, was brought forward to meet demand and went in at number one, cementing the meteoric rise of a fresh British talent. 'Foundations' opens with two simple piano notes and some handclap percussion, layering organ, strings and further piano flourishes as the tension of the story builds – the fights reveal the cracks in the couple's foundations, she knows she should let go but she can't. It's the lyrical details that catch your attention, the "intelligent input darling... have

another beer then" comments that make it so real. Nash had turned to songwriting while simultaneously recovering from breaking her foot and being rejected by drama school. Inspired by Regina Spektor and Buzzcocks, she combined sharp observation and frank home truths with a rich inner life that thought of pumpkin soup and skeletons, seeing the philosophical in the everyday. Singing with a distinct outer-London twang, her first gig was in her hometown of Harrow and from there she started performing with other new young singer-songwriters, from Adele to Jack Peñate. After writing to Xfm's X-Posure with a demo of what would be her first single, 'Caroline's A Victim', she got her first ever radio play. Xfm continued to play a part by playlisting second release 'Foundations' ahead of other radio stations, which waited until it was already a hit. The downside of the song's runaway success would be that, live, Nash would sometimes be pelted with lemons after singing about being "so bitter"!
JK

> The downside of the song's runaway success would be that, live, Nash would sometimes be pelted with lemons after singing about being "so bitter"!

New Order

New Order
Ceremony

! 1981 · 4:24 · Joy Division

When Joy Division singer Ian Curtis committed suicide in 1980, the rest of the band agreed to continue under a new name. As New Order, their first task was to record the final songs written with Curtis. Unbearably poignant, 'Ceremony' debuted at the very last Joy Division gig.

New Order
Temptation

! 1982 · 6:59 · New Order

Originally titled 'Taboo No. 7', this was New Order's first self-produced single, and showcases their increasing interest in electronic music. On the original 12-inch, you can hear singer Bernard Sumner yelp as manager Rob Gretton sticks a snowball down the back of his shirt.

New Order
Blue Monday

! 1983 · 7:29 · New Order

"I literally saw the light when I was in New York. Someone spiked my drink with a tab of acid and suddenly all this electronic music made sense." Following his epiphany, Bernard Sumner led New Order away from rock and towards the dancefloor. For the opening of the Haçienda club in 1982, they composed a heavily-sequenced track called '586' – the next step was 'Blue Monday', which used the same sledgehammer percussion. However, Stephen Morris's original drum patterns were lost when he accidentally unplugged the machine. "The drums that we did were never as good as the ones that were wiped!" bassist Peter Hook told Xfm in 2008. Nevertheless, the track became the biggest-selling 12-inch single ever – not that New Order saw much profit, thanks to the notoriously expensive sleeve, designed by Peter Saville and based on a floppy disk he'd seen in the band's studio. "The sound was being made by sequencers and the disk carried

"I literally saw the light when I was in New York. Someone spiked my drink with a tab of acid and suddenly all this electronic music made sense" – Bernard Sumner's electronic music revelation

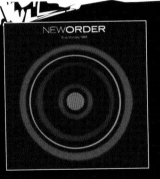  

From left: 'Blue Monday 1988', 'World In Motion', 'Ceremony'

the information," he explained, "so there was an intrinsic link between the disk and their new, more defined direction."

New Order
Bizarre Love Triangle

1986 • 4:22 • New Order

Recorded for the album *Brotherhood*, this song is better known in its single form, remixed by American DJ Shep Pettibone. A fine example of the band tapping into cutting-edge club culture, it's typical of their tracks in that its title has no relevance to the actual lyric.

New Order
True Faith

1987 • 5:55 • New Order – Hague

A slick collaboration between the band and producer Stephen Hague, during the session for this track singer Bernard Sumner went back to their communal flat to write the words. He found himself locked in until late evening when the

others returned. "By that time, besides being pretty pissed off, he'd actually cracked the lyrics," recalled Hague in 2005. One of the original lines was "Now that we've grown up together, they're all taking drugs with me", but it was thought this reference might affect radio play.

New Order
Touched By The Hand Of God

1987 • 3:44 • New Order

Recorded for the film *Salvation!*, the title is a sly reference to the Diego Maradona handball incident from the 1986 World Cup. The video features the band dressed as heavy metal rock gods and was directed by Kathryn Bigelow, now best known for the Oscar-winning movie *The Hurt Locker*.

New Order
World In Motion

1990 • 4:30 • New Order – Allen

Struggling to write the lyrics for the official

England song of the 1990 World Cup, frontman Bernard Sumner employed the help of actor Keith Allen. The original title was 'E For England', but football bosses feared the drug connotations would be controversial. Featuring the England squad on vocals, and a memorable "rap" by former Liverpool player John Barnes, the nation loved the combination of daftness and patriotism and sent the track to number one.

New Order
Regret

! 1993 • 4:08 • New Order – Hague

By 1993, Factory had gone bust and New Order were now on the major label London. Relationships were strained and the band was quietly put on hold following the release of the *Republic* album. Despite this, 'Regret' was one of their instant classics.

New Order
Crystal

! 2001 • 6:51 • New Order

New Order's last great single, which marked their comeback following their five-year hiatus, now minus keyboard player Gillian Gilbert. The video for 'Crystal' featured a group of kids miming to the track. This fake band's name was "The Killers", which gave a young Brandon Flowers an idea... MO'G

! Trent Reznor

Nine Inch Nails
Head Like A Hole

! 1989 • 4:59 • Reznor

Nine Inch Nails, despite appearances to the contrary, were never really a band. Instead the name was a blanket from under which intense, moody frontman Trent Reznor could unleash his inner demons and innate creativity. Asked in 1990 how the group's dynamic worked, Reznor told *Alternative Press* magazine: "Basically, if you don't like what you're playing, come up with something better. If I like it, you can play it. If I don't, play what I did." Nine Inch Nails' then drummer, Chris Vrenna, confirmed: "He wrote the music. It's his thing."

Reznor had been a solitary child and saw no reason for such an existence to change. Raised by his grandparents in Mercer, Pennsylvania – "a little patch of nothing", as he called it – his early years were spent dreaming of escape. His grandparents urged him into music and, eventually, he would end up playing saxophone and tuba in the school marching band. "It clicked with me immediately," he said. "My whole life, I always knew what I wanted to do: play

At first I thought, 'I can't fucking say these things'. But I also realised it was honesty that made it important."

The songs would make up his first release as Nine Inch Nails, 1989's *Pretty Hate Machine*, on which 'Head Like A Hole' was the tortured centrepiece. It was a spiteful blast of minimal electro-goth, a furious and candid outpouring of emotion set against a backdrop of electric chaos, which stuck out like a sore thumb against the then prevailing hair metal or stadium-rock of bands like Guns N' Roses. Clearly it was never going to make Reznor an overnight success. Instead, he and Nine Inch Nails went on

"If you don't like what you're playing, come up with something better. If I like it, you can play it. If I don't, play what I did"

– Trent Reznor on his group's dynamic

music and be in a rock band." Aged 23, Reznor had a string of mediocre bands behind him and was working in Cleveland's Right Track Studios. In exchange for doing the jobs there no one else wanted to do – cleaning the toilets, mostly – Reznor was allowed to experiment with his own songs in the studio's downtime. So it was that most nights would find him creating angular, angry sounds to counterpoint his own desperate lyrics. "I opened up my journal," he told *Kerrang!*. "It was full of bad feelings, honest feelings.

the road for five years, supporting acts like The Jesus And Mary Chain, playing on the first ever Lollapalooza tour and getting relentlessly booed when he opened, bizarrely, for Guns N' Roses at their August 1991 Wembley Stadium show. And as he toured, word began to spread while simultaneously grunge crept in to kill off the old rock guard. Reznor's influence – in part thanks to his helming of Marilyn Manson's early career – would continue to loom large over the decade.
TB

Nirvana

Nirvana
Smells Like Teen Spirit

! 1991 • 5:01 • Cobain – Grohl – Novoselic

 There had been little in Nirvana's debut album, *Bleach*, to suggest they would achieve so much with their follow-up. A scruffy, belligerent, unpolished collection, it had nonetheless earned them an underground reputation. But 'Smells Like Teen Spirit' would change things forever. Kurt Cobain has since claimed he was simply trying to rip off the Pixies, something he achieves in the song's quiet-loud dynamic, but it would lead to so much more. As Dave Grohl's stuttering drum intro unveils its classic opening, the song ushered in a new era of serious, emotional and raw rock whose influence remains today.

Nirvana
On A Plain

! 1991 • 3:16 • Cobain – Grohl – Novoselic

A song written by Kurt Cobain about, erm, writing a song. "Start this off without any words" run the singer's opening lyrics, penned in a hurry shortly before he was due to go into the vocal booth to start recording it. Later, he steals some of his own lyrics – "Black sheep got blackmailed again" and "I got so high, I scratched 'til I bled" from the then unreleased 'Verse Chorus Verse' – as he struggled with writer's block. This is perhaps *Nevermind*'s most immediate song, revelling in Cobain's desire that Nirvana should be "just a very, very heavy pop band".

Nirvana
Come As You Are

! 1992 • 3:39 • Cobain – Grohl – Novoselic

 Intended as a welcoming call to outsiders, whose number Kurt Cobain counted himself among, 'Come As You Are' (*Nevermind*'s second single) found the singer in more introspective mood. A simple guitar introduction unfurled into a contemplative lyric in which Cobain, with dark irony given his later suicide, maintained "I don't have a gun". However, much as 'Smells Like Teen Spirit' had drawn criticism for its similarities to Boston's 'More Than A Feeling', so 'Come As You Are' had its resemblance to Killing Joke's 'Eighties', something which would lead the British band to sue – unsuccessfully.

Nirvana
Lithium

! 1992 · 4:17 · Cobain – Grohl – Novoselic

Written during a previous incarnation of Nirvana – one not featuring drummer Dave Grohl – and subsequently reworked for *Nevermind*, Kurt Cobain claimed the story of 'Lithium' was fictional. However, its religion-bating lyrics seem more likely to have been inspired by a period spent in 1985 with the born-again Christian family of his friend Jesse Reed after he had run away from home. Cobain uses lithium, a treatment for manic depression, as a metaphor for the effect of religion on those with problems. The third single to be released from *Nevermind*, it reached number 11 in the UK charts.

Nirvana
In Bloom

! 1992 · 4:15 · Cobain – Grohl – Novoselic

Despite its apparently scathing lyrics about a man who would "sell the kids for food", 'In Bloom' was actually intended as something of a mark of respect to Kurt Cobain's friend and drug buddy Dylan Carlson, an early champion of the band who would, as the song goes, "like to sing along". Something of a weapons aficionado, Carlson was further honoured in the line "he likes to shoot his gun". More than that, though, 'In Bloom' was also a somewhat bitter attempt by Cobain to address the growing

numbers of fans from outside their scene who claimed Nirvana as their own.

Nirvana
Heart Shaped Box

! 1993 · 4:39 · Cobain

Nirvana's explosive rise had taken a toll on the band by the time they came to record third album *In Utero*. Kurt Cobain wanted to withdraw from what he saw as *Nevermind*'s commercial sheen, while his relationship with bandmates Dave Grohl and Krist Novoselic was ragged enough that he had been bullying them into reducing their songwriting royalties. So fractious were Nirvana that Cobain was bouncing ideas off new wife Courtney Love instead. 'Heart Shaped Box' was intended as a love song to her, but it was a curiously worded one in which he compared Love to diseases like cancer and drug addiction.

Nirvana
All Apologies

! 1993 · 3:50 · Cobain

A scathing and haunting attack on himself, 'All Apologies' was Kurt Cobain at his most emotionally open and revealing. Ever a singer who tended to explore his issues, to a greater or lesser degree, on record, it was here – on the track that closed *In Utero* – that Cobain shredded himself apart in a brutal and haunting display of self-loathing. "Everything is my fault, I'll take the blame", he sang

Cobain shredded himself apart in a brutal and haunting display of self-loathing

with weary resignation, in a song first written in 1990. He dedicated the track to his wife Courtney Love and daughter Frances Bean. Within four months of its release, he would be dead.

Nirvana
The Man Who Sold The World

! 1994 • 3:50 • Bowie

For many bands, MTV's *Unplugged* show was simply another step on the promotional treadmill – hence they tended to play their hits as they normally would, just on acoustic guitars. Nirvana were determined not to do that in their 1993 appearance and refused to play many of their songs, which they felt would not work in an acoustic guise. Instead, to MTV's concern, they played covers. Yet what emerged was a tender, intricate and stunning performance of which this David Bowie cover was one of the standouts. In fact, so good was it that many people thought it was a Nirvana original, much to Bowie's irritation.
TB

Noah And The Whale
5 Years Time

! 2008 • 3:34 • Fink

Listening to this sweet song, with its ukulele, shivering strings and poetically repetitive lyrics about young love, it's hard to imagine that all that joy could come crashing down so dramatically. Featuring a guest vocal from Laura Marling, then girlfriend of singer Charlie Fink, it was obvious that the pair of them meant every word. Eventually, however, they broke up and soon Marling began dating mutual friend Marcus Mumford of Mumford & Sons. Heartbroken, Fink wrote the band's second album, *The First Days Of Spring*, about the demise and aftermath of the relationship. A brutal, bleak record, it was musically a hand-break turn from the joy of the first, showing a very different side to the band. Fortunately it received rave reviews from all corners of the music press, which may have brought something of a silver lining to what, if this album is anything to go by, was a very dark cloud.
MS

It's hard to imagine that all that joy could come crashing down so dramatically

Oasis

Oasis
Supersonic

1994 • 4:43 • Noel Gallagher

And so it begins. This was the first anyone heard of the most popular British guitar band of the past 20 years, being their debut single and debut TV appearance (on Channel 4's *The Word*, presented by fellow Mancunian, Terry Christian) and after a fair measure of hype it was almost considered a disappointment, peaking at a mere 31 in the UK (their lowest ever). Despite unpropitious beginnings and lyrics that sound like a poor man's version of Shaun Ryder, the song has aged well, sliding in on a brilliant guitar line and providing early proof of Liam Gallagher's unique singing talent.

Oasis
Shakermaker

1994 • 5:08 • Noel Gallagher

The band's second single and an outing for Noel Gallagher's line in doggerel, namechecking everything from his 1970s toys to the Sifters record shop in Didsbury, where the brothers used to buy their music. Sadly, it was the use of another childhood memory, the Coca Cola ad music and, New Seekers hit 'I'd Like To Teach The World To Sing', which cost them a bundle in a lawsuit. "We all drink Pepsi now," shrugged Gallagher.

Oasis
Live Forever

1994 • 4:38 • Noel Gallagher

Conceived as an antidote to Kurt Cobain's "I hate myself and I want to die" line (though written before that became a self-fulfilling prophecy), this was a working-class celebration of life, penned while Noel Gallagher was nursing his smashed foot in the storeroom of the building company where he worked. Loosely based on The Rolling Stones' 'Shine A Light', it was the song Noel played to brother Liam as his de facto audition for the band. Despite having no chorus to speak of ("you and I are gonna live forever" is the sum of it), 'Live Forever' was the moment a million Oasis fans decided this was the band for them and it remains their ultimate anthem.

Oasis
Cigarettes And Alcohol

! 1994 · 4:48 · Noel Gallagher

Early proof that Oasis were more than just a bunch of Beatles obsessives. If there was one song that defined the lad culture of the mid-1990s, it was 'Cigarettes And Alcohol'. Hailing the joys of booze, fags and drugs (the coke reference was omitted from the title), Noel Gallagher's recent insistence that it's "social comment" seems fair enough, given that it's all about escaping the drudgery of work. Noel took a few shortcuts himself, the opening guitar riff being one of his more blatant lifts, this time from T.Rex's 'Get It On' anthem. Another great performance from singer Liam, who pronounces "imagination" like a man in love with every syllable.

Oasis Rock N' Roll Star

! 1994 · 5:23 · Noel Gallagher

First album, first track: as statements of intent go, 'Rock N' Roll Star' was unbeatable. Noel Gallagher later said that, 'Live Forever' and 'Cigarettes And Alcohol' summed up all he wanted to say; everything that followed was just variations on the theme. The song was about escape and self-belief, but also about the frustrations that lay just below, the fear of life being defined by a choice between dull work and the dole. "I live my life in the city / and there's no easy way out", Liam sang with rare conviction. And despite the occasionally clunky lyrics ("I take my car and I drive real far"), it was obvious from the off that they'd soon be living the dream.

Oasis Whatever

! 1994 · 6:21 · Noel Gallagher

Released at the end of a triumphant year for Oasis, 'Whatever' finds them in their full orchestral phase, shimmering with strings and an easy lolloping tempo. Despite its obvious similarities with mid-period Beatles, it wasn't their melody they pinched but that of Neil Innes, who

From left:
'Whatever',
'Cigarettes
And Alcohol'

! Above: 'Half The World Away'

Although Liam sings the verses, Noel insisted on taking the chorus himself, claiming Liam couldn't reach the high notes

– Oasis, 'Acquiesce'

wrote the songs for Fabs parody The Rutles and successfully sued for part-ownership. Never kid a kidder, Noel.

Oasis
Half The World Away

! 1994 • 4:21 • Noel Gallagher

As Noel Gallagher himself says, this isn't so much an Oasis B-side as the theme tune to one of Britain's best-loved sitcoms. A gentle acoustic number about the frustrations of family life, living when "my body feels young but my mind is very old", 'Half The World Away' slipped out as one of 'Whatever''s myriad flips, but only became famous when Caroline Aherne chose it as the theme for *The Royle Family*. Noel had suggested 'Married With Children' instead. Never shy about admitting his influences, he later said it was ripped off from Burt Bacharach and Hal David's 'This Guy's In Love With You' and expressed amazement he hadn't been sued.

Oasis Slide Away

! 1994 • 6:32 • Noel Gallagher

Only their belief that five singles off one album would be excessive kept 'Slide Away' back from its own release. But Oasis were so consistently, breathtakingly good in the early years that they could well afford to leave some of their best tracks lurking near the back of albums. 'Slide Away' is one such, with a furiously intense vocal from Liam that Noel later claimed was his best vocal performance ever. Written about a row Noel had with his girlfriend, he said the song was an attempt

to emulate The Smiths' 'Reel Around The Fountain', but with the kind of simple, brutal guitar play of Neil Young that turned it into a six-and-a-half minute epic.

Oasis
Some Might Say

! 1995 • 5:28 • Noel Gallagher

Their sixth single and first number one, 'Some Might Say' is Oasis at their most swaggering, with a T.Rex guitar intro, a rollicking rock-out and a gorgeous switch-up when Liam goes into "standing in the station" and the lyric descends into complete nonsense. Beneath all that there's more than a hint of beauty in the verses, with Liam mixing sympathy for the common man with optimism for better times. 'Some Might Say' sounded like it was written with one eye on the radio and one on the football stands. No wonder that ten years on Noel called it the "archetypical Oasis track."

Oasis Acquiesce

! 1995 • 4:24 • Noel Gallagher

One of the B-side (see 'Talk Tonight' on page 286) of 'Some Might Say' and easily its equal, 'Acquiesce' is a glorious celebration of friendship – not just about the brothers themselves, according to sleevenotes writer Paul Du Noyer – set to one of their hardest riffs. Although Liam sings the verses, Noel insisted on taking the chorus himself, claiming Liam couldn't reach the high notes. Used as promotion for *The Masterplan* compilation of B-sides, it reached number 24 in the US on radio play alone. Noel complained that Liam always skips the second verse when they play it live. Liam denied this, saying he'd never seen the words, blaming the "geezer who puts the words in front of me... I just sing what I read, man."

Oasis Talk Tonight

! 1995 • 4:21 • Noel Gallagher

Another B-side-only track of 'Some Might Say', 'Talk Tonight' was written after the first of Noel Gallagher's many famous walk-outs, when he left the band in LA and headed for San Francisco in 1994. It's another of Noel's gentle acoustic strummers, one in which he opens up about the friend who "saved my life."

Oasis Roll With It

! 1995 • 3:59 • Noel Gallagher

Remember the Britpop wars? It's ironic that the two biggest bands of the era went into battle over two of their least remarkable singles. Blur's 'Country House' won the absurdly hyped contest of middle-class Southerners vs working-class Mancs, going straight into number one while Oasis settled at two, though the ensuing albums rewrote it as a landslide win for the Gallagher brothers. 'Roll With It' is strong enough, with a searing guitar sound and a memorable tune, but perhaps the first sign of a certain predictability settling in. Blur mocked it as a Status Quo rip-off. Oasis said "ta very much", and printed the Quoasis legend on a T-shirt.

Oasis Morning Glory

! 1995 • 5:03 • Noel Gallagher

With lad culture in full flower, no one expected rock stars to hide their drug habits as carefully as they had in the 1980s. Sure enough, the title track of the biggest-selling British album of the 1990s was perhaps the clearest drugs reference since The Shamen's 'Ebeneezer Goode'. Apart from all those references to razor blades and mirrors, the helicopter effect that bookends the track is probably inspired by the famous *Goodfellas* scene. Noel Gallagher has never been coy about drugs and later claimed he'd popped into a Downing Street toilet for a quick line during the Blairs' famous party in 1997. We should tut, but the fact is Noel was on fire at this point.

Oasis Wonderwall

! 1995 • 4:18 • Noel Gallagher

The tune that proved even your mum could love Oasis, 'Wonderwall' is a lovely singalong song and, with its acoustic intro and deep strings, both the gentlest and the most romantic of their big records. It could've been so different: guitarist Bonehead remembers Liam Gallagher storming out of early sessions because it sounded too much like a reggae song, while brother Noel told BBC's *Seven Ages Of Rock*: "I don't know why it took on a life of its own; you'll have to ask someone who likes it." He later denied the widely reported story that it was about his then girlfriend Meg Matthews, saying the meaning of the song had been "taken away from me". Despite everything, it stalled at number two in the UK, held off by Robson & Jerome (busy week for mums, that one).

Oasis The Masterplan
! 1995 • 5:22 • Noel Gallagher

The B-side of 'Wonderwall' and, like its daddy, sung by Noel Gallagher. 'The Masterplan' is Oasis at their most Beatle-esque, slipping in on an acoustic guitar before building into a brass fanfare underpinned by a string section. All that for something that was just a B-side? Noel told a Dutch radio station that Creation boss Alan McGee insisted it was too good to waste that way, to which he replied: "I don't write shit songs."

Oasis
Don't Look Back In Anger
! 1995 • 4:47 • Noel Gallagher

Oasis have always been accused of being musical magpies, with critics likening them to a hip-hop producer sampling his tunes from bits of other people's records. Noel Gallagher would probably just shrug and say, "Yeah! And?" 'Don't Look Back In Anger' is comprised of the intro to John Lennon's 'Imagine', some scrapbook lyrics by the same author and a hint of their own 'Whatever'. Even brother Liam chipped in with "so Sally can wait" – ironically on the first Oasis tune his brother would sing. Despite all that, it was this track and 'Wonderwall' that came to define Oasis' ascension to the status of Britain's favourite band and their ultimate victory over Blur in the Britpop wars.

Oasis
Champagne Supernova
! 1995 • 5:08 • Noel Gallagher

Noel Gallagher's stab at psychedelic songwriting might not be up there with 'I

! From left: 'Roll With It', 'Wonderwall', 'Don't Look Back In Anger'

Am The Walrus' ("slowly walking down the hall / faster than a cannonball"), but no one ever went to him when they wanted great lyrics. 'Champagne Supernova' is still up there with the very best of his tunes, thanks in large part to an epic vocal performance from his brother Liam and a crashing guitar guest spot from Noel's dad-rock hero Paul Weller. Though the song has no distinct meaning, it works best as an escape fantasy, the far side of the journey begun on 'Rock N' Roll Star'. Sure enough, when Noel bought his house in Hampstead he changed the name (from number nine) to Supernova Heights. The song proved an epic finale to their record-breaking Knebworth gigs of 1996.

Oasis
Cast No Shadow

❗ 1995 • 4:52 • Noel Gallagher

Not a single, but a track from the epic *(What's The Story) Morning Glory?* album that stripped the band's sound right down and let Liam Gallagher loose on one of his most restrained vocals. There's a hint of melancholy in 'Cast No Shadow', about a man "bound with all the weight of all the words he tried to say." Dedicated to Richard Ashcroft (mercurial singer of nearby band The Verve), the song hints at his struggles, which reportedly included bouts of clinical depression. Ashcroft returned the favour with 'A Northern Soul' and when the inevitable "Noel is dead" rumours surfaced (you're no one in rock without a good death rumour), Ashcroft was said by the conspiracy theorists to be filling his role behind the scenes.

Oasis
She's Electric

❗ 1995 • 3:41 • Noel Gallagher

Just as The Beatles' albums invariably had a novelty track (generally with Ringo on vocals), so did Oasis (*Definitely, Maybe* even had two, in 'Digsy's Diner' and 'Married With Children'). 'She's Electric', though, took on a life of its own as a jaunty, funny track about a girl "from a family full of eccentrics". Liam Gallagher sang it with a knowing wink and tongue firmly in cheek.

Oasis
Little By Little

❗ 2002 • 4:54 • Noel Gallagher

While Oasis records generally divide the world into people who love the band and people who can't stand them, 'Little By Little' found plenty of haters on both sides of the line. With a sombre, almost Pink Floyd sound, it was certainly far from their most chipper and Noel Gallagher substitutes shouting for singing on the hook, with a particularly harsh *NME* review claiming "the gap between Oasis and Stereophonics perceptibly narrows". And yet the tune is undeniable and the sympathy-for-the-working-stiff lyrics are Noel at his most honest and affecting. One for the singalongs. SY

little by little/she is love

The sympathy-for-the-working-stiff lyrics are Noel at his most honest

Ocean Colour Scene
The Riverboat Song

1996 • 4:54 • Fowler – Minchella – Harrison – Cradock

Steeped in mod culture and with a reverential understanding of classic songwriting, this was the moment that Ocean Colour Scene propelled themselves into the national consciousness. The unmistakable and relentless riff of 'The Riverboat Song' became the most recognisable and enduring soundtrack to life in Britain during 1996. In the wake of Britpop, an enthusiastic media propelled their *Moseley Shoals* album to number two in the UK charts and onwards to become one of the biggest sellers of the year. That electrifying riff came to guitarist Steve Cradock in a dream, he told Xfm in May 2010: "I woke up with the whole song in my head."

Ocean Colour Scene
The Day We Caught The Train

1996 • 3:06 • Fowler – Minchella – Harrison – Cradock

A song written by singer Simon Fowler while Steve Cradock was away on tour with Paul Weller. Released in June 1996, it was the sound of the summer and totally hit a nerve with its anthemic reflection on friendship and possibility. It spent nine weeks in the UK top 40 and became *the* festival moment for Ocean Colour Scene fans for years to come.

Ocean Colour Scene
The Circle

1996 • 3:43 • Fowler – Minchella – Harrison – Cradock

Another Simon Fowler track about friendship and one that he told Xfm he wrote "in the time it takes to sing it". It was originally written in a more upbeat, Buzzcocks style until guitarist Steve Cradock mellowed it out into the summery breeze of a song that became their third UK top 10 hit in 1996.

Ocean Colour Scene
Hundred Mile High City

1997 • 3:58 • Fowler – Minchella – Harrison – Cradock

The opening track and first single taken from the band's hugely anticipated third album *Marchin' Already*. 'Hundred Mile High City' gave Ocean Colour Scene their fourth consecutive UK top 10 hit and helped its parent album reach number one while displacing *Be Here Now* by their good friends Oasis. OCS hit the lad-rock zeitgeist once again when 'Hundred Mile High City' was chosen by film director Guy Ritchie as the main song in his hugely successful 1998 British gangster movie *Lock, Stock and Two Smoking Barrels*. MW

"I woke up with the whole song in my head"

– Steve Cradock

The Offspring

The Offspring
Self Esteem

! 1994 • 4:17 • Holland

This was the track that really tore open a whole new pop punk scene in the US. 'Self-Esteem' did the unthinkable and enabled a punk band on an independent label, to cross into mainstream American rock radio and sell millions of albums. The album in question was *Smash*, The Offspring's third studio album and often referred to as the most successful independent album of all time with sales of over 10 million units. *Smash* was the record that took the Epitaph label from a bedroom business to one of the world's biggest music players in less than a year.

The Offspring
Pretty Fly For A White Guy

! 1998 • 3:08 • Holland

The Offspring's greatest success to date, 'Pretty Fly For A White Guy' achieved worldwide success and number one hits in nine countries. The single reached gold status in Austria and Germany, and platinum status in Norway, Sweden and the UK. The first single from fifth studio album *Americana*, the track's tongue-in-cheek vibe is captured brilliantly by the accompanying video, in which in which our hero drives through a typical suburban town, and with lots of female backing singers, desperately tries to be hip-hop cool and fails miserably.

The Offspring
Why Don't You Get A Job?

! 1999 • 2:49 • Holland

Released on March 30th 1999, and available on both CD and 12-inch formats, this catchy little number was based around The Beatles' song 'Ob-La-Di, Ob-La-Da', mixed with the trademark Offspring ska sound, and topped off with sarcastic, resentful and dark lyrics. Confused? You should be. It's certainly one to listen to when someone's wound you up. Another great track for angry, angst-y teens – and there must have been plenty of them in the UK in 1999, as the song reached number two in the UK singles chart.

The Offspring
The Kids Aren't Alright

! 1999 • 3:00 • Holland

Single three of album five from this great US punk rock group plays on The Who's hit song 'The Kids Are Alright', and featured on the soundtrack for 1998 teen horror film *The Faculty*. The lyrics came from a trip that lead singer and songwriter Dexter Holland took back to his hometown, Garden Grove in Orange County, where he came across many people who had met with tragic incidents in their lives. BdP / MW

The Only Ones
Another Girl, Another Planet

! 2006 · 3:37 · Perrett

Sometimes it seems that every band making music in the late 1970s has been, at some point, labelled "seminal" – but in this case the description is truly deserved. Although rarely mentioned in the same breath as the likes of the Sex Pistols and Joy Division, The Only Ones played their part in shaping the sounds of British rebellion, and bands such as Blur, Nirvana and The Libertines have all since taken a leaf out of their punk-pop book. Such credit is only bestowed on them now, with their cult status giving them a higher profile via various *Best of...* and compilation releases than their original albums. The song 'Another Girl, Another Planet' – thought to be about the band's experiences of heroin, which would later prove their undoing – is a fuzzy, fast-paced pop song full of teenage petulance and casual indifference, courtesy of Peter Perrett's Libertine-esque vocals. Media conspiracies and record company incompetence have taken some of the blame for the track's low profile, but it remains a mystery as to why this record, hailed by some as one of the greatest rock songs ever, was never a worldwide hit.
JS

The Orb
Little Fluffy Clouds

! 1990 · 4:21 · Paterson – Youth

A cockerel crowing; a plane flying overhead; and an American woman telling us what the clouds were like in Arizona. Not the most obvious recipe for defining a genre, but 'Little Fluffy Clouds' remains the seminal "ambient house" track. The Orb originally comprised Alex Paterson, ex-roadie for post-punkers Killing Joke, and Jimmy Cauty, former guitarist with the band Brilliant. Having abandoned traditional drumbeats for their experiments in house music, the pair explored the more freeform, atmospheric side of dance music: taking their cue from Brian Eno's experimental albums from the 1970s and acknowledging Pink Floyd's more left-field moments, they dubbed it "ambient house for the E generation".

Recorded after Cauty had moved on to success with the KLF and Paterson had hooked up with Killing Joke bassist Youth, 'Little Fluffy Clouds' was a more traditionally structured instrumental, based around an interview with US singer Rickie Lee Jones who was asked, of all things: "What were the skies like when you were young?" Although she was less than happy about being sampled, it's Jones's odd intonation (apparently the result of a heavy cold) that gives the track its trippy, "come down" feeling that made it a hit in the chill-out rooms around the world. Also in the mix are various BBC sound effects, some Ennio Morricone harmonica and snippets of avant garde guitarist Steve Reich's composition *Electric Counterpoint*. Having finally mastered some accomplished beats for the backing track, Patterson claimed he could never reveal where he sampled the drums from, for fear of mortifying Orb fans.
MO'G

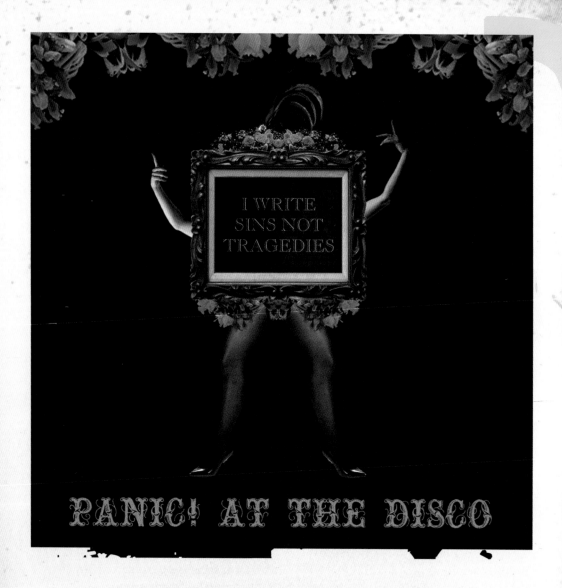

I WRITE SINS NOT TRAGEDIES

PANIC! AT THE DISCO

"I'd be lying if I thought back then that they'd go on to sell three million records and appear on the cover of *Rolling Stone*"
— Panic! At The Disco's manager Jonathan Daniel

Panic! At The Disco
I Write Sins Not Tragedies

! 2005 • 3:06 • Ross

Four Fall Out Boy fans had their world turned upside down after posting one of their demos on FOB bassist Pete Wentz's blog. Barely out of high school, the members of Panic! At The Disco quickly signed to Wentz's Decaydance record label and set about recording their debut album, *A Fever You Can't Sweat Out*. The record's meagre recording budget of $11,000 betrayed the modest expectations of all concerned.

"Sometimes you know when something's going to be super big, and other times you don't," Panic!'s manager Jonathan Daniel told Xfm. "I'd be lying if I thought back then that they'd go on to sell three million records and appear on the cover of *Rolling Stone*."

Helped considerably by Fall Out Boy's success and patronage, as well as the social networking explosion, US radio began playing album opening track, 'The Only Difference Between Martyrdom And Suicide Is Press Coverage'. Panic!, however, were keen to make a video for 'I Write Sins...' instead. "The band had done everything on their own up until that point," continued Daniel. "They clearly had the creative vision, so we stuck with it."

A cheap video, shot by director Shane Drake, saw the band causing havoc at a twisted, macabre wedding. It proved to be a huge hit that went on to score the gong for Video of the Year at the 2006 MTV Video awards. The success made 'I Write Sins...' one of the emo movement's biggest and best-loved songs, but the band had a far broader scope of ambitions. The ensuing tour, in a nod to the showbiz glitz of hometown Las Vegas, saw the band lug a windmill, dancers and numerous changes of costume around the world. It would inspire unwavering devotion among the faithful and seal a hugely successful album campaign for four unlikely heroes. OH

Pavement
Gold Soundz

1994 • 2:40
Malkmus – Kannberg – Pavement

Pavement's singer/guitarist Stephen Malkmus' sarcastic puncturing of pop culture endeared the band to a generation of music fans left cold by alternative rock's ascent into the mainstream. Over the course of five albums, a handful of EPs and singles, they became indie-rock's torch bearers in the most brilliantly nonchalant way. Formed in Stockton, California, by Malkmus and schoolfriend Scott "Spiral Stairs" Kannberg, Pavement would make enormous waves with their fall-indebted debut, *Slanted And Enchanted*, but the undying love they'd inspire gathered greater momentum following the release of second album, *Crooked Rain Crooked Rain*.

Having parted ways with loose drummer and even looser cannon Gary Young during the early stages of recording, the band took on an immediately more robust sound with the drafting of new sticksman Steve West. While the album's lead single 'Cut Your Hair' became a moderate (and utterly bizarre) MTV hit, 'Gold Soundz' would better typify the album's genius. On a bed of strumming, sunny indie-rock sat Stephen Malkmus' strange, strained vocal melodies. It was a beautiful example of the contradictions at the heart of the album. On the one hand, here was Pavement's most accessible, conventional-sounding work; on the other was the band's love of the unorthodox, the strange and the obtuse.

As a result, 'Gold Soundz' failed to follow 'Cut Your Hair' to MTV glory, or follow through on many people's prediction that *Crooked Rain...* would be Pavement's breakthrough album. What it did do, however, was cement their reputation as indie-rock godheads. Clutched to the bosom of the faithful – an influential faithful that would include band members, future band members, journalists and broadcasters – Pavement's deification continued unabated until their split in 1999. When they reformed in 2010, their biggest-ever shows awaited, with a welcome usually reserved for returning royalty. OH

Pearl Jam Alive

! 1991 • 5:41 • Gossard – Vedder

In 1991, guitarist Stone Gossard and bassist Jeff Ament were passing around a tape of five vocal-less songs, entitled *Stone Gossard Demos 1990*, in the hope of attracting a singer. It made its way to Eddie Vedder, a gas-station attendant and surfer, who was captivated by one track 'Dollar Short'. He recorded lyrics (about his experience of discovering the man he thought was his father wasn't his real dad) over the top of the instrumental and mailed it back to Gossard having changed the song's name to 'Alive'. Impressed, Gossard and Ament signed him up and the song became their debut single and first hit.

Pearl Jam Once

! 1991 • 3:52 • Gossard – Vedder

Another of the songs on guitarist Stone Gossard's demo tape, 'Once' began life as the instrumental 'Agytian Crave' before it was re-worked after Eddie Vedder lent the track his lyrics. Vedder was a surfer by day and would spend much of his time on the waves writing lyrics in his head and 'Once' was derived from what must have been a particularly feverish sea in which he envisioned what it might take for a man to go so mad that he became a serial killer. It would eventually go on to open the band's debut album, *Ten*.

Pearl Jam Even Flow

! 1992 • 4:54 • Gossard – Vedder

After the release of first album *Ten* in 1992, Pearl Jam had cemented themselves as grunge's "other band", something that always seemed to rankle with them and their fans. Perhaps stemming from the band's more classic rock influences and singer Eddie Vedder's rich, deep vocals, they were seen as the more mainstream, commercially acceptable rivals to Nirvana, peddling faux-angst and corporate chords – a theory that ignored founding members Stone Gossard and Jeff Ament's long Seattle scene history and the fact that both had earlier played in the Nirvana-influencing Green River (alongside two future Mudhoney members), and further dismissed Vedder's troubled upbringing. 'Even Flow' was their second single and another of the Gossard guitar tracks on the early demo that found its way to Vedder (it was originally called 'The King'). Lyrically powerful, 'Even Flow' marked Pearl Jam's singer out as more of a thinker than some of his peers; rather than simply write about himself, he would make an effort to empathise with those around him. Here he was writing about the homeless – a situation he hadn't been too far away from before he joined Pearl Jam in 1991 – while his band found a solid groove behind him.

Pearl Jam Jeremy

! 1992 • 5:19 • Vedder – Ament

'Jeremy' was frontman Eddie Vedder at his most affecting. Pearl Jam's third single was a haunted, haunting and bleak affair that their record company were initially reluctant to release as a single (they preferred the darkly pretty, but less controversial, 'Black', prompting Vedder to phone radio stations who played that song to demand if they were doing so at the record company's behest). In fairness, 'Jeremy' was hardly built from the stuff of which hit singles are made. It was written about the 1991 suicide of Texan schoolboy Jeremy Delle, who had walked up to the front of his high-school class, pulled out a handgun, and shot himself. Vedder had read the story in a newspaper and was affected by the fact that such an alarming death had been summed up in one small paragraph. He decided to make something more of Delle's actions. The song became their then biggest hit when released, making number 16 in the UK singles chart, but was not put out in America until the record company saw its success elsewhere. Consequently, they commissioned a high-budget video in dubious taste detailing the death of 'Jeremy', which – after heavy MTV-rotation – made Pearl Jam both huge and determined not to make another video again.
TB

Peter Bjorn And John
Young Folks

! 2006 • 4:39 • Peter – Yttling – Morén

Peter Bjorn And John formed in Stockholm in 1999 and by 2005 were being placed alongside bands like the Shout Out Louds and The Concretes as part of an uber-hip Swedish indie-pop movement. In fact, the female vocal on 'Young Folks' is the irresistible voice of The Concretes' singer Victoria Bergsman. PB&J's third album was signed in the UK by ultra-cool indie label Wichita (home of Bloc Party and The Cribs), and they were aided by being the first band on stage on the first day of the first Latitude Festival in July 2006. As Mark Bowen, Wichita label boss, told Xfm: "They didn't play to very many people on that Friday afternoon but for the rest of the weekend the only song that was coming out of every tent and food stall's stereo was 'Young Folks' or, as most people called it at the time, 'that whistling song'." The single release cracked the UK top 40 a month later but became a proper hit in September of the following year when it entered the chart at number 13 and stuck around for a very healthy seven weeks. With the help of a wonderfully simple animated video, 'Young Folks' also achieved some success in the US, and was named iTunes Song of the Year in 2006. As Bergsman is not a permanent member of the group, a number of singers have joined the band onstage to perform 'Young Folks' live over the years, including Swedish pop star Robyn, Tracyanne Campbell of Edinburgh indie band Camera Obscura, and – most bizarrely – Kanye West, who sang the track at 2007's Way Out West Festival in Gothenburg.
MW

PinkFloyd

Pink Floyd
See Emily Play

| 1967 · 2:53 · Barrett

Led by psychedelic visionary Syd Barrett, Pink Floyd became giants of the British underground scene in the late 1960s before developing into the now legendary million-selling progressive rock behemoth. 'See Emily Play' was their second single from June 1967 and while America's psych movement was all about cultural revolution, Britain's take on the music was much more whimsical. Featuring weird echoes, electronic noises and speeded up sections, Barrett's lyrics tell the apparently true story of seeing a young girl in the woods while he was taking an acid trip – although he later admitted he'd made the whole thing up.

Pink Floyd Time

1973 • 6:53
Mason – Waters – Wright – Gilmour

Having lost original singer Syd Barrett to an apparent breakdown and gained a new guitarist in Dave Gilmour, the Floyd moved into more experimental areas. After a series of ambitious and not entirely successful albums, they convened at London's Abbey Road studios to work on an album that they could take on tour. The impetus for *Dark Side Of The Moon* was bassist Roger Waters' interest in the pressures of life and the effect they have on individuals' mental health – a subject that was close to home, given Barrett's withdrawal from the rock star life. 'Time' expresses the universal fear that our days are running out... Starting out with a striking collage of clock sounds, the song grimly notes that "Hanging on in quiet desperation / Is the English way".

Pink Floyd Money

1973 • 6:30 • Waters

Kicking off the second side of the epic *Dark Side Of The Moon* album, 'Money' is one of Pink Floyd's more accessible songs, based around a decidedly funky Roger Waters bass riff and given a complex time signature that makes it a prime example of "progressive" rock. Tied into the concept of the album's examination of modern life and its resulting madness, the song is a satire on greed and avarice. 'Money' memorably opens with a rhythmic collage of cash registers and clanking coins that echoes the bassline – a tricky thing to pull off in the pre-digital days.

Pink Floyd Shine On You Crazy Diamond (Part One)

1975 • 13:31
Waters – Gilmour – Wright

The follow-up to the incredibly successful *Dark Side Of The Moon*, the influence of original Floyd frontman Syd Barrett hangs over *Wish You Were Here*. Opening the album with an extended, spacey intro, 'Shine On You Crazy Diamond' seemed to be about the singer's withdrawal from the world: "Remember when you were young? / You shone like the sun". Ironically, the man himself visited Abbey Road while the song was being recorded, but was initially not recognised by his former bandmates. Now overweight and with a shaved head, Barrett was a shadow of his former self, adding extra poignancy to this tribute.

Pink Floyd Wish You Were Here

1975 • 5:40 • Waters – Gilmour

The title track of Pink Floyd's ninth album relates to the overarching theme of absence and opens with the sound of a radio tuning away from the previous track ('Have A Cigar'), across a station playing Tchaikovsky's Fourth Symphony and on to Dave Gilmour playing the delicate acoustic guitar intro. Roger Waters later claimed that the song was about his grandmother's final years and how she would think Waters was her long-dead husband – the sighing introspection of the music sums up the mundane tragedy perfectly.

Pink Floyd
Another Brick In The Wall (Part 2)

1979 • 4:00 • Gilmour – Waters

As Pink Floyd turned into a million-selling-records band in the mid-1970s, they soon found themselves performing to larger crowds. At one stadium show in 1977, bassist Roger Waters became so aggravated with a noisy section of the audience in front of the stage, that he spat at them. The incident inspired the band's next album, which explored alienation in different forms. Featuring a character called Pink, *The Wall* depicts what happens when childhood trauma and the pressures of life become overwhelming, leading to self-imposed isolation from other people. 'Another Brick In The Wall' savagely criticises the "thought control" of school and authority, musing that the system produces just "another brick in the wall". One of the rare Floyd tracks to become a hit single, the song memorably features a choir of children from Islington Green School whose north London accents give the track much of its flavour.

Pink Floyd
Comfortably Numb

1979 • 6:24 • Gilmour – Waters

"Everything that I've ever written is very emotional and been tied to some real feeling that I've had about something at some point," bassist Roger Waters told Xfm. This was never more true than with the song 'Comfortably Numb' from *The Wall*, which many thought was a reference to heroin, but was actually inspired by a real event that took place on Pink Floyd's 1977 tour, as Waters explained to *MOJO* magazine: "I had stomach cramps so bad that I thought I wasn't able to go on. A doctor backstage gave me a shot of something that I swear to God would have killed a fucking elephant. I did the whole show hardly able to raise my hand above my knee. He said it was a muscular relaxant. But it rendered me almost insensible."

The song fitted in with *The Wall*'s concept, where the rock star protagonist has now alienated himself from the rest of the world and is seeking solace in sedation. The music for the song was written by guitarist Dave Gilmour, who had been working on the tune for his first solo album, but this was to be the last song he'd write with Waters as their working relationship became ever more fractured. Later given a disco makeover by the Scissor Sisters, the track remains one of the most powerful Pink Floyd ever recorded and was the very last song the band played together at Live 8 in 2005. MO'G

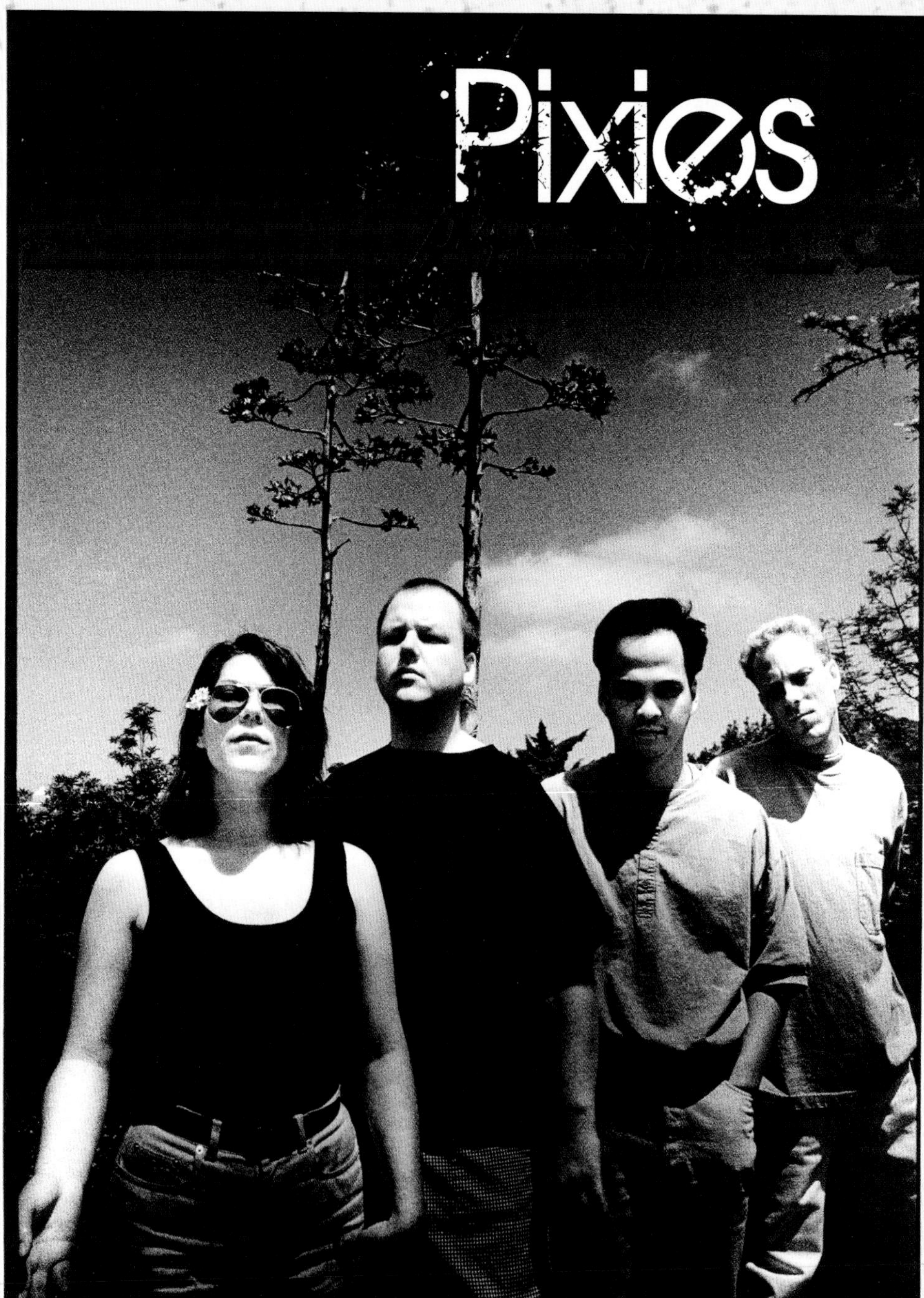
Pixies

> *"That came from me snorkelling, and having this very small fish trying to chase me"* — Black Francis

Pixies
Gigantic

| 1988 • 3:55 • Francis – Mrs John Murphy

Formed in Boston by singer and guitarist Black Francis, aka Charles Thompson IV, the Pixies were influenced by melodic punks Hüsker Dü, adding Francis' own surreal lyrics and unmistakable screeching vocals. 'Gigantic' features words by bassist Kim Deal – who was then going under her "married name" Mrs John Murphy – concerning a 1986 movie called *Crimes Of The Heart* in which a middle-aged white woman falls in love with a black teenager. Brilliantly, the dusty leather glove on the back of the 12-inch sleeve came about because photographer Simon Larbalestier misheard the lyrics – he thought the line was: "Gigantic... a big, big glove".

Pixies
Where Is My Mind?

| 1988 • 3:54 • Francis

"That came from me snorkelling in the Caribbean," recalled Black Francis to *Select* magazine in 1997, "and having this very small fish trying to chase me." Produced by underground legend Steve Albini, 'Where Is My Mind?' was recorded for the Pixies' first full-length album, *Surfer Rosa*. It's testament to Albini's lo-fi approach that the backing track to 'Where Is My Mind?' cuts off abruptly – the tape had simply run out and the take was kept on the finished album.

Pixies
Debaser

| 1989 • 2:53 • Francis

The opening track on the *Doolittle* album, 'Debaser' rewrites the notorious surrealist film *Un Chien Andalou*, which depicts a man slicing open a woman's eye with a razor. "The point of *Un Chien Andalou* was to debase morality," Black Francis told *NME* in 1989. "To debase standards of art." Producer Gil Norton told Xfm: "The word debaser doesn't exist and I like the idea of penning a new noun... Charles didn't like the song when we started recording, but once Kim's vocals went on he warmed to it, and really liked the way the song built." Although not released as a single at the time, the song's storming guitar attack and Francis' hysterical delivery had a massive influence on Kurt Cobain, who later admitted that 'Smells Like Teen Spirit' was "basically trying to rip off the Pixies".

Pixies
Monkey Gone To Heaven

1989 • 2:58 • Francis

"Someone told me that in the Hebrew language, you can find references to man in the fifth, Satan in the sixth and God in the seventh," explained Black Francis after the first single from the *Doolittle* album was released. "I don't know if there is a spiritual hierarchy or not. I didn't go to the library to figure it out." Part nursery rhyme, part apocalyptic environmental disaster, 'Monkey Gone To Heaven' pondered the consequences of man's destruction of the ozone layer, polluting of the seas and other ecological horrors. The subtle counterpoint to

Francis' Old Testament hollering was a delicate string quartet. "The idea came from Kim plucking piano strings with a plectrum," explained producer Gil Norton. "I really liked the idea of a different sonic landscape to this song so I suggested getting in a small string quartet. The band were excited and nervous about this at the same time, but when we recorded the section they all loved it."

Pixies
Here Comes Your Man

1989 • 3:22 • Francis

An early song by Black Francis, 'Here Comes Your Man' is a brief sketch about "winos and hobos travelling on the trains,

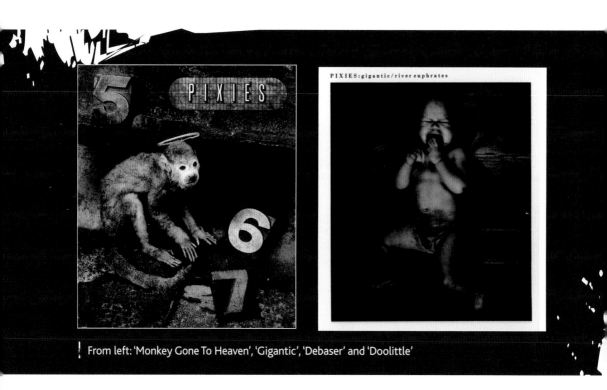

From left: 'Monkey Gone To Heaven', 'Gigantic', 'Debaser' and 'Doolittle'

who die in the California Earthquake". The band had already made three attempts to record the song, but feared it was too "pop". "I really liked the song and wanted to try a different arrangement," said producer Gil Norton. "We played around with it on a weekend while Charles was away. When he got back to the studio we had a new arrangement, which took all the best bits of the other versions and Charles got excited about it again. We were trying to develop different styles of music so when you put the album on, it was like you were on a rollercoaster ride that you didn't want to get off". MO'G

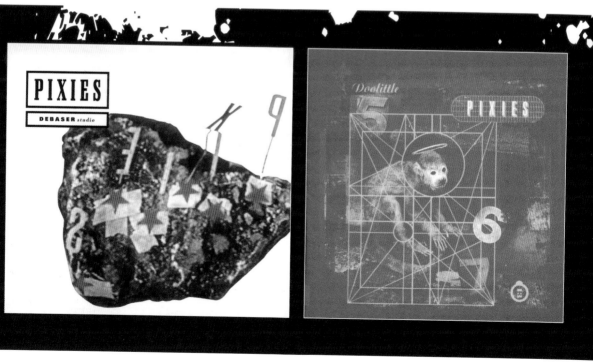

Placebo

such naïve pursuits. Again, it's a song now the band regret. In fact, the band's singer Brian Molko, is so embarrassed by it he's vowed not to play it again. "The days of the nonsense lyrics, like on 'Pure Morning', are just completely gone," he said in 2009. "I just can't write that way anymore."

Placebo
Nancy Boy

❘ 1996 · 3:48 · Placebo

With Britpop in the ascendancy and the laddishness of magazines like *Loaded* dominating the cultural agenda, the cross-dressing, make-up wearing, trash-talking Placebo were very much agents provocateurs when they emerged. "We wanted to stand up and be counted," said the band's singer Brian Molko. "There's no better way to do that than by putting a bunch of slap on, wearing a skirt and fucking with people's heads." This was the single that got them noticed, a gender-bending blast of power-punk that the band themselves now regret. "I just wish the song that propelled us into the limelight had been a little bit better written," cringed Molko.

Placebo
Pure Morning

❘ 1998 · 4:14 · Molko – Placebo

Having successfully got under the skin of much of the then-prevailing Britpop community, Placebo set about cementing their reputation as hedonists of the highest order. 'Pure Morning' set that ball in motion in stylish fashion, celebrating as it did friends with weed and further

Placebo
20th Century Boy

❘ 1998 · 3:40 · Bolan

Placebo may have got under the nose of much of rock's elite, but they did have one powerful ally. David Bowie had heard a demo of the band's first album and, impressed, he took them on tour around Europe and then, subsequently, asked them to open for him at his 50th birthday bash at Madison Square Gardens. Placebo seemed the obvious choice, then, to cover this Marc Bolan classic for the film *Velvet Goldmine*, which detailed the story of glam in the early 1970s and in which they even had a brief cameo, as a band called The Flaming Creatures. Placebo then performed this track with Bowie at the 1999 Brit awards.

Placebo
Every You Every Me

❘ 1999 · 3:33 · Molko – Campion – Placebo

Placebo's second album, *Without You I'm Nothing*, was recorded under a certain amount of stress as the band struggled to see eye-to-eye with their producer Steve Osborne. "There was a lot of frustration and depression there," said the band's singer Brian Molko. "Having said that, we're a band that does need a certain amount of friction on which to thrive." From that friction came one of their best-loved songs, in which the band found their feet as a power-trio, while Molko found himself on more certain lyrical ground in detailing a bitter love affair.

Placebo
Without You I'm Nothing
| 1999 • 4:08 • Molko – Placebo

Opening with a bruised guitar, 'Without You I'm Nothing' – the title track of Placebo's second album – further sealed their relationship with David Bowie, the singer duetting with Brian Molko over its initially monotone melody. Dark, pleading, edgy and epic, it would hint at more depth and introspection from Placebo to come.

Placebo
The Bitter End
| 2003 • 3:10 • Placebo

Frontman Brian Molko was in reflective mood as Placebo went into the making of their fourth album. Their past record, *Black Market Music*, had seen them indulge in a party lifestyle, while their next, *Meds*, would detail the aftermath of that life. *Sleeping With Ghosts*, in the middle, was the bridge between the two and found Molko carrying considerable baggage. The pulsating guitars and frantic driving rhythm of 'The Bitter End' belied what was, in fact, an exorcism of emotion as Molko exhumed, dissected and analysed the collapse of a relationship in a bid to free himself of its memories.

Placebo
For What It's Worth
| 2009 • 2:47 • Placebo

Clean, sober and with a new drummer in tow, Placebo remerged in 2009 with perhaps their strongest album in years. 'For What It's Worth', a taut and honed piece of songwriting, was the first sign of their newfound dedication. Both the track and the album it came from – *Battle For The Sun* – would spearhead a Placebo renaissance.
TB

Iggy Pop
Lust For Life
| 1977 • 5:14 • Pop – Bowie

Iggy Pop achieved notoriety with garage rock pioneers The Stooges. After releasing two under-appreciated albums at the turn of the 1970s, the band imploded due to lack of commercial success and rampant heroin abuse among the musicians. Winding up in London, Pop met David Bowie and the superstar agreed to record a third Stooges album. *Raw Power* was a major influence on punk, but it was the last gasp for the band, with Pop winding up in a mental institution. There, he was visited by Bowie, who suggested he accompany him on his US tour... and when Bowie relocated to West Berlin in 1976, Pop went too. Embarking on a (mainly) drug-free regime and recording in a derelict ballroom by the Berlin Wall, the duo produced four albums between them in just one year – Bowie's *Low* and *"Heroes"* and Pop's *The Idiot* and *Lust For Life*. Once content to write songs like 'Death Trip', the title track of the latter album represents the new, revitalised, more optimistic Iggy Pop. "I was living on coke, hash, red wine, beer and German sausages, had my own little place and I was sleeping in a cot with cold-water showers," he recalled in the 2007 book *Iggy Pop: Open Up And Bleed*. The title track was inspired by the Morse code message that would open the US Armed Forces TV network every evening, and was transformed by drummer Hunt Sales into a thunderous racket. Pop's hipster poetry makes little sense ("Johhny Yen" is a character from a William Burroughs novel, although former Doors manager Danny Sugerman contends that it's a reference to a former drug dealer he and Pop knew), but it's impossible to deny the joie de vivre that spills out of the record. Memorably used to open the film *Trainspotting*, this song about overcoming heroin addiction has since been used to advertise luxury cruises.

Iggy Pop
The Passenger

1977 • 4:44 • Pop – Gardiner

Written by Iggy Pop about his sojourn in West Berlin in 1977, 'The Passenger' depicts the star travelling through the German streets on the overground S-Bahn train and was inspired by a poem written by Jim Morrison of The Doors, which described a metaphysical car journey. Featuring David Bowie on piano and backing vocals, guitarist Ricky Gardiner came up with the song's riff while walking in the countryside near his home. "It was a case of the chord sequence 'slipping through' while I was lost in the glory of a beautiful spring morning," he recalled to *The Independent* in 2005. MO'G

"I was living on coke, hash, beer and German sausages"

– Iggy Pop

Portishead
Sour Times

1994 • 5:49 • Gibbons – Barrow – Utley – Schifrin – Brooks – Turner

In 1994, a new music scene – soon to be dubbed "trip-hop" by many – was emerging from Bristol, in south-west England. The sound was characterised by its experimental use of downtempo breakbeats alongside moody, atmospheric music and samples. Massive Attack's 1991 debut *Blue Lines* was the first album from the genre to be both commercially and critically successful. But it wasn't until Portishead's debut album *Dummy* that trip-hop truly crossed over into the mainstream. Initially released in 1994, 'Sour Times' was an unlikely candidate for mainstream success. Its shuffly beats, sinister guitar riffs and ethereal vocals weren't the sort of thing that sat easily next to contemporary chart-dominators Wet Wet Wet and Mariah Carey. In fact, on first release, it didn't make much of an impact. The album, released a week later, spent one week in the top 40 before dropping out. However, it was with the release of the following single, 'Glory Box', that things really began to turn around for the band. After its success, 'Sour Times' was re-released, hit the top 20 in the UK and went on to be an alternative rock hit in the US.

Portishead
Glory Box

1995 · 5:06
Gibbons – Barrow – Utley – Hayes

Portishead's label, Go! Discs, knew that 'Glory Box' was a hit, despite the band's own reservations. Recalls Geoff Barrows, "We had a row with the record company because we didn't want to release it because it felt too commercial. We lost the argument really. But we bought houses!" Strings and distorted guitar notes are layered over breakbeats, with Beth Gibbons' haunting voice crooning along. Coming out a month after album *Dummy* had topped end-of-year polls, the single debuted at number 13, in spite of little radio play and the band's refusal to do much press. It led to the album re-entering the UK top 40 and staying there for 44 consecutive weeks. In July, *Dummy* won the Mercury Music Prize. MS

The Presidents Of The United States Of America
Peaches

1996 · 2:49 · Ballew – The Presidents Of The United States Of America

It's commonly acknowledged that there just aren't enough rock songs about eating soft fruit. Lead singer Chris Ballew has said that he wrote the track about a girl he liked who had a peach tree; others have interpreted the lyrics less literally. Whatever the meaning, "Movin' to the country, gonna eat a lot of peaches" has become the band's most recognisable refrain. Formed in Seattle in 1993, the band broke the musical mould of the American north-west with an ironic originality and humour noticeably lacking in much of the area's prevalent grunge.

The Presidents Of The United States Of America
Lump

1995 · 2:14 · Ballew – The Presidents Of The United States Of America

Short, eccentric, catchy and slightly manic, 'Lump' was written by Chris Ballew after he had unusually vivid dreams while on antibiotics. The band themselves have called this their favourite song. The video made for the song, directed by Roman Coppola, is set mainly in a bog, where the band rock out while up to their knees in water and pond weed, singing about the eponymous lump, who sits alone in a marsh. A second, alternative, video was considered too dark to be used. JH

Primal Scream

Primal Scream
Loaded

1990 • 4:33 • Gillespie – Innes – Young

With its fervently indie purist scene, Scotland was the last place to look like it would get swept up in the acid house revolution. Primal Scream were self-confessed sceptics about dance music, but by the time Andrew Weatherall remixed their old 'I'm Losing More Than I'll Ever Have' into 'Loaded', they were converts. Built on samples from a Peter Fonda biker movie, *The Wild Angels*, and a bootleg mix of Edie Brickell's 'What I Am', it became a dance anthem the moment it was promo-ed, becoming the band's first hit in March 1990. Its similarity to Rolling Stones' 'Sympathy For The Devil' was much remarked upon, possibly influencing their decision to recruit the man who produced it, Jimmy Miller, for the subsequent album, *Screamadelica*.

Primal Scream
Come Together

1990 • 4:54 • Gillespie – Innes – Young

Dance music was about so much more than just dancing. 'Come Together' was essentially one long (very long – the album version ran for more than ten minutes) build-up where the beat is mostly replaced by dubby echoes and a church organ. This is dance music as

gospel: the sampled voice of Jesse Jackson booms out from the Wattstax concert as the bassline grows stronger, the pianos come in but still the beat never rises above a sedate tempo and the listener is left as if expecting the resurrection. Possibly the most E'd up record ever made. And on most versions, lead singer Bobby Gillespie doesn't even appear.

Primal Scream
Movin' On Up

1991 • 3:51 • Gillespie – Innes – Young

Radio never really got 'Loaded' or 'Come Together', big as they were. But 'Movin' On Up' suited them just fine. Where its predecessors had sampled dialogue, 'Movin' On Up' had a hook, a riff (Stonesy, again) and the kind of introductory line that gives the fans pins and needles. "I was blind, now I can see / You've made a believer out of me" wailed Bobby Gillespie, like a man who'd just been baptised... in the reviving waters of acid house. This was the fifth (count 'em) single off the album, but radio luv ensured it was the biggest hit of the lot.

Primal Scream
Rocks

1994 • 3:36 • Gillespie – Innes – Young

As if to prove they hadn't abandoned rock music, merely introduced it to some interesting new friends, Primal Scream yanked themselves right back to elementary rock'n'roll with their follow-up album *Give Out But Don't Give Up*. Lead single 'Rocks' was almost a pastiche of the Stones, with its slashing guitar and lyrics about junkies and whores. Their drug habits at the time were reputedly equally as Herculean as the Stones' in their prime too, and tales persist of them collapsing at record company meetings, shacking up with Hollywood madam Heidi Fleiss or being mysteriously stabbed at parties in Memphis. This was the sound of a band living the life so you don't have to.

Primal Scream
Jailbird

| 1994 • 3:46 • Gillespie – Innes – Young

Primal Scream later told *Uncut* they'd originally intended the follow-up to *Screamadelica* to be "down... redemptive and uplifting... slow and soulful". But a meeting with Black Crowes' producer George Drakoulias scotched that and the lead singles turned into straight-up boogie stomps, with 'Jailbird' soon following 'Rocks' into the charts. Once

again, this is rock at its most, er, primal, with singer Bobby Gillespie wearing his drug interests on his sleeve ("scratching like a tomcat I've a monkey on my back") while the riffs come hard and gospel-influenced backing singers turn the chorus into an instantly tangy addiction.

Primal Scream
Country Girl

| 2006 • 3:55 • Primal Scream

Having gone through dub, angry punk and electro rock, Primal Scream came back to the 1970s with *Riot City Blues*. With its banjos, po' boys and the pungent whiff of the Delta, 'Country Girl' is The Scream doing The Stones doing Dixie (and even sounds a little like their 'Sweet Virginia'). Derivative it may be, but it's also a blast, with a kick-ass intro and Gillespie in prime hell-raiser mode. "Never get to bed, never get to hell" is as good a summation of this most hedonist of bands as you could wish for. The cover was borrowed from Whitbread Prize-winning novel *The Accidental*, by Scottish author Ali Smith. SY

'I was blind, now I can see / You've made a believer out of me' wailed Bobby Gillespie, like a man who'd just been baptised... in the reviving waters of acid house

– Primal Scream, 'Movin' On Up'

The Prodigy

The Prodigy
Poison

! 1995 · 4:05 · Howlett

Up to this point, The Prodigy had only been using samples for vocals, but it was for 'Poison' that their MC, Maxim recorded the lyrics. Liam Howlett told Q magazine that "[Poison] was a turning point for us. Free-styling over the music. When we did that we thought, 'Why the fuck haven't we done this before?,'" The track was the fourth single from the album *Music For The Jilted Generation*. The group wanted to call the album "Music For Joyriders" but were persuaded against that title by their record label, XL Recordings.

The Prodigy
Firestarter

! 1996 · 3:45 · Deal – Dudley – Flint – Horn – Howlett – Jeczalik – Langan – Morley

Formed by Essex boy Liam Howlett in 1990, The Prodigy are one of the few big beat pioneers to break into the mainstream in the early 1990s. Known for their eccentric videos and enthralling live performances, their record sales matched their critical acclaim, with more than 20 million records sold worldwide to date – a feat that remains unparalleled in dance music history.

'Firestarter' was released on March 18th 1996, the first single from new album *The Fat Of The Land*. Their tenth single to date, it became The Prodigy's first-ever number one, staying at the top spot in the UK charts for three weeks. With success also came great controversy as the national fire service accused the band of promoting an incitement to arson. The video also featured Keith Flint looking menacing in a tube tunnel at Aldwych station. Notably, this was the first track to feature Flint on vocals: flint/firestarter, geddit...?

The Prodigy
Breathe

! 1996 · 3:59 · Howlett

'Breathe' was single number two from *The Fat Of The Land* and by this point, the group found themselves reaching godlike status across the UK festivals over the summer of 1997. Dance artists had rarely achieved such status in the past, so their seven years

"When we did that we thought, 'Why the fuck haven't we done this before?'"

– Liam Howlett on the decision to free-style over music

"We represent all that is great about Britain"

of work building up to this moment had truly paid off. 'Breathe' achieved number one status in Finland, Norway, Sweden and the UK. Looking back at the UK charts at the time, the previous number one spot had been held by Robson & Jerome for 'You'll Never Walk Alone' and 'Breathe' was succeeded by Peter Andre's 'I Feel You'. This could be interpreted in two ways: either the music tastes of the British public were in meltdown or it highlights what a huge achievement it was for such an unusual dance act to have achieved such mainstream success.

The Prodigy
Smack My Bitch Up

❕ 1997 • 4:45 • Howlett

Having achieved phenomenal worldwide success with 'Firestarter', 'Smack My Bitch Up' took The Prodigy back to the top of the charts, reaching number eight in the UK singles chart.

All this, despite a less-than-PC chorus sampled from the Ultramagnetic MCs' 1988 track 'Give The Drummer Some' and an eye-popping video from director Jonas Åkerlund which features a night out from hell seen from the eyes of a drinking, drugging, womanising protagonist… that turns out to be a woman herself.

The Prodigy
Omen

❕ 2009 • 3:14 • Howlett – Hutton – Palmer

On January 9th 2009, a newsletter was sent out to fans announcing the imminent arrival of the hotly anticipated new Prodigy single. 'Omen' was set to launch their brand new album, *Invaders Must Die*. With their history of mixing up genres, beats and sounds, their stalwart fanbase and the UK's expectant media were intrigued as to what the new album would bring. Liam Howlett was in no doubt as to their place in the nation's affections: "We represent all that is great about Britain, and we should be protected like a national heritage," he is quoted as saying, with a smile.
BdP / MOG

The Psychedelic Furs

The Psychedelic Furs
Pretty In Pink

1981 · 3:57 · Richard Butler

"It's not representative of what we do," recalled Psychedelic Furs singer Richard Butler, "but if somebody came up to me in ten years' time and said, 'You're the guy that wrote 'Pretty In Pink', I wouldn't be that upset." The Psychedelic Furs were based around London-born brothers Richard and Tim Butler, and their moniker hopefully evoked the spirit of their 1960s heroes, while Richard's studied cool and impressive cheekbones made him almost a pin-up version of the Sex Pistols' Johnny Rotten. Their first, self-titled album from 1980 was a minor hit in the UK, but the group reconvened the following year for its follow-up, *Talk Talk Talk*. Full of polished, clean-sounding rock, its most enduring moment was 'Pretty In Pink', an ambiguous sketch of a mysterious girl delivered in Richard's dry, Bowie-esque growl.

The single brushed the edge of the top 40, but it wasn't until five years later that the song became a bona fide hit. Director John Hughes was something of an Anglophile and had used many British bands to soundtrack his incredibly successful teen movies, most notably 'Don't You Forget About Me' by Simple Minds in *The Breakfast Club*. For his 1986 comedy drama starring Molly Ringwald and Jon Cryer, he took the title from The Psychedelic Furs and made 'Pretty In Pink' its theme song. Depicting romance across class divides in a US high school, the track encapsulated the character of crazy punk kid Ringwald and her attempts to bag a rich boyfriend, but despite pushing the song into the UK top 20 in a re-recorded version, Richard remained unimpressed with the film. "I don't think it's any good," he scoffed. "The girl in the song is very kind of low life and the girl in the movie is totally the opposite. It's too cutesy, too Americana. It's bubblegum." MO'G

Public Image Ltd
Public Image

1978 · 3:00 · P.i.L.

When the Sex Pistols came to an ignoble end following their US tour in 1978, and with manager Malcolm McLaren plotting to take the band to Rio to meet fugitive "Great Train Robber" Ronnie Biggs, disillusioned frontman Johnny Rotten quit. He jettisoned his "punk" pseudonym and insisted he was referred to by his real name, John Lydon, before enlisting old friend Jah Wobble on bass and former Clash guitarist Keith Levene. Their first single remains one of the finest rants in pop music, as Lydon rails against his uncaring ex-manager: "You never listen to a word that I said / You only seen me for the clothes that I wear". Given a scorching riff by Levene and a subsonic Wobble bassline, the bile audibly spills out of Lydon as he reclaims his own personality from the cartoons McLaren created. The door was officially closed on the Sex Pistols story... for a while, at least.

Public Image Ltd
Rise

| 1986 · 6:18 · Lydon – Laswell

John Lydon originally wanted P.i.L. to create the most inaccessible music imaginable – everything he wanted the Sex Pistols to be, in fact. But while 1979's *Metal Box* is one of the most harrowing albums ever and created "post-punk" as we know it, the "collective" began to disintegrate. Frustrated with the band's slow work rate, Jah Wobble left in mid-1980, while Keith Levene jumped ship a couple of years later when frequent clashes with Lydon became a problem. So P.i.L. became the former Johnny Rotten and a backing group, and subsequently veered off into poppier territory. 1986's *Album* spawned 'Rise', which became one of the band's biggest hits, reaching number 11 in the UK despite the lyrics concerning the controversial issue of apartheid in South Africa. The slow but insistent build-up of the music and the refrain "Anger is an energy" perfectly encapsulate the feeling of struggle. MO'G

Pulp Babies

| 1992 · 4:05 · Banks – Cocker – Doyle – Mackey – Senior

Fifteen long years after starting the band with a schoolfriend, Jarvis Cocker and Pulp would begin their ascent to mainstream fame with single 'Babies'. Recorded at Island Records' studio The Fallout Shelter with Suede producer Ed Buller, the song didn't set the charts alight when it was released by small indie Gift Records, but it did bring Pulp to the attention of the studio's owners. "I remember shopping the song around," Buller told Xfm, "but everyone apart from Island were saying they'd been around too long and that they wouldn't fly." The song's glitzy, disco-infused indie would soon become a Pulp hallmark and go on to spectacularly disprove the doubters.

Pulp Lipgloss

| 1993 · 3:34 · Banks – Cocker – Doyle – Mackey – Senior

Once signed to Island, Pulp embarked on recording their major label debut with producer Ed Buller. Inspired, according to Buller, to make a '90s version of Roxy

Music's 'For Your Pleasure'", they hunkered down in Pink Floyd's Britannia Row Studios in Islington. Keen to hitch a ride on Britpop's coattails, the record label released 'Lipgloss' as their first single. "The band weren't over-confident because they'd been doing it for a long time," Buller remembers, but the single charted at number 50, a surefire sign that Jarvis Cocker and Pulp's fortunes were changing.

Pulp
Do You Remember The First Time

| 1994 • 4:23 • Banks – Cocker – Doyle – Mackey – Senior

If album *His'n'Hers* was Pulp's breakthrough moment, then 'Do You Remember...' was its pinnacle. A hymn to the mixed experiences of losing one's virginity, it catapulted the band into the hearts of a nation, and cast Jarvis Cocker as an unlikely, bespectacled poster-boy for Britpop. The single also inspired a short film, which the band had decided to make during the album's six-week recording session. The result was chaos, according to their producer Ed Buller. "We had a collection of famous people – Jo Brand, Vic Reeves and Bob Mortimer, John Peel – walk past and give their thoughts on their first shag. It was a typical, and classic, Pulp moment."

Pulp
Common People

| 1995 – 5:50 • Banks – Cocker – Doyle – Mackey – Senior

As Britpop hit its commercial and cultural stride in the mid-1990s, Pulp introduced their second major label album, *Different Class* with a single that would establish them as one of the movement's big-hitters. Ironically, 'Common People' was an attack on the "class tourism" that seemed prevalent at the end, but the story of one of Jarvis Cocker's fellow students at London art college Central Saint Martins struck a large enough chord to take the song to number two in the UK charts. The result was a vindication of the band's progress and their decision to enlist the services of heavyweight producer Chris Thomas (Roxy Music, Pink Floyd, Sex Pistols). Toiling in London's Townhouse Studios, Thomas admitted that bringing 'Common People' to life was a struggle. "Various bits and pieces needed work to make sure it sounded cohesive," he told Xfm. "The lyric was the cherry and icing on the cake, but the cake had to be right in the first place."

Pulp
Sorted for E's & Wizz

| 1995 • 3:42 • Banks – Cocker – Doyle – Mackey – Senior – Webber

A song about going to an illegal rave, the title was a phrase heard by one of Jarvis Cocker's friends on attending The Stone Roses' legendary outdoor show at Spike Island. Many years later, Pulp would step into the Roses' vacated Glastonbury headline slot in 1995 after a mountain-biking accident in which guitarist John Squire broke his collarbone. The era-defining performance was the first time the band played 'Sorted...', which would go on to cause minor tabloid uproar with a single cover that had instructions on how to build your own drugs "wrap".

Pulp
Disco 2000

| 1995 • 4:33 • Banks – Cocker – Doyle – Mackey – Senior – Webber

'Disco 2000' was Pulp's third top 10 hit in a row; confirmation that a band that had now been going almost 20 years had finally hit the super league. A slight throw-back to the themes and sounds of *His'n'Hers*, 'Disco 2000' nevertheless propelled album *Different Class* to platinum status and the Mercury Music Prize in 1996.

Pulp
Something Changed

| 1995 • 3:29 • Banks – Cocker – Doyle – Mackey – Senior – Webber

During the making of *Different Class*, producer Chris Thomas remembers being presented with seven or eight songs – "the meat of the album" – which Jarvis Cocker had written in a 48-hour period. 'Something Changed' was among them and went on to become the band's fourth top 10 single. The song's success was buoyed by Cocker's stage invasion and protest at Michael Jackson's self-deification during his performance of 'Earth Song' at the 1996 Brit awards. Jackson's people were fuming; everyone else fell even harder for Cocker's charms. OH

> Jackson's people were fuming; everyone else fell even harder for Cocker's charms

Queens Of The Stone Age
Lost Art Of Keeping A Secret

| 2000 • 3:36 • Homme – Oliveri

The loose collective of members that make up Queens Of The Stone Age hit paydirt with second album and its lead single, 'Lost Art Of Keeping A Secret'. Ex-Kyuss guitarist and head Queen Josh Homme had established the band's desert rock template on their eponymous debut album, but 'Lost Art...' took it to another level entirely. "This was the first introduction of a real pop sensibility to our fans," he explained to Xfm. "We were venturing into places I'd usually have been afraid to go."

Queens Of The Stone Age
Feel Good Hit Of The Summer

| 2000 • 2:43 • Homme – Oliveri

Rated R's explosive opener, with lyrics comprised entirely of a narcotic shopping list, seemed to tie Queens' flag firmly to the hedonist's mast. The song, however, became the most unlikely anti-drugs anthem when the San Diego Sheriff's

Department used it on an instructional video documenting the dangers of substance abuse. Perhaps the greatest irony, however, was the drafting of Judas Priest singer and former chemical dustbin Rob Halford to sing backing vocals on the song. "He agreed without seeing the lyrics, so I wrote them down on a piece of paper for him – nicotine, valium, vicodin, marijuana, ecstasy and alcohol," said Josh Homme. "I wrote cocaine in big capital letters. He looked at it and said, 'Ah, a rock'n'roll cocktail. I think I invented that!'"

Queens Of The Stone Age
No One Knows

2002 · 4:38 · Homme – Lanegan

Since befriending Josh Homme in his Kyuss days, Foo Fighters' main man Dave Grohl had become a huge fan of Queens Of The Stone Age. He told Xfm: "There were such beautiful songs on [Rated R], we wore that record out." While he'd made no secret of wanting to participate in that album's sessions, he finally got his chance on third record Songs For The Deaf. Nowhere was the former Nirvana sticksman's presence felt more than on 'No One Knows', with its thunderous drum fills and countless air-drumming moments. It became an instant classic and remains one of Queens' greatest-loved tracks.

Queens Of The Stone Age
Go With The Flow

2002 · 3:07 · Homme – Oliveri

The unrelenting piano on 'Go With The Flow' introduced another classic single from Songs For The Deaf. Although the album was a huge critical and commercial success, it also signalled the end of singer/guitarist Josh Homme's working relationship with co-conspirator, bassist and loose cannon Nick Oliveri. "I knew Nick as a series of explosions of increasing size," Homme told Xfm. "The better we did, the bigger the explosions would get... Sadly, one of my skills has always been how to wield the knife."

Queens of the Stone Age
Little Sister

2005 · 2:54
Homme – Van Leeuwen – Castillo

With former Danzig drummer Joey Castillo installed in the band, his muscular groove and a ubiquitous cowbell (or 'Jam Block') rattled 'Little Sister' along at an impressive rate of knots. It was a huge improvement on the song's previous incarnation. "We tried a version of it on Songs For The Deaf," Josh Homme said. "It sounded like Molly Ringwald dancing... it was kinda lame." OH

It became an instant classic and remains one of Queens' greatest-loved tracks

– Queens Of The Stone Age, 'No One Knows'

The Raconteurs
Steady As She Goes

2006 • 3:37 • Benson – White

'Steady As She Goes' would be the starting point from which supergroup (a term the band themselves are not fond of) The Raconteurs would develop. According to the band's own account, White Stripes frontman Jack White had teamed up with old friend and solo artist Brendan Benson "in an attic in the middle of a hot summer" to help complete a song he was working on at the time. That song – at the time a reggae-style composition – was 'Steady As She Goes' and it proved to be the trigger to the pair forming a band. The addition of The Greenhornes' bassist Jack Lawrence and drummer Patrick Keeler completed the lineup.

Rock stars' side projects are often rather self-indulgent affairs that only diehard fans could pretend to enjoy, but with White and Benson at the creative helm, this would prove to be something special. The first taste of their music collaboration came in the form of a double A-side with 'Steady As She Goes' paired with 'Store Bought Bones' – and the former was undoubtedly the star of the show. White and Benson share vocals on a blues-tinged pop-rock track that bubbles along with a catchy 1970s bassline and a choppy guitar cutting in and out on the beat before the song explodes into a rock-fuelled chorus complete with symbol crashes. You can almost hear the enjoyment. Benson is able to rock harder than in his solo work while White, with increased personnel at his disposal, is given the freedom to experiment with more sounds than the sparse White Stripes set-up allows. Both the single and their debut album *Broken Boy Soldiers* achieved top 10 status in the UK and were followed up by second album *Consolers Of The Lonely*.
JS

Radiohead
Anyone Can Play Guitar

1993 • 3:37 • Yorke – O'Brien – Greenwood – Greenwood – Selway

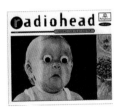

Radiohead's first UK top 40 single (number 32 in February 1993) was the sound of a band still finding their feet. Loved by many fans, 'Anyone Can Play Guitar' was the first single from the band's debut album *Pablo Honey*. Set against the backdrop of an increasingly diluted slew of American grunge and a relatively anaemic UK indie scene, the album showcased the emerging voice of a band that was special and distinctive.

Radiohead
Creep

1993 • 3:55 • Yorke – O'Brien – Greenwood – Greenwood – Selway – Hammond – Hazlewood

The song that Radiohead have arguably been reacting to since its success in 1993, 'Creep' is both their signature song and their albatross. It was omitted from their live set for many years before reappearing in the festival sets of 2006. 'Creep' was a radio hit in the US before it eventually gained the attention of the UK on its re-re-release in the September of 1993. Due to an unconvinced American record label, the single was almost not released in the US at all. David Field, a British A&R executive who was working at the label's LA office at the time, slipped a copy of the track to KROQ, LA's influential rock radio station. They started playing it immediately and word spread very quickly that 'Creep' was a hit.

Radiohead
Planet Telex

> 1995 • 4:22 • Yorke – O'Brien – Greenwood – Greenwood – Selway

Radiohead's second album *The Bends* was recorded with legendary producer John Leckie (The Stone Roses, Muse) at various sessions in RAK, Manor Studios and Abbey Road. The opening track on the album, the spacious and electrifying 'Planet Telex', was written and recorded in one night after an unusually boozy meal in a Greek restaurant. As Leckie told Xfm in May 2010: "After a few bottles of wine we ended up back in the studio where the whole of this track was written and recorded. It started with a sound at about 9pm and ended with Thom recording his vocal, a little worse for wear, at 2am."

Radiohead
My Iron Lung

> 1994 • 3:36 • Yorke – O'Brien – Greenwood – Greenwood – Selway

Producer John Leckie told Xfm that this was an unusual and difficult song to get right and it was only when they heard a live version, recorded at London's Astoria theatre for MTV in May 1994, that it made sense. The final version of 'My Iron Lung' that appears on *The Bends*, and which was released as the album's first single in October 1994, uses the intro and the verses from the Astoria live take and the chorus from the original studio session. A seamless piece of studio edit trickery by Leckie.

Radiohead
High And Dry

> 1995 • 4:17 • Yorke – O'Brien – Greenwood – Greenwood – Selway

'High And Dry' is the 'Creep' of *The Bends* – the album's biggest radio hit but unpopular with the band themselves. Thom Yorke later claimed that he was forced to include it on the album. A characteristically plaintive yet elevating Radiohead song, 'High And Dry' was written and recorded during sessions for *Pablo Honey* but was resurrected for the band's second album. The final version is simply the original demo but remastered.

Radiohead
The Bends

1995 • 4:04 • Yorke – O'Brien – Greenwood – Greenwood – Selway

An outstanding live song, 'The Bends' had been played live by the band for many months before it was recorded. John Leckie, Radiohead's producer, told Xfm that there was a lot of pressure from the label at the time to find Jonny Greenwood's "signature guitar sound". Many different amps, guitars and pedals were brought in before it was apparent that this long sought-after sound was simply him playing his original telecaster with his own Fender amp and an overdrive pedal. As powerfully demonstrated in the fierce awe-inspiring solo he gives towards the end of 'The Bends'.

Radiohead
Fake Plastic Trees

1995 • 4:50 • Yorke – O'Brien – Greenwood – Greenwood – Selway

The third single from *The Bends* in the UK and the opening single in America. This epic and beautiful song was built around a demo vocal recorded by Thom Yorke under duress from producer John Leckie at the end of a long day in the studio. There was a string section booked for the following day and nothing for 'Fake Plastic Trees' had yet been recorded. Yorke's original guide vocal was so perfect that it not only made the final cut, but also set the tone for the way

in which the whole song was then built around it. The organ on the track is Jonny Greenwood's own family organ and had to be transported from his mother's front room in Oxford to the studio in London.

Radiohead
Just

1995 • 3:53 • Yorke – O'Brien – Greenwood – Greenwood – Selway

The most straightforward rock track on the album was also the most straightforward to record – all five band members in a room hammering it out together without additional effects or overdubs. The enigmatic video was directed by Jamie Thraves and features a man lying down on a pavement having a heated (subtitled) conversation with passers-by. When he finally reveals why he is lying down, the subtitles disappear. Although the subject of much conjecture from Radiohead fans, the secret of why he was lying down will always lie with the director, who refuses to tell.

Radiohead
Street Spirit (Fade Out)

1995 • 4:13 • Yorke – O'Brien – Greenwood – Greenwood – Selway

The closing track on *The Bends* and an unlikely top five single. 'Street Spirit (Fade Out)' has been described by singer Thom Yorke as one of the saddest and darkest songs the band have ever made. It is

Just because you feel it, doesn't mean it's there

– Radiohead, 'There There'

certainly mournful but its fragile beauty anesthetises the listener from what Yorke has described as its true meaning of sheer hopelessness. Despite that, the song's final call of "Immerse your soul in love" actually leaves the listener in a better, richer and more positive place.

Radiohead
Lucky

1995 • 4:20 • Yorke – Greenwood – Greenwood – O'Brien – Selway

The penultimate track on *OK Computer* was originally recorded for charity War Child's *Help* album in September 1995. The concept behind the album was to release the recordings as soon as possible after they were made. Therefore, tracks were recorded on Monday September 4th, mixed the following day and in shops by Saturday September 9th. 'Lucky' was one of the first recordings the band did with Nigel Godrich, who went on to become a long-term collaborator. The band considered re-recording and re-mixing 'Lucky' but the original War Child version is what ended up on *OK Computer*.

Radiohead
Paranoid Android

1997 • 6:27 • Yorke – Greenwood – Greenwood – O'Brien – Selway

Six-and-a-half minutes of uncompromising genius. After the success of *The Bends*, Radiohead were in a strong position with a global media eagerly anticipating their next move, but nobody was quite ready for 'Paranoid Android'. In three distinct parts, it was a jaw-dropping epic, combining the ethereal and the aggressive with the darkest and the most uplifting sides of the band. Radiohead's American record label allegedly thought it was a joke and initially refused to release it. 'Paranoid Android' went on to be become Radiohead's biggest single to date, hitting number three in the UK in June 1997.

Radiohead
Karma Police

1997 • 4:24 • Yorke – Greenwood – Greenwood – O'Brien – Selway

'Karma Police' was the second single from *OK Computer*, an album that has regularly appeared highly in lists of the best albums of all time. Produced by Nigel Godrich, who was an engineer on *The Bends*, it's also by far Radiohead's most successful album. It introduced them to a wider audience without being in any way creatively compromised. This track was based on an in-joke the band had about "the karma police" coming to get you if you did anything bad. The audience singing the refrain of "For a minute there, I lost myself" always provides one of the most joyous moments at any Radiohead gig.

Radiohead
No Surprises

| 1997 • 3:50 • Yorke – Greenwood – Greenwood – O'Brien – Selway

This deceptively pretty song has a heavy heart – lyrically it underpins *OK Computer*'s anti-consumerist theme with a caustic weariness. One particularly memorable live outing for the song was during Radiohead's now legendary headline set at Glastonbury festival in 1997. It was one of the wettest on record, Thom Yorke had been frustrated with lighting and monitor issues but as 'No Surprises' was climaxing, the sky filled with fireworks from another field. Although not intended for the Radiohead set, the timing was perfect and for those of us who were there, it was a true Glastonbury moment to be treasured.

Radiohead
There There

| 2003 • 5:22 • Yorke – Selway – O'Brien – Greenwood – Greenwood

This dark and brooding song was the arresting first single from Radiohead's sixth studio album *Hail To The Thief*. 'There There' was also the first song in the set each night on the band's 2003/4 *Hail To The Thief* tour and set the tone for some of the band's most aggressive and powerful performances. Each song on the album was given a subtitle; for 'There There' it was 'The Boney King Of Nowhere'.

Radiohead
Jigsaw Falling Into Place

| 2007 • 4:08 • Yorke – Greenwood – Greenwood – O'Brien – Selway

Radiohead's seventh studio album, *In Rainbows*, was released digitally very quickly after its completion in October 2007 and was distributed in a unique "pay what you want" format from the band's website. 'Jigsaw Falling Into Place', the first single to be released from the album, was debuted live on the group's 2006 tour and its taut and infectious discordance is classic Radiohead.
MW

[In Rainbows] was distributed in a unique "pay what you want" format
– Radiohead, 'In Rainbows'

Rage railed against corporate America, cultural imperialism and government oppression

Rage Against The Machine
Killing In The Name

**1992 • 5:13 • De La Rocha –
Rage Against The Machine**

The marriage of rock and hip-hop may not have been revolutionary by the time Rage Against The Machine released their self-titled debut album in 1992, but few would argue that anyone did it better. Bringing a political conscience to the party of barechests and knobgags, Rage railed against corporate America, cultural imperialism and government oppression, armed with a muscular groove and a devastating sonic assault. 'Killing In The Name', a single inspired by institutional racism, was the world's wake-up call to one of the decade's most important bands.

Formed by four skilled musicians who'd paid their dues on LA's music scene, the recording of the song's definitive take was simply a matter of harnessing Rage Against The Machine's staggering live power. "We set up a whole concert PA system in the studio because I wanted to capture them playing together," the album's producer Garth Richardson told Xfm recently. "What you hear is what they played. They were as good then as they are now."

After a minor skirmish with their record company over axing the iconic pre-chorus chant of "And now you do what they told you" (the band won – it stayed in), the song was released as a single. Its rousing climax however, with 16 "fucks" and one "motherfucker", led to many red faces and complaints at the BBC after Radio 1 DJ Bruno Brookes played the full unedited version of the song on the station's chart show. Unsurprisingly, it only served to enhance Rage's reputation even further.

As if it wasn't iconic enough, 'Killing In The Name' won a legendary Christmas chart battle in 2009 when it toppled the offering of *X Factor* reality star, Joe McElderry, to claim the number one spot. The song had been chosen by Xfm listeners Jon and Tracy Morter to spearhead the protest against the TV show's chart dominance. A groundswell of support centred on the pair's Facebook group, which also encouraged followers to donate money to homeless charity Shelter. "We wanted the Christmas chart to be exciting again," Tracy told Xfm. "We wanted people to gather around their radio like they used to. And that's what we got!" Rage crowned their unexpected chart success with a free show on June 6th, 2010 at London's Finsbury Park – 40,000 revellers attended the victory party.

Rage Against The Machine
Bombtrack

**1992 • 4:04 • De La Rocha –
Rage Against The Machine**

'Bombtrack' was the incendiary opening song on the band's equally fiery self-titled debut album. A tension-building, muted guitar line slowly gives way to Brad Wilk's thundering drums before Tom Morello unleashes hell with a huge, roaring guitar riff. This vitriolic rant about social inequality featured a line that could easily have been the band's *raison d'être* – "dope hooks make punks take another look" – as Rage Against The Machine's political leanings were delivered with some of the most visceral, exciting music of the decade. OH

The Rakes
22 Grand Job

2005 • 1:45 • The Rakes

Short and sweet, the one-and-a-half minutes of '22 Grand Job' is some of the most energetic, spiky and clever debut music you're likely to hear. The Rakes' debut album *Capture/Release* dealt with working life and escapism – topics that are encapsulated in their first release, which nailed the band's colours to the mast.

Having formed in 2002, the four childhood friends released '22 Grand Job' as a maxi-single in 2004 before the release of the album (and the single's re-release) the following year. Among a sea of post-punk, post-Libertines bands coming out of the UK during the last decade, The Rakes were probably the closest to good honest punk, with their sharp vocals and simple buzzing guitars echoing bands like The Clash. However, their subject matter was slightly more middle class; the band cast an eye over the nine-to-five grind of unfulfilling work for their debut single with a sentiment that could become the anthem for faceless worker drones everywhere. Vocalist Alan Donohoe's yelping words are positioned high in the mix to allow listeners to hear his witty, instantly quotable lines: "What am I supposed to do / He's earning twenty-eight / and I'm on twenty-two".

Despite the insightful lyrics, the song was not written from personal experience but rather a job interview that Donohoe went for: "I wrote that song about a job I almost got. I've never ever earned anything near there. That song was written as celebrating if you had that much money!" The band released two further albums – the brilliant *Ten New Messages* and *Klang* – before splitting in 2009, claiming they could no longer give 100% to their live shows. JS

Ramones

Ramones Blitzkrieg Bop

1976 • 2:14 • Ramones

As debut singles go, it's hard to beat 'Blitzkrieg Bop'. Not only did it lay down the rule under which the Ramones would operate from inception to death (buzzsaw guitar, three-chord riff, driving bass, tub-thumping drums, repeat – quickly – to fade), it also remains perhaps the definitive New York punk track, an explosive call to arms wrapped up in the four-word chorus of "Hey! Ho! Let's go!". Commercially, it was initially a disaster and failed to chart. However, its influence, particularly on the nascent Sex Pistols and The Clash who experienced it firsthand on the band's 1976 UK tour, was profound.

Ramones
Sheena Is A Punk Rocker

| 1977 • 2:47 • Ramones

While those in New York's cognoscenti – particularly the patrons of clubs Max's Kansas City and CBGB – knew very well who the Ramones were, few people in the rest of America had much of a clue that Dee Dee, Joey, Johnny and Tommy Ramone existed in 1977. Only in England – thanks to 'Blitzkrieg Bop', a raucous tour and the booming punk scene – were the Ramones a name to drop.

But these four, non-related leather-clad punks were slowly dismantling the hippie scene that was still lingering in the US – not that the aforementioned lingering hippie scene necessarily knew much about it yet. The Ramones were the opposite of what was considered the prevailing mood. Where bands were extending their songs into epic jams, the Ramones would normally call it a day around the two-and-a-half minute mark. Onstage they would count off every song – "One... two... three... four" – before each member would apparently embark in a race to reach

the end before the rest of the band. "We believe in songs... not in, uh, boogying and, uh, improvisation and stuff like that, y'know," Tommy told the influential *Punk* magazine of their modus operandi.

Yet there was more to the Ramones than simply delivering raw, powerful and charged rock'n'roll in as few chords and little time as possible. Lurking beneath were far more diverse influences, which 'Sheena Is A Punk Rocker' became the first to exhibit. The band had grown up listening to bubblegum pop, surf music and girl groups and this, combined with the more visceral appeal of The Stooges and The MC5, all came together in what would become their fourth single. Still America cared little – it charted at number 81 – but England did. Soon the rest of the world would follow.
TB

Razorlight

Razorlight Rip It Up

2003 • 2:25 • Agren – Borrell – Smith-Pancorvo – Dalemo

One of the trio of tracks on the demo that was sent to X-Posure, 'Rip It Up' got Razorlight their first ever airplay the same night it arrived at Xfm in the autumn of 2002. Combining the power pop punch of The Strokes with a précised version of 'Television', it was clear that this was a band that was ready to go. Generating instant listener excitement they were invited in for a session while still unsigned. 'Rip It Up' went on to be the band's second single following another one of those first demo tracks 'Rock'n'Roll Lies'.

Razorlight Golden Touch

2004 • 3:25 • Borrell

While frontman Johnny Borrell's arrogant statements helped get Razorlight coverage in the face of initially hostile press, it was 'Golden Touch' that silenced the band's critics and connected them to a wider public resulting in their first top 10 hit. With a riff echoing The Cure's '10.15 Saturday Night', it was inspired by Mairead Nash, one half of London club promoters and DJ duo Queens Of Noize, who Johnny had once shared a house with alongside Pete Doherty before they were all in the public eye. Mairead's golden touch was most recently evident as manager of Florence & The Machine.

Razorlight Vice

2004 • 3:25
Agren – Borrell – Burrows – Dalemo

'Vice' was single number five from Razorlight's debut album *Up All Night* and was released on September 13th 2004. Frontman Johnny Borrell included his phone number within the lyrics towards the end of the track when they were performing 'Vice' at live events. He even wrote the number (or "the vice line") on his chest to see if fans would work it out and give him a call. *NME* magazine then printed it and Borrell was inundated with calls. Allegedly he liked to surprise fans by calling them back for a chat.

Razorlight Somewhere Else

2005 • 3:16
Agren – Borrell – Burrows – Dalemo

[Borrell] liked to surprise fans by calling them back for a chat

– After including his phone number on the track 'Vice'

RAZORLIGHT

"In the morning, you know he won't remember a thing"

With singer Johnny Borrell at the helm of the band's songwriting talent, Razorlight have produced some of the most iconic hits of the last decade. 'Somewhere Else' from the album *Up All Night* was released on April 11th 2005, and it swiftly shot to number two in the UK singles chart.

Razorlight In The Morning

2006 · 3:42

Agren – Borrell – Burrows – Dalemo

'In The Morning' is the opening track to Razorlight's critically acclaimed eponymous second album, released in 2006. As the lead single, it reached number three in the UK in July 2006. The album and in turn, the singles released from it, brought the band many nominations in the following

of radioactive poisoning were found on their scheduled flight from Moscow.

Razorlight America

2006 · 4:13

Agren – Borrell – Burrows – Dalemo

In 2006, Razorlight released their second album, the self-titled *Razorlight*, and it was at this point that the band's success really started to pick up. 'America' was single number two from the album and went straight to number one in the UK singles chart, as well as achieving similar success around the world. With its vibrant energy, 'America' soon became an anthem of the decade. Razorlight's then drummer, Andy Burrows, revealed how the song came about to the *Times* in July 2006: "We were in a

From Left: 'In The Morning', 'Rip It Up',' America', 'Rock N' Roll Lies'

12 months, including two Brit awards and two *NME* awards. Razorlight were fast becoming the superheroes of the indie rock scene but their superpowers let them down in November 2006 when the whole band had to be hospitalised after traces

hotel in Ohio and Johnny [Borrell] won't like me telling you this because he wants it all to be 'Ooh, it just came from the stars', but this Billy Joel record came on and he said, 'Why haven't we got a song with a drumbeat like this?' So I said, 'You can have one if you like'."

Razorlight
Before I Fall To Pieces

❗ 2006 • 3:22 • Burrows – Borrell

Following the fantastic success of their second album *Razorlight* and the two singles released from it previously, single number three beckoned. On December 18th 2006, they released 'Before I Fall To Pieces' – vying for that all-important Christmas number one spot in the charts. The track reached a respectable number 17 in the UK and remains a firm favourite among their fans.

Razorlight
I Can't Stop This Feeling I've Got

❗ 2007 • 3:25 • Agren – Borrell

'I Can't Stop This Feeling I've Got' was the fourth and final single from the album *Razorlight*. The least commercially successful of the four, it failed to make the top 40 in the UK. Despite that it is seen by many as being the defining track of the album and was described by *The Observer* as "gorgeous, huge and shamelessly sentimental". Following the release of Razorlight's third album, *Slipway Fires*, it was announced that drummer Andy Burrows had left the band, citing that favourite artist's euphemism "personal differences". Johnny Borrell's mixed relationship with the media led to some journalists claiming Burrows to have been the creative heart of the band, something Burrows himself has denied.
JK / BdP

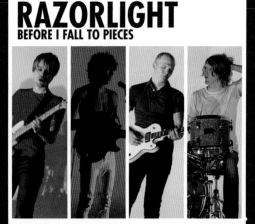

❗ From left: 'Somewhere Else', 'Before I Fall To Pieces', 'Stumble & Fall'

"Why haven't we got a song
with a drumbeat like this?"

– Johnny Borrell in awe of a Billy Joel record

Red Hot Chili Peppers

Red Hot Chili Peppers
Higher Ground

1989 • 3:22 • Wonder

Singer Anthony Kiedis met bassist Michael "Flea" Balzary in their first term at high school. Along with Hillel Slovak, they formed the band that would eventually become Red Hot Chili Peppers. Having created a buzz with their novel mix of funk, punk and rock, they released three albums that were critically acclaimed, if not commercially successful. In 1988, Slovak died of a heroin overdose. Despite Kiedis also battling drug problems, he and Balzary decided to continue and were joined by John Frusciante and Chad Smith. Michael Beinhorn became their producer for a second time, and focused on a cover of Stevie Wonder's 'Higher Ground'. In particular, he pushed Kiedis — a seasoned rapper, but not yet a confident singer — hard. It was worth it: the single became their first US hit and drew attention to the album which, within eight months of release, became their first gold record.

Red Hot Chili Peppers
Blood Sugar Sex Magik

1991 • 4:31
Kiedis – Flea – Frusciante – Smith

Great art needn't always involve great suffering. Writing fourth album *Mother's Milk*, said Anthony Kiedis, "it was squeezing blood out of a rock to get a song done", but 'Blood Sugar Sex Magik' was much more straightforward. Having enlisted Rick Rubin to produce — a relationship that would continue through all their subsequent

records — he suggested that the album should be named after this track. Lyrically the track pays homage to Kiedis' "incredible sexual encounters" with an ex-girlfriend, and the band didn't consider this grinding, guitar-laden, rap-covered album track to be the song they wanted people to focus on. But they conceded that the title best encompassed the "vibe" of the record.

Red Hot Chili Peppers
Give It Away

1991 • 4:20
Kiedis – Flea – Frusciante – Smith

A funky, joyful rap song, the lyrics of 'Give It Away' centre on the idea of enlightenment through altruism. It also includes a verse about River Phoenix, who was at that time a friend and big supporter of the band. The lead single from the album, it went on to be the Chili Peppers' first mainstream success both in the US and European charts. It also won a Grammy and two MTV Video Music awards.

'Blood Sugar Sex Magik' pays homage to Anthony Kiedis' "incredible sexual encounters" with an ex-girlfriend

Red Hot Chili Peppers
Under The Bridge

1991 · 4:34
Kiedis – Flea – Frusciante – Smith

Starting out as the grown-up equivalent
of teenage poetry, this song almost
never existed. Frontman Anthony Kiedis
would deal with emotional problems
by writing "song mantras" for himself.
This one, about having wasted love by
abandoning his girl to go and shoot
heroin under a freeway bridge, was
found by producer Rick Rubin who
convinced Kiedis to share it with the
rest of the band. They turned it into an
optimistic-sounding, but thoughtful
and slow rock song, which became
a huge success worldwide, pushing
the band firmly into the mainstream.
The Gus Van Sant-directed video was
placed on heavy rotation on MTV.

Red Hot Chili Peppers
Suck My Kiss

1991 · 3:37
Kiedis – Flea – Frusciante – Smith

By the time bass-heavy funk-rap-rocker
'Suck My Kiss' was released as a single
in Australia, the band were flying.
Warner-released album *Blood Sugar
Sex Magik* had gone top 10 in America
and the band were playing to packed
arenas, but behind closed doors not
everyone was pleased. The more popular
the band got, the unhappier guitarist
John Frusciante became. Succumbing
as he was to his drug addiction, he was
handling the increase in fame badly.

Red Hot Chili Peppers
Breaking The Girl

1991 · 5:03
Kiedis – Flea – Frusciante – Smith

Anthony Kiedis has been a lover of women
all his life – usually one at a time, almost
always wholeheartedly, but never for very
long. One day, while pondering his latest
break-up and wondering whether he would
follow his father's pattern of "hopping
from flower to flower", John Frusciante
approached him with a melody that led
him to express these emotions in the
form of the lyrics to 'Breaking The Girl'. A
melodic, acoustic guitar-led song, its riffs
were inspired by Led Zeppelin ballads.

Red Hot Chili Peppers
Aeroplane

1995 · 4:45
Kiedis – Flea – Navarro – Smith

In May 2002, guitarist John Frusciante
quit the band, overwhelmed by their
newfound popularity and struggling with
a heroin addiction. He was replaced by
Dave Navarro, of Jane's Addiction. The new
lineup began to write together, all the
while feeling an underlying pressure to live
up to the success of the last album. It hit
frontman Anthony Kiedis hard, and after
almost six years of being sober, he relapsed
back into addiction. The rest of the band
remained ignorant. But there were clues
in his lyrics, even in the rambunctious
'Aeroplane': "Looking in my own eyes /
I can't find the love I want / Someone
slap me before I decompose". "That,"
said Kiedis, "is a cry for help." Nonetheless,

it was a successful single from another successful album: although it didn't match their previous record's success, *One Hot Minute* still achieved top five placing in album charts across the world.

Red Hot Chili Peppers
Love Rollercoaster

1996 • 4:37
Williams – Satchell – Bonner – Jones – Middlebrooks – Pierce – Beck

"Huhhh huhh huh…" Readers of a certain age will almost certainly have laughed themselves silly watching animated MTV series *Beavis and Butt-head*. With each episode typically averaging six minutes, the show shouldn't have worked as a feature-length film. But a $20.11m opening weekend can't be ignored. The Chili Peppers were perfect for the soundtrack. Exactly the sort of band those TV losers would love, their cover of The Ohio Players' 1975 hit had all the funkiness and glitz needed for a Hollywood film, with enough rough edges to keep Beavis and Butt-head happy. The band were even immortalised in animated form for the video.

Red Hot Chili Peppers
Scar Tissue

1999 • 3:37
Kiedis – Flea – Frusciante – Smith

Getting sacked from your band can be brutal. But being immortalised in their next single might help make up for it. So it was for guitarist Dave Navarro – the "Sarcastic Mister Know It All". Having let him go and reinstated a now clean John Frusciante, the band released their most successful single to date. Musically calmer than the previous few, it spent several months at the top of various Billboard charts and won a Grammy award. Its success was repeated across the world.

Red Hot Chili Peppers
Around The World

1999 • 3:59
Kiedis – Flea – Frusciante – Smith

With John Frusciante back in the band and he and singer Anthony Kiedis (for the time being) sober, the Chili Peppers went back into rehearsals. *One Hot Minute*'s success hadn't replicated its predecessor, which somehow freed the group. "Everyone was having fun," remembered Kiedis. "It was as if we had nothing to lose, nothing to gain." *Californication* showed a shift in style and became their most successful album to date, selling over 15 million copies worldwide. This single, although markedly louder than 'Scar Tissue' and covered in Flea's trademark bass sounds, still has its more thoughtful moments in the chorus, reflecting their new direction.

"The song that makes John Frusciante cry"
— Anthony Kiedis on 'Otherside'

Red Hot Chili Peppers
Otherside

1999 · 4:16
Kiedis – Flea – Frusciante – Smith

The most maudlin of all of their singles, 'Otherside' tackles the subject of Anthony Kiedis' long-running battle with heroin. A mellow, thoughtful song, it showcased the band's new direction. Having recently rejoined the band after getting sober, it resonated strongly with guitarist John Frusciante: according to Kiedis, this is "the song that makes John cry".

Red Hot Chili Peppers
Californication

1999 · 5:22
Kiedis – Flea – Frusciante – Smith

Although this was the first song the band worked on for their new album, all but singer Anthony Kiedis were keen to scrap it. But he was determined: "This is the anchor of the whole record," he told them. "It has to be a song." John Frusciante came up with the gentle guitar riff, bassist Flea and drummer Chad Smith added their parts and the rest is history. A sparse, understated tune, the lyrics were inspired by Kiedis' trips to East Asia and his surprise at how his native city's culture had saturated theirs. "No matter how far away I go," he said, "I see the effects that California has on the world."

Red Hot Chili Peppers
By The Way

2002 · 3:36
Kiedis – Smith – Flea – Frusciante

There is a theory that, once a band gets sober, their music gets lame. Proof that the theory is a myth, this single came two years after Anthony Kiedis' Christmas Eve "moment of clarity" that saw him finally kick his heroin habit. It showcases both the band's funky roots – juggernaut basslines and quick-fire raps – and, in the choruses, their gentler, harmonic side. At the time, guitarist John Frusciante was spending his Wednesdays at LA drum'n'bass night Concrete Jungle. The energy he felt from the club stayed with him during the rehearsals where the song was written.

Red Hot Chili Peppers
The Zephyr Song

2002 · 3:52
Kiedis – Smith – Flea – Frusciante

The second single to come from phenomenally successful album *By The Way* started out with the working title 'Coltrane'. Gentle, almost syncopated verses lead into open, catchy choruses. Uncharacteristically, the song features a sampler – something the band weren't used to recording with.

Red Hot Chili Peppers
Can't Stop

2002 · 4:29
Kiedis – Smith – Flea – Frusciante

As nonsensical as the lyrics in 'Can't Stop' may seem, they in fact took Anthony Kiedis hours to write and ended up being part of the very last vocals recorded for the album. Influenced by Gang Of Four, this was the only song from *By The Way* to feature Flea's trademark slap bass, overlaid as it is with

'Dani California' is named after a character who first appeared in 'Californication'

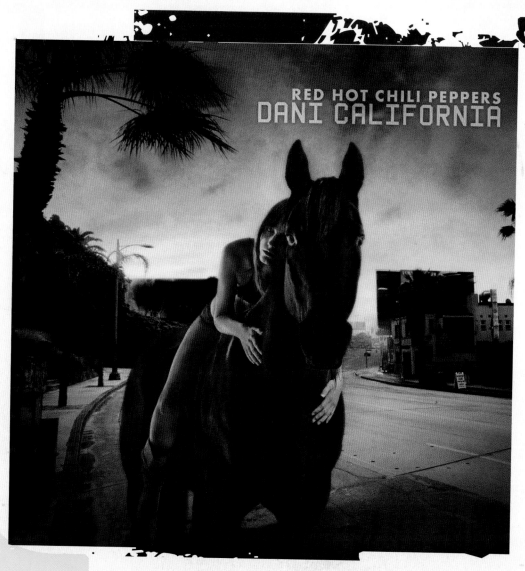

RED HOT CHILI PEPPERS
TELL ME BABY

According to Anthony Kiedis
'Tell Me Baby' is about the river of
humans that flow into Hollywood

Kiedis' rapping in a style more reminiscent of the band's early punk-funk sound.

Red Hot Chili Peppers
Universally Speaking

2002 · 4:18
Kiedis – Smith – Flea – Frusciante

One of the older songs on the album, 'Universally Speaking' is a thoughtful, pared-down rock stomper. Only released as a single in Europe, the video was directed by long-time band friend Dick Rude who also made their live convert DVD, *Off The Map*. It features actor Dave Sheridan reprising the crop-top-wearing comedy character first seen in the 'By The Way' video.

Red Hot Chili Peppers
Fortune Faded

2003 · 3:23
Kiedis – Frusciante – Flea – Smith

Like a fine wine, sometimes a song just needs to be left for a while. Originally written alongside the *By The Way* demos, 'Fortune Faded' didn't make it onto that album. But after a few live outings, it was re-recorded for 2003's *Greatest Hits*. Produced by Rick Rubin, it's an upbeat big rock song with a killer guitar lick.

Red Hot Chili Peppers
Dani California

2006 · 4:44
Kiedis – Smith – Flea – Frusciante

Producing a double album can be risky, but for the Chili Peppers it was a risk

'Universally Speaking' is a thoughtful, pared-down rock stomper

that paid off: *Stadium Arcadium* won five Grammy awards and was a worldwide hit. The first track to be released from it, 'Dani California' is named after a character who first appeared in 'Californication', then again in 'By The Way'. The almost country-sounding drumbeats and guitar rhythms were in fact inspired by Wu Tang Clan's *Enter The Wu-Tang (36 Chambers)*. Like the album, the single was an international hit and picked up another two Grammys.

Red Hot Chili Peppers
Tell Me Baby

2006 · 4:07
Kiedis – Smith – Flea – Frusciante

Another song about the band's beloved hometown, according to Anthony Kiedis, this is "about the river of humans that flow into Hollywood". 'Tell Me Baby' brilliantly showcases the two sides of the band: the verses are the punk-funk that got them recognised while the harmonic choruses echo those that first broke Red Hot Chili Peppers through to the mainstream.
MS

Lou Reed

Lou Reed
Walk On The Wild Side

1972 • 4:12 • Reed

The Kinks may have got there first with 'Lola', but the portrayal of transvestism in 'Walk On The Wild Side' was infinitely more shocking. Detailing the people Lou Reed met during his time with Andy Warhol's Factory, the song got properly down and dirty. Despite its depictions of oral sex and drug use (did radio programmers not know what "giving head" meant in 1972?), it was Reed's only hit single, thanks largely to the irresistible bassline. That proved particularly fruitful, being sampled many times down the years – notably by rap stars A Tribe Called Quest, who had to cough up 100% of the songwriting credit for 'Can I Kick It?'.

Lou Reed
Satellite Of Love

1972 • 3:39 • Reed

Originally recorded in the dying days of The Velvet Underground, 'Satellite Of Love' is a bitter tale of jealousy set to a deceptively lovely melody. It was released as the follow-up single to the huge hit 'Walk On The Wild Side' and instantly restored Lou Reed to his customary position as perennial chart-dodger.

But it deserved better: not only is it a to-die-for tune but the arrangement, produced by David Bowie, gives each element its space, letting the piano hold the body before flute and brass float it out a little further. Ironically, its B-side, 'Vicious', was later the reputed source for Sex Pistol Sid's nickname.

Lou Reed
Perfect Day

1972 • 3:44 • Reed

Whatever way you look at 'Perfect Day', it's a beautiful song about hanging out in the park with a loved one. The inamorata could be another human being or it could be heroin – given Lou Reed's habit of laying bare those things other singers would rather hush up, the smart money was always on the latter. Certainly the makers of *Trainspotting* thought so, when they used it to soundtrack Renton's overdose. But the BBC thought otherwise, using a specially recorded all-star version first to celebrate their music coverage, then as a massive Children In Need fundraiser, which went to number one for three weeks and raised more than £2m for the charity. Proof that a great song can be whatever the listener wants.
SY

Reef
Place Your Hands

1996 • 3:41 • Reef

Even though the four lank-haired members of Reef swept in on grunge's coattails, they were far more enthralled by the surf lifestyle and funk-rock of California's west coast. The band initially made waves after their song 'Good Feeling' was featured on a ubiquitous MiniDisc advert, but the modest success of promising debut album *Replenish* would pale in comparison to second album *Glow* and their breakthrough single 'Place Your Hands'.

The song's genesis came as a result of noted producer George Drakoulias (a former protégé of uber-hip knob-twiddler Rick Rubin) aborting recording sessions at Abbey Road to return to his comfort zone of LA. It bought the band some time to work on a promising riff that had surfaced at the venerable English studio. Fleshed out during rehearsals at Peter Gabriel's Real World complex, and with a set of

lyrics inspired by the death of singer Gary Stringer's grandfather, the band flew to LA's equally revered Sound City Studio to record the new song. With a soulful, ballsy sound so characteristic of Drakoulias' work, the one thing left to do was pepper the song with Stringer's primeval grunts, as the frontman explained to Xfm: "George had already dubbed me the 'King of the ad lib', but with 'Place Your Hands', its "Alright Now"s and the middle eight breakdown... I kinda took it to an extreme."

'Place Your Hands' became a huge hit and gained increasing infamy by soundtracking a feature to Chris Evans' zeitgeist-squeezing Channel 4 show, *TFI Friday*. On the back of the single, the album went on to attain platinum status, which put these four surfers from the West Country well and truly on the map.

"People still come up to me and ask, 'Aren't you fedup with that song now?'", Stringer told Xfm. "No way! Why would I be? I still love playing it!" OH

R.E.M.

"I wrote the most inane lyrics I could possibly write"
– Michael Stipe on 'Stand'

R.E.M. Fall On Me

1986 • 2:51
Berry – Buck – Mills – Stipe

Hailing from Athens, Georgia, R.E.M. quickly became one of America's greatest underground bands, thanks to their merging of post-punk with country rock. 'Fall On Me' is typical of their early work, with singer Michael Stipe's vocals uttering an obscure lyric about oppression, while bassist Mike Mills offers a counter-melody concerning the environment.

R.E.M. The One I Love

1987 • 3:18
Berry – Buck – Mills – Stipe

Michael Stipe's lyrics had often been buried under his strange and mumbled diction (which added to R.E.M.'s mysterious allure), but 'The One I Love' seemed clear enough – it was a simple love song, no? What about the line: "A simple prop to occupy my time"? As Stipe explained at the time, "It's very clear that it's about using people over and over again."

R.E.M. It's The End Of The World As We Know It (And I Feel Fine)

1987 • 4:08 • Berry – Buck – Mills – Stipe

One of R.E.M.'s last singles with indie label IRS, 'It's The End Of The World...' updates Bob Dylan's classic 1965 stream-of-consciousness 'Subterranean Homesick Blues'. The inspiration, however, was a dream that singer Michael Stipe had, in which he was at a birthday party populated by famous people who all had the initials "LB". Mixed up in Stipe's frantically delivered apocalyptic scenario are notorious 1960s comedian Lenny Bruce, former Russian leader Leonid Brezhnev, American music journalist Lester Bangs and – in the song's most memorable moment – US composer Leonard Bernstein, who wrote the score to *West Side Story*.

R.E.M. Orange Crush

1988 • 3:52 • Berry – Buck – Mills – Stipe

After releasing *Document* in 1987, R.E.M. signed with major label Warner Brothers.

"We'd play to 200 people in the UK and go to one or two record stores and they wouldn't have any of our albums," Michael Stipe explained to Xfm. "Warner Brothers offered us worldwide distribution and it took us from being an American band to being an international band." The first single from their debut Warner album *Green* was 'Orange Crush', a savage look at America's involvement in Vietnam. Agent Orange was a chemical used by the US military to pare back the jungle undergrowth in the war zones – the side-effect was countless birth defects and disabilities among the local population.

R.E.M. Stand

! 1988 • 3:13 • Berry – Buck – Mills – Stipe

'Stand' is a daft ditty relating to finding your direction in life and was deliberately written as a simple, bubblegum pop song. "I wrote the most inane lyrics that I could possibly write," Michael Stipe admitted, and he even came up with an idiotic dance for the video that fans could emulate.

R.E.M. Losing My Religion

! 1991 • 4:29 • Berry – Buck – Mills – Stipe

A solemn yet passionate piece, 'Losing My Religion' unexpectedly became one of R.E.M.'s biggest hits. The central motif of the song is Peter Buck's delicate mandolin riff, which was developed as the guitarist was trying to learn the instrument. Michael Stipe's lyrics are another dissection of obsessive love, while the phrase "losing my religion" is

"The reason the lyrics are so atypically straightforward is because it was aimed at teenagers"

– Peter Buck on 'Everybody Hurts'

an old Southern saying, meaning to get angry or frustrated to the point at which you could no longer believe in God.

R.E.M. Shiny Happy People

! 1991 • 3:46 • Berry – Buck – Mills – Stipe

"There's no irony or cynicism," says frontman Michael Stipe of R.E.M.'s most famous song. "It came from this guitar line Peter wrote that made me unbelievably happy. The challenge for me was to find words to match his music." With a guest vocal from Kate Pierson of The B52s, positive energy spills from the song. However, the band quickly tired of it and Stipe has since gone on the record to say that he now "hates" the track. Although that didn't stop America's greatest alternative rock heroes from performing the song on classic pre-school TV programme *Sesame Street*, changing the lyrics to "Furry Happy Monsters".

R.E.M. Drive

1992 · 4:32
Berry – Buck – Mills – Stipe

After the phenomenal success of *Out Of Time*, R.E.M. followed up the album with a collection of darker, more personal songs. The first single from *Automatic For The People* was 'Drive', a brooding, atmospheric track that was, according to Michael Stipe, influenced by David Essex's 1973 single, 'Rock On': "There were, before punk, a few songs that resonated with me," he explained. "'Drive' is a homage to that." The lyric also reveals who Stipe was backing in the forthcoming Clinton vs Bush presidential elections, thanks to the line "Smack, crack, bushwhacked", which echoed a newspaper ad he'd taken out back in 1988: "Don't Get Bushwhacked. Get out and vote. Vote Dukakis."

R.E.M. Man On The Moon

1992 · 5:14
Berry – Buck – Mills – Stipe

'Man On The Moon' concerns Andy Kaufman, an American comedian whose life began to border on crazy performance art. Best known for his role in the TV comedy show *Taxi*, Kaufman would do things like take an entire theatre audience out for milk and cookies, or challenge women to wrestling matches on stage. The song's lyrics also reference his mind-bending 1983 movie *My Breakfast With Blassie*, which features an endless and confusing meal with professional wrestler "Classy" Fred Blassie. Kaufman

died of lung cancer in 1984, but persistent rumours that he'd faked his death as another outrageous stunt led Michael Stipe to link him to the ongoing urban myth that the 1969 moon landings were a hoax.

R.E.M. The Sidewinder Sleeps Tonite

1992 · 4:09 · Berry – Buck – Mills – Stipe

One of R.E.M.'s most playful songs, 'The Sidewinder Sleeps Tonite' is heavily influenced by 1960s single 'The Lion Sleeps Tonight', whose roots go back to an old South African number from the 1930s, 'Mbube'. Michael Stipe attempts the song's distinctive yodelling on R.E.M.'s take, which is another stream-of-consciousness string of obscure references and details, including the well-known children's author Dr Seuss and a tale about a desert rattlesnake. Thanks to Stipe's erratic diction, the chorus has caused much confusion over the years, but the official lyric is "Call me when you try to wake her".

R.E.M. Everybody Hurts

1992 · 5:20 · Berry – Buck – Mills – Stipe

Direct, moving and uplifting, 'Everybody Hurts' now has a life beyond its inclusion on the massively successful *Automatic For The People* album. The majority of the song was written by R.E.M. drummer Bill Berry as a message to people in doubt or despair, with the climax offering a glimpse of hope. As guitarist Peter Buck explained: "The reason the lyrics are so atypically straightforward is because it was aimed at teenagers." The song has now been used by countless charities, including The Samaritans, as well as to aid victims of the earthquake in Haiti in January 2010.

R.E.M. Nightswimming

! 1992 • 4:18 • Berry – Buck – Mills – Stipe

A simple piano tune, 'Nightswimming' evokes instant nostalgia for youth and carefree times. Bassist Mike Mills, who plays piano on the song, originally wrote the melody during the *Out Of Time* sessions and he claims the lyrics relate to R.E.M.'s early days in Athens, Georgia. Former Led Zeppelin man John Paul Jones scored the string section, while apparently the piano was the same one Eric Clapton used on the classic 'Layla'.

R.E.M. What's The Frequency, Kenneth?

! 1994 • 4:01 • Berry – Buck – Mills – Stipe

After the introspective *Out Of Time* and *Automatic For The People*, R.E.M. decided they would like to tour for the first time since 1989 and worked on a "portable" album that would feature more upbeat, rock-based songs that could be played live. The first single, 'What's The Frequency, Kenneth?', features a distorted, clanging guitar riff from Peter Buck and some of Michael Stipe's most entertaining lyrics. The title is based on an incident from 1986 that saw American TV newsreader Dan Rather attacked by a mentally disturbed man who claimed the media were beaming signals into his head; he repeatedly yelled at Rather, "Kenneth, what is the frequency?"

R.E.M. The Great Beyond

! 1999 • 5:07 • Buck – Mills – Stipe

Another song relating to comedian Andy Kaufman, 'The Great Beyond' was recorded for the 1999 film based on his life starring Jim Carrey and named after R.E.M.'s earlier track, 'Man On The Moon'. Released between the albums *Up* and *Reveal*, this was R.E.M.'s biggest hit in the UK, reaching number three in the singles chart.
MO'G

R.E.M. performed 'Shiny Happy People' on *Sesame Street*, changing the lyrics to "Furry Happy Monsters"

Reverend And The Makers
Heavyweight Champion Of The World

| 2007 · 3:30 · Cosens – McClure – Smyth

There must be something in the Sheffield water. Something that makes its musicians cynical, sarcastic and blessed with the ability to write pop music with real themes. Standing shoulder to shoulder with the likes of Arctic Monkeys and Jarvis Cocker is Jon McClure, also known as the Reverend; making music with something to say.

A call to arms for anyone in a dead-end job but looking for a better life, 'Heavyweight Champion Of The World' started life as a bassline, running around in McClure's head. Enlisting the help of mate and band member Ed Cosens ("Cos I wasn't very good at playing music at that point," he confessed to Xfm), the pair met up with Arctic Monkeys and Pulp producer Alan Smyth, who helped work the ideas into a fully formed song. Later, Primal Scream and Kasabian producer Jagz Kooner gave the track a disco feel using the lyrical refrain of "Be like everybody else / Be like everybody else" as a drop. "He explained how music follows the trajectory of an ecstasy trip," McClure explained, "and the chorus is the release. It hit the nail on the head." The record does indeed do just that, dropping in pace and intensity before exploding again into a dancefloor-filling crescendo.

Clever and outspoken in its lyrics, the influence of Manchester performance poet John Cooper Clarke (Clarke even duets with McClure on the spoken word B-side 'Last Resort') can clearly be heard: witty references and clever delivery act as a sugar-coating for the song's bleak portrayal of everyday life delivered with a Northern swagger. A heavy funk bassline combined with atmospheric guitars and disco beats provide a backdrop for lyrics delivered with their own rap-like rhythm. Undoubtedly the band's signature song, the track peaked at number eight in the UK's singles chart.
JS

Damien Rice
Cannonball

| 2002 · 5:13 · Rice

During his time in indie band Juniper, Damien Rice lost belief in the music industry following label pressure to ensure their songs were radio-friendly. He quit, fled to Tuscany and seriously considered a career as a farmer, before music started calling him again. He sent some new demos to his second cousin, producer and film composer David Arnold, who was impressed enough to offer Rice his own studio, even stepping in to produce a song on his 2002 debut album O. As well as being a huge success in the UK (reaching number eight and staying in the chart for 97 weeks), it topped the US Billboard Heatseekers chart and won the prestigious Shortlist Music Prize. 'Cannonball' came out twice as a single, both times charting in the UK – despite Rice doing almost no press. With warm, strumming guitars, loose drums and Rice's strong but fragile voice, it managed to please music fans from every corner: gentle enough for mainstream radio stations, catchy enough for the top 40, "real" enough for haters of processed pop.
MS

The Rolling Stones

The Rolling Stones
(I Can't Get No) Satisfaction

1965 · 3:43 · Jagger – Richards

The Rolling Stones' most famous riff was one that nearly didn't exist at all. It was dreamed up, literally, by Keith Richards one night, when the guitarist rolled out of bed, recorded the guitar, mumbled a lyric, then fell back asleep. "On the tape you can hear me drop the pick and the rest is me snoring," he said. He and fellow Glimmer Twin Mick Jagger didn't think much of their subsequent tale of commercial rebellion and didn't want to release it as a single. "I thought the fuzz guitar was a gimmick," he said and Jagger agreed. The band, fortunately, overruled them.

The Rolling Stones
Get Off My Cloud

1965 · 2:57 · Jagger – Richards

Riding high on the success of '(I Can't Get No) Satisfaction', The Rolling Stones suddenly found themselves public property. This single was their reaction to that intrusion and, ironically, made their problems considerably worse given that it immediately went straight to number one in both the US and the UK. Somewhat typically of the band's 1965 singles (see 'Satisfaction'), Keith Richards didn't much like it, criticising the production and blaming the pressure of coming up with a follow-up to a hit single. "I never dug it as a record," he said in 1971. "The chorus was a nice idea, but we rushed it."

The Rolling Stones
Paint It, Black

1966 · 3:46 · Jagger – Richards

Until 1966, almost all of The Rolling Stones' work was directly inspired or derived from the US R&B, so beloved of the band. It was 'Paint It, Black' – curious comma added, asserted Keith Richards, by the band's record label – that would change things. First to instigate that shift was guitarist Brian Jones, whose use of a sitar to pick out the guitar line worked in a hint of the mysterious. Charlie Watts' pounding double-time beat, meanwhile, was originally a piss-take borrowed from another song. But it was the dark lyrics about a dead girlfriend that proved there was more to the Stones than the blues.

The Rolling Stones
Let's Spend The Night Together

1967 · 3:26 · Jagger – Richards

'Let's Spend The Night Together' marked the moment The Rolling Stones

"'Course it's subversive. It's stupid to think that you can start a revolution with a record. I wish you could" – Mick Jagger on 'Street Fighting Man'

began to really revel in their bad boy image. A tame lyric now, in 1967 this was revolutionary stuff – so much so that influential chatshow host Ed Sullivan banned the chorus from his show. Mick Jagger's subsequent eye-roll as he sang "let's spend some time together" for Sullivan got The Rolling Stones blacklisted from the programme permanently. Despite all this, the song itself is a simple, piano-led, harmony-heavy pop song and would soon be the sort of thing the Stones would jettison as they took a somewhat disastrous psychedelic direction a year later.

The Rolling Stones
Ruby Tuesday

! 1967 • 3:32 • Jagger – Richards

Because of the reluctance of 1960s radio stations to play the downright immoral, lascivious – and nowadays entirely tame – 'Let's Spend The Night Together', it was in fact that single's B-side that received considerable airplay and thus sent both to the top of the charts on each side of the Atlantic. Written in its entirety by Keith Richards, though he and Jagger share the credit, it was pieced together in an LA hotel room as Richards mooned after a free-spirited girl of the guitarist's more intimate acquaintance. The recorder comes courtesy of Brian Jones, teeing up the move to more whimsical work to come from the Stones.

The Rolling Stones
Jumpin' Jack Flash

! 1968 • 3:43 • Jagger – Richards

"That's a kind of end-of-the-world song, really," said the singer of the song's darkness

– Mick Jagger on 'Gimme Shelter'

The beginnings of 'Jumpin' Jack Flash' are somewhat less romantic than the song would have you believe. Rather than being born in a crossfire hurricane, Jumpin' Jack was actually Keith Richards' gardener – who startled Mick Jagger into awaking in a flash one morning. Jagger, more exotically, claimed the song was born from an acid trip. The riff, so punchy and violent, was actually recorded on a fuzzed-up acoustic guitar and is another dismissed by Richards. "It's really 'Satisfaction' in reverse," he said. "Almost an interchangeable riff." Though it is one, however, that bassist Bill Wyman claims he first wrote.

The Rolling Stones
Street Fighting Man

! 1968 • 3:18 • Jagger – Richards

Written as the uneasy mood in Paris was threatening to spill over into the May 1968 riots, and also set against a backdrop of American race riots, 'Street Fighting Man' was Mick Jagger at his, then, most political. "'Course it's subversive," he retorted to its critics, but added: "It's stupid to think that you can start a revolution with a record. I wish you could!" It's another Stones song played exclusively on acoustic guitars; the edgy, overdriven sound was in fact the result of recording the song too loud for the portable tape player recording them, while Charlie Watts' beat comes courtesy of a toy kit.

The Rolling Stones
Sympathy For The Devil

! 1968 • 6:27 • Jagger – Richards

Originally written as a folk song as Mick Jagger tried to imagine what a Bob Dylan tune written from the point of the Devil might sound like, it was Keith Richards who suggested changing the rhythm into a brooding samba. Inspired by Russian writer Mikhail Bulgakov's novel *The Master And Margarita*, a book referenced in Jagger's lyrics, it was also a cultural snapshot of the turbulence of the era along the same lines as 'Street Fighting Man'. Not that the press saw it that way at the time. They assumed the Stones had become devil-worshippers and attacked them correspondingly.

The Rolling Stones
Honky Tonk Women

! 1969 • 3:01 • Jagger – Richards

Conceived initially as a Hank Williams-style country song (and resurrected as such on *Let It Bleed*), 'Honky Tonk Women' was composed by Mick Jagger and Keith Richards after the pair had been drinking in a Brazilian cowboy bar and was intended as a reference to the prostitutes there. However, "honky tonk women" was a term they always meant to change before recording the song. "A lot of times you're fooling with what you consider to be just working titles," said Richards. "Then you realise there's nothing else that's going to fit in the same way. So you're left with this fairly inane phrase."

The Rolling Stones
Gimme Shelter

! 1969 • 4:36 • Jagger – Richards

After the edginess of their *Beggars Banquet* album, *Let It Bleed* opened with this brooding, apocalyptic salvo – as if, despite the peace and love elsewhere, The Rolling Stones had tapped into an altogether dark vein. "Rape, murder – it's just a shot away" (as backing vocalist Merry Clayton screams midway through) were not then staples of 1960s songwriting. Keith Richards had been toying with the riff while Mick Jagger was acting in the film *Performance*.

"All the nasty subjects in one go. I would never write that song now" – Mick Jagger on 'Brown Sugar'

When the pair came together, though, the song simply fell into place. "That's a kind of end-of-the-world song, really," said the singer of the song's darkness.

The Rolling Stones
You Can't Always Get What You Want

! 1969 • 7:30 • Jagger – Richards

A snapshot of London in the 1960s, 'You Can't Always Get What You Want' was a song pieced together by Mick Jagger from chords with which he had been fooling around with little purpose – he called it a "bedroom song". He had also wanted a gospel choir to sing it but, when none was available, the Stones enlisted the London Bach Choir "for a laugh", as Jagger claimed. Incidentally, the Mr Jimmy character mentioned was not, as everyone assumed, Jimi Hendrix. Instead, it was producer Jimmy Miller, who used the word "dead", as the lyrics assert, when he liked something. Miller also played drums on the track.

> "Beautifully played by everybody. When everybody hits it, that's one of those moments of triumph"

– Keith Richards on 'Tumbling Dice'

The Rolling Stones
Brown Sugar

! 1971 • 3:50 • Jagger – Richards

On the surface, 'Brown Sugar' is classic Keith Richards. It sounds like his riff, it was written in part about heroin – one of Richards' former favourite indulgences – yet this was pure Mick Jagger, from the guitars to the words. It was originally going to be called 'Black Pussy' given the song's intended subject matter of a woman having sex with a black servant. "But I decided that was too direct, too nitty-gritty," said Jagger of a song whose dark themes of sex, drugs and violence he later regretted. "All the nasty subjects in one go," he said. "I would never write that song now."

The Rolling Stones
Wild Horses

! 1971 • 5:44 • Jagger – Richards

Perhaps The Rolling Stones' most evocative ballad, there is some debate between Mick Jagger and Keith Richards over who wrote what. Richards has claimed it was a song about not wanting to leave his son and "old lady" to go on the road, adding that the chorus and guitar line were his. He has also said, however, that Jagger turned 'Wild Horses' into a song about not wanting to leave his then girlfriend Marianne Faithful. The singer, though, claimed that Richards wrote the melody and the phrase "wild horses", but that he wrote the rest – though denied it was about Faithful. Whatever, it's still their most beautiful single.

The Rolling Stones
Tumbling Dice

1972 • 3:47 • Jagger – Richards

When the Stones emigrated to France in 1971 for the distinctly un-rock'n'roll reason of tax issues, they decamped to Keith Richards' Villa Nellcôte mansion and there set about a period of bacchanalia in which they also happened to record arguably their greatest album, *Exile On Main St*. 'Tumbling Dice' was pieced together in Richards' basement, their makeshift recording studio, before Mick Jagger finished the lyrics in Los Angeles after a conversation about gambling with his cleaning lady. It remains one of Richards' favourites. "I really loved 'Tumbling Dice'," he said. "Beautifully played by everybody. When everybody hits it, that's one of those moments of triumph."

The Rolling Stones
Start Me Up

1981 • 3:33 • Jagger – Richards

If 'Start Me Up' sounds like the sort of classic rock The Rolling Stones were playing in the mid-1970s, rather than the weaker stuff they were writing in the '80s, that's because it was first pieced together in 1975. It started life as a reggae song but failed to make either 1978's *Some Girls* or 1980's *Emotional Rescue*; however, the band did record one lost take as a straight rock number. Mick Jagger unearthed it while putting together 1981's *Tattoo You*, mostly an outtakes album. "It was just sitting there and no one had taken any notice of it," he said in disbelief at his discovery of a gem.
TB

The Ruts
Babylon's Burning

1979 • 2:34
Fox – Jennings – Owen – Ruffy

They were not to last long, The Ruts. Cut down in their prime by the death of singer Malcolm Owen from a heroin overdose, their career spanned three short years. But what they left behind was seminal – and nowhere more so than 'Babylon's Burning'. The Ruts formed wanting only to blend their reggae influences with their punk ones but, increasingly, they took on a more political bent as the rise of the National Front movement began to appal them. Opening with a blare of sirens, 'Babylon's Burning' was their address – not to the neo-Nazi organisation, but to the problems in late-1970s Britain that had led to conditions where such an organisation could be formed. As racist and angry tensions bubbled beneath the surface of British life, so their guitars seethed with emotion and their lyrics spat with fury. It touched a nerve, the song crashed the top 10, but their influence would be limited by Owen's death.
TB

Seahorses
Love Is The Law

! 1997 · 7:43 · Squire

After leaving The Stone Roses, guitarist John Squire wanted to try something different. Having seen 20-year-old Stuart Fletcher playing in a York venue, he approached the bass player about starting a new band. "I didn't know who he was at first," Fletcher told Xfm. "A couple of my mates had to tell me he was in the Roses." The music media wanted Stone Roses part two, but Squire's intention in forming a band with relatively unknown musicians was to do something a bit different. The result was the Seahorses, the origins of which name have been widely speculated on. Claims that it is derived from an anagram of "He Hates Roses" or "The Roses Ashes" are denied by Squire.

'Love Is The Law' was the first single from the new project. Although it has a much more guitar-driven sound than the Roses' dance rhythms and influences, there are certainly comparisons to be drawn – not least in Squire's unmistakable twanging guitar (the album version features a guitar solo reminiscent of 'Fools Gold'). It's possibly closer in sound to *The Second Coming* rather than The Stone Roses' eponymous debut, albeit with a more melodic and tuneful sound courtesy of Chris Helme's vocals. The album received mixed reviews at the time, but the single charted at number three in the UK.

Seahorses
Blinded By The Sun

! 1997 · 4:38 · Helme

Despite being the main creative force in The Stone Roses, the Seahorses were not to become John Squire and band; other members of the group contributed songs, 'Love Me And Leave Me' was co-written with Liam Gallagher, and second single 'Blinded By The Sun' saw vocalist Chris Helme taking control. "Chris had some chords for 'Blinded By The Sun'," remembers bassist Stuart Fletcher. "We started playing along with him. John came in a bit later and quite liked how it was sounding so we started rehearsing." Squire's back-seat approach led to a single that sounded more like The La's than the Roses: a moody track with an obligatory string section that can be heard on many late-1990s Britpop classics. The band's existence was to be short-lived; after one album and three years together, they split. JS

Sex Pistols
Anarchy In The UK

! 1976 · 3:32
Jones – Cook – Matlock – Rotten

'Anarchy In The UK' was the debut single of the Sex Pistols, a band of misfits who gravitated towards the ultra-fashionable SEX boutique in London's Kings Road. The shop's owner, Malcolm McLaren, saw a chance to combine art, fashion and music by forming his own group. McLaren brought together Steve Jones and Paul Cook, two kids who frequented the shop, on guitar and drums respectively. Glen Matlock was added on bass and another SEX customer, John Lydon, auditioned to be the band's singer. Re-christened Johnny Rotten, his bile-filled, untutored vocals were ideal for the aggressive and offensive music McLaren had in mind – which quickly became known as "punk", after the American term for hoodlum.

Rotten also supplied lyrics for the band and, with encouragement from McLaren (who had studied conceptual groups like the Situationists at art school), worked up a terrifying rant for the band's first single. With mid-1970s Britain in a terrible state of financial crisis, unemployment and social upheaval, Rotten suggested the possibility of 'Anarchy In The UK'. The song opened with probably the most jarring half-rhyme in rock history: "I am an anti-christ / 'I am an anarchist'". "The first thing I wrote was I am an anti-christ," Lydon remembered in 1999 documentary *The Filth & The Fury*. "And I couldn't think of a damn thing that rhymed with it. 'Anarchist' fitted just nicely." Signed to major label EMI, the Pistols recorded the song in October 1976 with former Roxy Music producer Chris Thomas. "Putting the backing track down wasn't that easy," he told Xfm. "It involved quite a few edits of

different takes of the backing track. Then there were quite a lot of guitar overdubs put on to strengthen it. But the band were very easy to work with." A milestone single in British music, 'Anarchy In The UK' still sounds breathtaking today.

Sex Pistols
God Save The Queen

1977 • 3:18
Jones – Cook – Matlock – Rotten

1977 was the year of the Silver Jubilee – 25 years since Queen Elizabeth II came to the throne in the UK with a special day of celebration set for that June. With a royalist mood in the air, singer Johnny Rotten was determined to bring some reality to proceedings with his ultra-nihilistic lyrics. "I thought about it for weeks," he recalled, "and then it came out in one go." Taking the British national anthem in vain, Rotten equated the Royal Family with a "fascist regime" and claimed that for the common man, there was "no future". "You don't write 'God Save The Queen' because you hate the English race," he explained. "You write a song like that because you love them and you're fed up with them being mistreated." Banned by various broadcasters, the song attracted much controversy, but managed to make number two the week of the Jubilee – there remains a persistent rumour that the charts were "rigged" so that the less offensive Rod Stewart held the top spot instead.

Sex Pistols
Pretty Vacant

| 1977 • 3:16
| Jones – Cook – Matlock – Rotten

Apparently based on Abba's 'S.O.S.', this is the Sex Pistols' most straightforward pop song, despite Johnny Rotten placing much emphasis on the second syllable in "vacant" to make it sound very rude indeed. Producer Chris Thomas told Xfm that it was this recording that finally nailed the "Sex Pistols sound", as bassist Glen Matlock had recently left the band. "They'd asked him to come down as a session guy, but obviously having been kicked out of the band, he didn't turn up", remembers Thomas. "Without a bass player, I thought let's try Steve Jones. He played exactly the same root note at the same time as he played it on guitar. Bingo, the sound was absolutely immense. It was a simple combination and I realised that's what we were looking for." MO'G

Shed Seven
Going For Gold

| 1996 • 4:27
| Gladwin – Witter – Leach – Banks

Formed in 1990, York band Shed Seven were a real Britpop success story, with more hits in 1996, than any other act – a total of five entries into the UK top 40. In the March of 1996 the brass-laden laidback anthem 'Going For Gold' was the band's biggest UK hit at number eight. The track was the second single to be taken from their second album *Maximum High* – a top 10 album that spent a total of 26 weeks in the UK charts. One of the most memorable frontmen of the Britpop era, Rick Witter was the good-looking, maraca-shaking party-starter who memorably wore a gold lamé suit for all his TV performances of 'Going For Gold'... a suit that he still owns to this day. Unlike many of their peers, Shed Seven

"You write a song like 'God Save The Queen' because you love the English race and you're fed up with them being mistreated"

– Johnny Rotten

also had international success in Australia and the Far East; their fourth single 'Ocean Pie' kept Take That off the Christmas number one slot in Thailand in 1995.

Shed Seven
Chasing Rainbows

▌ 1996 · 4:24
▐ Gladwin – Witter – Leach – Banks

On a particularly wet and miserable night in an unmemorable German town in 1995, Shed Seven were coming to the end of an especially long and arduous European tour. Singer Rick Witter was pissed off and homesick – a mood not lifted by having to play to only 20 unenthusiastic German punters. After the show he retired to the tour bus and very quickly wrote all of the lyrics to 'Chasing Rainbows', a track based around a guitar line that the band had been playing with that afternoon in sound check. It became one of the band's most cherished songs, with fans singing every word at every Shed Seven gig. Witter also performed the song at the wedding of Inspiral Carpet member and Xfm presenter, Clint Boon, in September 2005. MW

Sigur Rós
Hoppipolla

▌ 2005 · 4:29
▐ Sveinsson – Birgisson – Hólm – Dýrason

Emerging in the late 1990s when post-rock offered an antidote to Britpop's '60s / new-wave sickness, Sigur Rós fitted nicely alongside others such as Tortoise, Mogwai or Godspeed You! Black Emperor – bands who looked to push music into new territories. Coming from Iceland gave them a certain mystique, but it was their sound that set Sigur Rós apart. While they too would build passages up slowly with waves of percussion and shimmering melody, they had a secret weapon that was vital to the group's impact: the voice of Jónsi Birgisson. An ethereal falsetto, it could send shivers down the spine, bringing their music an otherworldly yet human aspect that had a strong emotional effect.

By the time 'Hoppipolla' arrived on their fourth album *Takk...* in 2005, Sigur Ros had gone through several stages musically and already been critically lauded across the world, although they were still regarded as an underground band. This song changed that. A piano refrain rises and rises, lifted further by chimes and drums, and Birgisson's vocals soaring above, mirrored by stirring strings; it's a completely uplifting piece of music. Once married to a myriad of moving images, from the BBC's *Planet Earth* series to trailers for *Slumdog Millionaire*, it became the sound of awe and wonder. After being used so ostensibly in film and television, it was the group's biggest hit on re-release. Its true resonance, however, can't be measured merely by chart position. While ironically nicknamed "The Money Song" in the early stages of writing, as the band felt it had commercial potential, 'Hoppipolla' actually translates as "jumping in puddles", conjuring up the idea of simple joys, and most of the words are in the band's own made-up tongue of Hopelandic. The key to the appeal of Sigur Rós is that their music connects beyond language. JK

Siouxsie And The Banshees
Hong Kong Garden

1978 · 2:54

Sioux – Severin – McKay – Morris

Siouxsie Sioux was a punk star before she ever released a record. Part of the celebrated Bromley Contingent, a close-knit coterie of young punks and Sex Pistols fans whose fashion sense did much to define the more creative ends of the genre's look, Sioux played a central role in *that* infamous Bill Grundy TV interview, when the hapless host's fumbling flirtation with her ("I'll see you after the show") prompted Pistols guitarist Steve Jones' potty-mouthed outburst. By the time Siouxsie And The Banshees were signed to Polydor – hyped by manager Nils Stevenson's guerrilla campaign proclaiming them the "greatest unsigned band", spraying "sign the Banshees" on record company walls – they'd already been through two future stars (Sid Vicious drummed and Marco Pirroni, of Adam And The Ants, played guitar at their first gig).

Within weeks, the single 'Hong Kong Garden' appeared, soaring into the top 10 in September 1978, just as punk's limitations were being exposed. This, though, was part of a new sound, already pushing in other directions. Brash and colourful, the guitar riff competed for attention with the glockenspiel motif that underscored the lyrics' theme. Named after a Chinese takeaway in Bromley, it was part tribute, part amble through Orientalist culture and clichés: Confucius gets name-checked, as do "slanted eyes" and "a race of bodies small in size". Although it's unlikely some of these lyrics would've survived more sensitive times, Sioux insisted it was a tribute to the takeaway owners who were bombarded with racist insults every week. "I remember wishing that I could be like Emma Peel from *The Avengers* and kick all the skinheads' heads in, because they used to mercilessly torment these people for being foreigners. It made me feel so helpless, hopeless and ill," she told *Uncut* in 2005. The single has held up so well it was used in the soundtrack for Sophia Coppola's *Marie Antoinette* in 2006.
SY

Skids
Into The Valley

1979 · 3:17 · Adamson – Jobson

It was with something approaching good timing that Scottish art-punks Skids landed in the late-1970s post-punk scene and wangled themselves a deal with the formerly hippy label Virgin. Any earlier and their new-wave image might have denied them any attention at all – any later and their frequent lineup changes could have prevented their first hit being written. 'Into The Valley' caught them before guitarist Stuart Adamson disappeared to form Big Country and at a point when singer Richard Jobson's vocals were merely unintelligible rather than incomprehensible, as they latterly became. An anthemic, tuneful slice of new-wave punk, it was intended as a song about the recruitment of Scottish teenagers into the army – though as a statement about various local rivalries around the band's then native Dunfermline, it bore relevance, too. Since adopted by virtually any football club whose ground includes the word Valley – Charlton Athletic, Bradford City, et al.
TB

Skunk Anansie

Skunk Anansie
Weak

1995 · 3:34
Dyer – Kent – Lewis – France

The multicultural, London-based band Skunk Anansie formed in 1994 and went on to be one of the most successful rock acts of the decade, both at home and overseas. They were much more Britrock than Britpop during the UK guitar explosion of the mid-1990s. Skunk Anansie had far more in common with US heavy rock acts than they did with the British, Beatles and Kinks-inspired scene led by Oasis and Blur. Named after the West African folktales of Anansi the spider-man, Skunk Anansie were known for their powerful and anthemic songs, which dominated the festival scene of the late '90s. The band had a fierce live reputation that was led by Skin, the atomically charismatic six-foot black singer, who was unquestionably one of the great front-people of the era. 'Weak' was the fourth, final and most successful single from the band's acclaimed debut album, *Paranoid & Sunburnt*, and it was their first single to crack the UK top 20 in January 1996. Bizarrely, the song was also covered by Rod Stewart for his 1998 album *When We Were The New Boys*.

Skunk Anansie
Hedonism (Just Because You Feel Good)
! 1997 • 3:28 • Dyer – Arran

The first single to be taken from second album *Stoosh* and one of the band's most successful tracks. Skunk Anansie's song catalogue oscillates between aggressive rock records with serious political themes – such as 'Little Baby Swastikka', 'Selling Jesus' and 'Yes It's Fucking Political' – to incredibly tender and emotionally resonant power ballads. 'Hedonism (Just Because You Feel Good)' is a world-class example of the latter. It's one of the era's ultimate break-up songs, sung with huge openness and fragility by the otherwise quite intimidating Skin. Skunk Anansie disbanded in 2001 before reforming in 2009 with some new material, a greatest hits album and sold-out tours. MW

! From Left: *Paranoid & Sunburnt, Stoosh*

"The whole idea of rock and roll is to get people off their arses"

– Steve Marriott

The Small Faces
All Or Nothing

1966 • 3:03 • Marriott – Lane

By the mid-1960s, London's mod scene had ceased to rely on American R&B as its sole source of records and had begun to produce its own. The Small Faces were eager young mods, named after the colloquial term for a scene leader and the fact that its principals, singer-guitarist Steve Marriott and bassist Ronnie Lane, both stood at about five feet six inches. Despite all the band members being working-class cockney boys (Marriott's father even owned a jellied eels stall), Marriott had more than a hint of showbiz about him, having successfully played in the West End production of *Oliver!* But it was his voice rather than his acting that stood out and when the album version of the musical was released, Marriott was singing the famous Artful Dodger songs, such as 'Consider Yourself At Home'. By the time he reached manhood (or at least his late teens), his voice had blossomed into something only the prodigy Steve Winwood could rival. Deep, rich and round, it boomed out of his small frame like something trapped in an alien body, and 'All Or Nothing' took it to places it hadn't been seen before, including the very

pinnacle of the British singles chart, where it replaced 'Yellow Submarine'. Previous hits included songs like 'Sha-La-La-La-Lee', commissioned from Kenny Lynch by their manager Don Arden (then a somewhat notorious showbiz figure with roughhouse connections, now probably better known as the father of Sharon Osbourne), which were chirpy where The Small Faces longed to be authentic. "'Sha-La-La-La-Lee' was a good little Saturday night dance record, but it wasn't what we were really about, which was playing black R&B", said Ronnie Lane.

'All Or Nothing', by contrast, was the real deal, powered along by an impassioned vocal from Marriott. Written either for an ex-girlfriend or his future wife about her split from Rod Stewart (who later replaced Marriott when the band became The Faces), it's a tornado of a song, whipping around the ferocious combination of guitar and bass and atmospheric keyboard, seeming to slow down and speed up at various points. It's also a fairly blatant stab at persuading a girl into bed, which escaped the censors at the time – as The Small Faces so often did (see the blatant drug references on 'Here Comes The Nice' and 'Itchycoo Park'). Its passage to the number one spot wasn't all smooth sailing though. It was given the thumbs-down on *Juke Box Jury*, though Marriott joked they celebrated this with a bottle of champagne as the TV show had called all their previous records wrong. Despite the single's success, the band saw little money from Arden, leading to an infamous meeting between him and the group's parents (half of the band were still in their teens) where the manager explained their lack of funds by (falsely) claiming they injected it all up their arms.

The Small Faces
Tin Soldier

! 1967 • 3:22 • Marriott – Lane

An epic single that aped 'All Or Nothing' in many ways except chart-topping success (it peaked at a respectable number nine in December 1967). Another heartfelt love song, a powerhouse vocal – perhaps Steve Marriott's best ever – and the way guitar and keyboards seem to compete for attention make this a standout track in an incredible year for British rock. 'Tin Soldier' was originally written for P.P. Arnold, a label mate at Small Faces' new home Immediate, where the mercurial owner and former Stones manager Andrew Loog Oldham was using Marriott and Ronnie Lane as de facto house writers and producers. Reputedly, Marriott snatched it back when Dan Arnold's reaction was too favourable, replacing it with 'If You Think You're Groovy'. Arnold's voice can be heard on the backing chorus, a female counterpoint to Marriott's barnstorming performance. Long-time Small Faces fan Paul Weller named this his favourite record ever when he went on *Desert Island Discs*. SY

Smashing Pumpkins

Smashing Pumpkins
Today

! 1993 • 3:20 • Corgan

Chicago's Smashing Pumpkins were based around singer Billy Corgan and guitarist James Iha. Their first album, 1991's *Gish*, emerged several months before Nirvana's *Nevermind*, but its use of heavy guitar and traditional rock riffs led them to be touted as "the next big thing". Subsequently signing to Virgin, there was much pressure on Corgan to deliver a hit album. With the band in disarray – drummer Jimmy Chamberlin had a serious drug addiction, while bassist D'arcy Wretzky and Iha had just finished their relationship – Corgan was plunged into a depression. "I was really suicidal," he recalled. "I just thought it was funny to write a song that said today is the greatest day of your life because it can't get any worse." The distinctive guitar intro was actually the last part to be written for the song and popped into Corgan's head one day, fully formed.

Smashing Pumpkins
Disarm

! 1993 • 3:17 • Corgan

Although some observers have claimed that this song is about abortion, singer Billy Corgan explains that it's actually about his dysfunctional relationship with his parents. "Rather than have an angry, violent song," he recalled, "I thought I'd write something beautiful and make them realise what tender feelings I have in my heart, and make them feel really bad for treating me like shit."

transitory nature of life: "You can never ever leave / Without leaving a piece of youth". While Corgan's extraordinary feline voice implores us to embrace life while we have it, the enormous sound of a 30-piece string section from the Chicago Symphony Orchestra brings the song to an emotional peak.

Smashing Pumpkins
1979

! 1995 • 4:26 • Corgan

An introspective and low-key track from

> "I thought I'd write something beautiful... and make my parents feel really bad for treating me like shit"
> — Billy Corgan on 'Disarm'

Smashing Pumpkins
Tonight Tonight

! 1995 • 4:15

Recording the follow-up to *Siamese Dream*, Billy Corgan had enough songs stockpiled to make a double album. Loosely based around the cycle of life and death, *Mellon Collie And The Infinite Sadness* was an ambitious work that saw the Pumpkins broaden their horizons and once again record together as a band. Following the brief instrumental title track, 'Tonight Tonight' is the first proper song on the album and muses on the

Mellon Collie And The Infinite Sadness, '1979' almost didn't make the final cut as it was written towards the end of the sessions. As part of the album's "cycle of life" concept, the song details the transition into adulthood while the accompanying video features various teenage shenanigans in which the band are seen playing a house party. One of Smashing Pumpkins' more underrated singles. MO'G

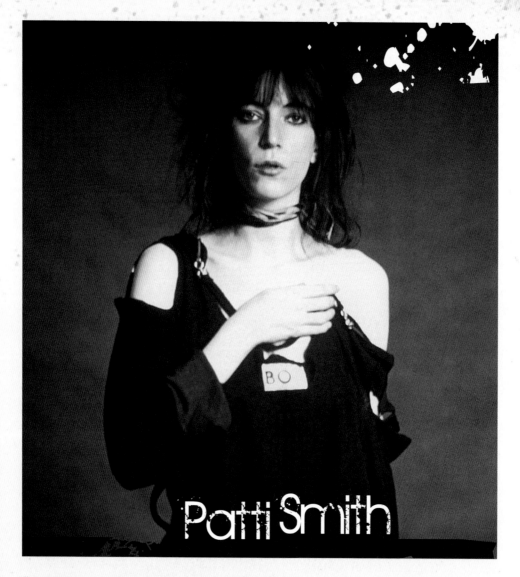

Patti Smith

Patti Smith Because The Night

1978 · 3:21 · Smith – Springsteen

On the Robert Mapplethorpe-photographed record cover of her third album, *Easter*, Patti Smith strikes a confidently sexy pose in a skimpy top. An even more provocative image that appears to be from the same photo shoot is used on the cover of 'Because The Night', her best-known single. This sultry persona also appears on the song, as she sings "Desire is hunger, is the fire I breathe / Love is a banquet on which we feed".

Both sexy and commercial, it is slightly untypical of her mostly hard-edged and intellectual oeuvre, but 'Because The Night' is all the more effective for its glimpses of unexpected tenderness. Bruce Springsteen originally wrote the song; it was never included on any of his studio albums, though he did perform it live. Producer Jimmy Iovine, who was working on albums for both artists at the time, passed Patti Smith a taped copy and she partly rewrote it. Many other artists have subsequently covered the track, including 10,000 Maniacs, Kim Wilde and KT Tunstall with the Buena Vista Social Club.

Born in Chicago in 1946 to a waitress mother and a factory worker father, Patricia Smith was brought up as a

Jehovah's Witness — a religious background she disowned as a teenager. By 1969, she had dropped out of college due to pregnancy, given up the baby for adoption and was busking in Paris, writing poetry and doing performance art. Her complex background and a status as an outsider set her up well to become the godmother of punk. She is angry and thoughtful in equal parts, rough-edged and acerbic. Smith's classic early records blended her influences into a challenging form of art-punk, not easy listening or radio-friendly, but exceptionally influential; a blueprint for so many female rock stars who followed her. *Horses*, produced by The Velvet Underground's John Cale, was Smith's debut album in 1975, and still rides high in most lists of all-time greats. It combined her fascination of poetry with a recognisably Cale rock sound: barbed and sparse. Smith's 1976 follow-up, *Radio Ethiopia*, mixed the increasingly experimental with some more conventional rock songs; 1978's *Easter* was a touch more conventional, while retaining her singular sound and was her most successful album to date.

'Because The Night' was the first single from *Easter* and reached number five in the UK charts and number 13 on the US Billboard chart. Opening with a solo piano refrain, Smith comes in with intimate singing before guitar riffs increase the tempo and the raw intensity. Her vocal and emotional range in the song is extraordinary, swooping from sensitive murmuring to strident lust, from romance to passion, from sandpaper to love.
JH

! Patti Smith's album *Horses*

Patti Smith Horses

The Smiths

The Smiths
Hand In Glove

1983 · 3:16 · Marr – Morrissey

On its release in 1983, The Smiths' debut single was as surprising as it was stunning. From nowhere there emerged a band with a vision, a poetic soul and a musical complexity that was then unrivalled. Just as The Smiths always seemed to, so the song would grate against what was then mainstream – Morrissey's haunted, yearning lyrics suggested loneliness, bleakness and something resolutely Northern and working class, very much not the staples of the time. "It should have been a massive hit, it was so urgent," said Morrissey. "To me, it was a complete cry in every direction. It really was a landmark."

The Smiths
This Charming Man

1983 · 2:42 · Marr – Morrissey

After 'Hand In Glove' topped the indie charts, a host of major labels began to court The Smiths. However, Morrissey stuck to his independent guns and instead the band signed a long-term deal with Rough Trade. 'This Charming Man', with its utterly danceable bassline and thrillingly jaunty guitars, was their first single once fully installed there. Concerning ever-present Morrissey themes of the fragility of masculinity and questions about sexual identity – the charming man in the song comes to the aid of a cyclist in distress and the pair uneasily flirt – it would also introduce the gladioli-clutching, hearing aid-wearing singer to a wary *Top Of The Pops* audience.

The Smiths
What Difference Does It Make?

1984 · 3:46 · Marr – Morrissey

With expectation for The Smiths' debut, self-titled, album almost feverish at the beginning of 1984, this January single worked as a teaser. Morrissey, bitter and resigned in equal measure, sticks it to an uninterested lover before admitting that "I'm still fond of you". The single, their third, would rocket to number 12 in the charts, but it wasn't one that either Morrissey or guitarist Johnny Marr much liked, both grumbling about murky production. "I thought [it] was absolutely awful the day after the record was pressed," the singer told *Q* magazine. "I didn't think it was a particularly strong one," agreed Marr.

The Smiths
Heaven Knows I'm Miserable Now

! 1984 • 3:35 • Marr – Morrissey

Possibly the definitive Smiths single, this track was nonetheless overshadowed by its B-side. 'Suffer Little Children' was a much lesser song but its subject matter, the Moors murders, caused some offence among the families of Myra Hindley's victims and considerably more in the tabloids, leading to the single's withdrawal in Boots and Woolworths. Its A-side, a hymn to the odiousness of working, deserved better than its number 10 chart-placing. Morrissey had discovered during his very occasional bouts of employment that he despised everyone he worked with. "You realise you're spending your entire life with people that you do not like," he said of day jobs, "which was incredibly distressing."

> "You realise you're spending your entire life with people that you do not like"

– Morrissey

The Smiths
How Soon Is Now?

! 1985 • 6:42 • Marr – Morrissey

An odd song in The Smiths canon as it remains one of their most enduring, without being particularly representative of the band. Very much a Johnny Marr song, its teaming, bubbling guitars and shimmering riff seethe with a masculinity and stridence that were rarely Smiths trademarks, yet seem entirely natural here. Marr had wanted to write a song with an "intro you couldn't forget", an ambition he achieved. However, The Smiths' record company were less sure and buried it on a B-side, only to realise their mistake later and give the track its just desserts as a full single release.
TB

The Smiths
The Boy With The Thorn In His Side

! 1985 • 3:17 • Morrissey – Marr

One of Morrissey's more obscure songs, 'The Boy With The Thorn In His Side' does, however, contain one of the writer's best couplets, which harks back to his days as a shy outsider: "When you want to live / How do you start, where do you go... who do you need to know?" Producer Stephen Street claims that the finished single is actually the demo recording, as Morrissey was happy with the original. The initial choice for the single's cover star was English footballer George Best – when the sportsman refused permission, writer Truman Capote was drafted in instead.
MO'G

> When you want to live? How do you start,
> where do you go… who do you need
> to know?
>
> The Smiths, 'The Boy With The Thorn In His Side'

The Smiths
Bigmouth Strikes Again

1986 • 3:14 • Marr – Morrissey

With a burgeoning reputation for controversy, Morrissey sought to address the trouble his comments were causing. Typically, though, he did so in suitably antagonistic fashion – he was hardly apologising, singing instead in faux self-chastisement. "I was only joking", the lyrics plead. "I would call it a parody if that sounded less like self-celebration, which it definitely wasn't," he told *Melody Maker* a year later. "It was just a really funny song." For the music, Johnny Marr was trying to write his version of 'Jumpin' Jack Flash'. "I wanted something that was a rush all the way through," he said of the song.
TB

The Smiths Panic

1986 • 2:20 • Morrissey – Marr

'Panic' managed to arouse the wrath of the UK music press, who claimed its "Hang the DJ" refrain was racist. However, journalists had the wrong idea – rather than slating black hip-hop DJs, Morrissey was attacking the crassness of daytime radio in Britain. Having heard a news report on the devastating disaster at the Soviet nuclear power station Chernobyl immediately followed by an inane pop single, the frontman vented his frustration at the vacuousness of the charts. The glam-rock stomp makes the rant more effective and the sweet-sounding children's choir on the lynch mob chorus is a typically hilarious touch.
MO'G

The Smiths
There Is A Light That
Never Goes Out

1986 • 4:02 • Marr – Morrissey

Certainly one of The Smiths' most tender and beautiful songs, this may also be the band at their best. By 1985, the Marr-Morrissey songwriting partnership was at its peak and, as an example of the form they were in, this was written during the same sessions as 'Bigmouth Strikes Again'. But where that song was a firecracker, this one was the converse: an introspective and lonely lyric underpinned by a delicate, intricate, acoustic-led band. It would never get its single release, but instead remained the highlight of The Smiths' astonishing and sweeping third album *The Queen Is Dead*.

The Smiths
Ask

! 1986 • 3:15 • Marr – Morrissey

A curiously African guitar sound and rhythm introduces 'Ask' – one that originated with temporary guitarist Craig Gannon, he claims – before Morrissey takes his own shyness to task in a gloriously catchy diatribe about his inability to cut loose. Released three months after the protest and alarm of 'Panic' had risen to number 11 in the charts, The Smiths were wary that they didn't want to be seen as a political band because, as Morrissey once said: "Regardless of the merits of the actual song, people would say, 'Here we go again'." It would reach number 14 in the UK singles charts.
TB

The Smiths
Girlfriend In A Coma

! 1987 • 2:03 • Morrissey – Marr

Used by critics as evidence of Morrissey's unrelenting miserablism, 'Girlfriend In A Coma' actually contains some of the singer's most moving lyrics, complemented perfectly by Johnny Marr's sweetly concise music. Written from the point of view of the boyfriend of the girl in question, the narrator muses about how he would get so annoyed at his partner, he'd often have murderous thoughts. Now that she's at death's door, he feels nothing but guilt. Despite clocking in at only just over two minutes, this is one of The Smiths' finest songs, and their last great single in the UK – Marr left the band a month before 'Girlfriend In A Coma' charted.
MO'G

The Smiths
Stop Me If You Think You've Heard This One Before

! 1987 • 3:32 • Marr – Morrissey

By the summer of 1987, The Smiths' perfectionism and intensity had bubbled irredeemably past boiling point and, in July, Johnny Marr left the band. Already in the can, though, was fourth album *Strangeways, Here We Come*, on which the guitarist had manoeuvred them away from their characteristic jangle. Despite the circumstances of its recording, the album would be Marr and Morrissey's favourite and this track was a highlight. However, 'Stop Me...' was prevented from a final, celebratory clamber up the charts because the BBC refused to give it airplay. They were concerned its line about mass murder would be inappropriate in the wake of the then recent Hungerford shootings.
TB

The Smiths didn't want to be a political band

SnowPatrol

Snow Patrol
Spitting Games

2003 · 3:48 · Lightbody – Quinn – Connolly – McClelland

Sometimes, you just have to be patient. Belfast-born, Scotland-based Snow Patrol signed to Jeepster while still at college in 1997. The assumption was that they could emulate the path of label stars Belle And Sebastian, achieving success purely through word of mouth. "We loved the idea of being on that sort of label because it was all under our control and we felt we weren't going to be pushed into anything we didn't want to do," remembers drummer Johnny Quinn. "But the downside of that was we didn't sell any records." Over the next four years they released

"Nobody thought anything was going to be a hit"

– Gary Lightbody on 'Run'

two albums. Both were critically acclaimed albums and resulted in a cult following, but that somehow failed to translate into sales. Jeepster dropped the band.

Having added guitarist Nathan Connolly, in 2003 Snow Patrol signed to Polydor's Fiction Records. That autumn they released 'Spitting Games', the first single from third album *Final Straw*. A bouncing indie pop tune about unrequited teenage love, its impact wasn't immediate. But something was stirring; the album was originally released without great fanfare, but managed to sell over 20,000 copies, mostly through word of mouth. And things were about to change with the release of their next single.

Snow Patrol
Run

| 2004 • 5:56 • Lightbody – Quinn – McClelland – Connolly – Archer

Fans were singing every word of this early favourite at gigs just weeks after the album had been released. A slow but solid guitar-led ballad, Gary Lightbody's breathy vocals over gentle verses made

way for a chorus so rousing, simple and memorable that it would be sung back at him by festival crowds for years to come. Yet before its release, the band had no idea they were sitting on gold. "It had been kicking about for years," says Lightbody. "Nobody thought anything was going to be a hit." The single debuted at number five in the UK chart. A re-issue of the album saw it hit number three, sending Snow Patrol on their way to being one of the most successful British bands of the decade.

Snow Patrol
Chocolate

| 2003 • 3:09 • Lightbody – Quinn – Connolly – McClelland

By the time this single was released in 2004, Snow Patrol were flying. As well as continuing to sell well in the UK, *Final Straw* entered the US top 100 album chart. 'Chocolate', a tuneful, gently rousing song with a thumping drumbeat, contains the lyric from which the album title was lifted. The accompanying video, where the band calmly count down the last three minutes on earth as panic ensues around them, was directed by Marc Webb, director of *(500) Days Of Summer* and the upcoming *Spider-Man Reboot*.

Snow Patrol
How To Be Dead

| 2003 • 3:24 • Lightbody – Connolly – McClelland – Quinn

At this stage, Snow Patrol's success was enormous. They had played at Live 8, been asked to tour with U2 and their album was selling hundreds of thousands. 'How To Be Dead' was the last single to be released from it – a quiet, reflective song, warm in tone despite biting lyrics. Of all of the songs on *Final Straw*, it's the one that producer Garret "Jacknife" Lee had the most input on.

Snow Patrol
You're All I Have

2006 • 4:33 • Lightbody – Connolly – Quinn – Wilson – Simpson

During the two years between album releases, the band worked non-stop, touring and writing for 2006 follow-up, *Eyes Open*. Its first single, 'You're All I Have', is an upbeat, joyful track. Lyrically, it seemed like Gary Lightbody had finally left some of his demons behind, although he claims it's still a bleak song "about a damaging but fulfilling relationship, something that terrifies you, but you

can't quite bring yourself to look away". Indicating how much their fanbase had grown, the single debuted at number seven in the UK charts, giving them their second-biggest hit to date. The album echoed its success, hitting number one in the UK and other international charts.

Snow Patrol
Chasing Cars

2006 • 4:27 • Lightbody – Quinn – Connolly – Wilson – Simpson

'Chasing Cars' was to become Snow Patrol's biggest success. This simple, gently building epic is, says Gary Lightbody, the "most pure and open love song [he's] ever written". Around the time of the album's release, the song was used over the final scenes of the season finale of TV show *Grey's Anatomy*. The band already had a solid US fanbase, but nothing could prepare them for the impact of this placing. Overnight the single went top

> "It's the most pure and open love song I've ever written"
> — Gary Lightbody on 'Chasing Cars'

10 on US iTunes. American radio stations began adding it to playlists. Within a few weeks of the episode being shown in Australia, the album shot to number one. Back in the UK, a change in chart rules during January 2007 saw download-only songs become eligible, leading to 'Chasing Cars' shooting to number nine. Its success helped the album to achieve platinum status in 11 different countries, including America, Australia and Argentina.

Snow Patrol
Set The Fire To The Third Bar

> 2006 • 3:23 • Lightbody – Connolly – Quinn – Wilson – Simpson

Written for and featuring Martha Wainwright (singer Gary Lightbody is a huge fan), this song flits between gentle, understated verses and urgent choruses filled with longing. It came as a surprise to those who considered Snow Patrol to be just another Colplay-lite. Musically, it seems closer to singer Gary Lightbody's pre-*Final Straw* side project The Reindeer Section than Snow Patrol's biggest hits. The band have performed it live with a number of notable guest vocalists, including Cheryl Cole, Andrea Corr and even comedian James Cordon.

Snow Patrol
Open Your Eyes

> 2006 • 5:38 • Lightbody – Connolly – Quinn – Wilson – Simpson

Snow Patrol know better than anyone that good things come to those who wait. Building understated guitar and bass notes with Gary Lightbody's singing, it's a full four minutes before the drums crash in, accompanied by strings and horns. For the video, footage was taken from 1976 cult classic fim *C'était Un Rendezvous* – the first-time director Claude Lelouch had granted anyone permission to use it. The song's popularity was cemented when it was used on *Grey's Anatomy* and the season 12 finale of *ER*.

Snow Patrol
Take Back The City

> 2008 • 4:38 • Lightbody – Quinn – Connolly – Wilson – Simpson

After their international hit with 'Signal Fire', the lead track from *Spider-Man 3*,

"A love song to Belfast... with a little bit of hate in there"

Snow Patrol returned in 2008 with their fifth album, *A Hundred Million Suns*. Preceding it, they released this rocky stomper, whose spiky, chunky chords were inspired by old Tom Petty and Cars records. Gary Lightbody described the track to Xfm as "a love song to Befast... with a little bit of hate in there as well, 'cause I grew up not really liking the place, but grew to love it." With Garrett Lee on production duties again, the album was an international success, achieving top 10 status in America and Australia, among other countries. MS

Soundgarden

Soundgarden
Spoonman

! 1994 • 4:06 • Cornell

As one of the earliest Seattle bands off the blocks in the late 1980s, most industry insiders were predicting that Chris Cornell and co. would be the first of the flourishing North West scene to make some commercial headway. Having paid their dues with a few indie singles on fledgling Seattle label Sub Pop and an album on LA's SST, their signing to a major label encouraged the band's Seattle peers greatly. A young Kurt Cobain reportedly eyed the move with particular interest.

'Spoonman' was a song title initially coined by Pearl Jam bassist Jeff Ament for the fictional band Citizen Dick in Cameron Crowe's Seattle-based movie' *Singles*. With a video that displayed the prowess of Seattle street performer and real life spoonman Artis, it set the scene for the staggering commercial success of fourth album *Superunknown*, which would follow a month later.

Soundgarden
Black Hole Sun

! 1994 • 6:17 • Cornell

Following the death of Kurt Cobain in April 1994, 'Black Hole Sun' seemed a fitting summertime song for a rock

scene in mourning. And, for a band who were initially marketed as a metal act before the *Nevermind* explosion, 'Black Hole Sun' was as "grunge" a moment as Soundgarden had produced. Black Sabbath and Led Zeppelin influences were still clearly audible, but singer Chris Cornell's abstract, poignant lyricism and exploding chorus was clutched to the hearts of those reeling from the Nirvana star's death, as well as fans of simple, good old-fashioned rock'n'roll. The cutting-edge video that accompanied the song was a huge hit on MTV. Directed by Howard Greenhalgh, it showed citizens of a twisted suburban enclave being slowly disfigured by a black hole in the sky. It catapulted the band into rock's super league and began the measuring of *Superunknown*'s sales in millions. The band's internal conflicts would see them split after one more album in 1997, only to reform in 2010 to play a few selected shows.
OH

The Soup Dragons
I'm Free

| 1990 · 3:58 · Jagger – Richards

Named after a character in classic British children's TV show *The Clangers*, 'I'm Free' was Scottish outfit The Soup Dragons' only UK top 20 hit. The song was originally recorded by The Rolling Stones in 1965, featuring on their *Out Of Our Heads* album. Hailing from the same town as Teenage Fanclub and the BMX Bandits (Bellshill, near Glasgow), The Soup Dragons started out as a pop-punk outfit in 1985, and had 12 singles and EPs prior to 'I'm Free'. These featured regularly in the UK indie chart, but failed to make any impact on the top 40. In 1990 the band absorbed the turn-of-the-decade "baggy" sound to create a landmark single very much of its time. With elements of reggae, rock and acid house, 'I'm Free' was an instant singalong dancefloor anthem, with a funky beat and a multi-vocal chorus. Featuring an overdub by Jamaican reggae star Junior Reid, it reached number five in the UK charts.

Rave culture had overflowed into the mainstream in Britain and the expression of freedom and love – "I'm free to do what I want, to be what I want, any old time" – slotted neatly into the ecstasy-fuelled, smiley-decorated, "second summer of love" atmosphere that pervaded music at the time. Covering a Stones song in an acid house style summed up the merging of rock and dance that the Madchester scene brought about. Twenty years on, 'I'm Free' has a rather dated, naïve charm to its fuzzy optimism and eclectic mix of sounds, but it's also possible to hear the beginnings of a newly confident British sound that would eventually evolve into Britpop.
JH

Space
Female Of The Species

| 1996 · 3:19
| Scott – Edwards – Griffin – Parle

While fellow Liverpool bands like The La's and Cast were following the city's Mersey beat tradition, Space were doing their own thing, sounding closer to their

Manchester neighbours than the Fab Four. Lead singer Tommy Scott had set out with the intention of creating a sound influenced by The Who, but ended up with character-driven storylines allied to Latin beats and feel-good guitars. This, the second single from the band's debut, was written by Scott as a tribute to his late father, who had always preferred the likes of Frank Sinatra to his son's own work. The result was unique: Britpop combined with crooning vocals, which original drummer Andy Parle was shocked ever saw the light of day. "We thought the record company were crazy," he said the year after the release of 'Female Of The Species'. "We thought it was too weird." But it was the weirdness that gave the song its charm and saw it stay in the UK top 40 for three months. Right up until the band split in 2005, it remained their signature tune. JS

The Specials
Too Much Too Young

! 1979 • 2:06 • Dammers

Many bands make great music but true innovators can be harder to come by. In the late 1970s, The Specials took the raw spitting energy of punk-rock and combined it with the walking bass and calypso rhythm of ska, which kick-started the ska revival in the UK (termed the "second wave" by some music historians). Forming in 1977, the seven-piece outfit, headed by keyboard player Jerry Dammers, attracted much attention from major labels after successful support slots with The Clash. But Dammers chose to set up his own label, 2 Tone, which would go on to sign many bands also following the ska movement, such as Madness.

Seemingly swapping at will between calling themselves The Specials and The Special A.K.A., the band produced a self-titled album and singles 'Gangsters' and 'A Message To You Rudy' before releasing EP *The Special A.K.A. Live* with 'Too Much Too Young' (a re-arrangement of the Lloyd Charmers' track 'Birth Control') as its lead track. It was their first UK number one. Although it is often reported that the song was banned by the BBC because of its pro-contraception stance, this is untrue (although the final line of "Try wearing a cap" did fall foul of the censors). Even vocalist Terry Hall proclaimed before a live performance of the song on BBC music show *The Old Grey Whistle Test*: "This should have been our next single but they wouldn't play it on the radio." The song itself is an embodiment of what made the band stand out from the UK punk crowd: incessant beats, ringing rock guitar riffs, shared vocals chopping between Hall's arrogant punk delivery of the skilful narrative and the casual Caribbean harmonies of Neville Staples and Lynval Golding. Topped off with Dammers' whirling keyboards, the song bubbles and soars with complex riffs and melodies.

The Specials
Ghost Town

! 1981 • 3:40 • Dammers

Two years later, The Specials returned with second album *More Specials* and a markedly different sound. The ska-punk scene was fading and the record showed a more experimental approach, with the band exploring genres such as new wave, lounge – even muzak. 'Ghost Town' was a non-album release the following year and a clear indication of the group's musical changes. A downbeat, doom-laden, politically-fired track, it was inspired by the financial problems of the band's home town of Coventry, and perhaps also of their record label. It was released amid race-related unemployment riots in Brixton

and Liverpool and seemed to embody the atmosphere of a nation, reaching number one in the UK charts where it sat for three weeks alongside upbeat synthesised pop.

An unusual arrangement saw the normal verse-chorus-verse structure abandoned for what was to be a very unique record. Jerry Dammers' keyboards are eerily atmospheric throughout and a chanting vocal provides a damning appraisal of inner-city life. The recording of the single had been traumatic with, at some stages, certain members of the band refusing to be in the studio at the same time. After three years of being one of the coolest bands in Britain, The Specials split. Later reformations without Dammers were mainly dismissed as money-making projects, but the influence of the band's early releases can still be heard in contemporary artists such as The Streets and Lily Allen.
JS

"This should have been our next single but they wouldn't play it on the radio"

– Terry Hall on 'Too Much Too Young'

Starsailor

Starsailor
Good Souls

2001 • 4:53
Walsh – Stelfox – Westhead – Byrne

Named after the 1970 Tim Buckley album, Starsailor met as a group of four 18-year-old music students at college in Wigan at the very end of the 1990s. One of the first songs they wrote together, 'Good Souls' was an unusually collaborative effort for the band: the powerful drive of the rhythm section here is just as important as James Walsh's vocals and melody. Walsh says that the lyrics are about staying positive when you have spent a lifetime as an outsider – keeping focused on what could happen and appreciating those supportive people around you. 'Good Souls' was undoubtedly the song that started the music business buzz that led to the band signing to the legendary Heavenly Records in 2000.

Starsailor
Alcoholic

2001 • 2:56
Walsh – Stelfox – Westhead – Byrne

The third single to be taken from Starsailor's debut album *Love Is Here* and the band's first UK top 10 hit. Written by singer James Walsh on an acoustic guitar, the dark nature of the lyrics was not born of bitter personal experience as many people assumed, but rather came from observing the damage done by the alcohol culture of his hometown. "You see a lot of babies being paraded around pubs in Warrington," Walsh told Xfm in May 2010. MW

"You see a lot of babies being paraded around pubs in Warrington"

– James Walsh of his hometown

Stereo MC's
Connected

1992 • 3:59
Birch – Casey – Finch – Hallam

Before 'Connected' came along, cool English kids didn't really get hip-hop. Listening now, it sounds modern but not that radical. At the time, however, it was a strikingly different British sound, blending American sounds and rhythms with a distinctly English attitude. Confident, cool, eloquent and unapologetically street, the Stereos were the first UK act to feature in the US R&B chart. In some ways they were a precursor to The Streets: rapper Rob Birch's refreshing vocals sounded as if that was probably how he talked to his mates down the pub on a Friday night. The band cemented their crossover appeal by polishing their live performances and playing festivals.

'Connected', their breakthrough single, also gave its name to their fourth album, a Brit award winner. The song has since been used in films and in a mobile phone ad campaign. Sampling Jimmy "Bo" Horne's 1978 song 'Let Me (Let Me Be Your Lover)', it's a funky-yet-chilled paean to being connected while not leaving your mind neglected. Somehow the single only reached number 18 in the UK charts on its release in 1992, but it remains a track that many people can happily sing along to two decades later.

Stereo MC's
Step It Up

| 1992 • 3:57 • Birch – Hallam

It may not be as well remembered as 'Connected', but the dancefloor-friendly 'Step It Up' was in fact Stereo MC's most successful single in the UK. Despite the references to dancing, the song appears to have saucier activity in mind, as Rob Birch sings about an "inflammation in my anatomy". Birch's somewhat drug-hazed demeanour, is, according to fellow band member Nick Hallam, entirely inaccurate: he says that Birch is in fact "one of the most health-conscious people I know".
JH

Stereophonics

Stereophonics
Local Boy In The Photograph

| 1997 • 3:22 • Jones – Jones – Cable

After years of learning their craft in South Wales' pubs and clubs, the Stereophonics rose to fame swiftly as the flagship act of Richard Branson's new V2 record label. "Before that, we'd had rejection letter after rejection letter," former drummer Stuart Cable told Xfm. "Kelly [Jones, singer] and I had even talked about ending the band. Bear in mind, we'd already written 'Local Boy...' and 'A Thousand Trees' by then." With the weight of the record company behind it, 'Local Boy...' was an attention-grabber that set the scene nicely for the runaway success of debut album *Word Gets Around*. Containing the key ingredients that would make the band a phenomenon – Kelly Jones' small-town tales and stadium-sized hooks – the UK music industry braced itself for the arrival of one of its biggest bands.

Stereophonics
A Thousand Trees

| 1997 • 3:03 • Jones – Jones – Cable

'A Thousand Trees' was another of the band's songs that was touted relentlessly when the band were called Tragic Love Company.

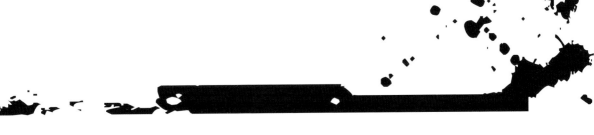

The change of name to Stereophonics helped immensely, but the A&R fraternity still couldn't get their heads around the song's meaning. "They thought it was about Greenpeace and sticking it to the big multi-nationals," bassist Richard Jones told us. "They obviously hadn't listened to the song, which was really about small-town rumours that escalate out of control."

Stereophonics
Traffic

! 1997 • 4:53 • Jones – Jones – Cable

Scribbled lyrics in the back of the manager's car transformed arduous journeys between record company meetings into one of the band's most well-known early anthems. The video, however, was a far more glamorous affair as the band were shipped out to LA for the first time... until disaster struck. "Stuart [Cable] had a nasty bug so he couldn't make it," explained Richard Jones to Xfm. "The drummer we drafted for the video turned out to be a relation of someone from [rock band] Grant Lee Buffalo, who we all loved. Cable was absolutely thrilled."

Stereophonics
The Bartender And The Thief

! 1998 • 3:07 • Jones – Jones – Cable

To crown the sweeping success of debut album *Word Gets Around*, Stereophonics organised a sold-out homecoming show at Cardiff Castle in June 1998. Already hard at work on their follow-up, the band debuted new song 'The Bartender And The Thief' in front of 10,000 committed fans. Inspired by two girls' drunken exploits in Neil Finn's Auckland bar, and channelling the metal fury of band faves' AC/DC, it went down a storm. The likelihood of a second album flop suddenly seemed remote at best.

Stereophonics
Just Looking

! 1999 • 4:05 • Jones – Jones – Cable

'Just Looking' followed 'The Bartender And The Thief' into the top five and became a firm fan favourite. While touring second album *Performance And Cocktails*, the song also became the cue for fans to throw Jelly Babies at the band. "The idea for the video was that we were all in a car and as Stuart [Cable] reaches for the Jelly Babies, he crashes it into a freezing cold lake," Richard Jones told us. "We occasionally still see a few airborne Jelly Babies now. It could be a lot worse!"

Stereophonics
Pick A Part That's New

! 1999 • 3:36 • Jones – Jones – Cable

As well as being *Performance And Cocktails'* poppiest moment, 'Pick A Part That's New' also heralded a significant change of approach for the band. The programmed intro riff signalled an interest in ideas and sounds generated outside the trio's immediate musical scope. "We drafted a keyboard player for the tour because we needed more people to perform these songs," said bassist Richard Jones. "It took us a while to get out of the three-piece mentality, but it was a step that we had to take to move forward."

Stereophonics
I Wouldn't Believe Your Radio

! 1999 • 3:51 • Jones – Jones – Cable

"The song title comes from an old saying in Cwmaman," drummer Stuart Cable told Xfm. "If someone was a huge liar, you'd say that you couldn't even believe their radio." The music, however, was a distinct change in pace for the band as

a shuffling rhythm ushered in a beautiful country-tinged ballad. The song surfaced in one of frontman Kelly Jones' dreams, where Cable sang the lead vocal. "In the morning Kelly'd got it all down – the guitar line, the lyrics, everything," Cable said.

Stereophonics
Hurry Up And Wait

! 1999 • 5:37 • Jones – Jones – Cable

A slow-burning epic that rounded off the hugely successful campaign for *Performance And Cocktails* nicely. The single was also notable for its B-side, where drummer Stuart Cable finally got to sing 'I Wouldn't Believe Your Radio', as per Kelly Jones' dream. "I may have been pissed at the time," said Cable of the Australian recording session that yielded the song's Johnny Cash/William Shatner delivery.

"It took us a while to get out of the three-piece mentality, but it was a step that we had to take to move forward"

– Richard Jones

Stereophonics
Mr Writer

! 2001 • 5:18 • Jones – Bird

'Mr Writer' was the first single from third album *Just Enough Education To Perform*, and the ensuing tour's live opener. A stinging ode to a journalist who'd hitched a ride on the *Performance And Cocktails* promo jaunt, the band admit it wasn't their greatest PR move. "It was the beginning of the end of our love affair with the UK press," Richard Jones told Xfm. "But if they were taking it to heart, then we'd obviously struck a chord with something they'd done in the past."

Stereophonics
Have A Nice Day

! 2001 • 3:26 • Jones

'Have A Nice Day' was recorded in Peter Gabriel's Real World Studios near Bath and produced by Marshall Bird and Steve Bush. It would be the band's final top five with the pair, crowning a successful partnership that stretched the length of their output to date. The song's unabashed pop sensibility did little to endear the band to a journalistic fraternity smarting from 'Mr Writer', but its glorious summer feel was a huge hit with the band's faithful.

Stereophonics
Step On My Old Size Nines

! 2001 • 4:00 • Jones

"'Maybe Tomorrow' was even the biggest radio record we've ever had"

– Kelly Jones

Bluesy ballad 'Step On My Old Size Nines' was played by Stereophonics at Wayne Rooney's post-wedding celebration, after being booked by wife Colleen as a surprise for her husband. As the band's number one fan, Rooney also has the album title *Just Enough Education To Perform* tattooed on his arm.

Stereophonics
Maybe Tomorrow

! 2003 • 4:34 • Jones

The band's fourth album, *You've Got To Go There To Come Back*, heralded the end of drummer Stuart Cable's tenure with the band and – for some – Stereophonics' descent into a mid-paced, Dad-rock quagmire. Singer Kelly Jones, however, remained unrepentant. "The fact is, it sold a million, it was a number one album, we had top five singles and we did the biggest arena tour of our career," he told Xfm. "'Maybe Tomorrow' was even the biggest radio record we've ever had!"

Remembering Stuart Cable

A few days after I interviewed former Stereophonics drummer Stuart Cable for this book, news broke that he'd passed away at his home near Aberdare, south Wales. It was June 7th 2010, and he'd recently turned 40.

He was a huge character. Hilariously funny, kind and generous, his booming voice and broad accent couldn't help but light up a room. I met him first when my band, The Crocketts, supported Stereophonics at Aberystwyth Arts Centre in 1997. From that point, through many tours together and at Xfm South Wales much later, it was clear that his wildly successful careers were as much a result of his sheer force of personality as his considerable skills. Thunderous drum grooves were coupled with excitable live performances and off-stage high jinks during the Stereophonics' rise to fame. Similarly, his encyclopaedic knowledge of rock and his immediately engaging tone on the mic made his many post-band broadcasting ventures such a joy to watch or listen to.

I will miss him greatly as will the many thousands of others he touched so profoundly. Most of all, and most sadly of all, he will be missed immeasurably by his brother Paul, mother Mabel and son Cian.

Owen Hopkin

Stereophonics
Dakota

! 2005 • 4:57 • Jones

If Stereophonics seemed adrift following Stuart Cable's departure, 'Dakota' was a triumphant-sounding resurrection. Looking lean in standard-issue black leather, with a cutting-edge new sound and taught grooves courtesy of Argentinean drummer Javier Weyler, it was the reinvention that continued the band's incredible success story. "I like being kicked up the arse by new bands," frontman Kelly Jones told Xfm mischievously, "but I like kicking them back, too." 'Dakota' became the band's first UK number one single and ensured that fifth album *Language. Sex. Violence. Other?* would become their fourth consecutive number one album.
OH

The Stone Roses

The Stone Roses
Sally Cinnamon

1987 • 2:55 • Squire – Brown

The Stone Roses' second single, released in May 1987, was not something that necessarily hinted at greatness to come. Singer Ian Brown's melody aside – a tuneful, almost folky offering that would become a familiar modus operandi – the song itself was a cod-psychedelic, indie jaunt whose guitars seemed inspired, in part, by The Byrds. In 1990, it made an unwelcome reappearance after The Stone Roses had become a success. The Midlands-based label FM-Revolver re-released 'Sally Cinnamon' without the band's permission, leading to The Stone Roses re-decorating their offices,

> "No wonder that LP sounds so mellow and laid-back. We were constantly stoned to fuck"
>
> – Mani

Jackson Pollock-style, with tins of paint. The band were arrested and fined £3,000 each for their artistic protest.

The Stone Roses
Elephant Stone

1988 • 4:53 • Squire – Brown

With bass player Gary "Mani" Mounfield on board by the time of its release, 'Elephant Stone' marked the moment The Stone Roses found their groove and direction. Opening with wonder-drummer Alan "Reni" Wren's clattering intro, before John Squire's tumbling, spiralling yet gentle guitars take the lead, this was the sound of a band whose feet were beginning to touch firm ground. Uplifting, catchy and full of pop nous, it hinted at the dance rhythms then flowing through Manchester, perhaps because of its production by New Order's Peter Hook.

The Stone Roses
Made Of Stone

1989 • 4:15 • Squire – Brown

The buzz surrounding The Stone Roses as their debut album neared its release date was building into something genuinely exciting. So when 'Made Of Stone' appeared in March, a month

before the album, it was leapt upon: its pounding, almost disco beat replicated the club sounds while its solo allowed John Squire a workout that added some much-needed meat to the band's sonic template. When that debut, *The Stone Roses*, was finally released in April, the band's blend of dance music and rock guitars would make them the leaders of the new "baggy" scene.

The Stone Roses
She Bangs The Drums

⌯ 1989 • 3:42 • Squire – Brown

For such a classic album, *The Stone Roses* was made in slightly surreal circumstances. The band relocated from Manchester to Willesden in north London, and would record only at night. Meanwhile, one of the studio's frequent guests was the former page three model Sam Fox. Lodging in a house in Kensal Green, The Stone Roses would smoke a lot of weed – "No wonder that LP sounds so mellow and laid-back. We were constantly stoned 'to fuck'," claimed bassist Mani – and meticulously plan their music. 'She Bangs The Drums' emerged from those sessions, a fully-formed indie anthem that reached number 36 in the singles chart.

The Stone Roses
Fool's Gold

⌯ 1989 • 5:24 • Squire – Brown

The definitive Stone Roses song, the definitive baggy track and the tune that would define Madchester wasn't, at first, even an A-side. Put out as a single seven months after the April 1989 release of *The Stone Roses*, it was initially the B-side to 'What The World Is Waiting For' before sense prompted the two to be released as a double A-side. From Mani's seminal bassline to John Squire's guitars, it already had the hallmarks of a belter, but when drummer Reni aped the beat of James Brown's 'Funky Drummer', a true classic was born. "I think it's one of the greatest things we did," said singer Ian Brown.

The Stone Roses
What The World Is
Waiting For

⌯ 1989 • 3:55 • Squire – Brown

Recorded, like 'Fools Gold', in the unlikely backwater recording suite of Sawmills Studio on the Fowey estuary in Cornwall, 'What The World Is Waiting For' was initially thought by the band and their management to be the stronger song and was thus readied for release. Stuffed full of biblical references – as, indeed, is much of The Stone Roses' work – it found the band berating capitalism and the "burned-out world". Drifting whimsically along, the records state that it hit number eight in the charts, but that was solely because it shared an A-side with 'Fools Gold'.

The Stone Roses
This Is The One

! 1989 • 4:59 • Squire – Brown

Written four years before the recording
sessions for *The Stone Roses* began, 'This
Is The One' was the result of the band
being locked in a room by the influential
Manchester producer Martin Hannett and
told to emerge with a song. The result was
a fast, brash and fiery rocker that was a
thrill live, but which The Stone Roses were
unsure how to capture on their album.
After a tricky recording session, it is now
frequently used to soundtrack Manchester
United's arrival onto the Old Trafford
pitch, something that lifelong United
fan Ian Brown is still delighted about.

The Stone Roses
One Love

! 1990 • 7:45 • Squire – Brown

By this point the biggest band in England,
The Stone Roses celebrated by playing to
30,000 people at Spike Island in Widnes
in 1990. Dubbed "the Woodstock of our
generation", the concert has attained near-
mythical status despite, erm, not being
very good. Dogged by sound problems
and technical issues, it nonetheless
was a cultural milestone that sealed
The Stone Roses' elevation to godlike
status – at least temporarily. Released
two months later, 'One Love' reached
number four in the singles charts but, in

John Squire's free soloing, would point
the way to the band's future rather than
acting as a celebration of their past.

The Stone Roses
I Wanna Be Adored

! 1989 • 4:52 • Squire – Brown

The Stone Roses had always been
possessed of an extraordinary confidence
and swagger, but to open a debut album
with a song entitled 'I Wanna Be Adored'
took some guts. After completing *The
Stone Roses*, that self-assurance was even
higher. "I remember finally finishing the
LP and [producer] John Leckie saying
to us, 'You're going to do really well
you know'," remembered Ian Brown.
"We just said, 'Yeah, we know'." They
were right, too. 'I Wanna Be Adored'
was pounding, sweeping and as good a
statement of intent as any, unfurling from
an opening bass growl into something
that would help define a generation.

The Stone Roses
Waterfall

! 1989 • 4:40 • Squire – Brown

Three songs into *The Stone Roses* and the
band were still operating on an almost
flawless level. With its lilting, shuffling
beat, cyclical guitars and floating vocals,
'Waterfall' was heavenly enough. Next,
though, they had the coolness to break
the song down into a languid jam before

> "I remember [producer] John Leckie saying to us, 'You're going to do really well you know'. We just said, 'Yeah, we know'"

— Ian Brown

building it back up again, reasserting that cyclical riff and heading off over the hills with it. Coming at the tail end of the 1980s, a decade in which guitar bands were either heavy rockers or virtually extinct, it suggested an independence of spirit and strength of mind unrivalled elsewhere.

The Stone Roses
I Am The Resurrection

| 1989 • 8:14 • Squire – Brown

The culmination of debut album *The Stone Roses* was its thrilling closer, 'I Am The Resurrection'. As a sign of a band with strut, a near 10-minute epic – including a thrilling four-and-half-minute psychedelic coda preceded by a singer proclaiming the glory and healing powers of pop music – is not a bad one. "I kept saying to them, 'Look you're great. Let's do a 10-minute song where you're just playing and playing and playing'," Ian Brown told *MOJO* magazine of the album's finale. "For

two days I watched them work out the ending of that song. It was just fantastic."

The Stone Roses
Love Spreads

| 1994 • 5:46 • Squire

'One Love' would be the last original Stone Roses song the world would hear for four years. A protracted legal battle with their record label and two years travelling around Europe had stalled progress on a follow-up to *The Stone Roses*. When sessions did begin, they were slow and frustrating, with producer John Leckie eventually leaving the band to their own devices. Marked more by John Squire's heavy blues guitars than the baggy beats of before, 'Love Spreads' – *The Second Coming*'s lead single – was considered a disappointment by some who felt the amount of time The Stone Roses had spent on the album had robbed them of their cultural significance.

The Stone Roses
Ten Storey Love Song

! 1995 · 4:29 · Squire

Second Coming may have attracted criticism for concentrating more on guitars (and songwriting) than its predecessor but, at least in terms of chart numbers, it was a much more successful offering. While 'Love Spreads' had gone to number two, the album itself went top five and this, its second single, landed at number 11. A gentle, flowing, electric ballad, its lightness of touch belied problems in the band. Their drummer, Reni, left shortly before this single's release and The Stone Roses would only carry on for another couple of years.

The Stone Roses
Begging You

! 1995 · 4:54 · Squire – Brown

Pulsing, pounding and driven by relentless dance beats courtesy of the departed Reni, 'Begging You' was the heaviest track ever released by The Stone Roses and, while it certainly captured their dance influences, its darkness also foreshadowed the band's split. This would be their last ever single and, with their drummer already long gone by the time of its release, guitarist John Squire would also jump ship less than six months later. As swansongs go, though, there are few more thrilling. Guitars squall, the bassline rumbles apocalyptically and Ian Brown is in fine form, urging the song to its thrilling finale. TB

The Stooges
I Wanna Be Your Dog

! 1969 · 3:25
Alexander – Asheton – Asheton – Pop

In Detroit, 1967, little-known singer James Newell Osterberg was inspired to form a band called The Psychedelic Stooges with brothers Ron and Scott Asheton, on guitar and drums respectively, and bassist Dave Alexander. After seeing The MC5 in concert in Ann Arbour, the band started calling Osterberg "Pop". He gained new first name "Iggy" soon after – a reference to a band he used to play in called The Iguanas. Iggy Pop became The Stooges' wild frontman, developing a reputation for incendiary live performances that included smearing his bare chest with hamburger meat and peanut butter, flashing his genitalia to the audience and even cutting himself with shards of glass while on stage. It was during this period that the band really developed their sound and legend has it that this is where Pop introduced stage-diving to American music fans.

In 1969, the band signed to Elektra Records and released their debut album, simply titled *The Stooges*. The record received poor reviews upon release and little critical acclaim. 'I Wanna Be Your Dog' was featured on this eponymous debut

'I Wanna Be Your Dog' has gone on to become one of the most covered tracks of all time

and stood out among the heavy metal/garage-rock tracks. Its simple melody and guitar riff of just three chords (G, F# and E for any budding guitarists) are played throughout the entire track, except for the bridge. Although now arguably considered the ultimate Stooges' track, it wouldn't last long if it was released in today's music industry. The intro is a heavily distorted simple guitar riff that lasts a ridiculous 33 seconds before Pop's vocals come in. 'I Wanna Be Your Dog' has gone on to become one of the most covered tracks of all time by artists including Red Hot Chili Peppers, Sonic Youth, The House of Love, Green Day, Ida Maria, Stereophonics and many, many others. R.E.M. performed the song with Patti Smith for their induction into the Rock and Roll Hall of Fame.

By the early 1970s, heroin was allegedly playing a major part in most of the band members' lives (with the exception of Ron Asheton) and their unique performance style became increasingly erratic and unpredictable. Elektra dropped them and The Stooges found themselves in something of a hiatus. During the subsequent four years, the band managed to release third album *Raw Power* while going through rehab. BdP

The Stranglers
Peaches

1977 · 4:03
Black – Burnell – Cornwell – Greenfield

The Guildford Stranglers – as they were originally known – were a dyed-in-the-wool pub rock band whose risqué lyrics and menacing demeanour gave them a leg-up into the rapidly rising punk scene. Their second single, 'Peaches', showcased Hugh Cornwall's sneering vocals as he – shall-we-say – "admires" bikini clad young ladies on a beach.

Produced as a seven inch single with the B-side 'Go Buddy Go', the BBC found the song slightly too offensive for their listeners and banned it from receiving any airplay. The radio edit was re-dubbed: "clitoris" became "bikini", "oh shit" was replaced by "oh no" and "what a bummer" with "what a summer".

The Stranglers
No More Heroes

| 1977 · 3:29
Black – Burnell – Cornwell – Greenfield

Despite the group's public popularity, the British media took a while to warm to The Stranglers, fearing sexist and racist innuendo in their lyrics, and a confrontational relationship developed between the press and the band. So much so that one of the band members punched a music journalist at a promotional event.

Dave Greenfield's keyboards recalled The Doors and such retro stylings merely added to their unfashionable allure. The public didn't care, however, and sent the iconoclastic 'No More Heroes' into the UK top 10 in September 1977.

The Stranglers
Duchess

| 1979 · 2:30
Black – Burnell – Cornwell – Greenfield

Despite The Stranglers' fractious relationship with the press, they maintained a constant presence in the UK singles chart in the late '70s and actually managed to become more successful than most "proper" punk bands. 'Duchess' was their sixth top 20 hit and was a melodic tale of a lady from the upper classes who'd lost all her money. The accompanying album *The Raven* was the band's most ambitious yet – songs about genetic engineering, nuclear weapons, Middle Eastern politics and heroin addiction made the record a heady concoction.

The Stranglers
Golden Brown

| 1981 · 3:28
Black – Burnell – Cornwell – Greenfield

Despite their reputation as the hard men of punk, The Stranglers' biggest hit was their most delicate composition yet. 'Golden Brown' was an intricate, ponderous harpsichord-led waltz that delighted the public (who sent it to Number Two in the charts) and even Radio 2, who made it their record of the week. As ever, though, there was a dark undercurrent – according to singer Hugh Cornwell, "The song is half about a girl I was having an affair with and the colour of her skin and half the colour of the heroin we were snorting at the time".

The Stranglers
Always The Sun

| 1986 · 4:51
Black – Burnell – Cornwell – Greenfield

'Always The Sun' was meant to be the hit to match 'Golden Brown' and critically, it had all the hallmarks of being a major success for the band. Yet somehow it didn't quite make it, instead limping into the UK singles chart at number 30. Founding member Hugh Cornwell recalled the band's surprise at the single's poor performance in his book *The Stranglers Song By Song*; he couldn't believe that their record company's prediction of how high it would chart was so off-centre. "We'd given [record label] CBS something great to work with and I could see in this guy's face that he knew he hadn't delivered."
BdP / MOG

Despite their reputation as the hard men of punk, The Stranglers' biggest hit was their most delicate composition yet

dry your eyes

please forgive me.
i know i fucked up
but all i can say
is that i'm sorry
i realised that i need
you more than anything
please don't leave me

mike x

THE STREETS

"I suppose it did make a lot of people think I was trying to be something I wasn't...."

– Mike Skinner on the name The Streets

The Streets
Dry Your Eyes

2004 · 4:32 · Skinner

Birmingham-born Mike Skinner is the unlikely star behind stage name The Streets. In a 2004 *Observer* interview, he acknowledged that his chosen name might have been misinterpreted by some: "I suppose it did make a lot of people think I was trying to be something I wasn't... it probably makes you think of the Wu-Tang Clan in New York or something. Whereas I suppose what my music is all about is saying life's not like that for most people." The second single from his second album, *A Grand Don't Come For Free*, 'Dry Your Eyes' was released on July 19th 2004 and went straight to number one in the UK singles charts. It stayed at the top for three weeks and became a garage anthem across the UK that summer. Skinner's desperately open and honest lyrics make his music accessible and endearing to a wide audience and the video for 'Dry Your Eyes' only adds to the pathos, depicting the singer after he'd just been dumped by his girlfriend – hurting and needy, your heart goes out to him. Oscars all round for this thoughtful classic.

The Streets
Blinded By The Lights

⎮ 2004 · 4:45 · Skinner

'Blinded By The Lights' was the third single from concept album *A Grand Don't Come For Free*. Each track tells part of the story — from Mike Skinner losing £1,000 to starting a new relationship, hanging out with mates, breaking up with his girlfriend, and finishing with the surprise discovery of the missing "grand". The album went str aight into number two in the UK, while 'Blinded by The Lights' entered the top 10 in September 2004. Another great promo video supports the track, with Skinner at a wedding taking various narcotics to get him through the evening's events. BdP

The Strokes
The Modern Age

⎮ 2001 · 3:32 · Casablancas

By the time The Strokes appeared on the music scene in 2001 with their three-song *Modern Age* EP, it was almost impossible for them to live up to the hype generated by the British music press. Excited by reports of their explosive live shows stateside and a unique brand of intelligent rock music that combined John Lennon-style songwriting with angular riffs and edgy guitars like those from The Velvet Underground, great things were expected from the New York five-piece. Somehow, they delivered.

The release of 'The Modern Age' would be one of the most important releases of the early 21st century. Something that Rough Trade label boss Geoff Travis, who first released the EP, recognised the very first time he heard the track: "[A friend] played me 'The Modern Age' over the telephone," he told Xfm. "I heard the first few chords and I said, 'That's something we want to do. Can we release this?'" Its rough, edgy sound (smoothed slightly for the album version) was in stark contrast to the pop music dominating the charts at the time. With its pulsing, driving guitars and Casablancas' distorted vocals, it became an instant classic and kick-started a garage-rock revival on both sides of the Atlantic.

The Strokes
Hard To Explain

⎮ 2001 · 3:47 · Casablancas

If excitement at the release of debut album *Is This It* wasn't high enough already, The Strokes released the first single from the record, 'Hard To Explain', to critical acclaim. With infectious and catchy guitar chords and a train-like rhythm, the band booked their place in music history with this track, proving that 'The Modern Age' was no fluke. The single's B-Side, 'New York City Cops', was replaced on the US release: the lines "New York city cops / They ain't too smart" were seen as inappropriate in the wake of 9/11.

The Strokes
Last Night

! 2001 • 3:17 • Casablancas

It wasn't just the music on debut album *Is This It* that was causing a furore. UK chain stores Woolworths and HMV had objected to the album's provocative cover art, which only served to build public interest. 'Last Night' is The Strokes' definitive song – encapsulating the band's talent for catchy guitar hooks and Julian Casablancas' ability as a songwriter. An unassailable rock'n'roll tune, it tells a tale of teenage confusion that, according to Rough Trade's Geoff Travis, instantly draws the listener in: "You kind of understand it, but you don't quite grasp it, like one of those murder mysteries."

The Strokes
Someday

! 2001 • 3:07 • Casablancas

Although more polished than the band's early EP, *Is This It* was in no way a glossy album – but of all its tracks,

'Someday' is probably the poppiest. The song showcases the band as a complete unit with Fabrizio Moretti's powerful drumming, the clanging guitars of Albert Hammond, Jr. and Nick Valensi, and Nikolai Fraiture's killer bassline all topped off with Julian Casablancas' effortlessly cool, almost disinterested, vocals.

The Strokes
12:51

! 2003 • 2:30 • Casablancas

In March 2003, The Strokes began work on follow-up album *Room On Fire* with producer Nigel Godrich (Radiohead, Beck) during the early sessions before returning to *Is This It* producer Gordon Raphael two months into the project. '12:51' was the first single to come from the new album. Containing all the hallmarks of their previous work, including frontman Julian Casablancas' "down-the-phone" vocals and the band's new-wave sensibilities, the track also experimented with a keyboard-like sound – played by Nick Valensi on

"[A friend] played me 'The Modern Age' over the telephone. I heard the first few chords and I said, 'That's something we want to do. Can we release this?'" – Rough Trade label boss Geoff Travis

guitar – following the vocal melody,
demonstrating The Strokes' willingness
to move in new directions rather than
create a carbon copy of their debut.

The Strokes
Reptilia

| 2003 • 3:41 • Casablancas

The Strokes do tight catchy guitar solos
and they do them well. Fans frequently
sing along to such moments at live gigs
and 'Reptilia' is a classic example. Often
credited as the highlight from *Room
On Fire*, Julian Casablancas' screams
crackle and distort over the track's
typical Strokes riffs and furious drums
– produced as if on a tiny budget and
reminiscent of the band's early releases.

The Strokes
Juicebox

| 2005 • 3:16 • Casablancas

After an internet leak forced an early
release, 'Juicebox' became The Strokes'
first single from their third album, *First
Impressions Of Earth*. Despite not receiving
the commercial or critical acclaim of
their previous two records, this single
was undoubtedly a high watermark, with
the band sticking their heads above the
lo-fi parapet, beefing up the guitars and
producing one of the most enjoyable
basslines ever written – reminiscent
of a 1980s television spy theme.
'Juicebox' is the sound of The Strokes
breaking loose, turning everything up
to ten and screaming at the world.
JS

The Subways
Rock & Roll Queen

| 2005 • 2:15 • Lunn – The Subways

We've all had the same idea at some point;
wouldn't it be great if you and your mates
could just pick up some instruments and
start a rock band? Well, sometimes it
works. Having grown up on a diet of AC/
DC, T.Rex and The Ramones, Billy Lunn and
brother Josh Morgan, along with Lunn's
girlfriend Charlotte Cooper, picked up
some instruments and started a band. A
series of home recordings and live shows
later and the trio had won themselves
a place at Glastonbury. The Subways
were on the rise and in June 2005 they
released debut album *Young For Eternity*,
produced by Ian Broudie, formerly of The
Lightning Seeds. 'Rock & Roll Queen' was
the third single to be released from the
album and delivered what the band do so
well: good, honest rock'n'roll with a nod
to the influence of Oasis and Nirvana.
Aggressive guitar playing and massive
sounding drums swamp the song, forcing
Lunn into a guttural scream as he struggles
for attention while bassist Cooper plays
the part of a rock'n'roll queen herself,
yelping backing vocals in support to
create a summery, feel-good rock song.
JS

From left: 'Animal Nitrate', 'Coming Up'

Suede
Animal Nitrate

1993 • 3:10 • Anderson – Butler

There was a touch of hype about early Suede. *Melody Maker* cover stars before they'd released a single, they benefited from a music press desperate for a band who were neither American nor dance. But 'Animal Nitrate' was no empty shell. A monster of a guitar riff slashes across the face of frontman Brett Anderson's lurid tale of rough, gay sex in a council flat. Anderson told BBC's *Seven Ages Of Rock* he was "obsessed with the idea of having a song that was sexually subversive in the top 10" and, although the video was banned for a man-on-man kiss, this landed at number seven. It also provided a stunning image

of them performing at the Brit awards to a bemused audience of stuffed shirts.

Suede
So Young

1993 • 3:40

With the album *Suede* going gold in its first week and proving the fastest-selling UK debut since Frankie Goes To Hollywood, Suede could afford to take a few risks with this, their fourth single. As they duly did: 'So Young' was the kind of stubbornly uncommercial slowie that record companies loathe and musicians love for separating the real fans from the casuals. With no obvious hook, 'So Young' foreshadowed the controversial album *Dog Man Star*

"I feel like a bisexual
man who's never had a
homosexual experience"

– Brett Anderson

in its romanticised view of childhood folly. It's hard to see the line "let's chase the dragon" as anything other than an explicit reference to smoking heroin.

Suede
The Wild Ones

! 1994 • 4:17 • Anderson – Butler

Suede were the Britpop breakthrough act. But just as the wave of bands they'd helped to inspire went truly tidal, Suede went obscure, releasing a dark, drug-addled second album that yielded just one major hit and culminated in guitarist Bernard Butler's departure. It divided fans, who either turned to the simpler, catchier sounds of Blur and Oasis or hailed it as one of the greatest albums ever. Though not the highest charter, 'The Wild Ones' proved

the album's most durable hit, a grand, sweeping hymn to doomed romance. "On you my tattoo will be bleeding and the name will stain", sang Brett Anderson, as if waving Butler off into the sunset.

Suede
Trash

! 1996 • 3:48 • Anderson – Oakes

From their inception Suede saw themselves as a 1990s version of David Bowie, patron saint of new romantics, gay rock and rejected youth – as encapsulated in frontman Brett Anderson's much-quoted comment about feeling "like a bisexual man who's never had a homosexual experience". If 'Trash' took that outsider chic to almost parodic levels (beyond it, some critics said), most doubts were

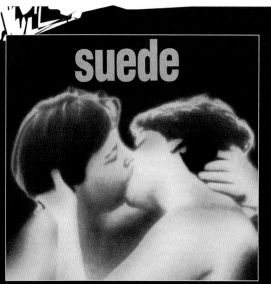

! From Left: 'Suede', 'Trash'

From left: 'Beautiful Ones', *Dog Man Star*, *Filmstar*

swept aside with a performance so overwhelming it ended up being their biggest hit. Anderson has described the song as being about Suede, both the band and their fans, and recently told *The Guardian* "it's about believing in the romance of the everyday".

Suede
Beautiful Ones

⦚ 1996 • 3:24 • Anderson – Oakes

With Bernard Butler gone, Suede honed their sound without changing their fascination with star-struck, glam-fixated, drug-guzzling youth. "I'd really like to write a straightforward pop album. Just ten hits," Brett Anderson said. Sure enough 'Beautiful Ones' reads like 'So Young' rewritten for the charts: the same obsession with wayward youth, this time the smack references replaced by kids necking E and sniffing glue. Most importantly, though, it has a hook that just falls into your arms and begs to be loved. Listeners returned the

compliment, sending it to number eight, and for the first time in their career' Suede scored back-to-back top 10 hits.

Suede
Filmstar

⦚ 1996 • 3:14 • Anderson – Oakes

Suede were always obsessed with 1970s glam, but in the run-up to *Coming Up*, singer Brett Anderson switched his listening habits from David Bowie's chameleonic waywardness to the focused whizz-bang pop of T.Rex, and 'Filmstar' is where that influence comes into its own. The crunchy, fuzzy guitars, courtesy of Butler's young replacement Richard Oakes, make 'Filmstar' one of Suede's most instantly addictive hits, while the lyrics play on the idea of stars losing their true identity as they become public property. Peter Saville handled all the artwork for the *Coming Up* album and this single was promoted with a series of posters depicting the legendary Factory designer reclining in a limousine. SY

Sum 41
Fat Lip

! 2001 · 2:58 · Sum 41

In order to make up for Céline Dion and Bryan Adams, Canada also gave us Sum 41. The pop-punk rockers from north of the border came pogoing onto the scene in 2001 with debut album *All Killer No Filler*. 'Fat Lip' was the first single from their record and remains the band's most successful track to date. On this teenage rebel's complaint about life in the suburbs, Sum 41 swing from the East Coast sunshine rock of Blink 182 to the New York rap core of Beastie Boys and back again. A great feel-good song and the soundtrack to air guitar in bedrooms up and down the country to this day.

Sum 41
In Too Deep

! 2001 · 4:08 · Sum 41

The follow-up single to 'Fat Lip', Sum 41 continued their pop-riffing, rap-edged, sophomore humour on second release 'In Too Deep', which looks at the difficulties involved in trying to end a relationship. In among the funny poses and spiky haircuts there lies some accomplished musicianship; an unusual tapping guitar solo not only shows off some nifty fretwork from guitarist Dave Baksh, but also the band's metal influences. Sum 41's later work would take a slightly heavier and more serious direction, but it's the releases from first album *All Killer No Filler* that remain their defining tracks.
JS

"We don't want to be a three cord punk band. We don't even call ourselves punk"

– Deryck Whibley, Sum 41

The Sundays
Here's Where The Story Ends

! 1990 · 3:55 · Gavurin – Wheeler

The inclusion of this song in this book of 1,000 great songs is significant for two main reasons. First, it's perhaps the only one to reference garden sheds and second, it is taken from possibly the most hotly anticipated album of a musical era. Following the split of The Smiths in 1987, the music industry was keen to find a new band to fill the jangly guitar pop hole they left behind and the bidding war surrounding The Sundays suggested that they might well fit the bill. Despite never getting a UK release following the collapse of record label Rough Trade, the second single from debut album *Reading Writing And Arithmetic* is probably the band's best-known release both sides of the Atlantic. Even though The Sundays never quite managed to meet early expectations, vocalist Harriet Wheeler's genuine one-off delivery effortlessly conveys a story of sepia-tinged nostalgia and unspoken sadness that's easy to love.
JS

Super Furry Animals
Something 4 The Weekend

! 1996 • 2:33 • Super Furry Animals

Cardiff-based Super Furry Animals introduced their DayGlo world to the UK with debut album *Fuzzy Logic*, emblazoned with multi-coloured pictures of notorious drug smuggler Howard Marks. While they were occasionally seen as Creation Records' lunatic fringe, their wonderful idiosyncrasies – bringing a full-size tank to festivals, for instance – soon gave way to the realisation that here was a musically literate collective with a fierce intelligence and contagious sense of humour. 'Something 4 The Weekend', their ode to narcotic indulgence, betrayed the influence of Cardiff's dance clubs, which the band would frequent and perform at, as well as favourite touchstones ELO, The Beach Boys and glam-rock. Having spent years toiling on the Welsh language music scene, *Fuzzy Logic* and 'Something 4 The Weekend' would drag the five members of Super Furry Animals and their extraordinary musical talents onto the world stage.

Super Furry Animals
Rings Around the World

! 2001 • 3:30 • Super Furry Animals

Following the lo-fi, low-budget release of the band's excellent fourth album *Mwng* (a record sung entirely in Welsh), the band pulled a characteristic volte-face and followed it with something reassuringly expensive. With Creation having folded and the reigns now in parent company Sony's hands, Super Furry Animals used their major label's considerable muscle to back something incredibly ambitious – the simultaneous release of an audio and DVD album, mixed in 5.1 surround sound. *Rings Around The World* is what emerged, with a DVD version that included an individually commissioned video for each song. Tying in with the theme of advancing technology was the single '(Drawing) Rings Around The World', a musing on how the planet would look if satellite and communication links could be visualised. The song's Status Quo/glam-rock stomp was brought to a crescendo with recordings of the band crank-calling random people around the world.
OH

Supergrass
Caught By The Fuzz

! 1994 • 2:17 • Supergrass

Supergrass might have been perceived by some as Britpop's class clowns, but the scene's child prodigies would have been closer to the mark. Singer Gaz Coombes and drummer Danny Goffey had tasted fleeting success with Oxford shoegazing wannabes The Jennifers when Coombes was just 16, but a meeting with bass player Mick Quinn in a local Harvester restaurant would formally kick off their next project,

'Alright' had jaunty piano and lyrics that struck a timely chord in 1995

– Supergrass 'Late in the Day'

Theodore Supergrass. A huge A&R buzz followed the shortening of their name and the release of indie single 'Caught By The Fuzz' – a tale of Coombes getting picked up by the police for possessing cannabis. Its frantic thrash tied in nicely with the tail end of the "new wave of new wave" scene but, as their next few singles were to attest, there were far more strings to this dazzling young trio's bow.

Supergrass
Alright

1995 • 3:01 • Supergrass

'Alright' was the breakthrough hit for Supergrass and one that, perhaps unfairly, nailed their flag squarely to Britpop's mast. The jaunty piano and its youthful rallying cry were traits that struck a timely chord, but it was also helped along by a video that almost became as famous as the song itself. Filmed in Portmeirion, home of TV series *The Prisoner*, the promo clip saw the band race around country lanes and beach in a large bed. Directed by drummer Danny Goffey's brother Nick and friend Dominic Hawley, its popularity catapulted the song to number two in the UK charts, thereby becoming the band's biggest hit. The video also drew the attention of director Steven Spielberg, who was keen to create a TV show in the vein of The Monkees, starring

Supergrass. The band decided to forge ahead with their second album instead.

Supergrass
Going Out

1996 • 4:16 • Supergrass – Coombes

Initially released as a stop-gap between debut album *I Should Coco* and second album *In It For The Money*, 'Going Out' bridged the upbeat enthusiasm of the former with the darker, slightly pessimistic tones of the latter. It was the final single to feature the knob-twiddling skills of producer Sam Williams, an instrumental figure in getting the band signed and bringing their debut album to life. The song, however, initially caused a little inter-band friction when drummer Danny Goffey took umbrage at what he perceived to be a swipe at his relationship with Pearl Lowe and the tabloid attention it gained.

Supergrass
Richard III

1997 • 3:14 • Coombes – Goffey – Quinn

In less then two years, Supergrass had gone from the jaunty pop of 'Alright' to the claustrophobic romp of 'Richard III'. A dark and menacing song – named after Shakespeare's unlikely hero for this very reason – it seemed to sum up the band's reported frustration at the protracted recording sessions for second album *In It For The Money*. The song preceded the album by two weeks and, like 'Alright', hit number two in the UK singles chart.

Supergrass
Sun Hits The Sky

! 1997 • 4:54 • Supergrass – Coombes

Recorded in Cornwall's Sawmills Studio with producer John Cornfield, 'Sun Hits The Sky' was one of *In It For The Money*'s more upbeat moments. Its recognisable keyboard solo came courtesy of Gaz Coombes' brother Rob, who'd been an unofficial member of the band since their debut album. Rob would join the band officially around the time of fourth album *Life On Other Planets*, but 'Sun Hits The Sky' was evidence that he was already indispensable.

Supergrass
Late In The Day

! 1997 • 4:44 • Supergrass – Coombes

One of *In It For The Money*'s most reflective moments was hilariously undermined by Britpop's greatest video. The opening black and white shot of frontman Gaz Coombes moodily strumming a guitar (so far, so appropriate) cuts to pogo-stick wielding bandmates who convince their singer to join them for a bounce around London. While some would argue the band's humour too frequently camouflaged their musical skill, 'Late In The Day' and its accompanying video showcased both traits enviably.

Supergrass
Pumping On Your Stereo

! 1999 • 3:02 • Supergrass – Coombes

A few months before the year 2000 was ushered in without the predicted catastrophes and disasters, Supergrass released their eponymously-titled third album, which seemed shot through with pre-millennial tension. While many unfairly considered it to be their weakest to date, it nevertheless contained the huge singles 'Moving' and 'Pumping On Your Stereo'. As newly-crowned masters of the music video, 'Pumping...' saw the band enlist Jim Henson's Creature Shop to design Muppet-like bodies for the band. In similar fashion to the video for 'Late In The Day', the hilarious promo clip did a wonderful job of undermining the song's paranoia-wracked lyrics.
OH

One of Supergrass's most reflective moments was hilariously undermined by Britpop's greatest video
– Supergrass, 'Late in the Day'

Jamie. T
Sheila

! 2006 · 3:30 · Treays

Revelling in the sound, rhythm and double meaning of words, Jamie Treays tells tales of urban youth and their lives, contrasting his colloquialisms with the sampled plummy sounds of former Poet Laureate John Betjeman reciting 'The Cockney Amorist'. The background noises, shouts and voices vividly conjure up the chaos that leads to tragedy for the likes of Sheila, Jack and Georgina, while a laidback reggae-tinged groove belies the serious subject matter. Seen by many as an amalgamation of Joe Strummer, Billy Bragg and Mike Skinner, 'Sheila' is a great example of why Treays is ultimately his own man.

Jamie Treays tells tales of urban youth and their lives

Jamie. T
Calm Down Dearest

! 2007 · 3:20 · Treays

Emerging from London with the likes of Mystery Jets and Larrikin Love in the mid-noughties, attempts to pigeonhole the just-into-his-20s Jamie Treays of Wimbledon into any particular "scene" soon fell apart. 'Calm Down Dearest' was his first UK top 10 hit, a downbeat shuffle pulling you in with its detailed one-line descriptions contrasting the minutiae of a night out with the physical and emotional aftermath. Debut album *Panic Prevention* displayed his musical magpie attitude; combining punk, ska, hip-hop and whatever else took his fancy, the result gained him a Mercury Music Prize nomination.

Jamie. T
Sticks'N'Stones

! 2009 · 4:00 · Treays

Ducking the limelight created by debut album *Panic Prevention*, Jamie Treays disappeared into the south London backstreets that had proved so inspirational. The first release from the follow-up *Kings & Queens* was 'Sticks'N'Stones', the title track of an EP, its rapid-fire delivery over a bouncy uptempo beat telling a typical Treays tale of drunken mischief-making along the train line from Wimbledon to Hampton Wick. Bigger and tougher sounding, despite being recorded in his garden shed, it was further proof of the singer's ability to capture the camaraderie, fun and foolishness of youth. JK

T.Rex
Get It On

1971 • 4:25 • Bolan

Mark Feld had one ambition – to be a star. But it wasn't easy for him – after an unsuccessful period as a solo artist and as part of would-be mod legends John's Children, the singer-songwriter reinvented himself as Marc Bolan and quickly jumped on the emerging psychedelia bandwagon.

Despite patronage from the mighty John Peel (then starting his long-term residency at the all-new Radio 1), Bolan's bongo-fuelled hippy ditties as Tyrannosaurus Rex only appealed to a limited audience of flower-children and underground scenesters. In September 1971, the now-abbreviated T.Rex released their second album, entitled *Electric Warrior*, which completed Bolan's transformation into a genuine pop star. Having ditched the bongos, his pure pop electric sound became the forefront of glam rock.

'Get It On' was the standout track on the album and went straight to number one in the UK and made the top 10 in the US Billboard chart. Its daft and vaguely raunchy lyric was considered a tad too smutty for the delicate Americans, however, who added the subtitle 'Bang A Gong'.

T.Rex
Children Of The Revolution

1972 • 2:29 • Bolan

'Children Of The Revolution' does what it says on the tin – this track is all about teenage rebellion. At a time when Marc Bolan's songwriting was becoming more sophisticated and the arrangement and production of tracks reaching unprecedented heights, his need for anti-society rock'n'roll was fuelled by his desire for adulation and superstardom. The track has since been covered by many of Bolan's rock successors including Violent Femmes, Bono, Elton John, Pete Doherty, Patti Smith and The Killers.

T.Rex
20th Century Boy

1973 • 3:24 • Bolan

Probably one of the greatest tracks to come out of the 1970s, '20th Century Boy' wasn't released on T.Rex's studio album until it proved to be a massive hit; it reached number three in the UK singles chart and was then added as a bonus track on the re-issued album *Tanx* later that year. This track appears in every "hall of fame" style listing and has also proven its timeless appeal by the number of cover versions it has inspired. Artists who have covered it include Placebo, Adam Ant and more recently Def Leppard. T.Rex also collaborated with David Bowie in a unique performance of the track at the Brit awards in 1999.

After the success of their *Tanx* album, the following years would bring tough times for T.Rex, with band members quitting, conflicts in musical direction and Bolan's cocaine and brandy addictions. On September 15th 1977, Marc Bolan and his girlfriend Gloria Jones went out drinking in Berkeley Square, London. They crashed on the way home to Bolan's house in the early hours, with Jones severely injured and Bolan killed instantly in the crash, just two weeks before his 30th birthday. BdP / MOG

Talking Heads
Psycho Killer

| 1977 • 4:20 • Byrne – Frantz – Weymouth

Talking Heads were the ultimate art-rock band. Meeting at college in the early 1970s, they became part of New York's nascent

punk scene but fused their angular guitar music with funk, soul and later "world music" to concoct a challenging series of albums that delighted critics, while also providing the occasional chart hit. Their singer was David Byrne, a deeply intelligent and creative songwriter who reinvented himself as a geeky-looking frontman and who would take on different personas during live performances. The band's second single, 'Psycho Killer', is a cod-horror story of a serial killer that throws in the odd French phrase for reasons that remain unclear. Kicking off with a creepy bassline, when Byrne claims "I hate people when they're not polite", you know you're in the presence of a genuine madman.

Talking Heads
Once In A Lifetime

| 1980 • 4:20 • Byrne – Eno – Frantz – Harrison – Weymouth

Intended to be a more collaborative effort than their previous LPs, sessions for Talking Heads' fourth album *Remain In Light* were influenced by bassist Tina Weymouth and drummer Chris Frantz's time in the Caribbean and the rhythms they'd heard there. Singer David Byrne had himself been experimenting with tribal percussion for his collaboration with Brian Eno, *My Life In The Bush Of Ghosts*. The different threads came together and, encouraged by producer Eno, the band turned in an ambitious album of polyrhythms and ethnic textures. "I found the music to be more trance-inducing," Byrne recalled, "and I changed my lyrical approach to reflect that." The second single, 'Once In A Lifetime'

TA LKI N GHE ADS

BUR NIN G DOW N
TH E HOU SE

"I found the music to be more trance-
inducing and I changed my lyrical
approach to reflect that"

– David Byrne

features Byrne disclaiming platitudes like a TV evangelist as he beseeches the listener to consider their materialistic life. The message was expanded in the famous video, which sees Byrne jerking his body like a broken puppet.

Talking Heads
Burning Down The House

1983 • 4:03
Byrne – Frantz – Harrison – Weymouth

While watching a show by George Clinton's P-Funk collective, drummer Chris Frantz was inspired by the crowd's chant of "Burn Down The house". This became one of Talking Heads' most funk-influenced tracks, while singer David Byrne worked up some stream of consciousness lyrics that play around with the fire motif. With its quirky video, the song became the band's only top 10 US hit. "That was the one that started getting popular on tour," Byrne remembered. "I could tell from the reaction of the audience that they'd been hearing it on the radio."

Talking Heads
And She Was

1985 • 3:36 • Byrne

Talking Heads' most straightforward pop song, the light, nursery rhyme-style

music hides a vaguely controversial story. The lyrics, according to David Byrne, apparently relate to a girl that he knew who would sit in a field and take the hallucinogenic drug LSD: "The world was moving, she was floating above it". Despite the potentially contentious words, the track was jaunty enough to make the UK top 20 in 1985.

Talking Heads
Road To Nowhere

1985 • 4:19
Byrne – Frantz – Harrison – Weymouth

With a pounding rhythm and airy accordion, 'Road To Nowhere' effectively evokes the feeling of travelling down an endless highway – although singer David Byrne thought the song was becoming a tad too monotonous and added a brief choral introduction to liven things up. The track had another excellent Talking Heads video, this time featuring Byrne pictured running on the spot – typical of his eccentric showmanship, which was born from shyness. "I had demons and felt socially inept," he explained. "In retrospect, I can see I couldn't talk to people face to face, so I got on stage and started screaming and squealing and twitching about." MO'G

"That was the one that started getting popular on tour"

– David Byrne on 'Burning Down The House'

The Teardrop Explodes
Reward

❘ 1981 • 2:47 • Cope – Gill

For a while Liverpool's post-punk music scene existed on nothing more than its own self-belief. The handful of key players shuttled between bands, rarely making records or even advancing as far as the stage. One of them, Julian Cope, described the scene in the book *Liverpool Explodes*: "We decided to have a group that didn't make music at all, but just got on other people's nerves... I had this song... I'd describe it to [Pete] Wylie and Griff and they'd discuss it and then we'd talk about another song or something else. That was rehearsing." It reached its peak in The Crucial Three, a group featuring three of the city's biggest egos (Cope, Wylie and Ian McCulloch) and no practical musicians.

All three found fame: Wylie fleetingly with Wah! Heat; McCulloch impressively with Echo & The Bunnymen. Cope eventually got his with The Teardrop Explodes, who scored a huge hit with 'Reward' in 1981. The Teardrops loved psychedelia, but Cope's limited, naturally buoyant vocals meant they always tilted towards the poppier, more exuberant end rather than the darker, trippier sound of his heroes like The Seeds and 13th Floor Elevators. 'Reward' is exuberance-plus, announcing its arrival with dramatic keyboards and a brass fanfare, then bouncing round the room like the kid that drank all the fizzy pop. Cope celebrated with more than that when they made it onto *Top Of The Pops*, where he famously took acid prior to performing and treated

the stage like his own little playpen. The Teardrop Explodes' time at the top was short-lived, but the armour-plated arrogance of Liverpool's players proved justified. Even the minor figures in their story went on to greater things: producer-keyboardist David Balfe would become the founder of Food Records and the subject of Blur's number one hit 'Country House' while producer-manager Bill Drummond was the leading light of avant-garde rave pranksters KLF and author of *The Manual (How To Have A Number One The Easy Way)*, something he managed, even if The Crucial Three came up short.
SY

Television
Marquee Moon

❘ 1977 • 9:58 • Verlaine

Television were right at the centre of the New York punk scene. Leader Tom Verlaine had played and written with punk poetess supreme Patti Smith; the band pioneered live gigs at the legendary CBGB's venue (even physically building the stage); and former band member

Richard Hell formed The Heartbreakers with ex-New York Doll Johnny Thunders, before splitting to go solo and writing punk anthem 'Blank Generation'. And yet Television's sound is a mile removed from punk's three-chord wonderland. 'Marquee Moon' was a frighteningly complex jam track (so complex it's said Hell left because he couldn't keep up), with elements of jazz and fusion in the endless sparring between Verlaine and fellow guitarist Richard Lloyd. Almost ten minutes long on the original album version, it was one of the first rock tracks ever to get a 12-inch release in the UK (the single was split into two parts), where it scraped the charts. But its influence could be felt for years to come, in the art-rock of fellow New Yorkers Talking Heads and a raft of acts that followed in the UK post-punk scene. SY

The Temper Trap
Sweet Disposition

! 2009 · 3:51

Hailed as one of the sounds of 2009, Melbourne quartet The Temper Trap have an epic, soaring sound, layered with Dougy Mandagi's falsetto vocals. Their debut album *Conditions* was produced by Jim Abbiss, who also produced Arctic Monkeys' stellar debut. Radiohead are the obvious influence, though The Temper Trap's is a softer, less abrasive and more cinematic sound. The band have been criticised for tackling subjects that don't match up to the grandiose scale of their sound, and 'Sweet Disposition' is as guilty of this as any of their tracks, dealing as it does with "a

moment, a love, a dream, a laugh". There's a precocious confidence to their music, however, that defies any such suggestions of immaturity. And the fresh and uplifting optimism of 'Sweet Disposition' is hard to be too cynical about. Aside from record sales (it was a top 10 hit in the UK, Ireland and Belgium), the single has had an extraordinary run of commercial success: as well as featuring in the film *(500) Days Of Summer* and British TV series *Skins*, 'Sweet Disposition' has been used in adverts around the world for Chrysler, Sky Sports, Channel 4, Peugeot, O2, Pepsi and Toyota. JH

Tenacious D
Tribute

! 2001 · 4:08 · Black – Gass

Despite meeting in 1989, actors/musicians Kyle Gass and Jack Black's unlikely genesis into band Tenacious D was a slow one, only playing their first gig as an unnamed duo in 1993. Further gigs, a TV series and Black's appearances in films such as *High Fidelity* resulted in their 2001 self-titled debut album, from which 'Tribute' was the first single. The track was apparently created as, well, a tribute to the "greatest song in the world" (which the duo claim they wrote in order to escape an evil demon, played in the accompanying music video by Foo Fighter Dave Grohl, but have since forgotten – hence the need for a tribute). It showcases some acoustic guitar with musical nods to 'Stairway To Heaven', courtesy of Gass and Black's theatrical vocal range.

Pastiche and satire are major elements of Tenacious D's act, but they are a long way from the "mock-rock" tag bestowed on them by some critics; their clever blend of folk, rock and metal and their ability to poke fun at self-important pomp-rock make them a worthy candidate for inclusion here. JS

They Might Be Giants
Birdhouse In Your Soul

1990 • 3:18 • Flansburgh – Linnell

Taking their name from the film of the same name (which was at the time being considered for a friend's ventriloquist act), TMBG's early days saw the duo playing accordion, saxophone and guitar along to a cassette tape backing track, and attracting a large cult following around New York. It was a biking accident that resulted in a change in their fortunes, with John Linell's broken wrist forcing a break from the live circuit. In this pre-MySpace world, the band sought another way to get their music heard and so recorded their songs onto an answerphone, posting the number in local papers under the name Dial-A-Song. Along with a favourable review in *People* magazine, the exposure led to the band signing their first record deal with Bar/None.

The band joined Elektra Records in 1990, and released third album *Flood* and its first single, 'Birdhouse In Your Soul'. The single showcases the duo's songwriting, with a slow chanting verse building to an instantly memorable chorus. The song's lyrical narrative takes centre stage, written from the rather unusual point of view of a nightlight that looks like a blue bird serenading the occupant of the room in which it sits. It's packed with clever rhythms and cultural references which, according to Linnell, were not always chosen as deliberately as they might appear: "The lyrics had to be shoehorned in to match the melody, which explains why the words are so oblique." He told *Rolling Stone*: "I didn't find out what the Longines Symphonette was until after the song was released. It rhymed with 'infinite' (sort of)." The happy coincidence works and the result is a charming, almost innocent view of the world rapped in cheerful pop melodies. It helped the album achieve gold status and saw the band become regulars on MTV in the early 1990s. At their peak the band sold over four million records; they have since regressed to their original cult status and are still recording and releasing music. JS

> "The lyrics had to be shoehorned in to match the melody, which explains why the words are so oblique"
>
> – John Linnell on 'Birdhouse In Your Soul'

Thin Lizzy

Thin Lizzy
Whiskey In The Jar

1973 • 5:44 • Traditional

Formed in the late 1960s by Irish singer Phil Lynott, Thin Lizzy's ancestry flowed through much of their work, not least in their intelligent portrayal of working class themes and emotions and in their string harmonies, but often also in their music's conception – as is the case with this release. While the band spent 1972 touring with the likes of Slade and Suzi Quatro, the band's record label made the decision to release Thin Lizzy's version of traditional Irish song 'Whiskey In The Jar' as a single. Despite the band's concern that the song neither represented their sound or their image, the track reached number six in the UK charts and became their breakthough release.

Thin Lizzy
The Boys Are Back In Town

1976 • 4:27 • Lynott

Despite not performing as well in chart terms as 'Whiskey In The Jar', 'The Boys Are Back In Town' has become Thin Lizzy's signature track (possibly due to its appearance in almost every single buddy movie soundtrack since its release). Who-like powerchords join the band's trademark double guitar harmonies and frontman Phil Lynott's rich, soulful vocals in a celebration of cutting loose during nights out. Despite Lynott's best attempts, Thin Lizzy never managed to recreate the formula and magic of 'Boys', but relentless touring and numerous releases have maintained a keen fanbase – throughout numerous lineup changes namely Phil Lynott dying in 1986 – to this day.
JS

The Ting Tings
That's Not My Name

2008 • 5:11 • De Martino – White

Against an infectious rhythm provided by Jules De Martino, Katie White turns pent-up anger at being patronised into one of the catchiest songs of the decade and a number one hit in May 2008. Success was never a foregone conclusion though. The Ting Tings were formed after a frustrated brush with the music industry as Dear Eskiimo. Re-emerging as a duo, they performed their first show at their home, the Islington Mill – an artist collective in Salford. It was here, while De Martino worked behind the bar, that they handed 'That's Not My Name' to DJ John Kennedy Xfm at a Friday night X-Posure Live gig in March 2007, which led to its first ever airplay the following Monday. Originally released by Switchflicker Records, the hit potential was obvious. That they would go on to sell millions and win an Ivor Novello Best Album Award for *We Started Nothing* was not.
JK

Travis

Travis
Writing To Reach You

| 1999 • 3:41 • Healy

Originally called Glass Onion, Travis hailed from Glasgow and went through a number of changes before eventually settling on the lineup of Fran Healy (vocals and guitar), Dougie Payne (bass), Andy Dunlop (lead guitar) and Neil Primrose (drums). Naming themselves after Travis Henderson, the character played by Harry Dean Stanton in the film *Paris, Texas*, their first album *Good Feeling* featured some great pop songs and made the top 10 album charts in the UK, but it was follow-up *The Man Who* that firmly put Travis on the map. Recorded with Radiohead producer Nigel Godrich at a chateau in the south of France, the album saw the band explore more acoustic textures as a contrast to the rockier side

they showcased on *Good Feeling*. The first song to be taken from the LP was 'Writing To Reach You', which Healy freely admits was inspired by Britpop giants Oasis and their classic track 'Wonderwall'. "It was December 1995 and I was sitting in the coldest flat in Glasgow," Healy told Xfm. "It was Boxing Day, and I was trying to play a song by The Connells, called "74-'75'. I quickly then swapped it to E minor and I thought, 'Oh that's good'. Then I realised they were actually the chords to 'Wonderwall' and I was like 'Ah, damn!' But then, Noel Gallagher's always talking about nicking chords from people, so I figured just using the chords was acceptable. But I doff my cap to the writer." Healy's delicate voice sings the achingly introspective lyrics, which namecheck the song's inspiration: "The radio is playing all the usual / And what's a Wonderwall, anyway?" And what did Mr Gallagher think of this musical tribute? "I remember meeting Noel years later," explained Healy. "He said, 'Nice chords'. And I was like, 'Right, OK!'"
MO'G

"Noel Gallagher's always talking about nicking chords from people, so I figured just using the chords was acceptable. But I doff my cap to the writer"

– Fran Healy on 'Writing To Reach You'

"It's a real love of each other and love of what we do, and it's a flame. There's times when it feels like it's nearly been blown out, but it's there"

– Bono

U2 New Year's Day

| 1983 · 5:36
| Clayton – Evans – Hewson – Mullen

Out of the chrysalis of an introverted post-punk band, born from the spark of 1976, came the *big* sound of a band looking outward and prepared to take on the world. 'New Year's Day' was U2's first UK top 10 hit, released in January 1983. A song about the Polish Solidarity movement of the day, it set a tone of political commentary as the first single off the *War* album. The video was shot in Sweden and temperatures got so low that at one point four local girls were recruited to body-double for the band during some of the horse-riding sequences.

U2 Sunday Bloody Sunday

| 1983 · 4:38
| Clayton – Evans – Hewson – Mullen

The opening track on *War* and by far U2's most politically charged – and misinterpreted – song. In the midst of the sectarian violence of the early 1980s, a Dublin band writing very specifically about the 1972 killings in Ulster was always going to be a brave move. "This is not a rebel song" as Bono, the self-proclaimed

"aggressive pacifist", famously said. This frustration was born out of a gross misreading of the song, especially within the ranks of American IRA sympathisers caught up in the myth of "the struggle". 'Sunday Bloody Sunday' is far from a call to arms ("I won't heed the battle call / it puts my back up / puts my back up against the wall"); it's a desperate plea for compassion on both sides of a very painful divide.

U2 Pride (In The Name Of Love)

| 1984 · 3:49
| Clayton – Evans – Hewson – Mullen

Stepping up yet another gear in a string of emotionally direct, heart-on-sleeve anthems, this homage to Martin Luther King was another benchmark release – the first U2 single to crack the US top 40 (at number 33) and the UK top five (at number three). It remains one of the band's most enduringly popular songs and has rarely been absent from a U2 set list since its live debut in Christchurch, New Zealand, in August 1984. Notably, though, it had to be dropped from the band's Live Aid set at Wembley Stadium in July 1985 after a version of their album track 'Bad' overran to 14 minutes due to Bono jumping off stage to dance with a girl in the crowd.

U2 The Unforgettable Fire

| 1984 · 4:56
| Clayton – Evans – Hewson – Mullen

Working with Brian Eno and Daniel Lanois for the first time, *The Unforgettable Fire* album marks the point when U2's sound went widescreen. This sweeping and epic production is captured most brilliantly on the title track, which is said to be inspired by the band's visit to an art exhibition by survivors of the atomic bombings in Hiroshima and Nagasaki. The album's potent mix of confident and impassioned songs with expansive and atmospheric production made it U2's pivotal record and the one that would set the stage for the next chapter in the band's incredible career.

U2 With Or Without You

1987 · 4:56
Clayton – Evans – Hewson – Mullen

It's hard to fully appreciate the impact that U2 had on the world in 1987. Their fifth studio album, *The Joshua Tree*, had them placed on virtually every radio station, TV channel and magazine cover on the planet. They even beat Mikhail Gorbachev to the front cover of *Time* magazine in April that year. The sound that kicked off this 25-million-selling album was the understated simplicity of 'With Or Without You'. The song builds through a deceptively uncomplicated arrangement to a climax of virtuoso vocals by Bono, leaving the listener in no doubt that here was a band meeting the highest of expectations. It became their first US number one.

U2
I Still Haven't Found What I'm Looking For

1987 · 4:37
Clayton – Evans – Hewson – Mullen

Like much of *The Joshua Tree*, 'I Still Haven't Found What I'm Looking For' delves into U2's obsession with American music – in this case, the spiritual imagery and soaring vocal melodies of gospel. The song was later re-recorded with a full gospel choir for the *Rattle And Hum* album. The lyrics are said to be about the conflict between Bono's roles as a touring musician and a domesticated man. The video showed the band walking around downtown Las Vegas and reportedly did wonders for tourism to the city that year, as well as improving its image among fellow musicians.

U2
Where The Streets Have No Name

1987 · 5:38
Clayton – Evans – Hewson – Mullen

The opening track on *The Joshua Tree* was notoriously one of the hardest songs on the album to record. Brian Eno estimates that at least half of the album sessions were spent on getting a final version of 'Where The Streets Have No Name'; to the point that he was about to delete the tape but was stopped at the last minute by the studio engineer. Famous for its spine-tingling intro, it is still *the* moment at most U2 live shows.

U2 All I Want Is You

1989 · 6:30
Clayton – Evans – Hewson – Mullen

U2 closed the decade with the fourth and final single from *Rattle and Hum*, a rich and darkly haunting love song. The album documented U2's journey through

U2

WITH OR WITHOUT YOU

"It's about how I feel in U2
at times – exposed"
– Bono on 'With Or Without You'

the FLY   U2

"We're going to go away
and dream it all up again"

— Bono, two years before the release of *The Fly*

American music. In true U2 style, it was an unapologetic and open-hearted expression of their bittersweet love affair with America. Despite its commercial success as an album and documentary film, it gave some critics fuel for a U2 backlash, calling it "pretentious" and "misguided". This experience of negative exposure most certainly informed U2's next reinvention.

U2 The Fly

1991 • 4:29
Clayton – Evans – Hewson – Mullen

On the last night of the 1980s, U2 were playing a New Year's Eve gig at Dublin's Point Depot when Bono announced that the band were going to "go away and dream it all up again". Less than two years later they released 'The Fly', and from the opening crunch of industrial guitar chords to the danceable rhythm track, nobody could argue that this was the same old U2. The song struggled to get traction with pop radio stations, but firmly hit the re-set button and still scored the band their second UK number one single.

U2 Mysterious Ways

1991 • 4:04
Clayton – Evans – Hewson – Mullen

Bono describes the album *Achtung Baby* as "the sound of four men chopping down *The Joshua Tree*" and it is fair to say that the silky sexiness and nodding funk of 'Mysterious Ways' would not have been welcome on their 1987 desert-based opus. As one of many *Achtung Baby* hit singles to receive mass radio play, the track exemplifies the slickness of the dirty yet clean production of Brian Eno and Daniel Lanois, which helped power the album to sales of over 18 million.

U2 One

1992 • 4:36
Clayton – Evans – Hewson – Mullen

'One' is the song that saved the *Achtung Baby* album and arguably saved U2. In October 1990, the band moved to Hansa Studios in Berlin (the legendary location of classic recordings by David Bowie and Iggy Pop) to find inspiration

From left: 'One', 'Mysterious Ways', *The Joshua Tree*

in a Germany on the eve of unification. Tensions within the band over quality of songs and artistic direction reached breaking point just prior to the emergence of 'One' – an improvised song that re-cemented the band's shared drive to make a new, forward-looking U2 album. 'One' went on to be regarded as one of the greatest moments in U2's entire catalogue.

U2
Even Better Than The Real Thing

| 1992 · 3:41
¦ Clayton – Evans – Hewson – Mullen

While on stage at the City of Manchester Stadium during their Vertigo tour of 2005, Bono described Manchester as "the city that taught the white man how to dance". This appreciation of the "Madchester" of the late 1980s was most apparent on 'Even Better Than The Real Thing'. An ecstatic rush of hedonistic energy firmly focused

on a dancefloor that the mid-1980s' U2 would have been far too self-conscious to go near. So club-ready was the track that an Oakenfold remix of 'Even Better' was released a month after the original single version and charted four places higher at number eight in the UK top 40.

U2 Beautiful Day

| 2000 · 4:08
¦ Clayton – Evans – Hewson – Mullen

It's the end of a decade (or in this case a millennium) and we are in a familiar part of the U2 cycle. After the critical bloody nose that they received from their dance-step too far with 1997 album *Pop*, it is time for another reinvention. With a renewed interest in the pop single (Bono claims that they wrote 11 singles for this album), they stormed the charts with the stadium-humping, platinum-plated pop bullet that is 'Beautiful Day'. Going to number one in pretty much every country on earth, it

U2//HOW TO DISMANTLE AN ATOMIC BOMB

U2 BEAUTIFUL DAY

440

introduced U2 to a vast new audience and reminded loyal fans why they loved the band so much in the first place. In terms of arrangement it was almost the anti-'With Or Without You': deceptively complex with an intricate set of Eno layers and a raft of new pedals for The Edge. The overall effect was that, at exactly 58 seconds in, you knew that the "biggest band in the world" were – as Bono put it – "re-applying for the job".

U2 Vertigo

2004 • 3:14
Clayton – Evans – Hewson – Mullen

Originally called 'Full Metal Jacket', 'Vertigo' is one of U2's heaviest, punkiest and most successful singles. Adrenalised high-octane guitars pound through the track as if The Edge had finally been taken off some imaginary leash. It went to number one in a record number of countries and heralded the band's 2004 album, another muscular back-to-basics collection called *How To*

Dismantle An Atomic Bomb – a title that Bono derived from his late father Brendan Robert "Bob" Hewson. In fact, Bono would sometimes refer to the album in interviews as *How To Dismantle An Atomic Bob*.

U2 City Of Blinding Lights

2005 • 5:48
Clayton – Evans – Hewson – Mullen

In January 2009, U2 played 'City Of Blinding Lights' in front of the Lincoln Memorial in Washington DC as part of President Obama's inauguration celebrations. The song is cited by Obama as one of his iPod's most played alongside the works of Bruce Springsteen and Marvin Gaye. Another hit single from the 2004 *Atomic Bomb* album, the track definitely harks back to the band's expansive mid-1980s' period. It encapsulates much of that early U2 wide-eyed optimism – now delivered by men in their 40s who have grown into their world-weary wisdom with aplomb.
MW

U2 ALL THAT YOU CAN'T LEAVE BEHIND

"We were just the right age at the right time.
It's the strength of the voice, and the urgency
of the drums and guitars, it seemed to
capture the moment"

– John O'Neill, 'Teenage Kicks'

TheUndertones

The Undertones
Teenage Kicks

1978 • 2:28 • O'Neill

It's 1978 in Derry, Northern Ireland, and Undertones bassist Mickey Bradley is on the phone to singer Feargal Sharkey trying to convince him not to leave the band. "He may have thought the band was going nowhere, or maybe he thought TV aerial installation was the career he wanted," remembers Bradley, but either way Sharkey was convinced to stay – at least until they had recorded a record.

The band had originally formed in 1975, just five mates playing cover versions in local pubs. The arrival of bands like Buzzcocks and The Ramones inspired them to make punk music, but the lack of a music scene in Derry almost forced the band to quit before it had really begun. That they managed to produce a record was only due to the intervention of Belfast record shop owner Terri Hooley, who financed the £200 needed to record the *Teenage Kicks* EP and release it on his own label, Good Vibrations. Even this good fortune might not have been enough to gain the band the attention they deserved, but huge support from legendary DJ John Peel (who would later have the lyrics "teenage dreams so hard to beat" inscribed on his tombstone) ensured the record was heard by the masses.

Like the bands that had inspired them, The Undertones took their song's key elements and filed them down to the bare bone – a short blast of punk-pop with no filler, no indulgence; Sharkey's singalong vocals over a summer shot of simple and catchy chords, fizzing and popping through two-and-a-half minutes. The energy of the performance is captured in the recording, reeking of teen vitriol and enthusiasm, which songwriter John O'Neill thinks was key to its success. "I still don't think the song's that good," he told *Q* magazine.

"We were just the right age at the right time. It's the strength of the voice, and the urgency of the drums and guitars, it seemed to capture the moment."

The band went on to release three albums in quick succession before a lengthy break and the release of 1983's *The Sin Of Pride*, which saw the band moving towards a more 1960s sound. It made little impact and soon after the band split, with Sharkey perusing a solo career while John and Damian O'Neill formed That Petrol Emotion. The Undertones reformed without Sharkey in 1999 with re-issues, documentaries and the first new material in 20 years released in 2003.

Although many argue that there are plenty of other Undertones' tracks equally deserving of the plaudits and attention that 'Teenage Kicks' received, there are few other records that capture the energy, spirit and angst of youth better. JS

Underworld
Born Slippy

! 1996 • 9:44 • Emerson – Hyde – Smith

Karl Hyde and Rick Smith have been making music together for more than 20 years, 14 of them under the banner of Underworld. Alongside the likes of The Prodigy and Orbital, they are pioneers of electronic music. But despite a number of single releases, it wasn't until 'Born Slippy' – the dance anthem of the Ibiza generation – that they became known for bringing dance music to the masses. You might say that 'Born Slippy' is to Underworld what 'Sunflowers' is to Van Gogh. The booze-culture legacy of 'Born Slippy' is all the more ironic given that the lyrics are so often heard as a celebration of drinking and partying (the repetitive line "Shouting lager, lager, lager" was effectively adopted as a battle cry for 20-somethings heaving over to the White Isle for a week of beer, sex and sunshine) when in fact they were born from Hyde's personal problems with alcohol.

Starting life in 1995 as the B-side to the instrumental version, 'Born Slippy (NUXX)' received its own single release a year later, thrust into the foreground by its appearance in the soundtrack to major Brit flick *Trainspotting*. Despite the band's original reluctance to be involved with the film – not wanting to strengthen the link between dance music and drugs – the single quickly became the definitive version, selling over a million copies and undoubtedly becoming one of the greatest dance tracks of the decade.

Part of the power of 'Born Slippy' is its relationship with a certain time, place and generation. I've lost count of the times the song has been played in the company of others and someone has started a hazy sun-tinged, half-remembered anecdote with the words: "This song always reminds me of...". It's the musical equivalent of smelling cut grass. JS

Vampire Weekend

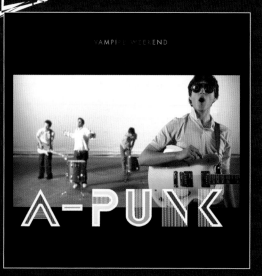 

From Left: 'A-Punk', 'Cousins'

Vampire Weekend
A-Punk

2008 · 2:17

Baio – Batmanglij – Koenig – Tomson

Vampire Weekend were formed in 2006, after the quartet met at Columbia University. Although they went on to enter the world of work as an eighth-grade English teacher (Ezra Koenig), an archivist for Sony BMG (Chris Tomson), a film composer's assistant (Rostam Batmanglij) and a Russian regional studies major (Chris Baio), the band continued to rehearse and write songs that they put out on self-produced EPs, to increasing buzz within the ska-punk music industry.

Their name comes from the title of a film lead singer Koenig made at university.

By November 2007, Vampire Weekend had been named the year's best new band by *SPIN* magazine – and that was before their debut album had even been released. It finally came out on January 29th 2008, and reached number 55 in the UK. It was met with a mixture of critical reviews, but one quote that sums up the general feeling came from Ben Blackmore at the *Times* who said, quite simply: "Do believe the hype."

'A-Punk' was one of four singles from their self-titled debut, and was released on February 28th 2008 when the band also made their debut TV appearance on *The Late Show With David Letterman*. The track is a current favourite on games such as *Guitar Hero 5*, *Band Hero* and *Lego Rock Band*. A great introduction to this preppy American band's creativity and unique sound, *Vampire Weekend* was voted as one of the top 10 albums for 2008 by *Time* magazine.

Vampire Weekend
Cousins

2009 • 2:25
Baio – Batmanglij – Koenig – Tomson

The single 'Cousins' was made available for download on November 17th 2009 and on seven-inch a month later. It's taken from Vampire Weekend's second album *Contra* and was recorded in the musically beating heart of Mexico City. 'Cousins' reached number 39 in the UK singles chart and number three in the UK indie chart. The video essentially features the band in an alleyway passing masks to each other while confetti falls from the skies. One that is perhaps better watched than described! BdP

Vampire Weekend met at Columbia University and are named after a film made by lead singer Ezra Koenig

The Velvet Underground
Venus In Furs

1966 • 5:12 • Reed

The Velvet Undergound were originally formed by Lou Reed, John Cale, Sterling Morrison and Angus MacLise in April 1965. However, by Christmas that year, the lineup had already changed in what proved to be an ever-changing band, with Maureen Tucker replacing MacLise on percussion while the group's sound was still developing. Their first real breakthrough moment came when, in 1966, they were chosen as the house band for Andy Warhol's Factory. With their outsider, non-complying attitude and unique sound, they gained a cult audience.

Released in May 1966, 'Venus In Furs' is taken from critically acclaimed debut album *The Velvet Underground & Nico*, which came out in 1967 and for which Warhol designed the iconic cover. The track's lyrics include the heady sexual themes of bondage, submission and sadomasochism, and the title comes from the novel of the same name by Leopold von Sacher-Masoch. One for the hall of fame vaults, the song has since been covered by many other artists.

The release of their album was marred slightly by a legal problem: in the background of the photo of the band that appears on the back cover you could see another Warhol work for which there were questions over clearance rights. Copies of the album were removed from record shop shelves and the image was airbrushed out.

The Velvet Underground
Sunday Morning

1966 • 2:56 • Cale – Reed

'Sunday Morning' is the opening track on debut album *The Velvet Underground & Nico*, and was released in December 1966. It was actually the last track to be recorded for the record and was written – no surprises there – on a Sunday $26 worth of heroin, with the "man" of the title referring to his drug dealer. Drugs were a common theme for many of the Velvets' songs. The song was recorded in two different studios: the original recording was done at Scepter Studios in New York, and was a shorter version of the track with the piano lower in the mix. On this version, Lou Reed sings the line "I'm waiting for the man"; on the album version, which was re-recorded at TTG Studios in California, this was changed to "I'm waiting for *my* man". The song has been covered by

> ## The intention was for singer Nico to take the lead vocals but in the end Reed sang the song himself, reportedly much to the annoyance of their manager, Andy Warhol
>
> – The Velvet Underground, 'Sunday Morning'

morning by John Cale and Lou Reed. The intention was for singer Nico to take the lead vocals, but in the end Reed sang it himself, reportedly much to the annoyance of their manager, Andy Warhol.

The Velvet Underground
I'm Waiting For My Man

1967 • 4:39 • Reed

Undoubtedly one of the band's best tracks, 'I'm Waiting For My Man' is thought to be about a guy purchasing many big names, including David Bowie, Beck, Debbie Harry, Smashing Pumpkins, Robert Plant and Jimmy Page. Individual members of The Velvet Underground have also produced solo versions.

Reed left the band in 1970 after just a few short years, but the original lineup reunited briefly two decades later. One of the most influential groups of the 1960s, the band is often name-checked by musicians and music industry aficionados today. BdP

'This is Music' is said to be about Oasis songwriter Noel Gallagher

The Verve This Is Music

1995 • 3:35 • Ashcroft

The turbulent history of The Verve started in Wigan at the dawn of the 1990s. Led by the distinctive and passionate voice of Richard Ashcroft, they honed their epic music across a pair of albums, coining a classic with *A Northern Soul* in 1995. The rousing lead single 'This Is Music' was something of a manifesto for the band, with the opening line claiming "I stand accused, just like you / for being born without a silver spoon".

The Verve History

1995 • 4:02 • Ashcroft

By the time of *A Northern Soul*, Verve had to rename themselves "The Verve" after the American jazz record label waved legal proceedings in the band's direction. Opening with an aching string section and boasting a heartbreaking lyric of failed love, 'History' is one of the tracks that defined the widescreen Verve style. Despite the success of the album and single, the band split for the first time a couple of months later, with the sleeve art claiming "All farewells should be sudden".

The Verve Bitter Sweet Symphony

1997 • 4:35 • Ashcroft – Jagger – Richards

After a brief hiatus, Ashcroft reunited The Verve in 1996 replacing guitarist Nick McCabe with Simon Tong. When McCabe returned in early 1997, the band was ready to start work on their magnum opus: *Urban Hymns*. The first the world heard of the new album was the majestic strings of 'Bittersweet Symphony'. A world-weary tribute to the healing power of music, the song ran into trouble by sampling Rolling Stones manager Andrew Loog Oldham's orchestral cover of the Jagger/Richards track 'The Last Time'. It was claimed that the track used a significant proportion of the original arrangement and awarded a partial songwriting credit to the two Stones. Its number two placing on the UK chart was therefore a bittersweet achievement for Richard Ashcroft.

The Verve The Drugs Don't Work

1997 • 5:05 • Ashcroft

The second single from *Urban Hymns* released in 1997 was the equally brilliant 'The Drugs Don't Work'. It went straight into the UK singles chart at number one and remains the band's most successful single. Back in 1995, singer Richard Ashcroft said in an interview: "There's a new track I've just written... It goes 'the drugs don't work, they just make me worse, and I know I'll see your face again'. That's how I'm feeling at the moment. They make me worse, man. But I still take 'em. Out of boredom and frustration you turn to something else to escape." While it's generally thought that song refers to the death of Ashcroft's father, the song was given added poignancy when it reached the number one spot the weekend of the funeral of Princess Diana.

while frontman Richard Ashcroft stands in the middle of the room strumming and singing his heart out. A US version of the video had to be created for fans on the other side of the pond who could not relate to leafy Hammersmith: it was replaced with the backdrop of New York.

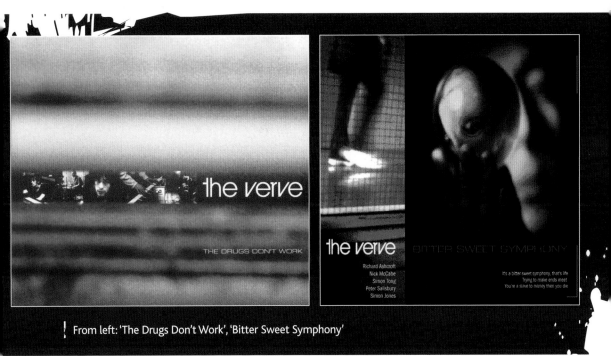

the verve

THE DRUGS DON'T WORK

the verve

BITTER SWEET SYMPHONY

Richard Ashcroft
Nick McCabe
Simon Tong
Peter Salisbury
Simon Jones

It's a bitter sweet symphony, that's life
Trying to make ends meet
You're a slave to money then you die

From left: 'The Drugs Don't Work', 'Bitter Sweet Symphony'

The Verve
Lucky Man

1997 • 4:53 • Ashcroft

Single number three from The Verve's highest charting album, 'Lucky Man' was released on November 24th 1997, peaking at number seven in the UK. The video for 'Lucky Man' was shot at Thames Wharf in west London. It shows the rest of the band lounging about in the background

'Bittersweet Symphony'. is a world-weary tribute to the healing power of music

The Verve
Sonnet

! 1998 · 4:21 · Ashcroft

'Sonnet' was the final single to be released from The Verve's third album, *Urban Hymns*, and proved to be another hit for this by now very established group. 'Sonnet' is another peerless ballad from Richard Ashcroft, which sees the singer beseeching the "Lord" as he's "looking at the heavens with a tear in my eye". *Urban Hymns* established Ashcroft as one of British rock's most charismatic and emotional troubadours.

The Verve
Love Is Noise

! 2008 · 5:29 · Ashcroft

After splitting in 1997, The Verve regrouped and returned to form ten years later with an inspired new album called *Forth*. With an opening line that recalls the hymn 'Jerusalem', 'Love Is Noise' was developed from a vocal loop that Ashcroft had recorded during a jam session with the band. Despite the success of 'Forth', The Verve split again just one year later – Ashcroft claims The Verve days are over and this song is a fitting epitaph.
MO'G / BdP

The View

The View
Same Jeans

! 2007 · 3:32 · Falconer – Webster

Although they might sound like an American rock band, The View are actually from Dryburgh in bonny Scotland. Originally the quartet got together during their school years as a covers band playing tracks by Squeeze and the Sex Pistols, to name but a few, before mutating into the band they are today. 'Same Jeans' was taken from the album *Hats Off To Buskers*, which was released in January 2007 and reached number three in the UK singles chart. It is still their highest charting single to date. The featured lines throughout the track –"I've had the same jeans on for four days now / I'm gonna go to a disco in the middle of the town / Everybody's dressing up and I'm dressing down" – have an appealing teenage ring to them.
BdP

The Vines
Get Free

! 2002 · 2:06 · Nicholls

Australian garage rockers The Vines were one of the lauded turn-of-the-century "The" bands, alongside The Strokes, The Hives and The White Stripes. Loud, intense, energetic and often angry, many hailed them as the saviours of rock. 'Get Free'

opens with powerful riffing and rasping and urgently delivered lyrics, and builds quickly to crashing crescendos. Performing the song on the *Letterman* show in the US, Craig Nicholls jumped onto and broke the drum kit. The band started off playing Nirvana covers, and though they may never match their predecessor's musical influence, here they convincingly share some of their anarchic punk energy.
JH

Violent Femmes
Blister In The Sun

! 1983 • 2:24 • Gano

Important songs don't always translate into record sales; 'Blister In The Sun' is proof of that. The song that became the anthem of teen outsiders for a generation was little more than an underground hit for many years, only reaching platinum status eight years after its original release. Inspired by his guitar-playing Baptist minister father, Gordon Gano was writing and playing guitar from the age of 15 ('Good Feeling' from the band's self-titled debut album was one of the first tracks he ever wrote). Bass player Brian Ricthie and percussionist Victor DeLorenzo made up the trio and the band spent their early days performing

Body and beats, I stain my sheets, I don't even know why

– Violent Femmes, 'Blister In The Sun'

in Milwaukee coffee shops until, after being spotted busking by Chrissie Hynde, they were asked to play a brief acoustic set before The Pretenders' gig that night.

In 1982, the band released their debut album, a collection of songs that struck a chord with listeners who connected to the frustrated themes and bitter lyrics. 'Blister In The Sun' was the standout track, full of raw, jittery energy with Gano's whining vocals built around a simple, instantly recognisable riff and clap-along beats. The album had little impact on the charts but its popularity spread by word of mouth, and the quivering delivery of "Body and beats, I stain my sheets, I don't even know why" echoed out of many teenage bedroom windows, getting quieter and quieter before the climatic final chorus, which only added to the opinion that the song is about masturbation. Claimed by some to be the start of a new chapter in alternative music, 'Blister In The Sun' is one of the most acclaimed cult tracks of all time and its wide-ranging influence can be felt on many contemporary artists as diverse as Weezer and The Libertines.
JS

The Walkmen

The Walkmen
The Rat

❗ 2004 • 4:28 • The Walkmen

Rocking and intense, Washington DC's The Walkmen released their debut album, the wonderfully titled *Everyone Who Pretended To Like Me Is Gone*, in 2002. Inspired, but occasionally rambling, comparisons were made with U2. Their noticeably tighter follow-up in 2004, *Bows + Arrows*, sounded like a band who'd found their feet. First single from the album and standout track 'The Rat' deals with an ex-friend or girlfriend: "You've got a nerve to be asking a favour, you've got a nerve to be calling my number" growls Hamilton Leithauser. Behind him, the drumming and guitars are extraordinarily fast yet immaculately sharp. Leithauser has said that the song was written in less than an hour, after drummer Matt Barrick started messing around in a jamming session. An electric organ adds a background of menacing atmosphere to the memorable intensity.

The band formed from the remnants of two split groups in 1998, one of which was the much feted Jonathan Fire*Eater. They set up a recording studio in New York City and added tweaks such as antique piano into the garage rock mix. Always inventive and evolving, the band have since done a track-by-track cover of Harry Nilsson and John Lennon's 1974 album *Pussy Cats*; their acclaimed 2008 album *You & Me* is softer, Dylan-tinged Americana. Self-critical and refreshingly modest, The Walkmen have spoken proudly about how David Letterman asked to have 'The Rat' added to his morning jogging tape after they appeared on his show. According to both *Pitchfork* and *NME*, 'The Rat' was one of the 20 best singles of the first decade of the 21st century. A wound-up, bristling knot of tight aggression, the song remains hard to follow. Anger seldom punched this hard or sounded this slick. JH

> When I used to go out I'd know everyone I saw / Now I go out alone, if I go out at all
>
> – The Walkmen, 'The Rat

The Wannadies
You And Me Song

❗ 1994 • 2:53 • The Wannadies

With its catchy pop chorus and lyrics of everlasting love, the youthful exuberance of 'You And Me Song' propelled this formerly little-known Swedish band to sell-out tours across the UK, Hollywood blockbuster soundtracks and frequent airplay on TV and radio for years to come. The Wannadies formed in Sweden in 1988 and had released two albums in their native country before they captured a sound on their third album, *Be A Girl*, which fitted neatly into the Britpop movement sweeping across the UK in the mid-1990s. Following in the footsteps of fellow Swedes The Cardigans, the feel-good, pop bliss of 'You And Me Song' and the memorable catchy chorus "It was always you and me, always, and forever", ensured it became one of the singalong anthems at festivals. On its re-release in 1996, it gave The Wannadies their highest UK chart single position, reaching number 18. The inclusion of the track on the soundtrack to Baz Luhrmann's film *William Shakespeare's Romeo + Juliet* gave the band further coverage, but they were unable to replicate its success and eventually split in 2009. MM

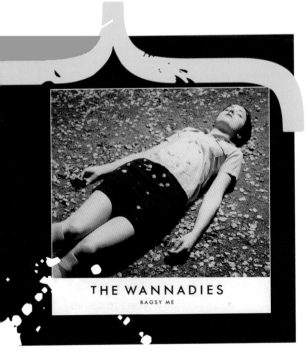

THE WANNADIES
BAGSY ME

We Are Scientists

We Are Scientists
Nobody Move,
Nobody Get Hurt
2005 • 3:16 • Cain – Murray – Tapper

Having moved to New York, the Californian band We Are Scientists began to build a cult following. But only after they came to the UK to tour with Editors did things really start to happen. As they told Xfm, they "were suddenly among a bunch of very like-minded bands" and British audiences began falling hard for excitable, emotional tunes like this one; a feisty, exhilarating rocker based around a catchy four-note riff. The band also became renowned for their hilarious chat, both live (more stand-up comedy than between-song banter) and online – leading to them reporting for *NME* and MTV. Their popularity grew further when they featured on the lineup for a now legendary *NME* tour in the UK, alongside Mystery Jets, Maximo Park and (by then the already very famous) Arctic Monkeys. "For us," they remember, "it was a pretty big step up." *With Love And Squalor* was released in the UK on Virgin and, within six months, had achieved gold status. MS

Weezer

Weezer
Undone – The Sweater Song

❚ 1994 • 5:05 • Cuomo

Not everyone in a rock band is cool. In fact, part of the appeal of Weezer's guitar-laden, metal-tinged pop-punk is their geekiness. Their clever, quirky lyrics mixed with sharp guitar riffs were developed as a result of garage rehearsals, university study and TV-watching. After forming in 1992 and signing their first record deal a year later, frontman Rivers Cuomo was in the middle of studying at Harvard when their self-titled debut album (also known as the *Blue Album*) was released. Originally, the label did not want to release a single, to see if it could gain momentum through word of mouth alone, but after positive attention from US radio, they relented and 'Undone – The Sweater Song' became the band's debut single. A grungy record with seemingly out-of-tune guitar riffs and Cuomo's casual vocal delivery, the singer describes it as his attempt at "A Velvet Underground-type song". The track became an underground hit in the US with its Spike Jonze-directed music video (shot in one continuous take) receiving heavy play on MTV.

Weezer
Buddy Holly

❚ 1994 • 2:40 • Cuomo

Although their debut had made the alternative rock world sit up and take notice, it was the release of second single 'Buddy Holly' that helped take Weezer into the mainstream. Again, an innovative video courtesy of Spike Jonze (this time featuring old footage from US sitcom *Happy Days*) ensured much MTV exposure and helped the album reach multi-platinum status. Only making it onto the album at the insistence of producer Rick Ocasek, 'Buddy Holly' shows a different side to Weezer when compared with their debut. The humour and self-depreciation are still there

I look just like Buddy Holly / Oh-oh, and you're Mary Tyler-Moore

—Weezer, 'Buddy Holly'

in lines like "I look just like Buddy Holly / Oh-oh, and you're Mary Tyler-Moore" but this time they're combined with catchy pop melodies and an upbeat vocal delivery.

Weezer
Hash Pipe

! 2001 · 3:06 · Weezer

Side projects, a three-year hiatus and a second album that disappointed commercially (although later gained a cult status) led to people asking the question, "Whatever happened to Weezer?" The perfect time, you might say, for a triumphant comeback tour. The album that accompanied the tour, known by fans as the *Green Album*, showed a band back at its geek-rock best. 'Hash Pipe' was a crunk guitar highlight on the record, with a choppy riff that could be heard emanating loudly from car windows throughout the summer of 2001.

Weezer
Beverly Hills

! 2005 · 3:16 · Cuomo

The Rick Rubin-produced album *Make Believe* was a sleeker affair than past offerings, with Rubin adding a new wave sound to Rivers Cuomo's traditional songwriting. Lyrically the album was also more mature – though 'Beverly Hills' was the exception, with Cuomo once more the geek-narrator. His status as an outsider and his unease with celebrity is never more evident than here but, as always, it's wrapped in cheery post-punk pop. A record full of LA sunshine and featuring a tongue-in-cheek "wha wha" 1970s-style guitar solo that shouldn't work – but does.

Weezer
Pork & Beans

! 2008 · 3:09 · Weezer

The band's third self-titled colour-coded record (the *Red Album*) promised to be something a little different from previous releases. Not only did Weezer experiment with new sounds and styles – from slacker rock to uplifting choral – but also, where previous albums had been songwriting vehicles for frontman Rivers Cuomo, this time the whole band would contribute. 'Pork & Beans' was the first single from the newly democratic Weezer. Inspired by a bust-up with their record label, the plan was to create a deliberately inane song using lines such as "Everyone likes to dance to a happy song / With a catchy chorus and beat so they can sing along". The result was insanely catchy pop-rock similar to the singles from Weezer's *Blue Album*, with a killer southern country-style hook and the usual Cuomo humour. JS

Paul Weller

"For the first time I didn't have this weight of expectation on me to write songs in a certain style"

– Paul Weller on 'Wild Wood'

Paul Weller Into Tomorrow

! 1991 · 3:12 · Weller

After an unhappy final few years with The Style Council, this is where the Paul Weller revival begins. 'Into Tomorrow' puts the jazz and funk to one side for a return to his R&B roots. Self-released on his Freedom High label, it was the only time in his career he came out on a completely indie label.

Paul Weller Wild Wood

! 1994 · 3:22 · Weller

If there was any doubt that Paul Weller was back to his best, *Wild Wood* settled it. Not only had his singing voice ripened with age, but he had a stack of great songs and a new direction, infused with the folk-rock of Traffic and John Martyn. "For the first time it felt like I didn't have this weight of expectation on me to write songs in a certain style, which was always there with The Jam and The Style Council," he recently said. The album was a triumph, the title track its most stunning moment of unforced bucolic beauty. It was even remixed by hip young beatmakers Portishead and given away as a free *NME* seven-inch.

Paul Weller
Out Of The Sinking

! 1994 · 3:51 · Weller

Issued at the exact mid-point between his *Wild Wood* and *Stanley Road* albums, it would end up on the latter but might well have given title to his next album,

Heavy Soul, being a densely layered guitar-led R&B tune. The lyrics – a lovely story about escaping the rat race with your loved one – explain its popularity.

Paul Weller
The Changing Man

! 1995 · 4:02 · Weller, Lynch

With the success of *Wild Wood*, Paul Weller wasn't just popular, he was hip all over again. His disciple Noel Gallagher sought him out, and he chipped in on 'Champagne Supernova' and elsewhere. His co-producer Brendan Lynch was also becoming fashionable for his dubbed-up Kosmos tracks, and his innovative, quirky style is evident all over 'The Changing Man', with effects shooting in and out. Lyrically, it's Weller's nod to his ever-changing stylistic moods, from new wave to mod to jazz-funk to house to folk-rock. Musically, it's pretty similar to his own brilliant 'Sunflower', both tracks owing a melodic debt to Eddie Floyd's Stax classic, 'Big Bird'.

Paul Weller
You Do Something To Me

! 1995 · 3:30 · Weller

Paul Weller has always had a romantic streak, which was generally subsumed in minor tracks like The Jam's 'English Rose'. But the third single from his acclaimed *Stanley Road* album takes it up a notch on a smouldering folk-rock tune infused with the soul music he'd been championing for the previous decade. By 1995, though, he was deep into his Traffic phase – a place where old English folk met psychedelic rock, notably in the brief mid-song guitar solo, which is perhaps the only weak spot on 'You Do Something To Me'. It's since become a standard, recently covered by soul girl Duffy.

Paul Weller
Broken Stones

! 1995 • 3:16 • Weller

Named after the street where he grew up, Paul Weller's *Stanley Road* album was probably his most nostalgic and 'Broken Stones' encapsulates that mood of quiet reflection perfectly. It's written about people tossed around by the currents and others' movements. The singer has often spoken about the break-up of the working-class communities where he was raised, council houses torn down or traded in. This beautiful single captures it all, the Rhodes keyboard and immaculate vocal demonstrating that Weller might have new influences but he hasn't slackened his grip on soul.

Paul Weller
From The Floorboards Up

! 2005 • 2:27 • Weller

There had been a time, when he was deep in his Traffic jam circa *Stanley Road*, when Paul Weller songs seemed reluctant to end. But 'From The Floorboards Up' was barely begun before it finished, ducking over the finishing line in less than two-and-a-half minutes, his shortest single since 'Friday Street' ten years earlier. A piece of gritty bar room R&B that wouldn't have been out of place in a Dr Feelgood set,

its driving guitar riff introduced a song celebrating music's most visceral qualities, its ability to grab hold of your senses and rattle them 'til there's nothing left. SY

White Lies Death

! 2008 • 5:00 • McVeigh – Cave – Brown

Sometimes you have to learn things the hard way. So it was for White Lies in their former incarnation. "Fear Of Flying basically got ignored by every record company there is under the sun," said singer Harry McVeigh. "It was a very hard thing to deal with." Deciding that the songs they were writing weren't suited to that band, the members decided to change their name – and how they went about conducting themselves. They thought about every detail months before their first gig: how they looked, what they would wear on stage, which lighting they would use. In the run up to it – a purposefully lengthy five months – rather than half-working on hundreds of demos and trying them all out live, White Lies methodically crafted just two songs in the studio. One of these was 'Death'. An epic, dark, atmospheric brooder that's punctuated by stabbing guitar chords, it builds for over three minutes before finally, exhilaratingly, kicking in.

White Lies
Farewell To The Fairground

! 2008 • 4:16 • McVeigh – Cave – Brown

On their frequent comparisons to Joy Division and Echo & The Bunnymen, White Lies are blunt: "We weren't alive during that period of music… I think our music's a lot more uplifting and euphoric." Listening to 'Farewell To The Fairground', it's hard to agree. Its exciting mix of military drums, piercing guitar notes, minor chords and serious vocals evokes the same desolate landscapes as those bands. This was reflected in the video,

filmed in Nikel – a bleak industrial town in one of the farthest northern reaches of Russia. It was during shooting that the band discovered they had hit number one in the UK charts with their debut album. Possibly not the best location in which to celebrate such uplifting and euphoric news. MS

The WhiteStripes

The White Stripes
Hotel Yorba

! 2001 • 2:10 • Jack White

Principally known for spearheading the garage-rock revival, Detroit's White Stripes were also knee-deep in American folk traditions, especially country and blues. 'Hotel Yorba' leans heavily on the former, with Jack White's powerful acoustic chords and Meg White's battered drumming sounding about as raw as anything could in the 21st century. The tune actually bears a striking resemblance to Country Joe And The Fish's *Feel Like I'm Fixin' To Die*, best known for getting hundreds of thousands of hippies to say the f-word on film at Woodstock. But since that was itself adapted from a traditional folk song, it's not really one for the lawyers.

The White Stripes
Fell In Love With A Girl

! 2001 • 1:50 • Jack White

While The Strokes were scooping the majority of public attention, The White Stripes were always the rawer, harder proposition, as evidenced on this sub-two-minute firestorm of guitar, drum and Jack White's coyote howl. But it took the ecstatic reaction of the UK alternative aristocracy (*NME*, who slapped them on the cover very early, and John Peel, who said nothing since Hendrix had so affected him) to hail the new heroes. 'Fell In Love With A Girl' is pure delirium, capturing that flush of love (albeit with a cheating girl) perfectly in its adrenaline-rush crash and bang. The rock star Lego video, directed

by Michel Gondry, won umpteen awards and was named best of the decade by *Pitchfork*, while the (retitled) song was covered by Joss Stone for her first single.

The White Stripes
Seven Nation Army

! 2003 • 3:52 • Jack White

The kind of tune by which decades are remembered, 'Seven Nation Army' took The White Stripes from alternative heroes to platinum-selling rock'n'roll superstars. For a man on the brink of stardom, Jack White sounds angry in the extreme, striking out at unspecified enemies and threatening to turn it all in to go and "work the straw". It also has possibly the most famous non-bassline in the business, Jack lowering the tone of his acoustic bass by running it through a pedal for the simple riff that would become a worldwide football chant, particularly famous for its association with Italy's 2006 World Cup winners.

The White Stripes
I Just Don't Know What To Do With Myself

! 2003 • 2:46 • Bacharach – David

The White Stripes may have been a two-person garage-rock revamp of folk traditions, but they were no strangers to the great American songbook, albeit a more modern version than Rod Stewart's. This classic, composed by Brill Building kings Burt Bacharach and Hal David, had already supplied hits for Dusty Springfield, Dionne Warwick and more, when Jack and Meg White made it the second single from their stellar fourth album, *Elephant*. This reads like a potential Pixies cover, beginning slow and sparse with the chorus before exploding into life on the verses. It was another boon for Bacharach, who had enjoyed the patronage of Noel Gallagher just a few years earlier.

The White Stripes
The Hardest Button To Button

! 2003 • 3:32 • Jack White

Another single built on a powerhouse riff, 'The Hardest Button To Button' crunches up on metallic chords and Meg White's typically carefree drumming. This is one of those odd songs that seems to mean different things to different people: some see it as a tale of childhood poverty and sibling rivalry; others as a critique of Ronald Reagan's foreign policy; still more as trying to find moments of silence (the hardest button being that used to fasten someone's lip). Jack White has given little indication, but he later said the video, again directed by Michel Gondry, "is the best because I had no idea what he was talking about when he was explaining it to me".

The White Stripes
My Doorbell

! 2005 • 4:01 • Jack White

The White Stripes had shown themselves more than capable of handling rising expectations before, but *Get Behind Me Satan* came after the global super-success of *Elephant* and difficult times for Jack White, who was in legal trouble for

fighting, in the tabloids for dating Renée Zellweger, and in the hospital following a car crash. If the album's first single, 'Blue Orchid', was an odd disappointment, 'My Doorbell' was reassuring, adding to their stripped-back recipe of guitar and drum with a simple piano line, giving it a flavour of mid-period Rolling Stones. In its catchy, singalong glory, it's an immediately jolly, almost pastiche, celebration of everything The White Stripes do best.

The White Stripes
The Denial Twist

! 2005 • 2:35 • Jack White

Perhaps the highlight of *Get Behind Me Satan*, 'The Denial Twist' is a glorious pile-up of guitars, drums, tambourine and piano with Jack White detailing a broken relationship that may or may not be his brief fling with Renée Zellweger. With its jaunty-yet-jerky rhythm and Jack's voice at its most piercing, 'The Denial Twist' seems more placatory than bitter, suggesting the injured party "take a mountain and turn it into a mole". There was a very limited three-inch vinyl pressing, which Jack distributed among friends and which is now an auction-house staple, where it routinely fetches several hundred pounds.

The White Stripes
Icky Thump

! 2007 • 4:14 • Jack White

By the time of their sixth album, The White Stripes seemed like just one of Jack White's many concerns. With new band The Raconteurs, outside production work and regular guest appearances, he'd relocated to Nashville with his new wife, while his bandmate Meg moved to LA. So *Icky Thump* was an album many thought would never get made, even if the cover (the first not to picture them in red, white and black) immediately announced how different things were. The title track, taken from Yorkshire slang, is a slamming anti-anti-immigration song and, in its mussed-up, gnarly way, the closest thing to metal they've done.

The White Stripes
You Don't Know
What Love Is
! 2007 • 3:54 • Jack White

Subtitled 'You Just Do What You're Told', this is one of the meanest songs Jack White's ever written. He told *MOJO* he wrote it on tour supporting his hero Bob Dylan, who gave a sharp intake of breath at the sourness of the lyrics. But beneath the clanging guitar noise and the tale of a lover just going through the motions, 'You Don't Know What Love Is' is beautifully moving, in the best traditions of country; a simple story well told. Whether it'll end up in the hands of White collaborator Loretta Lynn remains to be seen, though Jack did admit he'd love for "someone great to get hold of it". SY

The Who

The Who
I Can't Explain

1965 • 2:06 • Townshend

The first release under The Who name (a previous flop as The High Numbers was all but disowned) and their first top 10 hit, 'I Can't Explain' is a truly fantastic moment. Its choppy rhythmic intro was nicked off The Kinks' 'You Really Got Me', but everything else on the record screamed originality. This was cooler than the Stones and tougher than The Beatles, with an aggressive swagger already booming out of Keith Moon's drums. Its distorted guitar lines were actually the work of The Yardbirds' (later

Cooler than the Stones and tougher than The Beatles

Led Zep's) Jimmy Page, who producer Shel Talmy had roped in as a session musician in case his new protégés weren't up to scratch (the backing vocals were also the work of pop trio The Ivy League).

Although they loved their clobber as much as any self-respecting mod, there was something distinctly un-manicured about these four west London boys, whose R&B rawness was brilliantly channelled into immaculate pop. The song tackles that mainstay of every adolescent – mumbling inarticulacy and hopelessness in the face of love. Pilled-up, R&B-loving

teenagers looking for someone to put their frustrations into song knew that, with The Who, they had found their voice, if not their actual words.

The Who
My Generation

1965 • 3:18 • Townshend

The most famous stutter in rock and a youth anthem so blindingly obvious in intent it seems ridiculous it wasn't written back in the 1950s, when the teenager was officially "invented". In an era when even TV presenters swear, it's impossible to gauge the shock value of the stammered "f" on 'My Generation'; the sheer jaw-dropping, split-second thought that a singer might say the unsayable, before easing back into "Why don't you all just f-f-f-fade away". The stutter was the idea of manager Kit Lambert, who told Roger Daltrey to use his natural impediment to the record's advantage because "it makes you sound like you're pilled".

The Who had the physical edge to go with their attitude. There was simply nothing to compare to Keith Moon's explosive drumming in the mid-1960s, and Pete Townshend was already learning how to use his guitar as a bludgeon while letting John Entwistle carry the melody. Once again they proved you could make scorching pop records without sacrificing even a drop of R&B's brilliant reckless energy. Townshend has since offered many differing anecdotes to explain the song's genesis, but the most loveable (if not the most likely) is that it was written after the Queen Mother had his car, a hearse, towed away from his Belgravia home for being unsightly.

The Who
Substitute

! 1966 • 3:48 • Townshend

'Substitute' was The Who's first self-produced single and proof that they had more subtlety up their sleeve than the *sturm und drang* of their first recordings implied. Pete Townshend's 12-string guitar provides neat counterpoint to a tune that burns with class rage and his personal frustrations at being dubbed "a substitute for The Rolling Stones". It's among the best songs he ever wrote, Roger Daltrey sneering his way through the lyrics' succession of smart couplets (although "I look all white but my dad was black" was edited out of the American version). Keith Moon had no recollection of playing on 'Substitute' and accused the band of using a, er, substitute drummer.

The Who
I Can See For Miles

! 1967 • 4:06 • Townshend

The Who were never natural summer-of-lovers. Far too musically aggressive and politically dissident, peace and love just wasn't their thing. As singer Roger Daltrey later told *Uncut*, "Though we were all into the anti-war movement, every time we went on stage we were showing them what war was really like." 'I Can See For Miles' was their first stab at psychedelia, a hypnotic one-finger solo and a lyric that hinted at mind expansion. Although it gave

them their first notable American hit, coming in the wake of their Monterrey performance, guitarist Pete Townshend was said to be furious that it didn't give them a British number one, stalling at ten.

The Who
Magic Bus

! 1968 • 3:16 • Townshend

There is simply nothing more infectious in rock than the Bo Diddley beat, as The Rolling Stones ('Not Fade Away') and The Smiths ('How Soon Is Now?') would testify. Following 'I Can See For Miles', 'Magic Bus' was another track that dabbled in psychedelic waters, the title borrowing from author Ken Kesey and his Merry Pranksters, but that shuffling rhythm was the key, proving a live favourite and centrepiece for stage banter between Roger Daltrey and Pete Townshend. Not everyone was a fan, though, with John Entwistle bored rigid by the limited bass parts as the song grew in length through the live versions.

The Who
Pinball Wizard

! 1969 • 2:59 • Townshend

With its humming acoustic intro and pile-driver guitar chords, 'Pinball Wizard' is among The Who's most recognisable anthems. The standout track from the ponderous and pretentious rock opera, *Tommy*, 'Pinball Wizard' was everything that wasn't: concise, tuneful and fun. The tale of a "deaf, dumb and blind kid" was denounced as "sick" by DJ Tony

> "Though we were all into the anti-war movement, every time we went on stage we were showing them what war was really like"
>
> – Roger Daltrey

Blackburn but proved hugely popular in the US, where the success of the album got the band out of the financial hole caused by years of smashing their gear onstage. The pinball was inserted into the story for the benefit of friend and *New York Times* critic Nik Cohn (later the writer of *Saturday Night Fever*), who duly overcame his objections to concept rock and gave it a rave review.

The Who
Baba O'Riley

! 1971 • 5:05 • Townshend

'Baba O'Riley' was to have been the centrepiece of Pete Townshend's *Lifehouse* rock opera. That was nixed by the band, prompting Townshend to sink into depression, but when it finally surfaced, it was as lead track on the band's most revered album, *Who's Next*. The epic stadium-rock style – complete with enormous power chords, Roger Daltrey's skyrocketing vocals and multiple parts – was partially offset by Townshend's use of 'In C' by minimalist composer Terry Riley as inspiration for the song. Riley

is there in the title, the other half being a reference to Meher Baba, Townshend's spiritual guru at the time. Despite never being released as a single in the UK or US, the song is a Who mainstay.

The Who
Won't Get Fooled Again

! 1971 • 3:38 • Townshend

Pete Townshend's cynical diatribe about the realities of revolution is a kind of *Animal Farm* for the counterculture age, warning those "fighting in the streets" not to be hoodwinked by their leaders the way previous generations were. Right-wing magazine *National Review* recently placed it at number one in a list of the greatest conservative rock songs, but Townshend has denied that interpretation. He's described it variously as "the dumbest song I ever wrote" and one that is supportive of revolution, just wary of its consequences. No such qualms for the fans, who lapped up its edited radio length (newbies are directed to the eight-minute album version) and its innovative melding of guitar and synths.

The Who
5.15

! 1973 • 4:16 • Townshend

Though it has acquired cult status thanks
to the 1979 film, *Quadrophenia* was a
hugely overambitious double-album
and a disastrous stage show. '5.15' was
the only thing resembling a hit to be
found on it, detailing Jimmy the mod's
amphetamine-fuelled breakdown on
the train back to Brighton, scene of
the triumphant beach battle with the
rockers. It's heavy, almost sludgy rock,
lifted by John Entwistle's brilliant brass
playing. Having risen to number 20, The
Who were invited onto *Top Of The Pops*,
where they showed their lofty distaste
for the whole pop business by insulting a
producer (Pete Townshend) and attacking
a bar steward (Keith Moon), earning the
band a lifetime ban from the BBC club.

The Who
Who Are You

! 1978 • 5:06 • Townshend

Threatened by the rise of punk, Pete
Townshend (so the story goes) went
on a massive bender that included a
drunken apology for the sins of stadium
rock to Steve Jones and Paul Cook of
the Sex Pistols, and that culminated in
the collapsed guitarist swearing at a
policeman. Swearword removed, the insult
formed the title for their next single and
album. Despite its origins, 'Who Are You' is
very much in their synth-rock mode of the
1970s, the electronic introduction almost
hinting at a disco track before the epic

air-punching chorus brings it back
home. Keith Moon is very much a
becalmed presence behind the drum
kit and this was to be the last hit
before his death in September, less
than three months after its release.
SY

Wolfman
featuring Pete Doherty
For Lovers

! 2004 • 3:51 • Doherty – Wolfe

First meeting in a London bookshop some
years previously in a coincidence that
would melt the heart of even the most
hardened of PR professionals, Libertines
frontman Pete Doherty joined forces
with the relatively unknown poet and
songwriter known as Wolfman (Peter
Wolfe) to create an anguished and
beautiful love song. Doherty's vocals are
the star here, arranged over tinkling piano
and soulfully delivering Wolfe's lyrics
about the romantics he and his ex-wife
would watch from a bar in Paddington
station. Each meaningful syllable, full
of pain and hope, sends shivers down
the spine and black and white images of
chance meetings in cafés to the brain. It
was a top 10 single and was nominated
for a prestigious Ivor Novello Award.
Yet neither songwriter made much
money from the song, having sold the
publishing rights in a pub prior to release.
JS

The Wombats

The Wombats Moving To New York

! 2006 · 3:31 · Haggis – Knudsen – Murphy

Walking in on your girlfriend kissing another girl might be the stuff of fantasy for some young men, but not a young Matthew "Murph" Murphy. Especially not after he'd been told she was staying in that night – and yet there she was, in the middle of a bar, making out with another woman. The whole thing was made more complicated by the fact that she had previously had a romance with bandmate Tord

The WOMBATS
'Let's Dance to
JOY DIVISION'

'Let's Dance to Joy Division' was savaged by Joy Division fans, until Peter Hook professed his love of the song

Øverland-Knudsen. As Murph said, "If you can't write a decent song out of that, you can't write a song at all." The result was 'Moving To New York', a thundering indie-pop tune about running away from your problems. Initially released in 2006 as a limited seven-inch on the Kids Label, it caught the attention of Warner's 14th Floor Records (Damien Rice, David Gray) who duly signed them. After the release of their debut album, *The Wombats Proudly Present: A Guide To Love, Loss & Desperation*, a re-issue of the single in 2008 saw it reach number 13 in the UK charts.

The Wombats
Let's Dance To Joy Division

2007 · 3:11
Haggis – Knudsen – Murphy

Hell hath no fury like a disgruntled Joy Division fan. A fact discovered by The Wombats when they released this raucous indie tune in the autumn of 2007 – just as Anton Corbijn's Joy Division biopic *Control* was in cinemas. In fact the lyrics are born of a love of the band, say The Wombats in their defence: they are about "people dancing and having fun to songs they really find quite depressing [like] 'Love Will Tear Us Apart'". In the end,

Joy Division's Peter Hook had to step in. Professing his love of the song, he posted the video for the single on his website and even joined The Wombats on stage to play it live. According to singer Murph, "Since then everybody's kind of shut up." MS

The Wonder Stuff
Size Of A Cow

1991 · 3:12 · The Wonder Stuff

The Wonder Stuff were pretty much an instant hit in the UK; with their loud pop melodies and frontman Miles Hunt's equally loud personality, they grabbed the attention of the music press with debut album *The Eight Legged Groove Machine*. But it was for their first single from third album *Never Loved Elvis* that they are best remembered. On the surface, a playful, happy-go-lucky pop song, the lyrics tell of Hunt's disappointment in life using a tactic inspired by John Lennon. "[Lennon said] he'd got into people's homes with songs like 'Love Me Do'," Hunt told Xfm. "Then, once ensconced in people's lives, told them what was on his mind. I thought, 'How about trying to fuse that into one song?'." The single became the band's first UK top 10 hit. JS

"You know that I've been drunk a thousand times / And these should be the best days of my life" —The Wonder Stuff 'Size of a Cow'

The XX

The xx
VCR

| **2009 • 2:57**
| **Qureshi – Smith – Sim – Madley Croft**

Formed as teenagers at Elliott School in Putney, this south London trio (originally a quartet) is part of a generation of bands – from Hot Chip to The Maccabees – who grew up listening to Xfm and who, surprisingly, all went to the same school. The xx combine a variety of inspirations from Chris Isaak to Joy Division to R&B, electronica, dubstep and UK funky to create a warm, intimate sound that has won them a global audience. 'VCR' exemplifies the sensual quality of the hushed vocals of Romy Madley Croft and Oliver Sim and the powerful simplicity of the music. "I think

I think we're superstars/ you say you think we are the best thing

we're superstars / You say you think we are the best thing" they chime together, with an almost telepathic chemistry that can only spring from having been friends since they met at nursery. The album *xx* won the Xfm New Music award for the best British debut of 2009.
JK

Yeah Yeah Yeahs
Maps

| **2003 • 3:40 • Yeah Yeah Yeahs**

The sexiest woman in music is often a hotly debated issue. Kylie, Cheryl Cole and Rihanna are all often mentioned in the same breath, but really, there is only one woman worthy of that title... and that's Karen O, frontwoman of the Yeah Yeah Yeahs, alongside guitarist Nick Zinner and drummer Brian Chase.

The band were discovered in the garage-rock revival trailblazed by The Strokes (aside band members Nick Zinner and Brian Chase). Starting life as a folk band called Unitard, the trio thankfully dropped the terrible name and plugged in their guitars, opting instead for a sexy take on garage punk. After several EPs, the Yeah Yeah Yeahs' debut album, *Fever To Tell*, was released in 2004. 'Maps' was the star single. O's breathy, sexy vocals as she tells of her relationship with Liars frontman Angus Andrews are sung over a tense driving rhythm that seems always on the verge of exploding into chaos. The release, a year after the album first appeared, provided the perfect showcase of the band's ability: O's passionate voice and Zinner's sonic riffs produced a show-stealing performance at the 2004 MTV Movie awards and confirmed their arrival.

Yeah Yeah Yeahs
Gold Lion

| **2006 • 4:25 • Yeah Yeah Yeahs**

The Yeah Yeah Yeahs' second big hit after the breakthrough success of 'Maps' came from second album *Show Your Bones*. Despite rumours started by producer Squeak E Clean (really) that the record would be a concept album written about Karen O's cat Coco, 'Gold Lion' is the sole feline reference. The single sounded markedly different to the first album, which Nick Zinner says is down to their use of the acoustic guitar: "It was like a new tool we discovered," he said. "For us it felt kind of fresh." More subdued and reflective than their earlier work, singer O broods on recent heartache and Zinner's Jack White-style guitar licks offer a welcome venture away from the band's trademark sound.

Yeah Yeah Yeahs Zero

2009 • 4:25 • Yeah Yeah Yeahs

Not wanting to sit on their musical laurels for too long, the Yeah Yeah Yeahs released *It's Blitz!* in 2009 and had once more taken their sound in another direction – this time harking back to the raw energy and art-punk sound of their debut, but layering it with 1980s synths (bought by guitarist Nick Zinner on eBay) to create instant dancefloor-fillers, such as lead single 'Zero'. Gone are Brian Chase's driving drumbeats, replaced by synthesized beats from the off and glossy vocals nodding in the direction of Debbie Harry. The track blends rock credentials with glittery disco and brought the band closer to the mainstream then ever before.
JS

Neil Young
Rockin' In The Free World

1989 • 4:40 • Young

Neil Young concluded a decade that was a write-off for all but his most blinkered devotees with an album that suddenly made him relevant all over again. Young had always been wilfully perverse, but before his series of unloved genre-hopping albums that got him sued by his own label for making "unrepresentative" music, he'd been the only veteran of the hippy era to endorse punk, with 'Hey Hey, My My' – a tribute to Johnny Rotten. Like the *Rust Never Sleeps* album from which that came, 1989's *Freedom* is bookended by two versions of the same song: one acoustic, the other brutally noisy. Of course, with grunge just beginning to rear its head, it was the latter that became the anthem of its time, repeatedly performed live by Pearl Jam, often with Young himself guesting.

'Rockin' In The Free World' learned a trick from Bruce Springsteen's 'Born In The USA' – so long as the chorus is something Americans of all political stripes can pump their fists to, you can make the verses as sour as you like. Thus, the man who'd shocked long-term fans by supporting Ronald Reagan during the 1980s, redeemed himself by taking a long, hard look at some of the social conditions his economic policy had produced. By 1989, Reagan had ceded the presidency to his former vice president, George Bush (the first), and the reference to a "kinder gentler machine-gun hand" is an explicit mocking of Bush's promise of a "kindler, gentler America". The song also portrays the phenomenon of babies born to crack-addicted mothers and is an early example of rock singers expressing environmental concern (Young himself kick-started the trend with 1972's 'After The Gold Rush').

But none of this mattered for people who only heard the hook's uncomplicated exhortation. It was borne of TV pictures of Ayatollah Khomeini's funeral earlier that year, a crush of two million people that left eight dead and hundreds injured and saw mass burning of the American flag. Young and Frank Sampedro, of his backing band Crazy Horse, agreed they should avoid the Middle East for the foreseeable future, Sampedro saying they should "keep on rocking in the free world". With that one line repeated four times in every chorus, it's become one of rock's most recognisable hooks even though it was never released as a single outside the US – where it barely scraped the chart – and his homeland, Canada. In 2009, he headlined Glastonbury Festival, playing an incredible version of 'Rockin' In The Free World' that lasted well over ten minutes and included a wall of feedback and more false climaxes than a porn star's career. The lyrics were updated for America's new President Barack Obama, replacing the line about Jesse Jackson with his "yes we can" slogan.
SY

The Zutons

The Zutons
You Will You Won't

2004 • 2:54 • Chowdhury – Harding – McCabe – Payne – Pritchard

One of the UK's finest indie rock bands, the ability to not take themselves too seriously while producing some great tracks seems to stand The Zutons in good stead. Formed in Liverpool in 2001, they were a mainstay of the Liverpool live music scene and reached critical acclaim when they released their first album *Who Killed...... The Zutons?* in May 2004, from which 'You Will You Won't' was released as the second single. The album featured a 3D sleeve and fans also received Zutons-branded 3D glasses. Many fans took this a step further and brought the glasses to the band's gigs – the ultimate Zutons accessory, it seems.

3D glasses came with the album and soon were sported at gigs

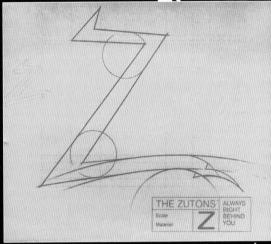

From left: 'You Can Do Anything', 'Always Right Behind You'

The Zutons
Don't Ever Think (Too Much)

2004 • 2:42 • Chowdhury – Harding – McCabe – Payne – Pritchard

Another Xfm favourite, 'Don't Ever Think (Too Much)' was later added to debut album *Who Killed...... The Zutons?* The track reached the top 20 and really introduced UK music fans to The Zutons. In the same year, the band had to change the Z from their logo to avoid any possible confusion with the Zenith company logo. Climbing up the charts throughout 2004 and 2005 with the album, the band were nominated for the Mercury Music Prize and Best British Breakthrough Act at the Brit awards.

The Zutons
Valerie

2006 • 3:56 • Chowdhury – Harding – McCabe – Payne – Pritchard

'Valerie' was the second single from The Zutons' second album, *Tired Of Hanging Around*. It was the second UK top 10 hit for the band from this pinnacle record and stayed in the top 20 for a whopping 19 weeks. A year later, Amy Winehouse and Mark Ronson collaborated at the Brit awards with a new arrangement of the track. Their version was later released as a single by Winehouse, giving her equally acclaimed chart success. BdP

INDEX

Xfm plays Music That Rocks
on 104.9 in London, 97.7 in Manchester,
across the UK on digital radio
and online at xfm.co.uk.

xfm.co.uk